THE

SELECTED

WORKS OF

GORDON

TULLOCK

VOLUME 7

The Economics and Politics of

Wealth Redistribution

THE SELECTED WORKS OF GORDON TULLOCK

VOLUME 1 *Virginia Political Economy*

VOLUME 2 *The Calculus of Consent: Logical Foundations of Constitutional Democracy* (with James M. Buchanan)

VOLUME 3 *The Organization of Inquiry*

VOLUME 4 *The Economics of Politics*

VOLUME 5 *The Rent-Seeking Society*

VOLUME 6 *Bureaucracy*

VOLUME 7 *The Economics and Politics of Wealth Redistribution*

VOLUME 8 *The Social Dilemma: Of Autocracy, Revolution, Coup d'Etat, and War*

VOLUME 9 *Law and Economics*

VOLUME 10 *Economics without Frontiers* (includes a cumulative index for the series)

Gordon Tullock

THE SELECTED WORKS OF GORDON TULLOCK

VOLUME 7

The Economics and Politics of Wealth Redistribution

GORDON TULLOCK

Edited and with an Introduction by

CHARLES K. ROWLEY

Liberty Fund

Indianapolis

This book is published by Liberty Fund, Inc., a foundation established to encourage study of the ideal of a society of free and responsible individuals.

The cuneiform inscription that serves as our logo and as the design motif for our endpapers is the earliest-known written appearance of the word "freedom" (*amagi*), or "liberty." It is taken from a clay document written about 2300 B.C. in the Sumerian city-state of Lagash.

Printed in the United States of America

Paperback cover photo courtesy of the *American Economic Review*

Frontispiece courtesy of Center for Study of Public Choice, George Mason University, Fairfax, Virginia

09 08 07 06 05 C 5 4 3 2 1
09 08 07 06 05 P 5 4 3 2 1

Library of Congress Cataloging-in-Publication Data
Tullock, Gordon.
The economics and politics of wealth redistribution / Gordon Tullock ; edited and with an introduction by Charles K. Rowley.
p. cm. — (The selected works of Gordon Tullock ; v. 7)
Includes bibliographical references and index.
ISBN 0-86597-526-4 (alk. paper)—ISBN 0-86597-537-X (pbk. : alk. paper)
1. Distribution (Economic theory). 2. Income distribution. 3. Wealth. I. Rowley, Charles Kershaw. II. Title.
HB523.T84 2005
339.2—dc22

2004057621

LIBERTY FUND, INC.
8335 Allison Pointe Trail, Suite 300
Indianapolis, Indiana 46250-1684

CONTENTS

INTRODUCTION

The Economics and Politics of Wealth Redistribution brings together Gordon Tullock's insightful contributions to the analysis of the determinants of income and wealth redistribution under democratic regimes. In these contributions, Tullock deploys public choice and rent-seeking analysis to challenge economists' strongly held egalitarian prejudices concerning the distribution of income and wealth within society.

The Intellectual Background

Prior to Tullock's public choice and rent-seeking insights, the large majority of economists approached the issue of the redistribution, with respect to both income and wealth, from the perspective of Paretian welfare economics.[1]

From the early beginnings of the utilitarian doctrine outlined in the late-eighteenth-century writings of Jeremy Bentham until the mid 1930s, economists believed that individual utilities were measurable on a cardinal scale and that they were interpersonally comparable.[2] They further argued, on the basis of the law of diminishing returns, that each individual's marginal utility declined with respect to income and wealth. In such circumstances, many economists forcefully advanced arguments in favor of government intervention designed to equalize the distribution of income and wealth across society.

Utilitarianism in its undiluted Benthamite form can be viewed as a combination of three conditions:

1. Welfarism, which requires that the goodness of a state of affairs be a function of only the utility information regarding that state;
2. Sum ranking, which requires that utility information regarding any state be assessed in terms of only the sum total of all the utilities in that state; and

1. See Charles K. Rowley and Alan T. Peacock, *Welfare Economics: A Liberal Restatement* (London: Martin Robertson, 1975), 7–66.

2. Jeremy Bentham, *A Fragment of Government*, ed. James H. Burns and Herbert L. A. Hart (1776; London: Cambridge University Press, 1988).

3. Consequentialism, which requires that every choice, whether of actions, institutions, or rules, be determined ultimately by the goodness of the consequent state of affairs, measured in terms of aggregate utility.

These three conditions remained the cornerstones of utilitarianism throughout the nineteenth century despite occasional concerns about the validity of the second condition. The early marginalists, such as William Stanley Jevons, Léon Walras, and Carl Menger, for example, though clearly aware of potential problems in measuring utility, continued to talk about utility as if it were measurable on a cardinal scale and fully comparable across individuals.[3]

In 1900, however, Vilfredo Pareto demonstrated that an ordinal notion of utility was sufficient for the construction of equilibrium theory and, in so doing, marked the trail for modern economic theory.[4] It is not clear, however, whether Pareto actually rejected the notion of cardinal utility or whether he thought that it was impossible to identify the appropriate function for measuring it. In any event, his 1900 insight would be recognized some thirty years later as the Pareto Principle.

Pareto's insight was not seized upon immediately by economists. In particular, Arthur Pigou, who was Alfred Marshall's successor at the University of Cambridge, adhered closely to the notion that utility was measurable on a cardinal scale and interpersonally comparable. In his book *The Economics of Welfare*, Pigou adopted aggregate real income as the "objective counterpart" of economic welfare and argued that

> the old "law of diminishing utility" thus leads securely to the proposition: Any cause which increases the absolute share of real income in the hands of the poor, provided that it does not lead to a contraction in the size of the national dividend from any point of view, will, in general, increase economic welfare.[5]

As in many areas of economics in which he worked, Pigou proved to be out of date with respect to this analysis. During the 1930s, economists became

3. William Stanley Jevons, *The Theory of Political Economy* (London: Macmillan, 1871); Léon Walras, *Elements d'Economie Politique Pure*, 1874; trans. William Jaffe (London: George Allen and Unwin, 1954); Carl Menger, *Grundsatze Volkwirtschaftslehre*, 1871; trans. James Dingwale and Bert F. Hoselitz (New York: New York University Press, 1981).

4. See Alan P. Kirman, *Pareto as an Economist*, in *The New Palgrave: A Dictionary of Economics*, ed. John Eatwell, Murray Milgate, and Peter Newman (London: Macmillan, 1987), 804.

5. Arthur C. Pigou, *The Economics of Welfare* (London: Macmillan, 1920), 89.

increasingly uncomfortable with the idea of cardinal measurement and interpersonal comparisons of utility. In 1934 John Hicks and Roy Allen used the technique of indifference curves, originated by Edgeworth and Pareto, to develop a theory of consumer behavior involving only ordinal comparisons of satisfaction. In 1938 Lionel Robbins imposed the final coup de grace on the felicific calculus and paved the way for economists, immediately following the end of World War II, to develop an approach to welfare economics based on the principles first outlined by Pareto.[6]

This so-called new welfare economics recognized that economists, henceforth, must work with only the welfarism and the consequentialist assumptions, while abandoning the sum-ranking assumption, thereby forging only a weak utilitarian criterion for policy analysis. The Pareto criterion states that social state A is to be preferred to social state B if at least one individual is better off in A than in B and if no individual is worse off. If this condition holds, social state A is said to be Pareto superior to social state B.

Given the impossibility of sum-ranking, a large number of Pareto-superior positions will exist, each corresponding to a previous distribution of wealth. Because the Pareto criterion cannot distinguish between such positions—a consequence of the ordinal nature of utility and the absence of a measuring rod for making interpersonal comparisons—the criterion offers only a quasi ordering of social welfare. Crucially, it appears to be silent with respect to evaluating alternative distributions of income and wealth.

For those economists driven by an egalitarian ethic, this restriction is anathema. They have devised a number of more or less convincing avenues of escape from the Paretian straitjacket without jettisoning the utilitarian principle. In one solution, John Harsanyi rationalizes social aversion to inequality by assuming that individuals are risk averse and favor equalizing income and wealth so as to protect themselves from possible adverse outcomes in an uncertain future.

In a more radical version of the same approach, John Rawls conducted a conceptual experiment designed to determine the nature of "justice as fairness." In this experiment, hypothetical individuals meet in the so-called original position behind a "veil of ignorance" that precludes their knowledge of

6. John R. Hicks and Roy G. D. Allen, "A Reconsideration of the Theory of Value," *Econometrica* 52 (1934); see Charles K. Rowley, "Wealth Maximization in Normative Law and Economics: A Social Choice Analysis," *George Mason Law Review* 6 (summer 1998): 971–96; Lionel Robbins, "Interpersonal Comparisons of Utility," *Economic Journal* 48 (1938): 635–41.

their relative positions within society with respect to such characteristics as sex, race, ethnicity, or physical or mental endowments. Rawls claims that under such circumstances extreme risk aversion will draw unanimous consent for a social contract that places the least-advantaged members in full control over the distribution of income and wealth within society.[7]

An alternative route to justifying equality rests on the presumed existence of interdependence among the utility functions of the rich and the poor. Harold Hochman and James Rodgers justify wealth redistribution through the political process in terms of the uncomfortable feelings of the rich regarding the living standards of the poor such that the rich gain utility when some of their wealth is transferred to that group.[8] Hochman and Rodgers claim that free-rider problems limit the effectiveness of private charitable donations in a large community, and that the rich, therefore, voluntarily endorse the use of government to overcome such free-riding externalities.

In yet another approach, economists simply ignore the Paretian limitations and introduce social welfare functions that openly encompass their personal views on wealth redistribution. In essence, they invite their readers to embrace egalitarian doctrine, even though this implies that utility is to be measured cardinally and treated as comparable across individuals.

The Economics and Politics of Wealth Redistribution

Tullock's contributions and responses to the redistribution debate consist of five parts.

Part 1, "Why Redistribute Wealth?" consists of five papers that focus critical attention on a variety of arguments advanced in favor of redistributing income and wealth away from the rich and in favor of the poor.

"Income Redistribution" reviews the argument that voters support the use of government as the principal agent of income and wealth redistribution in order to internalize free-riding externalities that impact adversely on the effectiveness of private charity. Tullock suggests that such a rationalization requires, de minimis, that political transfers actually do redistribute income from the wealthy to the poor. In practice, however, the bulk of government

7. John Rawls, *A Theory of Justice* (Oxford: Oxford University Press, 1971).

8. Harold M. Hochman and James R. Rodgers, "Pareto Optimal Redistribution," *American Economic Review* 54 (September 1964): 652–57.

transfers in the democracies involve the shifting of income among individuals in the middle-income bracket. This cannot be justified on the grounds of externalities. A better explanation is that the median-preference voters secure income transfers for themselves, thereby taking from both the poor and the rich.

"Helping the Poor" calls attention to the handicaps faced by most poor individuals in the political marketplace for income transfers. Tullock notes that many of the poor simply lack the necessary personal qualities to become well-off. These handicaps affect their bargaining power in politics, just as they hold the poor down in the private marketplace.

"Reasons for Redistribution [1983]" notes that most individuals are imbued with charitable instincts toward the poor, but only to a very limited degree. In the United States the combination of private charity and federal budget transfers specifically earmarked for the poor amount to less than 5 percent of gross national product. This leads Tullock to promulgate Tullock's Law: the average individual is willingly prepared to transfer no more than 5 percent of his income to the poor. Most political pressures for income redistribution are driven by the selfish desires of middle-income groups to secure transfers to their own kind.

"Reasons for Redistribution [1986]" focuses on the degree to which the redistributionist instincts of Western socialists stall at their respective countries' borders. In this respect, the behavior of the Western democracies closely resembles the apartheid policies of South Africa during the middle years of the twentieth century. For example, before its abandonment of the empire, the United Kingdom disenfranchised 85 percent of its subjects located in the dominions and the colonies and denied them the income transfers that their poverty surely justified. The United States currently disenfranchises illegal immigrants and denies them many income transfers, despite their evident poverty. In this sense, most well-intentioned socialists who argue in favor of the redistribution of income and wealth are predominantly arguing in favor of such redistribution strictly within the boundaries of their own country.

"Objectives of Income Redistribution" discusses the consumer surpluses that may be generated by efficient government policies and explores various methods—including Tullock's own demand-revealing method—whereby such surpluses may be distributed through society. As Tullock notes, governments rarely concern themselves with determining where the social surplus should go; indeed, they rarely even compensate those who suffer directly from such redistributive public policy initiatives.

Part 2, "Private and Semiprivate Redistribution Mechanisms," consists of five papers that focus on mechanisms of wealth and income redistribution that do not involve central government.

"Charitable Gifts" centers attention primarily on the nature of voluntary transfers, that is, those private transfers in which the government does not intervene. Tullock notes that such transfers are superoptimal, in the sense that the same product (the transfer) raises the utility of two individuals (the donor as well as the recipient).

Tullock notes that many voluntary transfers are in kind rather than in cash and thus carry significant excess burdens. He explains this phenomenon in terms of the desire of donors to achieve specific welfare outcomes rather than simply to increase the utility of the poor. He also notes that in cases involving tragic choices (choices over who shall live and who shall die) donors shrink from the consequences of their decisions and enter into nontransparent forms of transfer in order to conceal the heart-wrenching limits of their charitable instincts.

"Local Redistribution" explores the implications of providing transfers to the poor through local communities rather than through central government. Tullock acknowledges the standard argument against decentralization, namely, that the threat of outward migration by the rich and inward migration by the poor makes it impossible for one local government to provide higher relief payments than another. As a consequence, there would be a continual competition to lower payments (what is now referred to as a "race to the bottom").

In Tullock's judgment, however, the feeling of sympathy for the poor is strongest within the local community and falls off rapidly as geographical distance increases. Historically, this theory is borne out by the success of the English Poor Law system and the pre-1930 successes of local community poverty programs in the United States.

"Aid in Kind" rigorously explores the motivations of donors who insist on providing gifts in kind to the poor rather than providing them with cash transfers. Tullock deploys indifference curve analysis to evaluate the efficiency implications of in-kind transfers.

"Demand Revealing, Transfers, and Rent Seeking" demonstrates that the demand-revealing mechanism is superior to majority voting in limiting inefficient wealth transfers. The Clarke tax, implicit in this mechanism, prevents a number of transfers in which the transfer itself is not wealth enhancing, and in other cases it at least reduces their magnitude. In cases in which the donors obtain some benefit from the transfers, the demand-revealing process leads to larger transfers than the majority-vote method.

"Epilogue—The Grating People" notes that Washington, D.C., the capital of the world's largest welfare state, is also the place where the poorest people in the city (the grating people) are taken care of primarily by private charity. The graters are so well cared for privately that their numbers increased significantly during the middle years of the twentieth century. The *Washington Post*, simulating upset at the number of graters on the streets, systematically failed to suggest that its billionaire owner, Katherine Graham, and its wealthy editors and reporters, should transfer a large part of their wealth directly to these unfortunates. The *Post* also failed to recommend the establishment of earmarked government funds directed exclusively to the grating people, whose plight in bitterly cold winters it so vigorously deplored. Tullock leaves his readers to resolve this puzzle concerning the inconsistent attitude of the media toward welfare policy in the United States.

Part 3 of the volume, "Redistributive Politics," collects six papers that focus on the various forces of public choice that drive government programs of wealth and income redistribution.

"The Machiavellians and the Well-Intentioned" provides an explanation of why the democracies have shifted from transfer policies administered through means testing only to the poor to transfer policies designed to benefit everyone. Tullock rejects the standard explanation that generalized programs are designed to avoid stigmatizing the poor. Instead, he relies on the politics of deception as the correct explanation.

Two kinds of Machiavellians influence the political market in transfers through overtly deceptive behavior. The well-intentioned redistributionists seek to generalize government transfer programs as a means of securing otherwise reluctant middle-class support for programs that will help the poor. The selfish Machiavellians simply seek to secure government transfers for themselves. In both cases, they use deception by claiming that the transfer programs are designed primarily to assist the poor.

"Helping the Poor vs. Helping the Well-Organized" draws upon Tullock's earlier scholarship on rational voter ignorance, interest group behavior, rent seeking, and logrolling to explain how middle-class factions are able so effectively to subvert transfer programs to their own perceived advantage. Because the poor are unable to counterorganize effectively, they are often defenseless against such manipulations of the political process.

"Horizontal Transfers" focuses attention on coercive transfers of a horizontal nature, in that they occur primarily among and between members of the same (primarily middle-) income class. Such transfers (even cash transfers that take the form of marginal income taxes and subsidies, but especially transfers in kind) come with significant excess burdens, which implies that the transfer society will be less wealthy than the nontransfer society.

In Tullock's judgment, logrolling within the legislature, responding to rent seeking on the part of decisive interest groups, explains the generally perceived pattern of horizontal income transfers. Such logrolling behavior with respect to transfers is wealth-reducing for society as a whole, and therefore it tends to assume an opaque, noncash form that is not easily discerned by the general electorate.

"Information and Logrolling" examines the problems posed by the lack of information that plagues political markets and explores its implications for logrolling transfers. Tullock again emphasizes the incentives to be rationally ignorant that confront individual voters in a large democracy. Rational ignorance inevitably becomes even more prevalent when voters confront complex logrolling procedures within the legislature designed to obfuscate the pattern and overall cost of horizontal income transfers.

"The Mixed Case" explores the implications for transfer payments to the poor of a full democratic voting mechanism in which both the better off and the poor are enfranchised. In such circumstances, the outcome tends to be a large welfare state that transfers only a small amount to the poor. Tullock explores alternative voting mechanisms capable of ameliorating this outcome, notably that of providing individuals with voting power as a reciprocal of their respective incomes. He notes that there is no evident enthusiasm for such a solution among the middle classes.

"General Welfare or Welfare for the Poor Only" focuses attention on the differential implications for the poor of general programs as compared with means-tested programs. Tullock argues persuasively that means-tested programs—to the extent that they can be implemented in a majoritarian democracy—help the poor more than do general transfer programs. Because general programs are designed to satisfy the self-seeking motives of the middle-income groups, typically general programs serve those groups much more than they do the poor. In some instances, the poor may be worse off under such generalized transfer programs than under a zero-transfer system.

Part 4 of the book, "The Expanding Frontiers of Wealth Redistribution," brings together five papers that provide, from a public choice perspective, detailed analyses of specific programs that typify the modern welfare state.

"Old Age Pensions" critically analyzes the political implications of the social security system for old-age pensions in all Western democracies, but notably within the United States. Using a simple model, Tullock demonstrates that when the old-age system is first introduced all working individuals and all new retirees benefit, at a cost to all those below working age and all future generations. In addition, career bureaucrats, who stand to gain from the expansion of government services, lobby strongly for its implementation. Therefore, the initiative is politically popular.

Once the system is in place, any cessation would impose high transitional costs on the elderly, whose private savings will have declined as a consequence of the promised pension. Powerful political lobbying is predictable from this group and from career bureaucrats to retain the publicly provided pension scheme.

"Risk, Charity, and Miscellaneous Aspects of Social Security" advances the discussion further to take into account the dynamics of a pay-as-you-go social security system. Tullock notes that once the program reaches its maximum size, both in membership and in the percentages of income taken and income paid back in pensions, it becomes much less attractive to the (median) voter. In such circumstances, cuts in pension rates become a predictable public choice response.

If benefit cuts are imposed, the program is rendered even less attractive to younger workers and, ultimately, the viability of the entire program is threatened. If the program collapses, the poor will be the hardest hit, because before the program's inception the poor could rely on private charity networks to survive into old age.

"Education and Medicine" focuses public choice attention on two other major components of the modern welfare state. With respect to public education, Tullock notes that the transition effects are almost exactly the opposite of those for the pensions scheme. When public education is first introduced, those parents who have already educated their children suddenly find themselves paying taxes for which they receive no evident return. Parents whose children are advanced in the education process may also be net losers. The termination of the scheme also has opposite effects to the pension scenario, in that all posteducation individuals receive a net benefit from the transition.

In such circumstances, the selfish vote motive works against the introduction of public education. Tullock puts forward alternative explanations for the emergence of such programs.

With respect to medicine, Tullock explains how a government-subsidized health program may actually worsen the treatment of the poor. He illustrates his argument with empirical data drawn from the early experience of the British National Health Service.

"Administrative Transfers" reviews a number of important wealth transfers implemented through administered special privileges (rent seeking), for example, import quotas, farm-acreage restrictions, and airline regulation. Tullock shows how the stated objective of each of these regulations differs sharply from its actual purpose (and effect). He carefully identifies the public choice impulses behind such interventions.

"Giving Life" looks at the way in which voters confront the collective choice problem of making tragic choices (choices about who should live and who should die) under situations of resource scarcity. Tullock argues that voters rationally abdicate active decision making in such circumstances. He outlines the variety of alternative devices that are implemented in real-world tragic choice situations.

Part 5 of the book consists of one paper that summarizes Tullock's proposed solutions to the many public choice problems that trouble redistribution policy under democratic regimes.

"What to Do—What to Do" directly confronts the many paradoxes that dominate political wealth-transfer markets. Tullock assumes that individuals hold values that are charitable to some extent but that otherwise seek to attain as wealthy and as efficient a society as possible. On this basis, he speculates as to what kind of welfare state might best satisfy such underlying objectives. As one might expect, Tullock suggests a radical reform of the existing institutions of the modern welfare state.

Tullock's contributions to the economics and politics of wealth redistribution bring a refreshing antidote of realism to a field of economics that is overly dominated by utopian thinking. Only by thoroughly understanding the real-world impulses that drive redistribution policy, Tullock argues, can one hope to introduce reforms that have any expectation of effectively moving resources to the deserving poor rather than to allow such resources to be dissipated by self-seeking, rent-seeking struggles among the politically adept middle classes.

PART I

WHY REDISTRIBUTE WEALTH?

INCOME REDISTRIBUTION

Income redistribution is one of the most important activities of the modern state. For many people, this is both an observation of what states do and a normative judgment of what they should do. From this point of view it may seem odd that a discussion of income redistribution has been put off to the end of the book. The reason for this is not an effort to discriminate against this particular governmental activity, but the fact that it does raise unique issues. Although there are efficiency aspects and externalities of some importance in income redistribution, the basic problems are nevertheless radically different. It seems sensible, therefore, to discuss this rather special subject in a separate chapter rather than distributing it in little bits throughout the rest of the book.

The proponents of income redistribution are seldom clear as to exactly why they desire it. I think this is not because they are trying to conceal their motives, but because they think that their reasons are so obvious that they require no discussion. In fact, however, the reasons for desiring redistribution of income are rather complicated. Furthermore, I think that many of the programs we see in the real world have been organized under the slogans implying one particular set of motives but are actually aimed at serving another set. For this reason, it seems sensible to begin a discussion of externalities by a discussion of the reasons why we might want income redistribution.

The standard explanation for income redistribution is a desire to help the poor and downtrodden.[1] A person who wishes to help the poor may feel that it would be desirable that the poor have things given to them that they now do not have. Here, however, we come to a problem of the source of the gifts. I could, for example, be interested in helping the poor and deal with this desire by making a gift from my own pocket. This would be a free market activity. There is no reason why I cannot do it on any scale that I wish, and if things were that simple, we could leave this activity entirely to the private

Reprinted, with permission, from *Private Wants, Public Means: An Economic Analysis of the Desirable Scope of Government* (New York and London: Basic Books, 1970), 247–57.

1. Some "charitable" projects aim at helping people who are ill, regardless of their income level. The probable reason for this is a feeling that a person who is in pain is in a "bad way" regardless of the luxury of the surroundings in which he suffers.

sector. There are, however, some very great inefficiencies in both private and public charity, and they are perhaps worse in private charity.[2] Furthermore, as we shall learn, there are externalities involved. These externalities do not mean that I cannot make a gift to the poor, but they do provide a sort of external economy in giving gifts to the poor, so that I might be willing to make larger gifts to the poor through some kind of collective mechanism than I would be willing to make through individual gifts.

Let us now, however, pause to note that I might wish to have the poor helped but not wish to help them myself (at least not wish that they get the major part of their help from me). I might feel that someone else (in most cases, people who are wealthier than I) should help the poor. Now it will be noted that if I have the power, because I am a voter, or because I am in absolute control, to force some other person (let us say, Mr. A) to transfer income to a poor person, Mr. B, then probably I have the power to force him to transfer that money to me, and so (in a sense) I am making a direct charitable contribution to Mr. B. There would be, of course, cases in which I could compel Mr. A to transfer the money to Mr. B, but not compel him to transfer it to me. If this is so, then I am not engaged in charitable activity. In most cases, however, if I am able to manipulate the government to provide private transfer from Mr. A to Mr. B, I would also be able to divert the transfer from Mr. B to myself. Hence, I am in fact being charitable when I see that money goes to Mr. B. In any event, I shall for the present regard these two activities as being essentially charitable. A direct transfer of money to someone who is other than the person or persons who arrange the transfer, we shall call charitable, whether the source of the money transferred is the person who arranges the transfer or someone else.

If the income redistribution plans that are such a major part of modern state activity largely transferred money to the very poor, we could reasonably explain them in terms of this charitable motive. In practice, however, we find that the bulk of the beneficiaries of redistribution of income are not poor people. Undeniably some income is redistributed away from the very wealthy—although surprisingly little, given their voting weakness—and some income is redistributed to the very poor, but the bulk of the redistribution is a shifting of money among people in the middle income bracket. This naturally brings us to the second possible reason for favoring income

2. See Gordon Tullock, "Information Without Profit," *Papers on Non-Market Decision Making*, 1 (1966): 141–59.

redistribution. I might favor income redistribution because I anticipate that I will benefit from it. I am, let us say, a farmer, and I feel, correctly, that I will be much poorer if I have to sell my products in an ordinary competitive market. I therefore join with a number of fellow farmers and get from the government a program that raises my income. Naturally, I do not argue for this program in terms of the increase in my income. I may urge that it is necessary for the national defense or that it helps the poor, and, of course, there may be some poor who are helped. My basic motive, however, is to help myself. Most income redistribution activities in the government sector are motivated by pressure groups with this kind of simple, straightforward objective.

It is fairly easy to demonstrate that if a given redistribution of income is directed primarily by the people who receive it and who are not thought suitable objects of charity by others, then there is a loss to society from the transfer. If there are no persons other than Mr. A or Mr. B who are interested in the transfer from Mr. A to Mr. B, which would be true if Mr. B is not markedly poorer than Mr. A, then there are no externalities of a favorable nature, that is, no people who gain from the transfer except Mr. B. There are, however, some significant negative externalities: First, there is the excess burden of the tax that is used to raise the money for the transfer; second, is the excess burden caused by the delivery of the subsidy to Mr. B; and third, and probably vastly larger than either of these, is the large investment of resources in political maneuvering that is necessary to carry out the transfer. Thus, it would appear that those transfers of income, so common in modern states, that shift money from people who are politically weak to people who are politically strong are economically inefficient and cause significant waste. Needless to say, this argument is not conclusive in those cases in which money is transferred from one person to another, and a third person benefits from it because for some reason (normally because the recipient is poor) he feels that this improves the distribution of income in society.

Having clearly distinguished between two possible reasons for favoring the redistribution of income—a desire to make a charitable contribution, and a desire to gain money for myself—I am now forced to point out that these two motives have been inextricably entwined by a great many very well meaning scholars. The position was most clearly stated by Anthony Downs.[3] If I now discuss primarily the arguments offered by Downs, it will be because he states a widely held view with great clarity. If I am interested in helping a

3. *An Economic Theory of Democracy* (New York: Harper & Row, Publishers, 1957).

poor person, this is charity on my part. But from the standpoint of the poor person, his interest in receiving the money is not charitable, but simply a desire to benefit himself. The Downs argument points this out as true and suggests that we design governments in such a way that the poor are able to use their selfish desire to get money from the rich in order to compel the rich to make income transfers that are desirable for charitable motives. Downs assumes that ordinary majority voting provides the right amount of redistribution, but there is no reason to believe that this is so. It could just as well be true that we should give the poor (let us say) two votes for every one given to wealthy persons, or vice versa.

Furthermore, there is the question of the size of the government unit in which the transfer is to be made. Rothenberg engaged in unconscious circular reasoning with respect to this problem.[4] He started with an existing historically determined governmental unit to obtain the "right amount of redistribution," and then used this amount to design optimal governmental units. However, any application of this line of reasoning is necessarily circular.

It is probable that one could design a voting system to provide any given transfer of money to the poor from the wealthy. There is no obvious reason, however, to believe that any existing voting system is optimal in this sense. If I feel that the poor should receive (let us say) 5 per cent of the national income and I feel confident that the people who would be making gifts will, in fact, give only 2 per cent, I can probably arrange a constitution that compels them to make 5 per cent gifts. It is, however, hard to see any argument for this except simply my desire to force them to do something they do not want to do. It seems simpler to avoid all problems of voting procedures and just set up a flat rule that they must give whatever I feel is the right amount instead of concealing the imposition of my preferences upon them under a voting rule.

Regardless of these rules, what we actually observe in democracy is that majority voting does not redistribute much money to the poor and does redistribute a great deal of money to people who are by no means poor. This last activity, as we have noted, is almost a total social waste. It may seem perverse, after this discussion of what actually happens in a democracy, to confine oneself to discussing only that type of redistribution of income that

4. "Decentralization, Externalities, Equity, and Inter-Government Relations," presented as a paper at a Universities-National Bureau Conference, National Bureau of Economic Research, Committee of Production and Distribution of Public Products (April 26–27, 1968). To be published in a *Proceedings* of this conference.

actually benefits the poor, but that is the purpose of the remainder of this chapter. My point is simply that this is the only type of redistribution that can be justified by externalities. Redistribution from one group of middle-class people to another is not a way of generating favorable externalities, although it will usually generate unfavorable externalities.

Turning then to the pure problem of charitable redistribution, we should remember that there is no reason why any individual who is concerned with the poor may not transfer money to the poor himself. There are, however, two reasons to believe that the transfer of funds we would obtain in this manner would be less than optimal. In this sense, note that we are discussing the optimum for the man who is making a transfer, not the optimum for the poor person who is receiving the money. Clearly, any amount received will be gratefully accepted.[5] Thus, in determining an optimum, we must leave aside the preferences of the recipients. The poor person is simply a special example of those persons who wish transfers to themselves, and there is no reason why we should regard his desires as having any greater weight in designing the system than those of anyone else. The reason we help the poor is not that they wish to be helped—for, after all, I would like to be helped—but that other people wish to help them.

The externalities concerned with helping the poor are essentially twofold. In the first place, if I am made unhappy by a man starving in front of my door, and I give him some bread so that he does not die, this act not only benefits me, but it also benefits anyone else in the vicinity who is unhappy because of the starvation of this individual. Thus, I have created a positive externality for other persons, and as is generally true, this situation would lead to an underinvestment in helping that starving man. This is a fairly simple example of a consumption externality, and it is a situation in which my consumption of something benefits other people as well, and hence the social optimum would call for a subsidy.

The second type of externality is rather more special and as far as I know is found nowhere except in the single example of charity.[6] Briefly, let us

5. Anyone doubting this may experiment by sending the author a check.

6. For a detailed technical explanation, see my comment on Marglin's "The Social Rate of Discount and the Optimal Rate of Investment: Comment," *Quarterly Journal of Economics*, 78 (May 1964): 331–36. It may seem bizarre to cite a comment on another article as a primary source, particularly since my comment in this case is not original, but I think that this comment is clearer than anything else in the literature. Vickrey, who actually first thought of the idea, treated it in an extremely brief, even cryptic, manner.

suppose that I am contemplating giving money to a poor man. I would continue making gifts to him until the value to me of one dollar transferred to him (that is, an improvement in his well-being by one dollar) is exactly equivalent to the one dollar cost to me. Suppose, however, that I enter into an agreement with someone else and we jointly give him the money. Under these circumstances, the cost to me of improving the poor man's well-being by one dollar is only fifty cents. Hence, I would extend charitable gifts to him until the benefit to me of his receiving one dollar equals the cost of fifty cents to me. Here we have a modifying feature. Presumably I have some interest in the well-being of my cogiver and hence would take into account that he is also worse off by fifty cents, but my concern for him would be, in general, much smaller than my concern for the loss of a second fifty cents of my own. This is clearly a production externality. Note that this second type of externality in giving has two rather conspicuous characteristics: First, as the group engaged in making gifts grows larger, the effect on each member of the group falls off quite rapidly. In general, there is no great gain in increasing group size above a rather low maximum. A second point to be noted is that it assumes that the givers in a community all have exactly the same objectives. If I would like to make a gift to Mr. A, but the only agreement I can arrange with someone else is to jointly make a gift to Mr. B, I may indeed choose to make a larger gift to Mr. B than I would originally have given to Mr. A, but I will not be as well-off as if I could have obtained the same agreement for the aid of Mr. A.

But, having established the existence of an externality in charitable gifts, when we turn to deciding on the optimum size of the unit to make the gift, we find ourselves almost immediately in serious difficulties. It would seem per se that the average individual might have either one of two types of preferences with respect to poverty. First, he might simply be interested in helping the poor defined in terms of income. This would mean that the geographical location of a poor person would not be of any great interest to him, and he would make contributions entirely to an international charity that provided funds for the poor in low-income areas. Since most of the people in the world who are really poor live outside the Western countries, and since most of the people who make large charitable gifts live in the Western countries, one would anticipate that charity would very largely be a process of transferring funds from the Western countries to the Eastern and African countries. Needless to say, this is not what we observe. There are some transfers by governmental means from the wealthy Western countries to the backward parts of the world, but these transfers are trivial compared with the transfers within the Western countries themselves.

Even if we confine ourselves to that part of the transfer of income within the Western countries that actually goes to the poor, a rather small part, it is still true that this transfer is much larger than the transfer to the poor in other countries. This is particularly true since most of the foreign-aid programs are not aimed at helping the poorest people in the foreign countries. Thus, helping the poorest people is clearly not what modern democracies do.

The second possibility would seem to be that concern for the poor would vary inversely as the distance of the poor from the giver. The point of this particular preference pattern would be largely that I am distressed by the sight of the poor or by their near presence, and that the poor who live far away disturb me very little or not at all. Under these circumstances, one would anticipate that we would find charity lessening as we move away from individuals who are well-off. If this latter pattern of preferences existed among charitable people, one could very readily specify an appropriate system of charitable disposition. One would anticipate the participation of local governments in considerable charity for people in their immediate vicinity; a larger level (say, equivalent to the United States) engaging in a lower level of charity for everyone in their state; and finally a large government (let us say, national) engaging in very low level charity for all the people in the country. We would anticipate that there would be more charity in the first category than in the second, or in the second than in the third. This would occur because each voter was more interested in charity for people close to him than in charity for people who were at intermediate or great distances from him. Once again, this is not what we observe.

It may be, however, that the present institutions represent not a true expression of people's preferences but a rather accidental survival from the 1930's. During the Great Depression, expenditures of federal funds were, to all intents and purposes, free, since they contributed to recovery. Expenditures of local funds, however, did not have this fortunate effect, since the local governments could not print money. Under the circumstances, a transfer of many functions to the central government was sensible, and relief (apparently a temporary but large expenditure), particularly so. It may be that the present organization of our relief, then, does not represent the shape of individual desires with respect to charity but is simply a hangover from this period. But this is only a possibility. What we need here is more research as to whom people, in fact, do want to help. From this research we will be able to determine what the optimal unit for income redistribution is.

This chapter has been rather inconclusive. Charity may have externalities and hence may be a suitable area for governmental activity. We have been unable, however, to determine exactly what the government unit that is engaged in it should be, because it is impossible for us to tell much about the shape of individual preferences with respect to charity. This inconclusiveness is not a theoretical defect but an empirical one. We need further information about people's desires with respect to charity before we can make any definite decision.

HELPING THE POOR

In the last chapter we talked about a rather discouraging but important topic, the use of the government by private individuals to redistribute income for profit. In this chapter we are going to talk about a topic which is no doubt less important but which, nevertheless, is the traditional topic in the discussion of income redistribution: helping the poor. We are not going to talk only about the Robin Hood state, which takes from the rich and gives to the poor, but also about the making of gifts to the poor whether it is done by private individuals or by government.

In other words we are going to talk about transfers motivated by the desire to help other people. All of us have that desire to some extent. We are willing to make modest gifts to people who we feel are worse off than we are. We also frequently make gifts to people whom we just feel we should make gifts to. The President of the United States and the Queen of England are recipients of large-scale gifts by various private persons. In both of these cases their security officials prevent them from actual benefiting from the gifts. In an unusual case, after the Kennedy assassination, Officer Tippet's family received over $400,000 in completely unsolicited gifts from total strangers. More remarkably, Marina Oswald received $200,000 in similar gifts. It would be easy to feel sorry for either of these people—after all Mrs. Oswald was in no way responsible for her husband's crime—but it is not at all clear that they were particularly bad off. I don't know the Dallas police force arrangements for families of officers killed on duty, but I doubt that they faced any real poverty.

Note that we are not talking about intra-family gifts. That is not because intra-family gifts are unimportant; they are immensely important in both the family and the economy as a whole. They, however, do not raise any particular policy issues. We will therefore confine ourselves to gifts outside the family.

To repeat, most people do feel certain charitable urges and are willing to help people who are poorer than themselves. We will discuss this phenomenon and, in particular, whether it should be done privately or collectively. In this case, however, the collective provision is somewhat unusual. When we

Reprinted, with permission, from *Welfare for the Well-to-Do* (Dallas: Fisher Institute, 1983), 15–29.

talk about people who are motivated by charitable motives, the person who receives the charity is not an example. In other words, if we think of a democracy in which everyone can vote, which is the normal practice, we do not get an expression of pure charity but an expression of charity on the part of some people and a selfish desire to get more money on the part of the people who receive the transfers. In order to simplify the discussion, we will leave that case until later. Here, we will assume that people receiving charity do not vote and that any democratic voting is entirely on the part of those who are making the gift. This is, in general, not our normal procedure in the United States. Interestingly enough, it was the law in England until the end of the 19th century, and it was in practice, although not in theory, the procedure in many parts of the United States.

As an example, let's use one obvious case in which American citizens engage democratically in making charitable gifts and in which the recipients of the charity are not permitted to vote. This is foreign aid. Foreign aid goes to people who are much poorer than the average American (at least that part of it which is not siphoned off by the higher government officials in the recipient country), but these people are not permitted to have any role in the decision process as to how much they will receive. So when we talk about democratic voting for charity in this chapter, think not in terms of the payment to poor Americans, who are permitted to cast their votes and are apt to vote primarily for congressmen who want to raise that amount, but in terms of aid to poor citizens of, let us say, Bangladesh, who do not have that right to influence the decision.

Of course, not only democracies engage in helping the poor. Indeed, almost every government of which we have any historic record has done this to some extent. In fact, the evidence on the matter is weak, but apparently the poor did relatively about as well in the United States in 1850, before we had what we call the welfare state, as they do today. Incomes, in general, have risen, including the incomes of the poor, but individual poor persons appear to receive about the same relative share. There don't seem to be any data on other countries from which this comparison can be extended, but it is certainly true that aid to the poor has been part of the government agenda in most societies of which we have any record. That, of course, does not prove that government aid to the poor is desirable, and it certainly does not prove that the poor are better off with government aid than with private gifts.

Regardless of that, let us start with private gifts. As I mentioned in the last chapter, private gifts have an intriguing characteristic of super-efficiency; i.e.,

$1 produces $2's worth of net utility. The giver gets $1's worth of satisfaction out of his gift, and the receiver also gets $1's worth. If we consider private charitable organizations as they have existed in the past and exist now, we quickly observe a phenomenon which involves limited collectivization. For example, a wealthy man will agree with his alma mater that he will match gifts from other people to the university. Once he has done this, if I make a gift of $1 to the university, the university in fact will get $2. I can buy gifts to the university in a cheap store.

It is not absolutely certain that this technique would lead me to give more money to the university, but it seems highly likely that it will. Note, by the way, that the wealthy man is also receiving matching utility; i.e., every $1 he gives actually benefits the university by $2. Assuming that neither I nor the wealthy man cares about the other's well-being, we are each buying our charity in a low-price market by making this joint gift.

Because this technique is widely used to raise money, it appears that it actually does lead people to make larger net gifts than they would if they were not so matched. Suppose, however, that there was not just a $1-for-$1 matching as in our wealthy case, but that my $1 gift would be matched by, let us say, $10 million. If I chose to give $5, $50 million would go to the poor, and if I chose to give $7, $70 million. It seems likely that under these circumstances, I would choose to make a larger gift to the poor than if my $5 merely meant that the poor were better off by $5.

What has this to do with the choice between private and collective gifts? Oddly enough, Milton Friedman, in his famous book *Capitalism and Freedom*,[1] produced the first really intellectually respectable argument for government charity. Governments have been doing it for some 5,000 years without having any respectable argument, but now there is a suitable rationalization. The argument is based on the phenomenon of matching given above.

Let us see how this is so. Consider the situation of an imaginary state which has 10 million citizens, all of whom are permitted to vote, and it is considering making a charitable gift to citizens of another state who, of course, do not have the vote in our first state. Each individual in a country of 10 million can, if he wishes, make a gift to the citizen of the poor country. Citizens of the wealthy country might well feel, however, that they would be happier making gifts collectively, because each individual could feel that his gift was being matched by 9,999,999 others.

1. Milton Friedman, *Capitalism and Freedom* (Chicago: University of Chicago Press, 1962).

It is not certain that they would feel this way, but it is reasonably probable. Indeed, if they have normal preferences, it can be demonstrated that they would shift from the individual gift, let us say, every person giving $5, to a collective gift, in which each person was taxed $7 which was then distributed. The recipients of the charity would also be better off. This argument is a strong one, but it should be kept in mind that it only applies to those polities in which the recipients of the charity are not permitted to influence the amount of the transfer. That is not the way the United States deals with its own citizens.

There are some difficulties with this demonstration, two of which I do not intend to discuss at any length. The first is simply moral principle. Most Americans feel that the government has a moral duty to help the poor, but there is a minority of Americans who feel it is morally wicked for the government to take money from its better-off citizens to help the poor. I shall let these two groups fight out the moral issue among themselves.

The second problem I will not discuss here in any detail is the difference between the model I gave above, in which the citizens directly vote on the amount they will give to citizens of another country, and the actual circumstances of our complex representative democracy. Here, I leave the subject aside not because it is uninteresting but because I have devoted much of my life to writing books and articles about the functioning of representative democracy. We can, I think, simply offer the generalization that because of the complexity of the American representative government, the majority preference is subject to a lot of random noise and disturbance in the process of being implemented. The result is that variance from the preference of a majority of the people can go either way when special interests are not involved.

Let me turn to the problems more relevant to our discussion. The first of these is the fact that the different citizens of our charitable country presumably want to give different amounts of money to the poor in the other countries. I might feel, for example, that it is desirable that everyone give $9, and you might prefer $5. The actual vote might come out with $7 per person, or $70 million for society as a whole. Neither you nor I would be perfectly satisfied with this outcome.

This particular problem is inevitable in this kind of collective matching as a method of charity. Of course, it is not necessary that every individual pay the same amount. We might have a matching scheme under which the wealthy paid, let us say, twice as much as the poor, and still have everyone fairly happy. We cannot, however, adjust to individual preferences in the system.

This is clearly an objection, but it seems doubtful that discontent about the exact size of the gift on the part of individual citizens would cause them to abandon this super-efficient way of increasing the value of their gift. Given my choice of making a $9 gift to the other country or joining with the other citizens to each give a $7 gift, with the result that the country gives $70 million, I would surely select the latter.

Consider briefly this difference between a private charitable gift and a democratically voted gift. In the case of making a private charitable gift, I know that if I give $7 or $10 to Bangladesh, it receives $7 or $10. The cost to me is also $7 to $10. On the other hand, if I vote for a tax on everyone of, let us say, $7 to be distributed to Bangladesh, the cost to me is $7 and the benefit to Bangladesh is $70 million.

If I were thinking of using the private charity method, I might well assume other people would also make gifts, but the net effect of my gift would still always be exactly what it cost me, while in the democratic process that is not so.

The above argument impresses many people as paradoxical, but it can be formally demonstrated to be correct. I suppose the fact that Milton Friedman invented the argument in and of itself should be strong evidence that it is correct. He is, in the first place, an extremely competent economist and, secondly, not noted as a believer in all-encompassing state control.

The second problem I want to discuss at length is somewhat more important. So far I have been talking about foreign-aid programs in which the recipients of the charity are not permitted to vote. Transfers within the society in most democracies are not run that way. The recipients of the transfer may vote. In the United States they vote at a lower percentage than other groups, but still a great many of them do vote. Further, there is no doubt that their votes influence outcomes. Politicians do talk and vote in the legislature as if they were concerned about these recipients of transfers.

It is obvious if the recipients of charity participate in the decision as to how much charity they will receive, the givers of charity no longer are necessarily unambiguously benefited by collectivization. Instead of the givers deciding how much will be given, the givers and the receivers will jointly make the decision. Thus, the argument given above for collectivization is weakened and, some would say, made invalid.

Now, here we have constitutional and legal, not to say moral, problems. Surely the poor have a legal and constitutional right to vote, and most people would say they also have a moral right. I am talking here about what is desirable policy, however, not what is the current law. Further, I don't want to enter into moral debates. I will leave that problem to clergymen. Thus, I am going to confine discussion to the fact that the poor can vote on gifts to them if the gifts are made by the American government and they are American citizens. They cannot vote on gifts to them made by the American government if they are citizens of Bangladesh—as a policy question, not as a question of either morals or constitutional rules. Those who feel that the moral and/or constitutional principles should take priority are quite free to debate these issues among themselves, but they are not my topic.

In practice, the vote of the poor on charitable matters does not seem to make all that much difference. The actual numbers show that the poor do not do well in the United States. In 1981, the average American family of four that was completely dependent on our basic welfare program received about $4,000 in cash for the year and food stamps with a nominal value of about $2,000, for a total of $6,000—if you regard the food stamps as having a true value equal to their nominal value, or perhaps $5,500 if you evaluate the food stamps at a lower level. Clearly, this is not an immense amount of money.

The amount received is remarkable because it is not much more than such a poor family would have received if the total amount currently being transferred by the American government as part of its many "welfare" plans had simply been divided among the whole population. I mentioned that before the development of the welfare state the poor were doing about as well as they are now. (The welfare state will be discussed at considerable length later, but I should point out now that its actual inventor was Prince Bismarck, not a man notable for a desire to help the poor. Bismarck, normally called the Iron Chancellor, is primarily known for having united Germany under the leadership of Prussia in the mid-nineteenth century. In addition, however, to his great diplomatic skills and his ability to plan wars so that he won easily, he also founded the modern welfare state. His social reforms introduced around 1880 were copied throughout the world, and our Social Security Administration and government provision of medicine are simply distant echoes of his work.)

Of course, the poor do not receive only the direct cash transfers that I have listed above. They get various government services, for example free schools, that are available to all. Most of us, however, pay taxes roughly equivalent to our receipt. That is not true with the poor, because they pay relatively few taxes. Further, by a tradition going back to the Middle Ages, the poor in general receive free medical attention, currently under a combined state and federal program. Still, the total amount is by no means remarkably large.

Why the poor do not do much better than they do in a democracy in which they can vote is a little mysterious. One would think that they would receive a certain amount of money through pure charity from the people who are better off than they, and then that they could use their votes to add to that by political power. In practice, though, it looks as if they don't receive much more than they would probably receive if they were deprived of the vote. Indeed, I have on occasion argued that they would do better if they depended solely on the charitable instincts of the "better off" than they in practice do in our functioning democracy.

There are two apparent reasons why the poor do not do better than they do: one technical and one having to do with the poor themselves. To begin with the technical problem, modern government in a democracy to a large extent involves complicated bargains among different people. For example: the building of the Tombigbee Canal is traded off against a new repair contract for an anti-aircraft carrier in Philadelphia and the expansion of the wilderness areas in Idaho. The poor have a technical disadvantage in these bargains because it is obvious exactly how much they benefit from any increase in payments to them. It is not obvious how much the citizens living along the Tombigbee benefit from the construction of that canal. Thus, in the bargaining, the poor aren't able to keep any of their cards covered, whereas the people they are dealing with have almost all of them covered. Under the circumstances, it is not surprising that the poor do badly.

This technical problem is severely reinforced by the simple fact that the poor are normally poor because they lack the necessary characteristics to be well-off. Some of them are ill, which makes it difficult for them to keep their jobs and also makes it difficult for them to engage in political maneuvering. Others are not very bright which, once again, makes it difficult for them to get jobs or engage in political maneuvering. A third group lack motivation, possibly because of the absence of suitable role models, which is such a fashionable topic at the moment. This handicaps them in making a living, and also handicaps them in politics. A fourth, and in my opinion small group of the poor, are intelligent and reasonably strongly motivated, but their motives lead them to play a role in society which is not highly rewarded. This fourth group, of whom some artists are examples, normally are not motivated to become active in politics.

Thus, the poor are, in general, a group of people who don't do well in any aspect of life. The artists may do well in what interests them, but they are not likely to be effective outside that narrow sphere.

So, just as they are poor because they lack the role models, intelligence, and drive necessary to make a decent income, they are also handicapped equivalently in doing well in politics. They have failed in the economic market, which is what we mean by saying that they are poor. There is no reason to believe that they will succeed in the political market. We should not be surprised that they are not able to get a high return on their votes.

Now all of this sounds like an unkind thing to say about the poor, and certainly it is not praising them, but we should not regard this as meaning that they are to be discriminated against or punished. We feel charitable motives to help those who are worse off than we are. Normally, the reason that they are worse off is irrelevant.

To summarize, there is a quite good argument for collectivizing charitable distribution when the distribution is to somebody like the citizens of a foreign country who can't vote in American elections. The argument deteriorates if we turn to the actual situation in the United States in which the recipients of charity, the poor, can vote and their vote influences how much they receive. Looking at the matter realistically, however, it does not appear that they are able to get much of a return on their vote and hence may not make much difference. It is certainly true that the genuine poor in the United States do not benefit much from the various programs which have been enacted in their name.

It may well be that the low return the poor get in the United States is simply what the voters want. The whole welfare state system may, in fact, exist not to help the poor but to make transfers to more politically influential people in the middle class, while the discussion of the poor is to a large extent camouflage. This cannot, of course, be proved and in fact may be an unjust statement. The politically influential people who get so much out of Congress may honestly be in favor of helping the poor but primarily are concerned with other matters. Certainly there is some transfer of funds to the poor.

As an example of public policy advocated to a large extent by labor unions and people who normally would refer to themselves as representatives of the lower classes, consider the "voluntary" quotas on Japanese automobile imports. Beneficiaries of these quotas, so far as they have beneficiaries, are primarily the employees of the automobile industry, who are among the most highly paid workers in the United States, and the owners of stock in the automobile companies. The stockholders are a rather more diverse group, income-wise, than the employees. Indeed, the employees by way of their pension trusts hold a good deal of stock. Nevertheless, it does not seem likely that many poor people will benefit because of the improved values of automobile company stock.

The poor people, in fact, will be injured. It should not be forgotten that the United States is a very wealthy country, and many of the people we classify as poor own cars. That is particularly true in rural areas. These cars are basically second-hand cars rather than new ones, but nevertheless a rise in the price of new cars tends to "trickle down" to the purchasers of used cars.

But the quota has not actually raised the price of all cars in the United States, only some cars. The Japanese automobile industry is not managed by stupid and inept people. Being compelled to restrict the total number of cars they can ship to the United States by these quotas, they realized they could make more money on each car if they shipped in expensive cars instead of cheap cars. In consequence, they have increased their shipments to the United States of the more expensive cars and reduced their shipments of the cheaper kind. The result is that the more expensive cars in the United States aren't quite as much more expensive as they used to be. In other words, the producers of the higher priced American lines face stronger competition from Japanese companies, whereas producers of lower priced lines face much less competition. Of course, the industry as a whole faced less competition before, because the total number of cars entering is restricted, but there has been a distortion of the Japanese car exports to the United States in such a way as to benefit upper income purchasers of new cars.

Now I don't want to argue here that the people who pushed this program through, presumably all of them in the top half of the income distribution, were consciously trying to injure the poor. It was just that the issue's effect on the poor was of less interest to them than its effect on their own well-being. A significant redistribution was enacted by government regulation in this case rather than by tax. The beneficiaries were automobile workers, owners of stock in automobiles, and people who buy expensive new cars. The losers were people who buy cheap new cars and, secondarily, the people who buy used cars.

This situation is not atypical. Lip service is paid to helping the poor, and, of course, we in fact do help the poor a good deal, but the really big transfers made by the American government do not go to the poor. A tax on the rich and allegations that we should take money away from them, which I think come very largely from a feeling of envy, are also common. As a matter of fact, the total income by people in "the $200,000 to $500,000 bracket" is small enough that even if we could confiscate all of it, the effect on the budget would be insignificant.

The income transfer system in the United States is very largely a transfer from one group of middle-class citizens to another. We do help the poor to some extent, and we do to some extent take money away from the wealthy, but both of these are minor phenomena compared with the transfers among the middle class.

But I cannot leave the problem of helping the poor without turning to another essentially economic problem. This is well summarized in the current issue of *Public Interest*:[2]

> . . . (I)ndividuals certainly do have an interest in work if they have no other way to support themselves or if they can make much more by working than not. Once social programs exist, however, those meeting the eligibility rules have an alternative to work. And if they are low-skilled, they are unlikely to make much more by working than by going on relief . . .

In other words, this is the problem which the common man refers to as the welfare loafer. So far as I know, no one desires that people be permitted to draw relief in idleness, although there are, of course, some people who for physical reasons simply cannot work.

As a result of the general feeling that people should not be left idle while they are on relief, most of these programs have some kind of arrangements under which the people are required to work. To quote the current issue of *Public Interest* again:

> . . . In fact, the requirements are not effectively enforced and few recipients take them seriously . . .[3]

The problem here is a real one, although I do not think the current welfare administrations make any serious effort to actually enforce the working rules. Still, if they did it would be difficult. Consider the problems which someone attempting to get the unemployed to work faces. First, the number of "jobs" that you require varies sharply from day to day, depending on how many

2. Lawrence M. Mead, "Social Programs and Social Obligations," *Public Interest*, No. 69, Fall 1982, p. 28 (New York: National Affairs, Inc.).

3. Ibid., p. 22.

people happen to have lost or found jobs. Further, we would like to have them vary even from hour to hour because we would like to have it possible for someone on relief to take off at any time to investigate a job opening.

Secondly, the jobs, of necessity, must be low-skilled. That is not because there are not highly skilled people who become unemployed, but because it is unlikely that their skills will exactly fit the particular jobs available and, hence, they will have to be given unskilled jobs outside their specialty instead of skilled jobs in their specialty while on relief.

These requirements mean that the jobs we give to the unemployed must be ones in which capital investment is low and which are easy to supervise, because we cannot afford to keep immense amounts of capital and supervisory capacity available for the maximum number of unemployed we expect to be helping. Further, supervision is of necessity a little difficult here because you have to be willing to say to someone who asks for relief, "You take that rather dirty, low-paid job which we have provided for you, or you and your children will starve." Most people, and certainly most welfare supervisors, don't want to do that.

The outcome of all of this is that we can provide work for the unemployed who meet all these requirements, but probably they will not be very productive jobs. Indeed, some people writing on this subject have suggested providing completely make-work activity of the sort that involves, let us say, turning a crank against a resistance for eight hours a day. The purpose is not to produce anything but to make certain that people do not receive money in idleness. I think we could do better than that, but it would be true that we could not expect high productivity from the people on relief. Rubbish removal and picking up litter impress me as areas which meet our requirements. A man who spends his day walking 20 miles along one side of a freeway picking up litter probably will not contribute much to the national product, but at least he will not find that he is getting relief money along with a day's leisure.

If my suggestion is taken, we will provide a number of unskilled, fairly strenuous jobs for all people on relief who are physically capable of working. Then not only will the number of people interested in relief payments fall sharply but, as a matter of fact, we can raise the amount we pay them. As I mentioned above, $6,000 a year is the current average payment to a family of four in the United States. One of the advantages of this system, believe it or not, is that you can afford to be more generous. Six thousand dollars a year, with leisure (and we must remember that leisure can be partially filled with various productive activities which can be concealed from the relief administration) is probably no more attractive than, let us say, $8,000 or $9,000 combined with a fairly strenuous, not very productive job. Thus, by putting a work requirement in, even if the work requirement does not involve much addition to G.N.P., we make it possible to increase the amount of money available to people who truly need it without attracting a bunch of welfare loafers.

REASONS FOR REDISTRIBUTION [1983]

Redistribution is probably the most important single function of most modern governments. Further, it is a very traditional government function, with all recorded governments having done at least some of it. Indeed, as I shall discuss later, it seems quite probable that the original motive for forming governments was the desire for special types of redistribution.

In spite of the prominence of redistribution among the activities of the government, it has received relatively little scientific study. People have collected statistics on the distribution of income and wealth and made various proposals for changes in this distribution. There has been some work on the efficiency effects of income redistribution. Basically, however, the total amount of serious research in this area is low, both in quality and in quantity.

I suspect that the reason for the sad state of research on redistribution is a belief that essentially it is a moral rather than a scientific issue. People favor or oppose particular income redistribution programs essentially on moral grounds and tend to believe that science and morals do not mix very well. Most people believe that science should be the servant of morals, and this leads to a de-emphasis of scientific research on the foundations of income redistribution programs. They are thought to be morally required, or morally wicked, depending on the particular moral code used to judge them. This gives an adequate motive for favoring or opposing the programs, so there is no need to consider the foundations further.

It is perhaps this emphasis on morals that has led most discussions of income and wealth redistribution to concentrate on what is in fact a small portion of all income and wealth redistribution. There is no doubt that most modern states do engage to some extent in helping the poor, the classic moral objective of income redistribution, but there is also no doubt that this is a relatively small part of their total program of income redistribution.

In the budget year 1981, the United States spent an amount officially classified as transfer that was enough to give every person in the bottom

Reprinted, with kind permission of Kluwer Academic Publishers, from *Economics of Income Redistribution*, Kluwer-Nijhoff Studies in Human Issues: An International Series in the Social Sciences (Boston: Kluwer-Nijhoff, 1983), 1–15. Copyright 1983 Kluwer Academic Publishers.

10 percent of the population $12,000 and every person in the bottom 20 percent of the population $6,000. This meant that a family of four in those two categories could have received transfers, respectively, of $48,000 and $24,000.[1] In fact, according to Department of Health and Human Services' figures, a family of four on AFDC with no source of support except government payments received $4,728 in cash and enough food stamps to bring the total up to $6,432 if food stamps are counted at their nominal value.

Further, although this is what the federal government classifies as transfers, there are many, many other transfers carried out in our society. Right now the prospect of restrictions on Japanese automobiles entering the United States is being very strenuously canvassed. I do not know whether such restrictions will go through or how restrictive they will be, but it is clear that their basic effect will be to transfer funds from the American who is thinking of buying a car to members of the United Auto Workers and owners of stock in automobile companies. This transfer will not appear in the budget. Further, it is only a single example. It seems likely that regulations, protective tariffs, various biases in government purchasing programs, etc., lead to a further massive transfer of income within the United States. It may well be as large as that which is officially listed as a transfer. Once again, it is clear the poor are not the principal beneficiaries.

Still further, most government expenditures confer benefits on people in a manner that is not proportional to the taxes paid. In public education, for example, there is an immense program, mainly funded by local governments, for which the recipients overlap with, but are by no means identical with, the people who pay. Once again, although the poor receive free elementary education like everyone else, they are by no means the principal beneficiaries.

I do not want to be misunderstood. The poor do indeed receive substantial amounts of money in the United States,[2] but nowhere near the total amount transferred. The bulk of the transfer goes to the politically influential and well organized.

1. Total welfare expenditures from *The Budget of the United States, Fiscal Year 1981* and its *Appendix*. Calculations of actual payments from *Washington Post*, Wednesday, June 23, 1982, p. 16.

2. To avoid another misunderstanding, I am going to use American data in this book mainly because it is readily available. As far as I can see, the situation in the European welfare states is similar but more extreme than that in the U.S.

The major motive for government income transfer in the modern world, and in fact throughout history, is simply that the recipients of the money would like to get it, and they have the political power, or in some cases the luck, to implement their desires. Indeed, even the transfers to the poor in a democracy that permits the poor to vote have certain aspects of this kind of a transfer. Apparently the poor are not very good at getting a return on their votes.

The general intellectual confusion about transfers is well illustrated by a very prominent scholar, Thomas Schelling. He says, "Policy issues are preponderantly concerned with helping, in compensatory fashion, the unfortunate and the disadvantaged."[3] In the same article, he says:

> Most people probably devote most of their policy interest to the things that concern themselves and do it with a clear conscience. They do not get drawn into ethical abstractions. They may have strong ethical views on a limited number of subjects that do not flow from their stake in the outcome, but on matters called "bread and butter" they accept the ethic that in politics it is fair to look out for your own interest, expecting others to look out for theirs! Many of us in academic environments, though, try to take distributive issues seriously but not personally. Students rebelling against higher tuition are reluctant to say it is to save their own money; they join the picket line in behalf of somebody poorer. And professors concerned to protect their own salaries are thought not to be playing the ethical game, but the tobacco farmer concerned solely with his own family's welfare is excused from scholarly disinterest.[4]

The bulk of Schelling's article is a discussion of whether economic policies do or do not help the poor by transferring income downward. He is aware, of course, that most government policies are not concerned with helping the unfortunate and disadvantaged but with helping college professors, students, tobacco farmers, and so on. It perfectly illustrates the almost schizophrenic approach to income distribution that has dominated the literature so far.

The motives for income transfer, then, are more complicated than simply aiding the poor. Most people are, to some extent, charitable and are willing

3. Thomas C. Schelling, "Economic Reasoning and the Ethics of Policy," *Public Interest*, no. 63 (Spring 1981): 37–61.

4. Ibid., 39–40.

to make some sacrifices to help those who are worse off than themselves.[5] Further, most people are willing to make gifts, not only to the poor but to other people who for one reason or another they favor.

The obvious case, of course, is the intrafamily gift that in total adds up to an absolutely immense share of the national income. Although the intrafamily gift is not dealt with in this book, mainly because I am primarily concerned with governmental transfer, there are many cases in which gifts are given to people who are not poor. The Queen of England is one of the wealthiest persons in the whole world and regularly receives from the British people a large transfer that normally goes through Parliament without a murmur. When Oswald shot Officer Tippet, in Dallas, a deluge of gifts from private persons descended on the wife of Officer Tippet but, interestingly enough, over $200,000 was also sent to Marina Oswald. Similarly, the gifts to various political organizations in the United States, ranging from the Sierra Club to the Liberty Lobby, are intended by their donors to benefit the country as a whole. It should, of course, be said here that in many cases the individuals' definition of "benefitting the country as a whole" is a particular policy which will also benefit the giver, but this simply indicates that human motives are frequently mixed. This mix will preoccupy us a good deal in the latter part of the book.

Although there can be no doubt that people are interested in making gifts to others and, in particular, to those who are worse off than they themselves, the actual observed behavior seems to indicate this is a relatively minor argument in most utility functions. The reader should think of exactly how much of his income he has given away in the last year to sources outside the immediate family. For this purpose, eliminate religious gifts, because to some extent the religious gift is not an effort to benefit other people but an effort to protect oneself from hell. Still, even including religious gifts, if you have given more than 5 percent of your income away you are quite exceptional.

The total amount of voluntary gifts in the United States is considerably less than 5 percent of personal income, and not much of that goes to the

5. My rather simple use of charitable motives here may be regarded as an oversimplification. See *The Economics of Charity*, by Thomas R. Ireland and David B. Johnson, Blacksburg, Center for Study of Public Choice, 1970, for an effort to untangle the complex reasons that may lead somebody to feel charitable. A more recent discussion of the same subject was presented at the Southern Economic Association Meeting, 1981, by Orley M. Amos, Jr., "Empirical Analysis of Motives Underlying Individual Contributions to Charity."

poor. If we add in that part of the federal budget that is specifically earmarked to the poor, it will still be less than 5 percent of GNP.[6] It is, of course, true that various activities undertaken by the federal government indirectly help the poor, but it should be said also that many of them injure the poor. Five percent is probably a generous estimate of the total amount of transfers to the poor.

There is no reason why we should be particularly disturbed by the discovery that people are interested in maximizing their own income. We observe it in all walks of life. People are, in general, charitable but only mildly so, and their primary consideration is benefitting themselves. We should not be surprised to discover that political power is used to a small extent to help others and to a large extent to help oneself.

There is, in addition, another motive for income redistribution: envy. We have at least some tendency to envy those who are better off than ourselves, and there is no reason why we should not make use of the government to equalize the situation. It is true that most people do not like to admit that envy is one of their motives, and, indeed, there is a considerable industry in providing rationalizations for envy in income distribution matters. A political advertisement by the American Federation of State, County and Municipal Employees is a good example.[7] This ad is largely an appeal to envy, with a picture of a cake and emphasis on the fact that the Reagan policy for reducing taxes will lower the tax burden of a family with $100,000 income by $3,300 and a family with $15,000 by $185. The ad continuously returns to this aspect and refers to this as being "discriminatory," all of which should lead the reader to feel that he is not really envying the rich but that he is doing his moral duty in suggesting that they pay more and avoid discrimination.

Another interesting feature of this particular ad is that it does not seem to be very concerned about the poor. The text begins, "Sure, we have to cut the fat out of the budget. But do we have to cut the heart out of middle class working people while we're at it?" Later it says, "If middle income people

6. Danziger, Haveman, and Plotnick show the federal budget portion as about 2 percent of GNP. I do not totally agree with their classification, but then I do not think any two people are in full agreement with respect to classification of expenditures in this category. Sheldon Danziger, Robert Haveman, and Robert Plotnick, "How Income Transfer Programs Affect Work, Savings, and the Income Distribution: A Critical Review," *Journal of Economic Literature* 19, no. 3 (1981): 976–77.

7. *Washington Post*, Tuesday, May 5, 1981, p. A10.

suffer . . . let 'em eat cake." This union has almost all of its members in the top half of the income pyramid and, presumably, is attempting to benefit them. It is notable, however, that their principal arguments are envy and additional income for median and above-median members, while help for the poor is almost completely ignored. This is not atypical.

Although envy is undeniably a real motive for redistribution, it is, in my opinion, a rather minor one. It affects primarily the transfers away from the wealthy which, in turn, are but a small part of our total income redistribution. The major motive for the redistribution of income and wealth in the United States is almost certainly that the recipients want to receive it. The second motive is the desire to help various people, primarily the poor (i.e., charity). Envy is, I am sure, a poor third in this trio. In the latter part of this book, my technical discussion will only rarely deal with envy and will be primarily concerned with the first two motives. It will be unique among discussions of income redistribution because it will give emphasis to that part of the income redistribution machine which does not, and is not intended to, help the poor.

I think the reason other scholars tend to ignore this issue is their essentially moral approach. There does not seem to be any moral reason why millionaire American farmers should be receiving transfers from the far poorer people who buy bread. Nevertheless, there is a program to this end. Moralists are apt to ignore the program except perhaps to denounce it, but if they do mention it, they rarely do so in the context of studies of redistribution.

I will make an effort, probably not completely successful, to avoid moral judgments and confine myself to a discussion of the economic and political aspects of various redistribution programs. Thus, from my standpoint, the desire to help the poor—which I think most people have—is simply a motive that is no different from the desire to eat chocolate. I will try to discuss the redistribution program, insofar as it helps the poor, in much the same spirit as I would discuss the part of our economy that satisfies the demand for chocolate.

I am perhaps not able to be quite so objective in discussing the transfers that do not go to the poor. Theoretically, I should regard them as just another example of people engaging in profit-maximizing activity. I must confess, however, that personally I dislike these activities, and this bias may well slip through my effort to take a strictly scientific attitude toward it.

My three motives (the desire to receive transfers, charity, and envy) are not by any means the only ones that will be found in the discussion of income transfers. It seems that no careful scholar has ever explained such things as our farm program in terms other than that of the farmers' wanting to get money and using their political power to get it.[8] Transfers motivated by charity, or to a lesser extent by envy, have been frequently argued for on grounds other than these very simple motives, however. Indeed, one very high-paying activity among modern intellectuals has been the invention of new rationalizations for income redistribution to the poor.[9]

There are, however, a number of "justifications" for income redistribution to the poor that are not simply a restatement of the charitable motive. Hochman and Rodgers[10] are famous for having examined the charitable motive with some care, and they may have misled some noneconomist readers by referring to it as the "interdependence of utility functions." This is, in fact, simply charity or altruism under a more complicated name.

There have, however, been several efforts to produce arguments for helping the poor that do not depend simply on charity. The oldest, really carefully worked out one is Abba Lerner's.[11] He pointed out that if income has a declining margin of utility, then equal redistribution of income would maximize the total utility received by a society out of a given amount of production. Lerner is, of course, convinced that equality tends to lower total product and feels that a society should seek the optimal point where utility is maximized.[12]

This argument is plausible, particularly in the more modernized version offered by Breit and Culbertson.[13] The problem with it is that nobody really believes in it. If it is desirable to maximize total utility, then there are several

8. At the time the American farm program was built (and there was a similar argument in Switzerland), the idea that the farmer should be subsidized because farming was somehow superior, or, in any event, that our society required a certain number of farmers in existence, was pushed. This argument, however, would only be valid if it were assumed that the farmers were about to quit because they were not making enough money, hence an indirect proposal to help poor farmers. As such, it has relatively little to do with the programs that actually eventuated.

9. John Rawls, *A Theory of Justice* (Cambridge: Harvard University, 1971); Lester C. Thurow, *The Zero Sum Society* (New York: Basic Books, 1980).

10. H. M. Hochman and J. D. Rodgers, "Pareto Optimal Redistribution," part 1, *American Economic Review* 59, no. 4 (Sept. 1969): 542–57.

11. There were a number of economists who offered the same idea before Lerner, but he was the first one who worked it out in full.

12. A. P. Lerner, *The Economics of Control* (New York: Macmillan Co., 1944).

13. W. Breit and W. P. Culbertson, "Distributional Equality and Aggregate Utility: Comment," *American Economic Review* 60, no. 3 (June 1970): 435–41.

techniques in addition to equalizing income that will do so. For example, increasing the total population would, using Lerner's assumption of declining margin utility, raise total utility even if it had no effect on the actual product. In fact, it would increase total production even if not by very much. Lerner himself, on being asked about this, simply said that he had proposed maximizing utility as a goal when discussing income redistribution. He did not think it was a suitable goal for population policy. This would seem to indicate that he does not really value maximizing total utility very much.

A second problem with maximizing total utility as a goal is that in order for the Lerner theorem to work, even as modernized by Breit and Culbertson, it is essential that all people have exactly the same ability to generate utility out of a given income or that we have no information at all about that ability. If different people are able to generate different amounts of utility out of the same income, then the Lerner rule might lead to a radically unequal income redistribution in order to concentrate income in people who are efficient utility-generators.

With one distinguished exception, all the people who favor the Lerner proposal invariably refuse to agree that such unequal distribution would be desirable. They usually mask their reluctance by saying that it is impossible to make such judgments, and, of course, it is impossible to make them with any degree of accuracy, but it is fairly obvious from simple, superficial observation of human behavior that there are some people who get a great kick out of things and others who do not. There does not seem to be any obvious law of nature that implies that we could never work out a scientific way of distinguishing these two categories of people.[14] I think that the reason most proponents of the Lerner scheme refuse to admit this possibility is simply that if one could tell people who are efficient utility-generators from people who are inefficient, we would probably feel sorry for the inefficient utility-generators and would feel that more funds should be transferred to them. This, in any event, would be my own response.[15]

14. As a matter of fact, there are real decisions in which utilities are measured, to some extent in any event. Juries regularly give damage awards for "pain and suffering" as well as for measurable physical damage. It is clearly based on the view that we can, to at least some extent, evaluate other people's utility and compensate for loss of it. See, for another example, the now obsolete but nevertheless voluminous literature on Conubium.

15. It is also the response of Amartya Sen. Although his basic argument is mathematically more complicated, it is clear he, too, feels that more should be given to the inefficient utility-

Let us, for example, take a fairly clear-cut case in which income generates rather little utility: people who are seriously and permanently crippled, such as multiple sclerosis victims. It is fairly obvious that the marginal utility derived from each dollar put in the support of such people is low. If we were attempting to maximize total utility, we would surely cut back on our expenditures to them and increase our expenditures to the beach boys of Malibu. I take it that there will be not one single reader of this book who is in favor of that policy.

There is one distinguished exception to the rule. John Harsanyi argues very strongly that we should maximize utility and that we should quite deliberately transfer income to people who are efficient generators of utility and away from people who are poor generators of it. He tells a little story in which he has the opportunity of giving a small toy to one of two children. One is a happy, cheerful little boy who seems to enjoy almost anything that happens, and the other is a morose little fellow who shows little sign of getting satisfaction out of anything. Harsanyi recommends giving the toy to the happy, cheerful little boy on the grounds that this will lead to more total utility.[16]

Altogether, I think we have to put this particular line of argument down as rationalization. People are charitable, and they do not like to simply admit this is their motive, and hence they need some cover. There are a couple of other similar motives. It is alleged that a transfer of money to the poor will make it less likely that they will revolt or commit crimes. Evidence that either of the effects would occur is extremely weak, and, in any event, in both cases a totally uncharitable person would select pitiless repression rather than the transfer. It is only the person with a strong "interdependence of utility" who will think of transfers as alternatives to machine-gunning rioters in the streets and severe penalties imposed with great frequency for all crimes. From a straight cost-benefit analysis, the machine gun and the lash would dominate in an income redistribution system.

This is not in any sense a criticism of those against pitiless repression and for helping the poor. I am not suggesting that they change their attitude, merely that they abandon certain rationalizations. It is particularly absurd in this case since charity is, in general, thought to be a virtue, so there is no point

---

generators. In his case, however, there is no effort to equalize their utility, simply to make the inequality in their utility caused by their inefficiency less than would be with equal incomes. See his *On Economic Inequality* (New York: W. W. Norton, 1973), 15–23.

16. John J. Harsanyi, *Essays on Ethics, Social Behavior, and Scientific Explanation* (Dordrecht, Holland, and Boston, Mass.: D. Reidel Publishing Co., 1976), 75.

in concealing your charitable motives under a scientific screen. Many people, however, apparently feel that some sort of rationalization is necessary. Unfortunately, I don't think they have found any good ones.

In a more recent rationalization of income redistribution, Rawls[17] suggests that we should consider ourselves behind the veil of ignorance and then make a number of calculations that some economists think are incorrect[18] and get a good deal of equality out of it. Of course, it is not certain that the Rawls line of reasoning would lead to a great deal of equality. The maximum criteria that he uses could lead to very great inequality if it turned out that the incentive effects of equalizing income taxes were very great. I think, however, that Rawls believes, as do most economists, that these incentive effects, although certainly significant, are not large enough so that one could get a good deal of equality out of his line of reasoning.

Still, there are a number of problems here. First, behind the veil of ignorance, oddly enough, we know we are American citizens or at least citizens of the developed world and not members of the very poor part of the world.[19] Second, Rawls does not really confront the possibility that we might find we are in bad health when we come out from behind the veil of ignorance. We might be permanently crippled, dying of cancer, or have multiple sclerosis. If we have the kind of motives that he alleges, we would favor an income transfer distribution scheme that not only provided such people with medical care and perhaps minimum sustenance, but that also made a real effort to raise their utility to a level somewhat similar to that of people who are not so ill. In other words, we would favor a tax on the well-off that provided the ill with an income which is markedly higher than that of the well-off, with the advantage in pure income being proportional to how ill one is. The objective would be to give approximately equal utility. Rawls is not in favor of such a program, although, given his general line of reasoning,[20] it is hard to see why not.

17. John Rawls, *A Theory of Justice* (Cambridge, Mass.: Harvard University Press, 1971).

18. Kenneth Arrow, "Some Ordinalist–Utilitarian Notes on Rawls's *Theory of Justice*," a review article in *Journal of Philosophy*, no. 9 (May 10, 1973).

19. I may be a bit unjust to Rawls here but I do not think so. The text is not completely clear. See my "The Rhetoric and Reality of Redistribution," *Proceedings of Southern Economic Association Annual Meeting*, Washington, D.C., April, 1981.

20. One of my colleagues, David Friedman, has suggested that most people in fact think that they are less efficient generators of utility out of income if they are injured than if they are well and, hence, would favor programs that to at least some extent tend to concentrate their income in the period when they are well. If this is correct, and I have been unable to either

There is a more serious problem with Rawls's justification: it is actually a moral theory. He does not say that we are behind the veil of ignorance but that we should act as if we are. I do not quarrel with his moral principles, but there are, of course, other people with different morals.

There are various other justifications for income redistribution that are offered in the literature. Lester Thurow[21] has recently suggested an essentially political argument. Since I have discussed it in some detail elsewhere,[22] I shall not discuss it here, but it does seem to me that the great popular success of Thurow's book comes from a new rationalization for something that most people want to do anyway.

It is, of course, possible to write best-sellers on the other side, too. George Gilder[23] is an example. He offers essentially a moral case against significant redistribution although he is not opposed to helping the very poor. One could cite many other examples on both sides, all really rationalizations for charitable feelings.

I have, of course, not completely exhausted all of the arguments for greater equality. To take one offered by Le Grand in personal correspondence: "If it is believed that some people are getting more than they 'deserve' while others are getting less, then this can be a powerful motive for transferring income or resources from the former to the latter. This is not the same as charity; for if people get what you think they deserve, then you are also likely to think they are not suitable objects of charity." Although this is logically different from charity, I cannot avoid a feeling that the "deservingness" essentially comes from charitable feelings combined possibly with a certain amount of envy of those better off than we are.

Having discussed what I think are the basic reasons behind redistribution, I should like now to turn to two reasons for setting up programs that may appear to be redistributive or that in fact have redistributive aspects, but are basically not redistributive programs. The first of these is exemplified by the pension scheme used by the American government, particularly for the military. It is clear that the existence of these very elaborate pension arrangements

---

verify or contradict it by empirical methods, it would provide a justification for Rawls's approach to the people who are seriously ill.

21. Lester Thurow, *The Zero Sum Society* (New York: Basic Books, 1980).

22. G. Tullock, "Two Gurus," *Policy Review* 17 (Summer 1981): 137–44.

23. George Gilder, *Wealth and Poverty* (New York: Basic Books, 1981). Also reviewed in "Two Gurus."

means that people who go into the Army intending to stay for long periods of time can be paid much less during their active service than they would be without these schemes. I do not believe this is an efficient trade-off, but the pension received is to a very considerable extent simply a delayed payment for services performed earlier. Similarly, the various arrangements that now exist to provide education to military personnel, for example by sending them to some college in return for their agreeing to serve a certain period of time at wages well below what they could get in the private market, should be counted as part of the compensation of those people and not in any sense as a welfare program.

It has to be admitted, however, that in practice these programs are not quite this simple. Most people feel some kind of moral obligation to the military, particularly those who have fought in wars and, more so, those who have been wounded. Thus, there is some charitable motive involved here. Further, the ex-members of the armed forces are very well organized and push for increases in their own pensions and other benefits, and hence we have here a further admixture of a desire on the part of the recipients of the transfer to receive it.

Thus, this program is mainly a compensation program that permits us to pay active-duty military personnel less than we otherwise would. It does, however, have some charitable aspects and some aspects of people who want transfers receiving them. It would be very hard to separate these three aspects out. This is particularly so since Congress tends to pay active-duty military personnel the least it can, and they take into account their pensions when they decide whether or not to join or stay in the armed services.

The confusion of motives here is, I think, characteristic of many of the programs we will discuss. I will attempt to separate them out, at least conceptually, but a great many programs have a number of motives behind them. Further, as we shall see, a great many are in a way mistakes. For example, the present arrangements that make it possible for civil servants to obtain significant social security payments on top of their regular pension, without having made anywhere near proportionate contributions to the social security funds, were apparently originally built into the social security system without any particular idea that they would have this effect. Thus, this was originally a mistake. It should be said, however, that civil servants, an entrenched and very powerful group, fight with great vigor to retain this rather unfair privilege, which means that a group of decidedly upper-income people receive transfers from a group whose average income is markedly lower than theirs.

As another example of transfer by mistake, let us consider the original oil price control program as it was immediately after the OPEC cartel became effective. With the sharp rise in the price of imported oil, the prospect that owners of American oil wells would become very wealthy was obvious. The owners of such wells, although politically influential, are not anywhere near as numerous as the people who would be paying the additional gasoline prices, and a program was put in hand to restrict the rents that would otherwise accrue to the owners of the oil wells. The program, however, had the unfortunate characteristic that it also subsidized, somewhat indirectly, the import of oil from the Arab countries.

At the time, I made a study in which I looked over the relative elasticities and came to the conclusion that for every $3 that the oil well owners would otherwise have received and did not receive because of the program, the amount paid for gasoline by customers fell by $1, and the amount received by Arab oil well owners rose by $2. Clearly the transfer aimed at was the $1, and the $2 going to the Arabs[24] was an accidental by-product. Further, whenever I talked to American car owners about it, they were always furious on discovering that the program had this effect. It should be noticed that although they were furious, they rarely agreed that abandoning the price control scheme would be desirable.

It is interesting that this program continued, but, with time, the $2 that was going to the Arabs was gradually diverted to support a group of American entrepreneurs who put up special oil refineries designed to take advantage of the program. It should be said that although the entrepreneurs did well they did not get anywhere near the $2. The design of the refineries that fitted best to the program was inefficient technically, and there were no restrictions on putting up new refineries, so the result was the eventual fall of return on these refineries to approximately the normal rate of return on capital, discounted very severely for what was clearly a very severe political risk. Deregulation presumably will lead to the scrapping of all of these special refineries.

These are simply two examples of accidental redistribution. Both, I think, were initially enacted without any idea as to this particular redistributive effect, although in both cases redistribution was the basic objective of the program. In the first of these, the beneficiaries fought hard to keep their

24. This program also, no doubt, had a strong tendency to stabilize the cartel that conceivably would have collapsed without it.

privileges. As far as I can see, the Arabs never did anything in the way of operating in Washington to keep their advantage, but, of course, this may simply mean that they worked quietly. In any event, there is no overt evidence of any activity on their part. There is a good deal of similar accidental redistribution. We should, however, always keep in mind that some redistribution is not intended but is an accidental by-product of policies adopted for other reasons.

There is another category of government behavior that is frequently thought to be redistributive, but is, I think, best considered as an effort not to redistribute funds between A and B but to compel A to expend income in a way thought desirable by the government. An obvious case of this is compulsory insurance, an important aspect of many modern government programs. This differs from voluntary insurance, whether carried out privately—like fire insurance—or by the government—like flood insurance or the insurance on bank accounts.[25] The difference between these programs and fire insurance is not great. It is, of course, true that any insurance program of this sort can be regarded as redistributive. Those people whose houses do not burn down transfer funds by way of an insurance company to the people whose houses do burn down. As a result, wealth is more equally distributed across society than it would be if this institution did not exist. Nevertheless, I do not think it is what most people have in mind when they talk about income redistribution.

It is an interesting fact that this particular type of redistribution, or insurance-type activity, has many of the same inefficiency-generating characteristics that the more normal income redistribution to the poor has. Indeed, Samuel Colt always refused to insure his factory because he alleged that as a Christian it was his duty to act as a steward for assets on this earth, and if he had insurance he would work less hard to that end. Most people, today, do not have these religious views, but his statement about the incentive system is correct. If you have fire insurance, you will be less careful about avoiding fires than if you do not. This is exactly analogous to the person who does not try hard to get another job because he has unemployment insurance.

25. Neither of these programs is completely voluntary, since they are both tied in with other aspects of government policy, but it is also true that in neither case are you really compelled to buy the insurance if you do not want to and are willing to sacrifice the benefits of certain other programs.

But this is voluntary insurance. Compulsory insurance is rather different. We will be discussing the Social Security System in great detail later, but in one aspect it is an example of such compulsory insurance. In the stable state, individuals are compelled to pay 11 percent, more or less, of what they would otherwise earn (up to $36,000 a year) to the government, and in return they are promised a pension, which before 1977 was not too bad an actuarial repayment of these tax payments over their lifetime. The effect on lifetime income of individuals was small, and it could have been regarded as an insurance policy.

This is, of course, by no means a complete description of the Social Security System, but confining ourselves simply to this single aspect, it is clear that the motive was not to redistribute income between groups but simply to interfere in expenditure decisions in order to compel people to buy a particular type of insurance. Whether the activity is desirable or not must be decided, not in terms of whether redistribution is desirable or not, but whether we want people to make their own decisions in this area.

There are many other programs that restrict people's freedom of choice in what they purchase, such as laws against drugs or requirements that automobiles have certain safety equipment. These rules can be analyzed economically, but they really have little to do with redistribution except, perhaps, by accident. Some rules, those connected with the Social Security System in particular, are so intimately interconnected with redistributive programs that it will be necessary to discuss them at length later. However, requiring one to buy insurance is simply one example of the efforts made to change people's consumption patterns.

There is one special case, however, where most people would regard insurance as income redistribution. Suppose an insurance arrangement is made where if you make a great deal of money, part of it will be taken from you, and if you end up making little or no money, you will get a supplement. Further, assume that, actuarially, the payment and the subsidy are brought into balance. This is the kind of insurance that I think a great many people would want to buy, although it is by no means certain that a private company could offer it. Insofar as a government redistribution program does indeed transfer money from the wealthy to the poor, it is somewhat like this model.

This program, like the fire insurance program, does not literally transfer funds from the same person at one stage of his life to another person but rather among persons, depending on their general fortune in life. Although, so far as I know, it did not appear in print until I invented it in the course of working on *The Calculus of Consent*,[26] I think that this idea is in the back of the minds of many people who have favored what we could call a "Robin Hood"-type activity, i.e., taking from the wealthy and giving to the poor. It is, in my opinion, almost impossible to disentangle programs that would be motivated by these kinds of insurance considerations from those that are motivated by charitable motives or those that are jointly motivated by charitable motives and by envy of the rich. I can only express my own opinion, that although this particular motive is certainly intellectually respectable, and I think at least present in the back of the minds of a great many people interested in distributing funds downward, it is less important than altruism.

It is, of course, true that most real-life redistribution programs are driven by a mix of motives. Analysis, however, requires us to attempt to disentangle them. The early part of this book will deal with redistribution programs in which only one of these motives dominates. Specifically, in Chapters 2 and 3 we will start by considering those cases in which the sole motive is the desire of recipients to receive the transfer. The reason for starting with this motive is that it is the most important and analytically the simplest. In Chapter 4, we will turn to those programs that are motivated solely by a desire to help those less well off—the gift motive. We will then, in Chapter 5, turn to the more realistic cases in which various motives intermix, and for that purpose we will analyze a number of specific programs in Chapters 7 through 10. Some suggestions for reform will be found in Chapter 11.

So much for motives. There remains one task for this chapter which is essentially definitional. Almost all government acts, and a great many private acts, lead to a redistribution of resources. Which ones are to be called redistribution and which ones are not? To give two examples, the opening of the Western Sizzlin Steak House, in Blacksburg, led to the bankruptcy of the Rustler Steak House. That was a private act which led to a redistribution of wealth.[27] Similarly, the interstate road system, when it was laid down, had a very significant effect on the wealth of the owners of different parcels of real estate. As a matter of fact, the owners of these parcels did a good deal of active lobbying in order to affect locations of exits in the system, but it is clear that the advocates of the interstate system were not basically trying to create these transfers.

26. Gordon Tullock and James M. Buchanan, *The Calculus of Consent: Logical Foundations of Constitutional Democracy* (Ann Arbor: University of Michigan Press, 1962).

27. As a matter of fact, I also had my wealth reduced slightly. I preferred the Rustler.

How, then, do we tell a government action that we shall call redistributive from just any old government action that, as a matter of fact, changes the distribution of wealth even if only slightly? Essentially, we must look at the motives of the act. We can perhaps conceive of a government that is totally and completely uninterested in redistribution and takes all of its positions on the basis of other motives. Perhaps it engages in cost-benefit analysis and always undertakes those projects which have a positive sign. I do not think we will find governments in the real world that behave this way, but we can use this as our benchmark for transfers. When we observe a government activity that does not seem to be solely aimed at improving the efficiency of the economy, defending the country, suppressing murders, etc., we call it redistributive. Thus, under the ancien régime, those government expenditures that simply maintained armies on the frontiers of France would not be regarded as redistributive, although some of the officers seem to have been overpaid. We would, however, regard those portions of the taxes that were used to build a spectacular residence for the king as redistribution to the king.

But note here that there is no assumption in my analysis that the system that exists before a redistributive act is taken is efficient or that the redistribution necessarily is inefficient. Let me take an extreme case. After the Spanish conquest of much of the new world, a system called the *encomienda* was established under which the Spaniards, in essence, owned Indians, but for a term of years rather than permanently. This meant that the Spaniards, who frequently got their *encomienda* by some kind of competitive bidding, were motivated to get as much work out of their workers as possible and had no strong motive to keep them alive or in good health after their period of ownership terminated. The period in which this system was adopted was one in which the population of Indians in the Spanish-speaking part of the new world fell very sharply. It seems likely that the *encomienda* system was one of the reasons for this fall, although there were several other contributing factors.[28]

Clearly, this system was extremely inefficient by anybody's standards. There were advisors to the king who pointed out this inefficiency, but they were far more likely to talk about the moral aspects and to argue that it was unjust to the Indians. If the king had decided, for purely moral reasons, that he would abolish the system and, let us say, free all the Indians, this would have greatly improved the efficiency of the Spanish Indies. I would call this a redistribution, in spite of the fact that it led to great improvements in

28. Alfred B. Thomas, *Latin America: A History* (New York: Macmillan Co.), 101.

efficiency if the king's motives were essentially moral, a desire to transfer wealth from the Spaniards to the Indians. The status quo was inefficient, and the change would have led to greater efficiency.

In general, this is our technique. We will look at any change in the status quo and inquire whether it is redistributive or not. There is no assumption that the status quo itself is efficient and no assumption that redistributive changes necessarily lower efficiency. It is, on the whole, likely that changes in distribution that are motivated by a desire to change that distribution will lower efficiency rather than raise it, but this is a mere probability statement. There are many cases, such as our *encomienda* example, in which the redistribution may actually improve efficiency.

But we can sensibly pause here for a few moments to consider the actual meaning of efficiency in these circumstances. Suppose the king, instead of freeing the Indians, had converted their slavery for a period of years by rotating free Spaniards into permanent enslavement? This also would have been a large income redistribution, and it would have been efficient. The Spaniard, who now owned the Indian and all his children for life, would be motivated to invest resources in keeping his labor force alive just as he would not have underfed his horse.

Clearly, these two systems are radically different. Unfortunately, it is not clear which of them is most efficient. The problem with discussing redistribution and the switch from either the complete freedom system to the slave system or the slave system to the complete freedom system is that the traditional economic measure, Paretian efficiency, doesn't work.

It was said that free men automatically worked harder than slaves, but recent work on the antebellum slave system in the United States has raised doubts about this proposition. If free men did work harder than slaves, however, then the slaves would be able to purchase their freedom from their owner on some kind of credit arrangement, but that would not have involved any transfer. If the king freed them, the transfer that they received would not be the full value of their services as free men but their value as slaves. The Paretian system in which we consider potential or real compensation does not work, because the person who receives the transfer gets just exactly what the person from whom the transfer is extracted loses. If compensation was arranged, the transfer would be cancelled. Further, granted that most transfers involve at least some administrative costs, the net effect would be that the cost of making the transfer would be greater than the benefit.

In consequence of this difficulty, most people writing on income redistribution, wealth transfers, etc., have used a rather old-fashioned measure of efficiency, i.e., how much is apt to be produced. This is frequently combined with a subjective measure of utility. This old-fashioned measure of efficiency is normally presented without any particular argument that it is real efficiency, and I will continue this tradition. Thus, if I say that a particular transfer is inefficient, I am not saying that the beneficiary could not compensate the loser, although that very well may be true, but that the total output will be less. It is quite possible that although the total measured output is less, the total utility will be greater.

All of this is confusing to the economist. The subject of income redistribution raises these problems for efficiency measurement, and I will make every effort to make clear, as I go, the various aspects of efficiency or inefficiency. For example, a transfer that might lower measured product but increase utility will normally be described on both dimensions and not just one.

But this chapter is entitled "Reasons for Redistribution." In my opinion, there is no doubt that some redistribution is motivated by genuinely altruistic motives, although I think far less than is motivated by selfish desire on the part of the recipients to get the money. Envy also plays a part. This book will mainly be concerned with charity and selfishness.

REASONS FOR REDISTRIBUTION [1986]

If I am correct, redistribution is a slogan behind which there is really very little rational thought. Most, albeit not all, people seem to be in favour of redistribution, but I am unable to find any significant agreement among them as to what they mean by the term or how much redistribution there should be. Either most people who present arguments for redistribution normally present very confused arguments or, in those cases where they are not confused, they in fact refuse to apply their own line of reasoning. Further, no real-world redistribution system even remotely resembles the kind of redistribution which would be called for by, let us say, Rawlsian reasoning. This is not to say that one could not present arguments of redistribution, even arguments for the particular pattern of redistribution we see before us. It is only to say that people who favour redistribution have not done so.

I believe the explanation for the non-rationalised characteristic of redistribution is simply that for most people either it is a private good in the sense that they hope to receive redistribution, or it is a public good. The individual for whom redistribution is a public good—the wealthy man who feels that the poor in India should be helped, for example—has little or no motive to think carefully about the project, because of the usual arguments for poor information in political procedures. We shall see below that these arguments are even stronger in this case than they usually are. The person who hopes to benefit from redistribution has reasons for thinking about the distribution programme, of course, but in general he is better advised not to state publicly his true motives for favouring particular redistribution programmes. Hence, the public debate on the subject shows very little thought and a good deal of emotion.

I hope that the rational consideration with respect to redistribution which I propose to discuss below leads to an improvement in clarity in this field if it does not lead to any change in policy. I am attempting to find out what views on redistribution are held publicly in the hope that this will make it possible for me to provide a better discussion than I can on my present, rather

Reprinted, with permission, from *The Economics of Wealth and Poverty* (New York: New York University Press, 1986), 15–41.

feeble base. But before talking about various technical aspects of redistribution, let me very briefly take you on a tour of South Africa.

The South African economy is a complex one, and I do not want to go through it in detail. Basically, there are two white groups, the Afrikaaners and the English-speaking, with the English-speaking group making up about 40 per cent of the whites and being markedly more prosperous than the Afrikaaners; together they compose 20 per cent of the total population. The remaining 80 per cent of South Africans are mainly black, although there are two other groups—Asians and coloureds, who get special treatment, and whom I shall not discuss here. The blacks' income is very low, probably on the order of 20 per cent of the whites'. In part this reflects a much lower level of skill and other kinds of human capital on the part of the blacks, but in part it also represents discrimination. The most important aspect of the discriminatory system is the confining of about half the black population to what used to be called the native reserves and are now called homelands where they engage in subsistence agriculture at very low returns.[1] The blacks who live in the cities are subject to discrimination and are classified in a number of different categories which affect their employment opportunities, but in general their income is probably closer to that of the whites than that of the "Homeland" blacks.

Redistribution is, however, what I would like to talk about. The government of South Africa has an active programme for income redistribution, a part of which is referred to as income redistribution and part of which is hidden under other titles. The main recipients of these income redistributions are the Afrikaaner population, about half of whom are employed by the government. The government farm programme takes care of a large part of the remaining Afrikaaner population. In addition, the so-called poor whites, defined (more or less) as whites whose income is no more than three times the black average, are recipients of direct welfare payments of the type we are accustomed to in the United States and Europe.

It should not be said that the blacks themselves are totally ignored. There are welfare programmes directed to both the blacks and the whites to provide them with education, etc. There is a net transfer of tax funds from the white

1. Although the living standard is undeniably low it did not impress me that their life is all that unpleasant. The native reserves are usually fairly pretty, the climate is pleasant and the work requirements of the rather primitive form of subsistence agriculture are low. Thus, the citizens of the reserves are better off than inhabitants of a Chinese or Indian agricultural village. This does not, of course, mean that they are well-off.

population to the black. It is, however, utterly trivial compared with the transfers that occur within the white population. Further, it is by no means obvious that the blacks gain from the whole system, since various redistributional arrangements, particularly in agricultural areas among the white population, raise the price of food, and this may more than compensate for the rather small direct transfer to the black population. There is also the fact that the aid to the black community is largely administered by white civil servants, and it may well be that the gain to that small part of the white population involved in this work is as great as the net profit that blacks make on the redistributional activities which aim at benefiting them.

I find that most people on hearing about this system tend to get rather indignant. As a matter of fact, however, it is roughly the system that is used by all democratic countries, if you simply realise that the blacks in South Africa are not citizens. It very closely resembles the attitude of Switzerland or Sweden to their so-called guest-workers. The government of Sweden, for example, does not permit all Turks to enter Sweden and take jobs, and once Turks arrive in Sweden they are paid less than Swedes, partly because their human capital is less, but also because they are subject to various discriminatory rules on the type of jobs they may take. Sweden, of course, engages in a large-scale income redistribution within their population and has a foreign-aid programme. The foreign-aid programme is comparatively small, and among its beneficiaries surely are those Swedes who are administering it. The only difference between Sweden and South Africa is that some people regard the blacks in South Africa as citizens of South Africa,[2] but do not regard the Turks as citizens of Sweden.

There is an apparent radical difference in the way in which we redistribute to people who are regarded as citizens and those who are not.[3] We are indignant with South Africa for treating people in two different ways and restricting the immigration of some of their blacks to their major cities, but we are not particularly indignant with the Americans for treating people differently when one group are the Mexicans. Indeed, the American-Mexican problem is very similar to that of South Africa with respect to the blacks. American cities, like South African cities, have a certain number of the discriminated-against Mexican group present legally, and a large number who are there illegally. Our attitude towards these illegal Mexicans is again very similar to

2. Legally they are not.

3. West Germany, interestingly enough, treats those guest-workers who actually get into Germany much the same as its own citizens, but it is, I believe, unique in this respect.

the South African attitude towards the illegal blacks. We alternate between trying to get rid of them and feeling sorry for them. In both cases, if they are caught they can be removed (deported from the United States, and signed out in South Africa) by administrative officials without a court intervention, although once again in both cases it is possible to have the administrative decisions reviewed by a court.

The reasons for sharply limiting the immigration of Mexicans, Jamaicans, Asians, etc., are exactly the same as those used in South Africa to keep out the blacks. We do, however, keep out far more of them. The average major city in South Africa has about three blacks for every white, while only something like 4 or 5 per cent of the population of the average American city is non-American. The fact that we keep more out than do the South Africans, however, certainly is no argument that we are morally superior.

It is notable that the South Africans, having observed this particular oddity in the western moral system, have been attempting over recent years to convert South Africa into a situation in which the blacks are foreigners, and hence their being kept in subordinate positions, or even kept out of the major cities, would therefore be in conformity with western practice. The great indignation that this has aroused indicates that there is something further in this distinction that they have not fully understood.

Another example of redistributionist muddle concerns the dismantling of the European empires. Let us consider only the British case, because in some ways it is the most extreme example. When a socialist party took control of the government in London, the inhabitants of India were as much subjects of George VI as were the inhabitants of Britain. It is true, strictly speaking, that they were subjects of the Emperor rather than of the King, but this was really not a distinction of much importance. A socialist government, interested in helping the poor, should have noticed that of the population subject to its control, something like 85 per cent were much poorer than anybody living in Britain; in fact, many of them were on the verge of starvation. Hence, it should have made immense transfers to this portion of the population. As democrats it would also have been sensible for them to agree that the Indians should send representatives to Parliament in proportion to their population. Needless to say, this prescription was not only not implemented, it was not even thought of. I talked at the time to a few British socialists about this, and they showed a certain amount of embarrassment, but characteristically argued that the Indians did not want to be put in complete control of the British government which is what such a voting method would provide. They wanted independence. This was clearly simply a rationalisation.

It is, I suppose, clear that the reason that the empires were dismantled rather than granting to the subjects full citizenship was a simple selfishness on the part of the population of the central metropolitan power. It would have caused an immense drop in the living standard of the English, the French, the Portuguese, the Dutch and the Belgians if they had simply integrated the colonies into the whole society with an equal role.[4]

Why, then, other than for selfishness did the colonial powers not make large transfers to their colonial subjects once they came under the control of socialists? Why not permit them to vote? Indeed, why do we not permit foreigners to vote? We pass a number of bills in our Congress which are of great interest and importance to foreigners—the foreign-aid programme is perhaps the most significant example—but we do not permit them to vote on it. When I talk to people about this issue, the normal, immediate reaction is one of complete incredulity that I should raise it. When I point out, however, that for most egalitarians (and I usually talk about this subject only with egalitarians) it is contrary to their own ideas of equality to make distinctions on accidents of birth or geography, they normally simply become embarrassed and turn away. One particularly clear-cut example of this occurred when I visited New Mexico. A liberal member of the faculty of the university there, obviously intending to embarrass a visiting conservative, asked me if I thought the illegal Mexicans in the state should be permitted to vote. I was, of course, to say no, thus indicating how backward and contrary to advanced modern thought I was. Instead, I said that I saw no reason why mere position on either side of an arbitrary line should make any difference, and asked him whether he thought the Mexicans in Mexico should be permitted to vote in the New Mexican elections. He paused, looked somewhat shaken, said, I never thought of that, but I suppose we should let them vote, and then quickly changed the subject. I am sure he had the whole incident erased from his memory by a little later that afternoon.

Why don't we permit Mexicans to vote in those American elections where something directly concerning them is involved? The only answers that one can find are simply that we believe in nationalism in a strong sense, which most

4. The United States faced some of the same problems with the first colony it gave independence, the Philippines. But, of course, the population of the Philippines was small enough so that although representatives and senators could have played a significant role in our Congress, they would not have dominated it the way the empires I have discussed above would have been dominated by the former subject people if they had extended the vote to them.

moderns deny, or that we are selfish. We realise that they would use the vote to obtain money from us, and, even though we talk about egalitarianism, we don't really want to have our income reduced that much. South Africa again is a clear-cut case. The white South Africans, as I have mentioned above, do make some transfers to blacks, but egalitarianism in South Africa would mean transfers of something in the order of 80 per cent of the wealth of the whites to the blacks. They may be interested in equality, but not that much. We are the same.

The point of the above discussion is not to urge that we make large transfers to the poor who happen not to be American citizens, or that we permit them to vote. It is to point out that the standard explanations for egalitarian behaviour do not fit the real world. Those Americans who are receiving grants of various sorts from the American government on the grounds that they are poor are uniformly higher in income than the world average. In other words, if we had a really egalitarian programme, almost every single American who now is being aided by the state would in fact be taxed in order to transfer what little he has to people who have even less. Obviously, that is not our policy. Furthermore, most people who tell you that they are interested in equality are shocked when it is proposed.

Rawls's book is a particularly clear example of this kind of thing. As almost everyone knows, he turns to the original position in which you do not know who you are and then discusses the type of policy you would propose. He does not, however, discuss whether you know you are a citizen of the United States, Italy, India, etc. If you actually do not know who you are, and you think, therefore, that the likelihood of your being a citizen of India or of Communist China is as great as the likelihood of your being an American citizen, you would be in favour of very drastic transfers of funds away from the American citizens.[5] The best policy would be removing at least two-thirds of the present after-tax income of American citizens and giving it to the poorer parts of the world, and very likely 80 per cent would be a more reasonable figure. Swedes, even if members of the socialist party, or members of the British Labour Party, etc., all would find themselves impoverished.

In all of the published discussion of Rawls's book by people who favour income redistribution, I've seen this matter discussed only once. Beitz[6] talks to some extent about such redistribution, but his discussion seems to be

5. John Rawls, *A Theory of Justice* (Cambridge, Mass.: Harvard University Press, 1971).

6. Charles R. Beitz, *Political Theory and International Relations* (Princeton, N.J.: Princeton University Press, 1979).

based on the theory that we should redistribute to poor foreigners only if their poverty is caused by a lack of raw materials in their country. He does not suggest an 80 per cent of income transfer to them. But with this exception, income redistribution is implicitly, but almost never explicitly, confined to within the nation-state. In most cases there are people within the nation-state who are not made subjects of redistribution. The blacks in South Africa and the bulk of the Arabs of Israel are particularly clear examples, but there are others. The guest-workers in most European countries, the illegal immigrants in the United States and for that matter legal immigrants to the United States whose status is such that they can still be deported if they become public charges are examples. Really, however, the distinction is as to location on the map, which is as arbitrary a distinction as I can name.

The rule followed by substantially every wealthy country in the world is to restrict immigration in order to provide to their labourers a small amount of protection from competition.[7] This is, of course, a distinction which increases the total inequality in the world. There are, then, elaborate welfare schemes in almost every wealthy country in which only people within the boundaries of the country—and in general only citizens who are within the boundaries—can share. These schemes probably also increase total world inequality, although that is not absolutely certain.

To see the increasing inequality caused by these schemes, consider Figure 1. I have drawn here on the vertical axis income, and on the horizontal axis we simply have people designated by name. They are arranged from left to right on the horizontal axis, with the people with the highest incomes on the left. (The actual shape of the line I-I which shows the income of each individual arranged in this way would be a fairly complex curve, but for simplicity I have drawn it in as a straight line.) Let us suppose now that a club of millionaires, i.e., everyone to the left of the vertical line R-M, became concerned by the fact that some millionaires are only just millionaires while others have 10, 15 or 20 million dollars. They therefore set up a redistribution programme which changes the income distribution to the left of point M as shown by line R-R. The result of this redistribution, however, is a reduction in the total efficiency of the economy, and in consequence the income received by the people who aren't millionaires (i.e., those to the right of M) is also reduced, as is shown by the dashed line. The post-income distribution then is shown by line R, a vertical drop at M and then the dotted line whereas before it was I-I.

7. There are people who argue that this does not actually benefit the labourers.

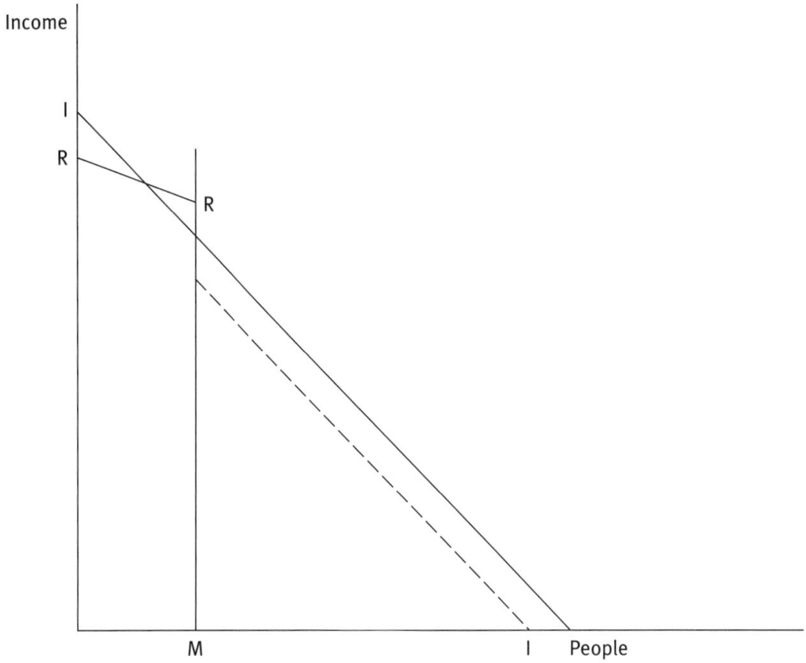

FIGURE 1

The income distribution is thus certainly lower for the lower-income groups and probably more unequal for society as a whole. When I have presented this proposition orally to various groups of economists they have agreed that the consequences that I specify occur, but some of them have thought that it might lead to more income equality. This would be purchased at the cost of lowering the incomes for substantially everyone except the poorer millionaires.

The question of whether this increases or decreases the income equality seems to me unimportant, but to some people it might be thought to be important. One of the criticisms of Rawls's book has been that he attempts to maximise the income of the citizen who is worst off. This has been criticised by various people on the grounds that an increase of the income of a wealthy man by 5 dollars might be accompanied by an increase of the poorest man by 1 dollar, and these critics feel that that would be undesirable. I have great difficulty in having much sympathy with this criticism, but it has been made.

The point of Figure 1 is that equalisation of income within the upper-income groups, i.e., the citizens of the United States, Italy, Germany, etc., is roughly equivalent to our equalisation of income among the millionaires.

Lowering the efficiency of the world economy lowers the income of the poor people who may live in such countries as India and Communist China. Thus equalisation of incomes in the United States is probably a way of increasing the degree of inequality of incomes in the world and certainly impoverishing the poorer people in the world, which means in essence that their death rate, which is already high, will rise further.

I should perhaps pause here to say a little bit about the efficiency effects of equalisation. They are debated to some extent, but so far as I know the debate is always won by the people who argue that equalisation will lead to a lower total income. It is not obvious, however, that maximising world income is the thing we would want to do. We must be careful about offsetting equalisation against efficiency.[8]

Changing a person's income by an income tax lowers the marginal return on effort for him and at the same time lowers his wealth. In general we think that people who are wealthier tend to work a little less hard than people who aren't so wealthy, although the empirical evidence on this is not very good. On the other hand, we would anticipate that people would work harder if the marginal return on effort was greater. Thus, for people whose income is lowered by a proportional income tax, it is not clear whether their work effort would be increased or lowered. Further, the empirical evidence is also not clear.

Income redistribution, however, also includes giving money to the poor. They receive what is the equivalent to a negative income tax of some sort (i.e., their income is supplemented), but the supplement is so arranged that it either declines as their earned income rises or is cut off entirely at some point. In either event, in their case the income effect raises their income, which would tend to mean that they would work less hard, and the reduction of a marginal return on their effort also would mean that they are likely to work less hard. Thus, the people who receive the transfers will work less vigorously than they would had the transfers not been paid to them.[9]

8. See Arthur M. Okun, *Equality and Efficiency: The Big Tradeoff* (Washington, D.C.: The Brookings Institution, 1975).

9. There is a partial and possible offset to this having to do with the extremely poor people, such as those living in South India, Communist China, etc., who may actually not have enough income to maintain reasonably good health. They might work harder if their income was raised. The problem does not arise with respect to American citizens, however. There are Americans who are poor because their health does not permit them to work very hard, but in most cases they are not suffering from a disease, such as malnutrition, which can be easily cured with a small increase in income.

The empirical evidence on the declining work effort of people who are receiving some transfer is not as voluminous as we would like; but it is clear. For example, the negative income experiment seems to indicate the withdrawal of labour power of about 15 per cent from the market when the negative income experiment was introduced. Since the people who were receiving the negative income payments had to a considerable extent been eligible for other transfers before, this is not a measure of the reduction in labour offerings caused by the negative income tax, but the difference between that and a somewhat less generous programme. Our efforts to measure the reduction in efficiency by the other types of relief and welfare programmes have on the whole not been very successful, because of the rather disorderly nature of these programmes. It is, however, clear that they do reduce the total product of the economy. It has been suggested, for example, that a good deal of unemployment is caused by unemployment benefits. Employment of people over the age of 63 and under the age of 72[10] is very markedly lower than it was before the social security programme was introduced. We have all also heard of welfare cheaters, and at least some of the loud indignation is well justified.

But so much for the inefficiency effects of equalising income transfers. A brief discussion is necessary here because of the demonstration that equalising incomes within an upper-income group (for example, the citizens of the United States) tends to lower the incomes of the poorer parts of the population (for example, the citizens of India or Communist China).

Why then do we observe so much interest in equalisation of the incomes of Americans and so little interest in equalising world incomes? Note that there is some interest in equalising world incomes; we do indeed make gifts to various foreign countries as the South Africans make transfers to their blacks. We also make some transfers to the illegal immigrants in the United States.

In order to understand these phenomena, it is essential that we consider the actual motives behind income redistribution. Here I should say that I have spent several years attempting to find a coherent discussion of the motives behind income redistribution among the writings or the oral expressions of proponents of it. One of my techniques was to read a paper before a number of audiences composed of economists, almost all of whom would at least purport to be in favour of income equalisation. In it I raised the question of why we gave only very small amounts of money to the very poor

10. Over the age of 72, social service payments are paid regardless of your income.

people in the world and quite a lot to our co-nationals who are very much wealthier than these poor people. I never found an answer to this question, even from people who were highly motivated for equality.

Two of them, Les Thurow and an English left socialist whose name I didn't get, showed considerable embarrassment about the question and then eventually took refuge in political possibilities, saying that it was difficult enough to get equalisation within the United States and England let alone working on equalisation in the world as a whole. We must concede that their political judgement about the difficulties of getting equalisation for the world as a whole is correct, but if it is difficult, it must be difficult because it is an unusual desire. Surely, there would be no great difficulty in getting the citizens of the United States to make large payments to the poor of Bangladesh if their actual motive is literally to reduce the amount of inequality. It would simply be necessary to point out to them that the people who live in Harlem are immensely better off than the people who live in the Sahel. The fact that these two well-intentioned people had given up on the problem indicates that their judgement of the actual motives of people who are willing to vote for income redistribution was that they are really not interested in treating all humans alike.

But these two were my prize exhibits. Most of the people with whom I raised this question either refused to answer it at all or took the view that it was perfectly obvious that, let us say, the Canadians should not transfer money to India. They couldn't imagine why I raised the question. They then might rearrange their previous remarks about eliminating poverty because all human beings are equal to say that they are eliminating poverty in the sense that all Canadians are equal. In these cases, however, I then said (as part of my experiment), "You meant that the Wogs and Gooks and other lesser breeds without the law can be permitted to starve quietly in their villages." They invariably rejected the implication vigorously. The inconsistency of their position did not lead them to reconsider, but merely to terminate the conversation.

A particularly interesting example occurred in Puerto Rico, where a communist[11] attacked the visiting American lecturer (myself) by saying the United States should transfer more money to Puerto Rico. I immediately replied that Puerto Rico was well above the average world income level and should transfer large sums of money to Bangladesh, which at the time was in

11. I am not insulting him; he was very proud of being a communist.

the middle of its post-independence disaster. He responded by saying, "Transfer money to Bangladesh?" paused briefly and then said, "You don't understand; they are used to their present way of life." I responded, "You mean that if everybody in the village dies of starvation they think it is a local custom and don't mind?" This terminated the discussion.

In judging these conversations, it should be kept in mind that I have a good deal of experience. They were far from my first attempt on the subject, but they frequently were the first trial by the people on the other side.

These two accounts are typical of my experience. No one seems to have any explanation for this matter based on the kind of reasons that are normally given for income redistribution. As I shall explain below, if one takes a more realistic view of the motives of income redistribution, then it is not at all impossible to explain it.[12] But it is possible that some reader may have a better explanation. If so, I would appreciate his telling me what it is. I should say here that I rather anticipate that a good many people will say simply that my line of reasoning is absurd, but without communicating wherein that absurdity lies. I would appreciate anyone who thinks that this line of reasoning is absurd or erroneous kindly explaining to me why. It is possible that I am wrong. I don't think I am, but it is possible, and certainly if I have made a ghastly error here, I am unlikely to recover on my own without the aid of my betters who realise what the error is.

It should be said here that there is a rather dishonest way of avoiding the whole problem. One can allege that what is important is relative poverty and not real poverty.

> Poverty can be defined objectively and applied consistently only in terms of the content of relative deprivation. That is the theme of this book. The term is understood objectively rather than subjectively. Individuals, families and groups in the population can be said to be in poverty when they lack the resources to obtain the types of diet, participate in the activities and have the living conditions and amenities which are customary, or are at least widely encouraged or approved, in the societies to which they

12. There is a small sub-section of people who are able to explain current income redistribution, but they are in general people who are not particularly interested in redistribution at all. They quite directly introduce distinctions among different groups of human beings, with the result that those who are closer to you are treated better than those who are farther away. I believe this is a correct statement of human motives, as I shall explain below, but is not an argument that is used by proponents of income equalisation.

> belong. Their resources are so seriously below those commanded by the average individual or family that they are, in effect, excluded from ordinary living patterns, customs and activities.[13]

The problem with this is that I have never found anyone who will stick to it. Thus, the statement that poverty is relative poverty, that what is important is that you don't feel poorer than your neighbours, does not withstand investigation.

Let us consider a few obvious examples. Our first is Newport in the 1890s. Poor Mr Smith's yacht is only 95 feet long, and the shortest other yacht on the sea off Newport is 150 feet long. He is, by the relative poverty definition, a deprived person and should, of course, receive government aid. Let us contrast his situation with a man whose name is Wong. He lives in a village in the Sahel, and every single person in the village is now dying of starvation. There is, of course, no poverty in this village, because, relatively, they are all in the same position. Indeed, perhaps we should argue for transfer from this village where poverty has been abolished to Mr Smith.

Suppose that you happen to be near Mr Wong's village and happen also to have a camel caravan with food. The food, however, would be enough to save the life of only 90 per cent of the villagers. Clearly, you should not take the food to the village, because your arrival would immediately create an impoverished class of 10 per cent of the population.

This particular definition of poverty has interesting and most striking consequences for the American aid programme. This aid, as you no doubt know, is aimed at abolishing, or at least reducing, poverty. Simply raising the wealth of a country is not likely to serve this goal because, of course, it will raise the wealth of the wealthy too. But the contrary activity, having our armed forces destroy all material wealth in, let us say, Peru, would indeed abolish poverty.

As you can no doubt deduce, I have never run into any relative-poverty proponent who would stick to his argument when pressed. I usually characterise this school of thought as one in which it is believed that if everybody has a toothache, it doesn't hurt. The view that a person in Harlem who does not have a colour TV feels worse about it than the citizen of a Sahel village who is watching his child die, but knows that child death is very common in his village and that he is not worse off than the other villagers, is a really

13. Peter Townsend, *Poverty in the United Kingdom: A Survey of Household Resources and Standards of Living* (Berkeley and Los Angeles: University of California Press, 1979), p. 31.

extraordinarily heartless one. To repeat, I have never found anybody who is actually willing to maintain it, although I have found people who refuse to discuss the problem.

It should be said here that there was, for a while, some evidence which supported the toothache theory. There were polls taken around the world which implied that people's satisfaction with their position in life was affected almost not at all by their absolute wealth but very heavily by their wealth as compared with their neighbours'. The Gallup organisation, however, obtained funds to rerun these experiments, and the results of their rather careful work have demonstrated that although people's satisfaction is indeed affected by comparison of their own wealth with that of their neighbours it is also affected by their absolute wealth.

Gallup explains the difference between their results and the previous results as derived from the rather technical way in which the problem was presented. In fact, however, I think this technical difference (the difference between a stair and a ladder) was relatively unimportant, and the problem was that the earlier poll asked individuals to compare their well-being with that of other people in a somewhat similar situation to their own, and the latter poll permitted comparison with people in other countries, etc. It may be, of course, that the time-lag is important here also. People today living in South India have a better idea of the difference between their living standard and the living standard of the Americans than they did 20 years ago. Indeed, the whole relevance of the relative-deprivation argument would collapse if we simply assumed that people all over the world are informed by movies and TV about upper-class American living standards.

This argument implies, and indeed sometimes it is directly stated, that progress is either undesirable or at least neutral. The invention of a cure for cancer would not reduce poverty. The immense reduction in transportation cost which occurred recently, and which probably will continue to occur, has not reduced poverty. The man who used to vacation in Brighton and envy his neighbour's trip to Paris now holidays in Spain and envies his neighbour's trip to Rio. His situation has not improved.

Earlier, I spoke of Rawls and the fact that his line of reasoning simply avoids the problem of international comparisons of income. This is, I think, probably the most blatant and obvious defect in his reasoning. I can, of course, understand why he did treat the problem this way. Living in the Harvard community he was going to be given kudos for having invented a new rationalisation for equality; but if this new rationalisation implied that his friends and neighbours should have their income reduced significantly, he would be given the silent treatment. If he had specifically considered the situation in which behind the veil you don't know what country you are going to turn up in, he would not have received all those favourable reviews. On the other hand, if he had said directly and openly that he was going to assume that behind the veil of ignorance you know you are going to be an American citizen, he would have been regarded as a heartless racist. His technique was tactful and adroit.

As a minor aspect of this problem, a member of the Virginia Polytechnic Institute philosophy department, Professor Carson, does believe that international equality is important, and Rawls should take it into account. He has succeeded in obtaining substantially no interest in his point of view. People do not in general disagree with him, but they also don't talk about it. This is in keeping with the general picture we have drawn above.

There is, however, another defect with the Rawlsian procedure. Behind the veil of ignorance I would not only take into account the possibility that I might be born un-American, I would also consider the possibility that I might have some other grave misfortune, particularly a serious injury or a serious illness. In a way we are, in fact, behind the veil of ignorance with respect to these things. We all know that terminal cancers are a normal risk of life. Science is making progress, but not very much, and a lengthy and lingering death by an unpleasant form of cancer is something which we all know can happen to us, and which we also know is more or less a simple matter of luck. In other words, with respect to this particular problem, we are behind the veil of ignorance.

There is, of course, no reason why a programme could not be put in hand to tax the healthy for the purpose of not simply providing medical attention to those who are ill—something which many people are in favour of—but actually to provide exceptional facilities for the ill, with the result that their net well-being is raised either to the same level as that of people who are well, or, at the very least, as high as is feasible. Seriously ill cancer patients could be taken to Hawaii, where they would be put in a hospital located on a beach served by topless nurses and have symphony orchestras play while they eat meals prepared by famous chefs.

That this programme probably sounds as silly to you as it does to me does not affect the relevance it has to the discussion. If we really had a Rawlsian attitude, we would be in favour of such programmes. The fact we are not indicates that Rawls has not properly accounted for either our or his own preference function.

I have found substantially no discussion of efforts to transfer enough money to people who are severely ill or badly injured, so that their net utility is equal to the average citizen's. Indeed, in a number of cases there are direct statements that this should not be taken into account. We are to equalise everyone's utility insofar as the disutility that a person suffers does not come from disease or deformity. Why this exception should be made is not clear. It seems contrary to the line of reasoning normally proposed, which is that everyone should be made equal regardless of their natural talents, etc.[14]

What I am doing is showing that there are a number of ostensible reasons for being in favour of income redistribution which are not false, but that the people who offer them are not, in fact, willing to apply them outside a very narrow area. What we observe is a feeling that a certain amount of income equalisation in the United States is desirable (or at least it is desirable to advocate it), together with an incoherent set of reasons for such redistribution. Part of my research in this area has been financed by the National Science Foundation. In one of my grants I said that I proposed to investigate the reasons for income redistribution by various methods which involved asking people what their reasons were. This particular grant proposal attracted a very negative referee comment, and one of his negative comments was that obviously this part of my research was nugatory and that I would have to begin by working out a theory of why redistribution is desirable.

This was rather odd, granted the fact that the question was directed to me. It is, however, typical. One of the intellectual activities of the modern intellectual is to provide rationalisations for income equalisation. The fact that the reasons he gives do not actually fit his behaviour or his desires is largely ignored. What we have is a desire either to redistribute income or, alternatively, at least to talk about redistributing income without any coherent explanation for this activity. This leads to a certain amount of intellectual tension and a very vigorous grasping at straws, such as Rawls's book.

Let us then turn to what I believe are the actual motives behind income redistribution in most modern societies, and indeed in the most ancient societies. One special motive which should be mentioned in passing is carrying out religious duties. A number of religions require specific charitable acts for salvation. The Bible, although not very specific about it, nevertheless argues strongly for the desirability of helping the poor. The individual who takes

14. Of course, in many cases this does not mean true equality, but that the inequality should be reduced. This leads to the same conclusion.

gifts to the poor because he thinks he will burn in hell if he does not is not actually being charitable, albeit the effects of his act are the same as if he were charitable.

Highly religious communities have traditionally had quite elaborate charitable activities. It should be pointed out, however, that in most cases in which highly religious communities have collected large amounts of money (the Moslems with the WACF, the Mormons, the Roman Catholic Church in the Middle Ages, etc.), the bulk of these funds have not gone to help the poor, but to build elaborate cathedrals, maintain the hierarchy of the Church, issue propaganda on the Church's doctrine, etc. Nevertheless, a good deal of the money has always helped the poor. Indeed, it seems likely that societies of this sort actually help the poor more than we do now.

But it should be pointed out that even with the sanction of hellfire and strong religious belief, formal tithing arrangements have never called on people to be very charitable. The net effect of being a Mormon in the United States today is that you are supposed to put about 16 per cent of your income into the various programmes of the Church. The amount is, of course, tax deductible, so the actual contribution is smaller. Under the Moslem rule it is 2.5 per cent; most Protestant churches take 10 per cent. All of this is no doubt desirable, but these are not large transfers, granted what is said about them. Willingness to spend 10 per cent of your income on saving your soul by charitable donations while you spend 90 per cent selfishly may be admirable, but it is nevertheless 90 per cent selfish.

Here we must, if we are going to talk rationally about redistribution, begin by saying that churches are not out of line in talking to an immense degree about charity but actually taking only 10 per cent. Most people in discussing income redistribution are extremely charitable. It is the amount they actually give away which is modest.

Some time ago there was a member of the political science department who could without any doubt at all be listed as a sloppy liberal. He was very much in favour of all redistributional programmes, felt the poor should be helped, etc. In the course of several long conversations (he was a neighbour) he revealed to me that he thought that means-testing should be eliminated from most programmes because it wasn't fair for people in his income bracket not to get the various free services given to the poor. On my pointing out that his point of view was contrary to his announced belief in progressive income redistribution, he agreed that it was, but repeated that the present system was unfair to people in his income bracket. I should perhaps say that he also on one occasion told me that he felt that private charity was immoral. All income transfers should be done by way of the government. This permitted him to be very charitable in his language and attitudes while making no sacrifices at all, because, of course, his political effect was nil. Note, I am not accusing this man of conscious lying. He wasn't that bright. He was, however, in the true sense of the word a hypocrite.

This kind of hypocrisy, albeit in less aggravated form, is widely found among the population as a whole. Another colleague of mine, in the Polytechnic's political science department, expressed the view that he would be willing to have very large parts of his income go to prevent starvation in India, but, of course, he was not willing to spend it on institutions which wasted it on administrative costs. He was here somewhat misinformed. He thought that all of the institutions which you can turn to to transfer money to the poor people in India would spend 60 per cent of your transfer on themselves. When I explained to him that there were also institutions called banks, and that by simply getting the names of some poor people in India he could arrange to transfer funds to them at a negligible cost, he laughed and changed the subject. In this case I should perhaps say that the man is not only in the political science department, but a perfectly genuine church minister. He gives sermons on Sunday on the desirability of charity and tells his classes about it. I believe also that, by American standards, he is a charitable man, probably making much more sacrifice of his own living standard to help others than most people do. Nevertheless, these sacrifices are strictly limited and much below the ones that he theoretically approves of.

But to return to our main subject, which is the real motives for income redistribution, I think there is no doubt at all that the most important single such motive is the desire of the recipients to receive the funds. Note that I am not criticising the recipients for having this desire; I like to receive transfers myself and so does everyone else I know. It is not making invidious distinctions to say that the people who in fact receive transfers want to receive them, nor that they will work towards obtaining them and, hence, wanting to receive transfers can be one of the motivating forces. Indeed, it would be very surprising if this were not so.

The only issue then that is raised by the view that those who desire to receive government transfers are the major source is simply the word "major." The evidence for this is, I think, very strong, however. First, most of the transfers in most societies, democratic or dictatorial, do not go to the poor. They go to people who for one reason or another are politically well organised.

As an academic I am particularly well prepared to testify to this point because like most academics I spend my time making a transfer from the average taxpayer who supports the university system to a group of students, all of whom have been selected for having better than average general talents. They are therefore people who would have higher than average incomes even without any educational advantages, and the taxpayer is compelled to subsidise their receipt of an education which further raises their lifetime incomes. This is a clear-cut case of regressive income transfer with which all academics are familiar. It is, after all, how they make their living.

But this is by no means a deviant case. The Department of Health and Human Services is very largely engaged in transferring funds back and forth within middle-class areas in accordance with various political pressures. It does indeed make some payments to the poor, but these are relatively modest. Indeed, if all its transfers were concentrated on the poor, the poor would cease to be poor and might even become members of the upper class.

While we are on the subject of the Department of Health and Human Services we might mention the largest single transfer activity in our society, the social security scheme. It should be said to begin with the fact that the Social Security Administration is characteristically advertised not as a transfer mechanism, but as an insurance scheme in which you pay your contribution during your working lifetime and then are paid back when you retire. If this were all there is to it, there would indeed be no transfer, and the social security scheme should be removed from all consideration of transfers or aid to the poor in our society. It would, of course, be true that the older people who were receiving the funds had less income than the young people who were paying in, but this would no more be a transfer from the well-off to the poor than the payment which implicitly goes from those policy-holders of fire insurance whose houses have not burned down to those whose have.

But this is not all there is to be said about social security. There is actually built into the system two transfers, one small and a second gigantic. Both of these transfers are probably progressive, but the larger one is in essence progressive by accident. In fact, it is a transfer from a group of people who do not have votes to a group of people who do.

Let us begin with the smaller transfers. Assume that social security remains unchanged at its present basic structure for a long enough time so that a person who entered as a young person taking his first job finally retires and dies. Within his generation there would be a very large payment made by all individuals during their working lives and an equally large receipt by all of them when they retired.[15] Within this group, however, those who had the higher incomes while they were working would find that the total pension they receive will not repay them for their investment, while those who had the lower incomes would find that they receive more than they put in.

The actual measure of this transfer is quite difficult owing to the complicated nature of the social security arrangements. For example, there is a significant transfer from families in which both the husband and wife work to families in which only one works or in which there is only one person. Secondly, there is a significant transfer to civil servants and army personnel who get very much larger amounts out than they put in. Civil servants and army veterans are not among the poor of the population. This transfer is probably, although not certainly, regressive. The major progressive part of the programme involves quite substantial transfers to the poorer part of the population, however. Note, by the way, that any person whose income comes entirely from property is not a member of the system and hence does not participate. A wealthy man, on the other hand, who was on the board of directors of a couple of companies, and hence very much a part-time employee, might take a profit out of the system.

An immense transfer which has been associated with the Social Security Administration, however, has been a transfer from future generations to the present (immediately past?) generation.[16] Assume that you are in a society in which there is no social security system and that the current general structure of the social security is suddenly imposed. Further, and only temporarily, let us assume that the economic growth of society is as high as the rate of interest. This means that almost everyone makes a net gain. The pay will be highest for elderly people who would immediately begin receiving pensions without making any payments. Other age cohorts will gain roughly in terms of their age. The 50-year-olds would have to put in 12 or 15 years of paying taxes, but the return that they will receive will be equivalent to what they would have received had they been saving the full amount of their payments from the time that they first started working and had invested it at the

15. With true stability of everything, the receipt would be the same as the amount paid out; i.e., there would be no interest payment. If we assumed the economy continues to grow this period, however, there would be an implicit interest payment equivalent to the rate of growth of society.

16. There is a much more detailed discussion of this point in my *Economics of Income Redistribution* (Boston, Mass.: Kluwer-Nijhoff, 1983).

interest rate which, remember, is temporarily held to be equal to the rate of social growth.

Similarly the 21-year-olds would receive in pensions an amount which is slightly higher than the actual present value of the payments they will make through the rest of their working lives. Even the 18-year-old youngest voters would gain because the average working life includes some work before the age of 18, and they would not pay taxes on that part of their lifetime income but will receive a repayment which will include the average amount of work below the age of 18 as part of its base. There is a qualification to this rather simple picture due to the fact, as I have said before, that there is a progressive transfer in the social security system itself. Someone who was young and who had a fairly high income throughout his life might find out that he paid in more than the present actual value of what he received. The small group of people who would suffer in this way would actually suffer only a small decrement in their lifetime income.

Who, then, pays this transfer? The answer is that it is a modification of the Ponzi scheme, but with legal compulsion to make it work. The members of the first generation who receive these large payments receive them from people who enter the system later. Keeping our current set of assumptions, the latter generations all receive amounts[17] equal to the actual value that they put in as long as the system continues. Thus, as long as the system continues, no one is injured, and it is always true that the existing population would be very badly injured by termination. The continuing transfer from those now working to the retired all works out actuarily except in the first and last generations. Further, since the future generations in general will be wealthier than the present generations, the net effect can be called a transfer which is of a progressive nature as a continuing matter by those who are not too critical.

There are two serious problems with this. One is that the rate of growth is unlikely to be as high as the effective interest rate, with the result that people entering the system actually pay in more than they get out. It seems likely, however, that with the amounts of interest in fact available to the average person, only younger people are injured by this and that at any given point in time the majority of the population would favour continuing the system.

The second problem is, of course, that this system leads to much less capital accumulation than would a fully funded system. Suppose, for example, the government simply compels people to buy insurance policies with the

17. Once again with the exception of those injured by the transfer from upper-income to lower-income groups.

same net return as the present social security pensions. For any individual now entering the system this would be better, in the sense that it would cost him less because he would receive interest on his initial payments and because capital investment in society would go up with the result that his labour income would rise. Individuals whose income came from capital would, of course, suffer to some extent because the return on capital would be lowered by this sharp increase.

Whether the social security system reduces the total investment to anywhere near this extent, given that insurance purchase is not compulsory, is a much-debated question and one into which I do not want to enter now. Most good economists agree that there is at least some reduction in capital investment as a result of the scheme.

Thus, we have a system which benefited the first generation and which will remain in existence as long as possible because it is always in the interest of the majority of the population to keep it going even though once it has reached an equilibrium, it no longer benefits them. The last generation, or the generation which is in existence when the system is cut back for some reason, will suffer severely.

But does this resemble the American system? The answer is yes. The programme before 1977 was expanded not all at once in one fell swoop, but step by step. Each time it has been expanded there has been a group of people over 40 who gained, and the losses are clearly well concealed and perhaps nonexistent. Further, politically, the drive behind this has almost entirely come from older people, which is an indication that the purpose is not to help the poor but to help certain people who are very anxious to be helped and who are willing to vote in terms of whether congressmen helped them or not. Since 1977, the programme has suffered a very considerable number of minor cuts and one quite major cut.[18] Which way the future will go is by no means obvious.

As further evidence that the scheme is not basically a charitable one, motivated by the desire of young people to help impoverished old people, but a desire by old people to help themselves, it should be pointed out that it was actually inaugurated by Prince Bismarck in Germany. Bismarck has never been noted for a desire to be charitable to the poor and downtrodden, although as a traditional aristocrat he doubtless felt it his duty to engage in a certain amount of paternalistic activity.

18. See my *Economics of Income Redistribution* for a more thorough discussion.

There is a further bit of evidence here. If I ask people the advantages of the social security scheme as opposed to letting people save money themselves, I invariably get the reply that a number of people wouldn't and that we would then have to take care of them. This is indeed, as far as I can see, the strongest single intellectual argument ever offered for the social security system, namely, that it makes it unnecessary for those of us who are provident to take care of the improvident.

This argument may conceivably be true, but note what it says: first, that without social security we would be called upon to make transfers to the poor. We force them to save money which they don't want to save in order to avoid this transfer for ourselves. In other words, the standard argument for the social security system is that it reduces the amount of transfers actually made to the poor. In fact, the bulk of the transfers goes to people who are reasonably well-off one way or another.[19] This is reinforced by the fact that those poor people who are so poor that they actually receive financial aid from the state of one sort or another have the social security payment which they receive deducted from that amount so that the net effect is that having paid social security payments all of their lives they end up receiving no more than they would had they, let us say, been living in Korea until their retirement and hence made no payments at all to the American government or social security system.

All of this is not atypical. Public opinion polls show clearly that the one and only part of the social welfare system which is unpopular is the direct payments to the poor. (I should say here that in talking to people about this I usually find that once I tell them how small those payments actually are they suddenly become in favour of increasing them!)

But so much for the drive to redistribute simply because the recipients want it. This is an immense phenomenon in all modern welfare states, but it is theoretically, at any event, a relatively simple motive. Let us now turn to some other motives, most of which are much less important than the desire to receive transfers, but which nevertheless do have an effect on redistribution. Note that although I have given pride of place to redistribution to people because they want it, because I do think that is the most important motive, I do not have any clear idea as to the relative importance of the

19. In many cases their asset situation has been adjusted to take advantage of the social security, but they would have no difficulty in providing for their retirement if that had been necessary. There are, of course, many individual cases for whom this is not true, and for whom charitable provision might well be made if the social security system did not exist.

motives I am going to discuss below, and hence have put them in random order.

The first of these additional motives is undeniably charity. No one who looks at human behaviour can deny that most human beings are willing to make at least some transfers to people who are less well-off than they are out of purely charitable motives. Presumably this would affect their vote as well as their private actions. Note, however, that what data we have seem to indicate that the amount they will give away is really quite small. The amount of talk about charity is great, but the amount that is actually given is small. Further, this amount does not seem to have changed very much with movement from the old-fashioned puritan-capitalist state in the mid-nineteenth century to the welfare state of today. This latter is based on a study by Lebergott[20] which shows that there has been some sort of minimum income in the United States for a long time and that this has remained, roughly speaking, a fixed fraction of the wage of the average workingman.

There is in the literature an argument[21] that government redistribution would be larger than private redistribution because of the neighbourhood effect. The explanation can be seen on Figure 2. We assume a three-person society composed of one poor person and two well-off people. The two wealthy people both have a "demand" for charity to the poor person shown by the line CC. The line P shows the cost of providing loaves of bread to the poor person in order to avoid his dying of starvation. Each individual well-off person would be willing to purchase bread for the poor person as far as point O. If both of them are individually purchasing the bread and they are informed of each other's gifts, the outcome is indeterminant, but it looks likely that the individual would receive only quantity O. How the cost would be distributed between the two wealthy persons is not clear.

Suppose, however, that the two wealthy people get together and form a collective organisation. For each of them, then, the cost of buying a loaf of bread for the poor person is only P′. With the same demand for charity as they had before they will jointly purchase O′. They will be better off and so will the poor person.

Let us turn now to my second genuine motive for redistribution, which is simply envy. I should say that most people who are in favour of redistribution

20. Stanley Lebergott, *Wealth and Want* (Princeton, N.J.: Princeton University Press, 1975), pp. 53–69.

21. I first read this in Friedman's *Capitalism and Freedom*, but I here use an apparatus for explaining it which is somewhat different from his.

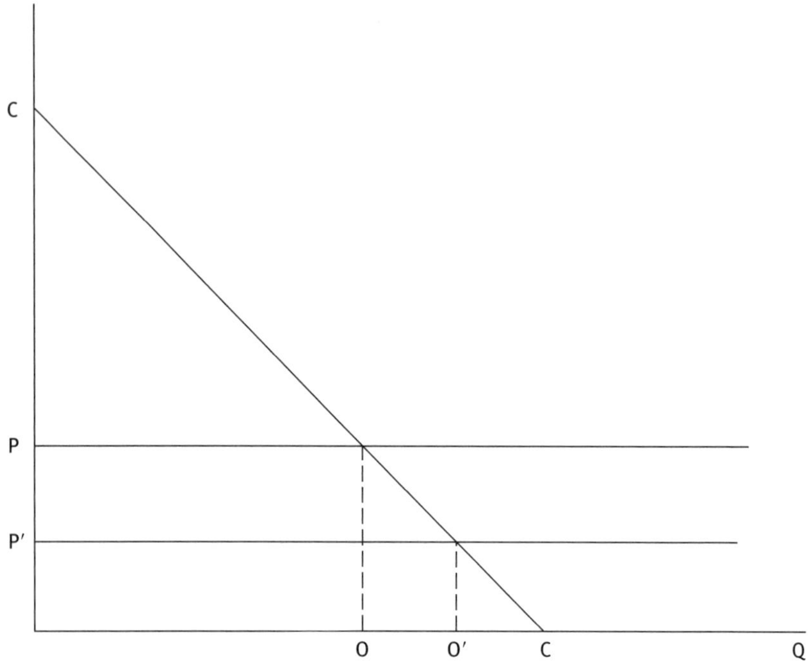

FIGURE 2

of income very strenuously disavow envy as one of their motives. I regret to say that I do not believe them. In redistribution literature there is at least as much discussion of the vicious spending habits of upper-income people as of the poverty of the poor. Partly this comes from simple intellectual misunderstanding, but more accurately I think it is an expression of annoyance and irritation with the rich, which comes from envy. For example,

> The chief conclusion of this report is that poverty is more extensive than is generally or officially believed and has to be understood not only as an inevitable feature of severe social inequality but also as a particular consequence of actions by the rich to preserve and enhance their wealth and so deny it to others. Control of wealth and of the institutions created by that wealth, and therefore of the terms under which it may be generated and passed on selectively or for the general good, is therefore central to any policies designed to abolish or alleviate the condition.[22]

22. Townsend, op. cit., p. 893.

Once again I do not wish to blame people for being envious. I frequently find myself envying those who have more than I do, and I am not surprised at being envied by people who have less. Envy is no doubt a deadly sin, but it is equally no doubt widely present in the human race. That it leads to redistributive attitudes is obvious, although in this case the redistribution, of course, is only away from people who have more than you have.

The combination of charitable motives and envy, I think, jointly leads to another explanation for income redistribution which, in my opinion, is largely a rationalisation of these two motives. It is frequently said, for example, by Henry Simons, the man who taught me economics, that it is desirable to have a greater degree of equality within the society simply because wide variance is, in and of itself, undesirable. I may be wrong in believing that this is simply a rationalisation of the two motives of charity and envy, but I don't think so. In any event, once again, this desire to have a greater degree of equality would normally appear to terminate at the national boundaries, but I have never found an advocate of egalitarian policies who will actually stand up and be counted as arguing for such a break.

I have only one more argument for income redistribution, but if any of my readers have others I would appreciate their sending them to me. This one is the insurance motive. I realise that there is at least some prospect that I will become impoverished in the future. Since I am risk-averse, I am willing to put up at least some resources now to provide myself with insurance against this.[23] One way of organising such an implicit insurance policy is some kind of a state floor under incomes.

The question of whether this kind of income insurance could be provided by private insurance companies is somewhat open. The problem would, of course, be adverse selection of risks, with individuals having—or at least thinking they have—better judgement than the insurance companies as to what type of income they will receive in the future. It is not clear whether this type of adverse selection of risk would make the provision of such insurance by private companies impossible, but it certainly would make it difficult, and it is arguable that a government programme would do better, because, being compulsory, it would eliminate this particular problem. The problem of individuals with this kind of insurance tending to work less hard would, of

23. As far as I know, I am the inventor of this particular rationalisation which, to my knowledge, first appeared in *The Calculus of Consent*, pp. 192–97.

course, be characteristic of both models, but the individual himself would carry the principal cost of this through his premium payment, and if he voluntarily chose the programme, we could assume he was better off. A compulsory system would, of course, deprive us of any way of determining whether individuals were better off under income insurance than without, but it certainly is quite possible that they would be.

This argument is relatively invulnerable to refutation on any other than empirical grounds. Further, it is very hard to think of a way to perform the empirical investigation to prove whether it is true or false. It has another advantage. It alone of all the arguments we have produced so far applies to justification for the break at the national boundary or at the ethnic boundary in countries where one ethnic group is in control. You know that whatever else happens you remain an American citizen unless you voluntarily choose to cease to be one,[24] just as a South African knows that his skin colour is not going to change. Therefore, if you favour income redistribution for this reason you need suffer no embarrassment about your unwillingness to include the citizens of Mexico in the distribution scheme.

It should perhaps be said in passing that all insurance policies have some equalising effect on net wealth. I mentioned the fire insurance policy before, but health insurance, life insurance and, for that matter, marine insurance on super-tankers all have the characteristic of leading to a somewhat more equal wealth distribution than would exist without the insurance. Income insurance would be simply one example.

The other thing to be said about income insurance is that I very rarely run into it in the literature. Note that I said rarely; it is not totally absent, but it does not seem to be a major argument offered for income redistribution by those who are in favour of it. I discovered that when I ask ordinary citizens about their reasons for favouring income redistribution (if they do) this answer comes up somewhat more frequently than it does in the formal literature, but still it is not very common.

The general theme of this chapter so far has been that the usual reasons given for income redistribution are muddled and not in accord with the actual income redistribution that we observe. The actual motives imply a very large volume of transfers in the society which don't necessarily help the poor, some probably minor transfers to the poor for charitable motives together with another unknown component of transfers to the poor because the poor

24. Or unless the United States is conquered and hence the citizenship vanishes.

want it and transfers away from the wealthy regardless of whether these transfers are beneficial or not; i.e., taxes may be put on the wealthy which are high enough so that the total revenue that is derived by the majority of the population for spending these taxes would be higher if the taxes were lowered.

Why all the confusion? The answers, I think, are fairly simple. Let us begin with the transfers to people who simply want them. On the whole it is unwise for them to say that their gain is the reason that the transfer should be implemented. This is not in general a good political ploy. The people who receive the transfers can no doubt be expected to figure that out, and hence they will become allies where we propose this kind of transfer, but it is best to keep other people confused.

Thus, Dr Townsend, proposing the famous Townsend plan during a period of great depression, offered it primarily as a way of curing the depression, and the very large transfers to the elderly which he proposed are merely a step towards that end. As he had expected, the elderly who were in favour both of ending the depression and of receiving large sums of money in general pressed for the plan. The rest of the population, as it turned out, were not confused enough so it could get through, but it seems quite likely that the Townsend plan episode was one of the reasons that the social security scheme was enacted later.

In this the programme is similar to almost all efforts to redistribute funds to people which are initiated or argued for by the recipients. They have a strong motive for concealing their real motive from the general public and if possible also from themselves, and hence they are rarely candid in their explanations.

But to return to the other reasons for transfer. Considering the desirability of acquiring accurate information about them on the part of the voter, we immediately realise that it is very weak.[25] An individual who purchases something or other for his own use almost immediately has brought to his attention any defects of that commodity. If he purchases something for someone else (i.e., engages in a charitable act), however, the defects of his purchase will be felt by that other person.

If we turn to envy, his motives for being well informed are no greater. Here he is attempting to injure someone, and the act which he undertakes in order to injure them is in general, in and of itself, a source of satisfaction. The actual

25. For an elaboration of this argument see "Information Without Profit," Chapter 4, below.

injury, unless it occurs directly in his sight, is not something from which he gets much satisfaction, because he doesn't have much information about it.

Here again he will be irritated if he finds out that he has not been successful. Indeed, the general attention of the media to loopholes and tax evasion seems to indicate that the general irritation which he feels if the object of his envy escapes his malice is stronger than his irritation if charitable funds are, in his view, wasted. Nevertheless, once again he does not have very strong motives for becoming informed of the actual results, and it is hard to do.

With respect to the insurance motive, which, as I have pointed out above, does not seem to be very much in the forefront of the minds of most people engaged in this activity, the individual would have strong motives for being well informed if there were a private market in income insurance and he were considering whether or not to purchase it. Once it becomes a public matter, however, the usual public good argument against becoming well informed applies. Of course, the public good argument against being well informed applies also to people who are interested in income redistribution for the motives I have listed above. In these cases, however, there is an additional argument for being badly informed. The individual who is considering whether there should be an increase in the appropriation for the local police force would not be well informed because of the public good argument. If he is considering an increase in the appropriations for the charitable contributions, the public good argument is reinforced by the fact that he himself is not going to benefit directly or be injured by the results of the appropriation.

My theme has been that the arguments for income redistribution are chaotic. It is widely believed that income redistribution is desirable, and I have said nothing here which indicates that that belief is false, but the discussions of the subject tend to involve a great deal of muddle and inconsistency. Further, we do not observe people behaving in a way which would be implied by the arguments insofar as their arguments are clear enough to imply anything. This does not, of course, indicate that income redistribution is undesirable, merely that the intellectual discussion of it is very poor. It seems to me that proponents of income redistribution should make an effort to clean up their act.

OBJECTIVES OF INCOME REDISTRIBUTION

The purpose of this chapter, oddly enough, is not so much to inform its readers as to solicit their assistance for the author on what our goals should be when we talk about income distribution in society and, in particular, the distribution of burdens and benefits of government activity. I am not able in this case simply to examine my own ideas in this area, because it would appear that my ideas are rather eccentric. I am not particularly in favour of income redistribution. I feel that some aid should be given to the poor, but clearly my position is not that of the average intellectual.

I am, however, a positive economist and am willing to advise other people on how to achieve their goals. In particular, since a great many people talk about various redistribution objectives, and since the demand-revealing process[1] permits much more precise adjustment of governmental behaviour to desires of the citizenry, it should be possible to achieve whatever goals are desired in the area of income distribution much more precisely with the demand-revealing process than with other methods.

The problem I have encountered, and for which I wish to request your assistance, is that there does not seem to be anything in the literature which indicates what redistribution we should desire, granted this greater precision made possible by the demand-revealing process.

The demand-revealing process makes it possible to make use of a close approximation of Lindahl taxes for public goods. Note that I say a "close approximation." There is some doubt as to how close an approximation we would be able to achieve, but it seems to me that it is only sensible to assume that the approximation will be very close indeed. If we assume that it is close and then develop a set of criteria we would use on that assumption, and it later turns out to be somewhat more difficult than we expected, we can easily correct our reasoning for this inaccuracy. If, on the other hand, we assume that the approximation is very rough, and therefore only a very crude set of

Reprinted, with permission, from *The Economics of Wealth and Poverty* (New York: New York University Press, 1986), 42–56.

1. See T. N. Tideman and G. Tullock, "A New and Superior Process for Making Social Choices," *Journal of Political Economy* 84 (December 1976), for an explanation of this process.

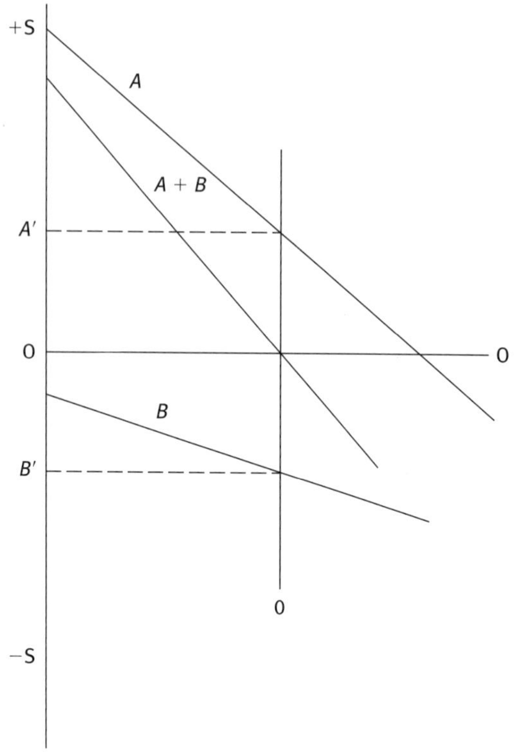

FIGURE 1

criteria is necessary, if we later discover that the approximation is very good, we will have to go through the whole process again. I would therefore like to ask that you bear with me and assume that the Lindahl taxes will be very closely approximated—indeed, for ease of explanation, we might assume that they will be reached perfectly.

Note that although we seldom mention this, the Lindahl taxes can be negative. In Figure 1 we show a two-person, A and B, society, in which there is some public good to be purchased which will benefit A and injure B. The demand curve for B, then, is negative, as shown in Figure 1. We sum the two demand curves to A + B and note the point where it crosses the 0 line. This gives us the optimum shown by O. We then charge A a tax of A′ and B a negative tax of B′.

This procedure, although geometrically different, is a mapping of the usual method of computing the optimal amount of pollution. Furthermore, it gives A and B roughly the same consumer surplus on this social improvement. It is, of course, simply the application of the Lindahl tax scheme, except that one of the taxes is negative.

Distribution of costs and benefits of this sort is not what most people mean when they talk about redistribution of income. In a moment I shall turn to the more normal meaning of redistribution, but I should like to raise questions here as to the appropriate distribution of benefits and costs of government action. In a way, I am going to follow the traditional economic distinction between discussion of an efficient change and of deliberate income redistribution; but, in my case, later I am actually going to talk about deliberate income redistribution. I simply want to clear the decks by talking about certain problems of efficient change first.

Note, then, that although public finance specialists (including myself) have always been deeply enamoured with Lindahl taxes, this has been essentially because they are theoretically so nice. Everybody is paying his true marginal evaluation of some particular public good, because the different evaluations of the public good by different people lead to their paying different prices for the same quantity. Furthermore, we can, in the demand-revealing process, obtain that quantity of public goods which is optimal, so everything seems fine.

When one begins thinking about it, however, it is not so obvious that the Lindahl tax is a sensible tax. Suppose that we have some public good for which A's demand is high and B's demand is low, as in Figure 2. We sum the two demand curves, using the demand-revealing process for the project, find the optimum (which turns out to be 10 units), and charge B $10 (or $1 a unit), which is the value of the marginal tenth unit to him, and we charge A (the high demander) $100 (or $10 a unit), which is the value of the marginal unit to him. For $11 a unit, we can produce the 10 units. B is paying $10 total and A is paying $100, and there is no obvious reason for us to believe that A has a higher consumption surplus than B. Indeed, the first approximation would be to say that they are probably about the same.

This certainly has little or no resemblance to what happens in the private market. Nor is it obvious to me that distributionally this is a good idea, whatever else may be said about it. Thus, my first problem with respect to income distribution under the demand-revealing process is to ask if it is indeed a good idea to use Lindahl prices, granted we can do so. Before trying to answer this question, remember that just at the moment I am only talking about changes in government process and *not* about the kind of redistribution we think of as assistance to the poor. I will turn to that in a moment. We should

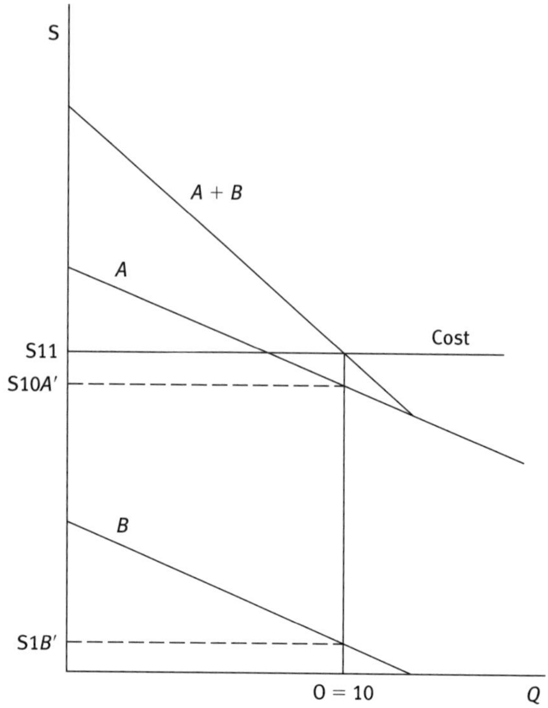

FIGURE 2

assume, then, that the income distribution before we contemplate purchasing this public good from A and B was one which had been socially accepted, although up to now I have not explained how we will obtain such an income distribution.

We also have the question of what we would do if we decide against the Lindahl price. But there is an even more difficult problem. In many cases of government action, there is a net social benefit of a unitary nature; i.e., we cannot carry the production of the public good out to the point where the marginal price—summing all individual demand, positive *and* negative—is equal to the cost. For example, suppose it were decided to abolish the Common Agricultural Community. Clearly, the benefit from this action would be much greater than the loss, and it is hard to think of any way to regard this as generation of a continuous type of public good.

This raises very real problems for income distribution. As an example, suppose that A has an Interstate Commerce Commission–granted monopoly on trucking between two cities in the United States. His income from this government-granted monopoly is $10,000 higher than what we would achieve in a competitive trucking market. B and C, on the other hand, are users of this truck line, and the cost to them of the monopoly is $9,000 and $6,000, respectively. This would, I take it, be roughly the typical situation, although normally there are many more parties involved. If we obtain the actual values the parties would place on the abolition of a monopoly, which is −$10,000 for A and a sum of +$15,000 for B and C, we note that it is clearly a socially desirable act, because there is a larger profit than there is cost.

But having decided that it is socially desirable, which is all that traditional economics has done, we now have the problem of determining who should get the $5,000 social profit. Indeed, we could ask who is to get the full $15,000, since it is not inevitable that we will compensate the loser. Nevertheless, most economists have argued in such cases that the loser should be compensated, and I am going to adopt this assumption. Note that the problems I raise later would not be changed particularly if we decided not to compensate A, but the amount of money to be distributed would be increased.

What, then, do we do with the $5,000? The traditional economic explanation is that we would let it remain in the pockets of B and C, with B getting $4,000 and C getting $1,000, and simply compensate A for his losses. But surely there is no strong argument for this. Why not divide it into three equal parts and give one-third to each of them? Or, if we think that A is a nasty man and should not be compensated, why not arrange that B and C will each get $2,500? Note that all of this is perfectly possible with the demand-revealing process.

Even these proposals are fairly modest. Why should any one of these three people have control over this fund? Why not contribute it to the well-being of the untouchables in India? Or why not pay it into a fund which is designed, when many further similar contributions are made, to be divided among all citizens of the world on a so-much-per-head basis? Or we could even concentrate it on the poor—that is, this money will be paid (once again, together with similar funds from the elimination of other uneconomic institutions) to, let us say, the 5 million poorest people in the world.

I can find no significant discussion of this problem. What is the objective which would be recommended by a person who believes in a great deal of equality or, for that matter, an economist who does not have any particularly strong feelings about equality but who just wants a "good" outcome? If you happen to be a property right devotee, for example, *who* has the property right in this fund?

There is, by the way, another candidate for the money—a candidate whom I would regard as exceptionally deserving, although administratively hard to locate. Presumably the abolition of the United States Interstate Commerce Commission would be the result of entrepreneurial activity by some group or individual. Giving them the bulk of the social profit, or at least enough social profit to motivate this kind of work, would seem to be highly desirable. This would mean that the present situation in which, in general, it is easy to organise a minority to push for some act which is contrary to the public interest, and very difficult to organise one which benefits the public interest, would be reversed. Granted we are going to compensate the losers, there would be no significant interest group organised to avoid this change in the law; and if we used the profit to compensate the political agency that brought about the change, then we would motivate political entrepreneurs to go into this business, and we might end up with a massively more efficient government.

The problem here is essentially administrative. Even with the demand-revealing process, very few people are motivated to become well informed. Thus, the reward might well go to the wrong people, and therefore it would not serve its motivating function. Still, I would think some experimentation along these lines would be desirable. Note that if we decide to give half of the social profit to whoever pulls off the political *coup* that makes the social profit possible, we would still have the other half for other distribution, and the questions I have raised above would still be important ones.

Having whetted your interest (I hope) with these subsidiary but nevertheless intellectually challenging problems, I would now like to turn to what I regard as the major problem in redistribution, which is conscious, deliberate redistribution of income for the benefit of the recipients.

I should like to begin by pointing out that there is one great advantage of the demand-revealing process: it does not permit transfers which are motivated *only* by the desire of the recipients to receive money. If we look at modern democratic states (and, also, for that matter, at dictatorships), we observe an immense amount of transfer from party to party which is motivated entirely by the desire of the recipients, with the people who involuntarily make the contribution not having any interest in the matter at all or being opposed. The Common Market agricultural policy is an example; almost all protective tariffs are further examples.

All of these transfers, so far as I know, can be justified only on the grounds that the political process does indeed grind them out because the recipients want them, and under democracy it is hard to organise any opposition to them. It is a case of an intense minority getting transfers from a dispersed and not deeply interested majority. All of these things would vanish if we used the demand-revealing process, because the mild opposition to these various programmes of the average man would, when added up, be greater than the intense desire for them by the minority. This seems to me an immense step forward.

Still, so far as I know, there is absolutely no rational explanation for any of these transfers, except that the recipients want them, and the political process happens to be such that they can get them. The change in the political process that eliminated them would, I think, be widely supported. Even some professors of economics would be willing to back a programme which would surely greatly reduce the demand for professors of economics.

We are thus left with transfers to people who, for one reason or another, attract the favourable attention of the donors. Mainly, these are the poor and the ill. There are other groups, of course, but I trust you will not object if I confine myself to these particular groups. It would be one of the advantages of the demand-revealing process, then, that transfers would be concentrated in a group of people who are, at least by some, thought to merit the transfer. Farmers, so far as I know, are not thought to merit transfers by anyone except the farmers themselves nor are the beneficiaries of various protective tariffs thought to merit the money by anyone but themselves. However, that is not true with respect to people who are sick and/or poor.

Here again I have frankly to confess that I am not very much of an egalitarian, and therefore I would probably choose a fairly low level of transfers. It is not obvious that I would choose as low a level of transfers to the poor as we actually observe in most democratic states—where the transfer tends to be of the order of 2 to 3 per cent of GNP—but, in any event, I would not be in favour of a very high transfer rate. My objective, however, is not to present my own preferences but to use this chapter in an effort to solicit the views of people who do believe in considerable transfers, so that, having found out what they have in mind, I can design a political process based on the demand-revealing process which will tend to generate that outcome.

There is, however, one problem with which I should begin. Suppose that Professor Bleeding Heart tells me that he knows perfectly well what income transfers should be. We should find the world average income and tax everyone who has an income above that amount by 90 per cent of the excess, and then use the funds derived to give to all people who have less than the average income 90 per cent of the difference between their income and the average income. I have not looked at the numbers recently, but I suppose that the average yearly income in the world is something like $500 per family.

There is nothing easier than designing a governmental structure which does this. We simply put the requirement that this be done into the constitution. To say it is easy to design is not to say that it is easy to implement. I doubt very much if such a constitution would be acceptable in any country which has an average income much above the world average, and I also doubt that we could get world acceptance simply because the wealthier countries, such as the United States and France, would object very strongly to this large transfer to poverty-stricken countries, such as China and India. Thus, although it is easy to design such a procedure, it is very unlikely that we would get beyond the design stage.

Furthermore, I am sure we would find that although Professor Bleeding Heart regards this as a good system, many other people would have different ideas. What we need, then, is a constitution or a method of making decisions on income transfers which has acceptable elements in itself and which succeeds in aggregating in one way or another the preferences for redistribution of many different people. Selecting one dictator for this subject is an easy course. Furthermore, selecting a single first preference is particularly attractive if we are going to use ours. In other words, we could all stand around, and each one of us could offer his own personal preference for redistribution.

The fact remains, however, that we are not dictators, not even collective dictators, and there is no obvious reason why our decision as to how much redistribution we think should be carried out is the socially binding one. And, in practice, it would not be. We can only hope to get some particular method of redistribution adopted if there is some procedure of aggregating the preferences of at least a large enough or powerful enough group so that there is some possibility that the procedure will be implemented. Since I take it none of us prefers the dictatorial route, that means that we must aim at a policy which a great many people will adopt.

But note here a particular problem with what we might call Rawlsianism. Since *The Calculus of Consent* also talks about things "behind the veil of ignorance," I might be regarded as a premature Rawlsian.[2] There is a difference, however. We talk about establishing a constitution in *The Calculus of Consent* to deal with future problems—these problems, of necessity, not being fully

2. J. M. Buchanan and G. Tullock, *The Calculus of Consent* (Ann Arbor: University of Michigan Press, 1962). Note, however, that although we wrote before the present surge of Rawlsianism, we were, at the time we wrote the book, familiar with Rawls's ideas from his previous work.

known at the moment. As it happens, we argue that there is a particular set of constitutional arrangements which is more efficient than others, and, hence, the present discounted value of this constitution from the standpoint of a person who is uncertain of the future would be positive. Furthermore, there is a set of side-payments which could be used, granted that we were going to use the optimally efficient constitution, to compensate people who, being able to make calculations about the future, realise that they will not do as well as other people. Thus, in our case, we are simply using a sort of variant of Pareto optimality, which we call Pareto optimality in large.

The Rawls proposal, however, does not claim that there is any particularly efficient level of income redistribution; and, indeed, I believe from my personal knowledge of Rawls that he would probably argue that a zero income redistribution would generate the largest total income; hence, in a way—a very special way—it might be regarded as the most efficient. Thus, he is not attempting to solve a problem with a solution which in fact could be to the benefit of almost everyone, but he is suggesting that people act as if they did not know in order to improve their morals. I doubt very much that any practical government is ever going to do this. In a way, Rawls has made a contribution to the way we should think and talk in the event that we decide that we will devote some time to the discussion of what is the optimal income redistribution in some ethical sense. He has not produced a method which we could expect to have any great effect on income distribution in the real world.

From the standpoint of the egalitarians this is fortunate, because the Rawls method surely would lead to less income redistribution than we now have. The point of the veil of ignorance is to make it impossible for people to make their decisions in full knowledge of their real-world circumstances. We do not have the veil of ignorance, and decisions are therefore made with this forbidden knowledge. Since the median income is below the average income, this would mean that we would anticipate in a democracy that there would be more money transferred than would be transferred behind the veil of ignorance.[3]

We need, then, a method of aggregating people's preferences: one method in general use today is the market; another is democracy. For redistribution of income, there is indeed a market solution—voluntary charity—and, in those cases in which there are not large government transfers, it tends to be quite extensive. However, I am going to ignore the market as an income transfer mechanism and concentrate on government or coerced income transfer.

3. R. E. Wagner, "Politics, Bureaucracy, and Budgetary Choice," *Journal of Money, Credit, and Banking* 8 (August 1974).

Traditionalists like Anthony Downs sometimes argue that the amount of income transfer generated by simple majority voting is the optimal amount. Downs, of course, then supplements this argument by arguing that a democracy is desirable because it transfers the optimal amount. The circular nature of this line of reasoning is clear. So far as I know there is absolutely no reason to believe that majority voting or any of the variants of democratic government transfer an "optimal" amount. Indeed, I would argue that they do very badly, since the bulk of the transfers they generate are transferred back and forth within the middle class; and, so far as I know, there are no arguments that would indicate that these transfers are desirable.

However, there is in democracy a very important problem which is normally ignored, i.e., the weighting of the individual votes. Characteristically, in democracies people's votes are weighted either 1 or 0. I can think of no argument for this except tradition, together with the fact that it might be politically extremely difficult to get any kind of agreement on a particular modification. In a way, this particular voting scheme is a Schelling point.

So far as I know, however, no justification has ever been offered for it other than that. There are occasional justifications for weighting all votes at 1, but the fact that we do weight some votes at 0 and some at 1 is, so far as I know, completely unjustified. Perhaps the reader knows of some discussion of this point. Speaking personally, I would rather prefer that if we are going to weight people at different weights, we have more than two weightings. For example, a person who believed in very large transfers of income might argue that individual votes should be weighted inversely with income ($1/N$),[4] so that the poor have much higher voting power than the wealthy, and they can use this to extract additional transfers from the wealthy. Another method which is used in most corporations weights people's votes in terms of their economic interest in the matter at hand, with the result that large stockholders have many more votes than small stockholders. If we look around, we can find many other cases of differential weighting of votes which have used continuous variation, but the dominant one in the present-day world of politics is the 0,1 weighting.

With the demand-revealing process, different people's votes are weighted differently, depending on their demand for various government services, including transfers. The 0,1 dichotomy, however, is very easy either to implement in the demand-revealing process or to leave out.

4. David Chapman has in fact so argued in an unpublished paper.

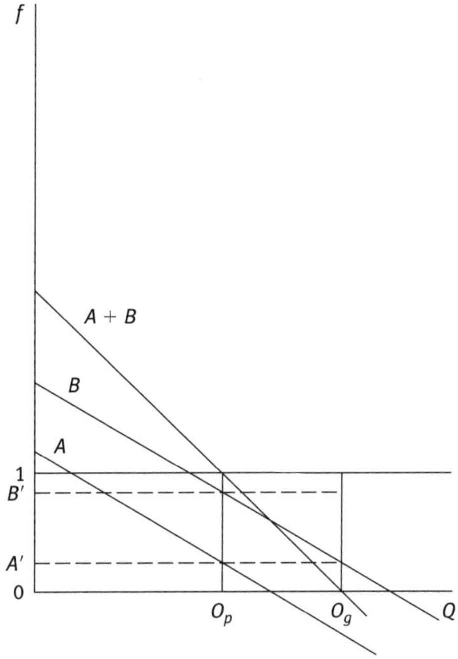

FIGURE 3

Let us suppose, then, that we are in France, where the poorest part of the population is Algerian immigrants. Suppose that the French citizens are interested in benefiting the Algerians who are, after all, very poor and live badly. Let us discuss how this should be done. For simplicity in diagrammatic exposition, I am going to assume that there are only two Frenchmen and one Algerian, but the demand-revealing process usually works much better with large numbers than it does with small numbers, so I trust the reader will accept this as merely a convention.

Consider Figure 3, which shows the demand for charitable transfer to the Algerian by two Frenchmen, A and B. The transfer itself is assumed to be done in franc units, and we will assume that the Algerian's demand for the transfer is simply 1 franc per unit; i.e., the horizontal cost line is his demand curve.[5] In a world of private charity, the situation is fairly simple: B would

5. This is not a necessary assumption, but without it, things become quite complicated graphically.

probably make a contribution to the Algerian, equivalent to the point where his demand curve crosses the cost curve; and A, observing that the Algerian has received a transfer larger than he wanted to pay, would pay nothing.

There is, clearly, a Pareto-optimal move from this. We sum the two demand curves to get the line A + B, which is the social optimum. We then charge B a per unit transfer, marked B′, and charge A a per unit transfer, marked A′. If we have presented their demands correctly, the Frenchmen will be better off, and the Algerian, who is now receiving more money, will be better off.[6] This amounts to using Lindahl taxes to pay for the transfer.

The demand-revealing process can very easily achieve this particular result—a result which I believe cannot be achieved by any other method. Note that, of course, there is the problem of approximating the Lindahl taxes, and it might turn out that we are rather bad at doing this with respect to transfers; but, once again, for the purposes of this paper let me assume that we can do it very well. If it turns out that later experimentation indicates that we cannot, our results can be appropriately modified.

It is interesting that in this particular case, we have now generated the result that Milton Friedman uses to justify government coercion in the field of income transfers. He points out that income transfers have neighbourhood effects, which show up in our diagram by the fact that the line A + B lies above B at the point where it crosses the cost line. Thus, the demand-revealing process in this case achieves a goal which has the interesting characteristic of neighbourhood effects, such that I cannot think of anyone really being opposed to it. One can argue that there should be more transfers than this, and I shall turn to such arguments in a moment, but surely it is hard to argue against this particular use of coercion which benefits everyone and injures no one.

This is the demand-revealing process equivalent to the way the French democracy currently treats the Algerians; i.e., the Algerians are not permitted to vote on various transfers given to them. It should be noted that the French are not unique in this. The guest-workers, who are the poorest part of the population all over Europe, face the same situation. The United States, as it

6. Note that it is not really certain that A would be better off. If B is already making a gift to the Algerian out to the point where his demand curve crosses the 1 franc line, then A clearly can gain (as can B) from an agreement under which further payment out to the line O_p is made, with A paying the amount A′ and B paying amount B′ on the increment. It is possible, however, that movement to the line O_p, if it is accompanied by payment by A of A′ for the entire range of payments, would be, from A's standpoint, inferior to leaving the situation as it was.

happens, does not have any guest-workers, but it has illegal immigrants. The exact number is not known, of course, but it is thought to run into millions. They are treated this way, although, interestingly enough, they are frequently able to obtain full services of various government bureaux which deal with income transfers, because the bureaux do not realise that they are illegal immigrants.

The problem is more significant in the world as a whole when it is realised that the nation-state itself is simply an artificial creation. There is, as far as I can see, no justification whatsoever, other than tradition,[7] why the citizens of India are not permitted to vote on transfers of funds from the United States and/or France to India. I am sure most "egalitarians" would be horrified at any such proposal, but I have never read any egalitarian explanation as to why we should *not* do so that, quite frankly, does not abandon all egalitarianism. Limited egalitarianism within the group traditionally permitted to vote is what is normally aimed at, together with some modest income transfers to the really poor people who are not permitted to vote. For the modest transfer to the relatively poor people who are not permitted to vote, the demand-revealing process would obviously work very well.

It is notable that the present situation in which recipients of transfers within the society are permitted to vote is not universal and has not been historically universal. Until quite recently people who were on relief or receiving other kinds of public charity were automatically deprived of their vote. Furthermore, in many states government employees were deprived of the vote for the same basic reason.

I am not arguing for deprivation of the right to vote, but I am asking the people who favour income redistribution to explain to me who they think should be permitted to make decisions on income transfers, and I would also prefer that they tell me why. Perhaps they feel that the "Wogs," "Wops" and "Chinks" and other lesser breeds without the law should not be permitted to interfere in the decision processes as to how much will be transferred to them.

In democracy the actual situation we have is that some of the beneficiaries of charity are permitted to vote and some are not, and there is no reason why the demand-revealing process could not be adjusted to permit exactly the same people to vote or to permit all people to vote. Therefore, let us assume that France changes its constitution and permits Algerians to vote in French elections, and thereby to influence the transfers to them.

7. I realise, of course, that tradition in this case has been built into constitutions and laws.

Turning once again to Figure 3, you will note that there is a portion of the diagram which is normally omitted, i.e., the part below the 0 line. Furthermore, the A + B line crosses the B line instead of stopping at B in the traditional way. The explanation for this is simply that the demand, after a while, becomes negative. A regards transfers to the Algerian—even if they come from his own pocket—as worth more than their cost, left of the point where the A demand curve crosses the 1 unit cost line. He regards them as worth something, albeit less than a unit, to the point where his demand curve crosses the 0 line. For example, at O_p he regards the transfer of 1 franc to the Algerian as worth, let us say, 10 centimes.

Eventually, however, he gets to the point where he is positively annoyed by the transfer, and therefore he would be willing to pay something to bring the transfer to a halt. For example, suppose a government programme were inaugurated to take $100 from each reader and use it to make a gift to Gadhafi on his next birthday. I suspect that most of the people, if given their choice, would prefer to put up a sum of $100.01 to avoid making this particular transfer which would be positively annoying to them. I may be wrong in this judgement. Perhaps people are nicer than I think they are, but I do think that there are many people who have positively negative feelings about some recipients of money drawn from their pockets. It is on the basis of this feeling that I have drawn Figure 3.

Thus, our donors at some point become positively annoyed by the transfer. If we are going to count the Algerian's preferences, however, his preference will, to at least some extent, counterbalance this annoyance. Using the demand-revealing process but including the Algerian's preferences, the amount transferred will be the amount O_g. Note that this is a case where the donors as a class cease to get any gain at all from the transfer; i.e., the annoyance of those who are annoyed by that size of transfer just exactly counterbalances the gain of B, who is in favour, still, of transfers (although he regards them as worth less than their cost). He has squeezed out the entire social satisfaction from the transfer, because, from this point on, although the Algerian will continue to gain 1 franc for every franc paid to him, the cost of A and B is greater than 1 franc.

The allocation of the tax cost between A and B can be carried out in such a way that they do not pay true Lindahl taxes, but in such a way that the cost to them is equal; i.e., each one will be paying about 50 centimes more than his personal demand for the transfer, which in this case would mean that A was paying about 25 centimes and B about 75 centimes. This amounts to each one paying 50 centimes more than the gain he receives, which in A's case is negative, which sums to 1 franc, exactly the gain which is being made by the Algerian.

So far I have simply talked technically about the way of applying the demand-revealing process to either of the two possible vote-weighting systems now in use in democracy. The choice between them would, of necessity, mean that we would have to make up our minds on this issue, and, as far as I can see, most intellectuals simply have not given the matter any thought. There are various possible reasons for this, but, rather than looking into these issues, I would prefer simply to urge that some thought be given.

I have read this paper in three Canadian and one American university. In each case I asked the audience to vote on whether they think that recipients of transfers should be permitted to vote on the size of the transfers or whether they think they should not. The question is usually hard to put over, because most Canadians, let us say, think it perfectly obvious that all Canadians—whether they are recipients or not—should vote on income transfers, and that it is perfectly obvious that all non-Canadian citizens—whether recipients of transfers or even contributors to the Canadian tax base—should not. This is the traditional *legal* situation; but, so far, in the various discussions on this matter, I have never encountered a single argument for it except that this is the way it has been done for some time.

Having got through this barrier, I find that the people voting on the issue do split roughly equally. About one-third are in favour of permitting the recipients to vote on transfers, about one-third are opposed and about one-third don't know. I take it that this is a reasonable indication that they had not given any great thought to the matter before the question was raised. I also take it that this would be true of the present readership also. However, I believe it is an important question and suggest that it be given thought.

Indeed, it seems to me, all three of the questions I have raised in this chapter are important and that all three are cases where people interested in income redistribution *should* have an answer but apparently do not. The Chinese sage, Mencius, argued that before a person takes action, he should first clarify his thoughts.[8] I would suggest that before proposing any income redistribution, its proponents first clarify their thoughts on these issues. Once they have done this, I think the demand-revealing process will reveal its superiority over ordinary voting in achieving whatever goal they have chosen. But in order to use the demand-revealing process, they first have to make up their minds on what will be the basic parameters of the redistribution they favour.

8. Mencius, *The Great Learning*.

PART 2

PRIVATE AND SEMIPRIVATE REDISTRIBUTION MECHANISMS

CHARITABLE GIFTS

The last two chapters, although undeniably very important in the discussion of real-world transfers, were rather depressing. In this chapter we turn to a more cheerful subject. Basically, the chapter is to be about government income transfers, but it is only sensible to begin with a few words about purely voluntary transfers in which the government does not intervene. We will then turn to reasons why charitably inclined people might choose to use the government as a technique for transfers.

The first thing to be said about charitable gifts is that they are what I might call superoptimal. Suppose that I earn $1, and the expenditure that gives me the greatest utility is to make a gift to some other person. I will receive $1's worth of utility from the gift, and the person to whom I give it also receives a full dollar's worth of utility. The same product has served at its full value to raise the utility of two different people. Clearly, this is much better than we could normally expect out of transactions between self-interested parties.

It could be said that there is a sort of mirror image in this situation. Suppose that I envy you, and the $1 that you receive lowers my utility. Under these circumstances, the return, looked at socially, from your income may be less than dollar for dollar. Indeed, it is possible that if a number of people envy a wealthy man enough, every dollar he makes actually lowers total utility. Further, these speculations about utility are not entirely empty of empirical content. By use of the demand-revealing process, we could measure how much individuals gain or are injured by payment of $1 to other individuals. The measurement would not be in utility terms, but in money or some other numeraire.[1] Unfortunately such measures, although quite possible, turn out

1. See Richard D. Auster (ed.), "Revealing the Demand for Transfers," by Gordon Tullock, *American Revolution, Papers and Proceedings* (Tucson: University of Arizona, Department of Economics, 1977), pp. 107–23, and "The Demand-Revealing Process as a Welfare Indicator," Gordon Tullock, *Public Choice* 29–2 (Supplement to Spring 1977): 51–63. These two papers deal only with the demand for transfers without including envy, but extension of the reasoning to include envy is fairly routine.

to be expensive, and there is no reason why we should undertake them except, perhaps, in a few experimental circumstances. The general direction of the effect is obvious, and there is no need for exact measures.

It is an obvious observation of human beings that they do indeed make gifts to people. A great many of these gifts are made to people who are worse off than they are, but some of them are not. The president of the United States is regularly deluged with gifts that those concerned with his security always prevent him from receiving. Surely he is not worse off than most of the people who make the gifts. When I was in Korea, a poor peasant gave a gigantic ginseng root that he had found to President Rhee. The president was duly grateful, and the peasant returned much better off than he had come up, but certainly received less than he would have had he sold the root commercially. For the purpose of this chapter, however, we are going to deal primarily with gifts to people who are worse off than the giver, i.e., those gifts whose net effect is, to some extent, to equalize income distribution in society.

The subject of the economics of the nonprofit sector and gifts requires, in my opinion, a good deal more research.[2] But in spite of this great need, I propose to leave that problem to other times and other scholars. In this book we will deal primarily with government income redistribution, and in this chapter primarily with that part of the government distribution that is motivated, in whole or in part, by charitable feelings. We will not, for example, discuss particularly the transfer from the British taxpayer to the Queen of England, even though I am sure that is as close to a voluntary gift from the voters as any governmental transfer ever is.

But why should the private citizen use the government as a mechanism rather than simply making direct gifts to the poor? There are, of course, possible administrative advantages, but I doubt that they are very significant. There is a real and significant explanation, however, which rather ironically was first invented by Milton Friedman and appears in his *Capitalism and Freedom*.[3]

2. See Barry P. Keating and Maryann O. Keating, *Not for Profit* (Glen Ridge, N.J.: Thomas Horton and Daughters, 1978), for a survey of what we currently know in this field. It is no criticism of the book to say that we should know more.

3. Milton Friedman, *Capitalism and Freedom* (Chicago: The University of Chicago Press, 1962). It seems to me that Friedman's argument is, although ingenious, not entirely free from criticism, and, indeed, in an unpublished paper I have raised some questions. See my "Elaborations on a Theme by Friedman," Center for Study of Public Choice, Working Paper No. CE 80-12-2. For our purposes here, however, there is no need to consider these rather detailed doubts, and we can simply accept his general position.

Consider then, a society of three people, A, B, and C. C is poor, and A and B both desire to give him gifts. We shall begin with a very simple procedure in which only the preferences of the people making the gifts are counted. The reason for this is simply that, at the moment, we are talking about charitable gifts. If the recipient is counted, his motive is, of course, to receive the gift, and hence we have a mix of the pure charitable transfer and the transfer that is motivated by the desire of the recipient to receive it. This is more complicated than either of the two simple cases and will be discussed later.

In considering gifts in this early discussion in which the recipient is not permitted to influence the outcome, consider yourself in a situation such as an American contemplating foreign aid (we do not let foreigners vote on this matter) or a citizen of England before 1900 contemplating helping the poor (receipt of government aid payments automatically disqualified Englishmen from voting). This is, of course, not the modern world with regard to domestic gifts, although it is the modern world with regard to international gifts. The problem of the two motives intertwined, however, is complicated, and it is much simpler to start with this simple situation and proceed on to the more complicated.

In Figure 1 we show by line A, A's demand for gifts to the poor person, and by line B, B's demand.[4] Line CC shows the cost of the gifts in the usual $1 per unit form. If the two parties engage in private gifts to C and if they know of each others' existence and gifts, the outcome is rather indeterminant because it will depend on various strategic decisions made by the two parties, but surely the total gift will not be greater than the amount 0.[5]

If the two parties collectively decide to make a gift, then we would add their individual demand curves vertically in order to get a social demand curve.[6] With the two demand curves added vertically, then with the line $A + B$ for the social demand, the total amount transferred would be $0'$. Assume that Lindahl taxes are charged—i.e., A is charged T_A and B is charged T_B for each $1 of transfer—then each of the two parties will be perfectly

4. In the following discussion we ignore any gain in utility from the act of giving. We assume the gain in utility of the donor comes from making the recipient better off.

5. Note the importance of the assumption that the two parties know of each other's gifts for the conclusion. This is, indeed, one of the more important problems discussed in "Elaborations on a Theme by Friedman."

6. Note this is an incomplete society. It is a demand for the gift of A and B, not the demand by C. The elaboration in which C is introduced will come later.

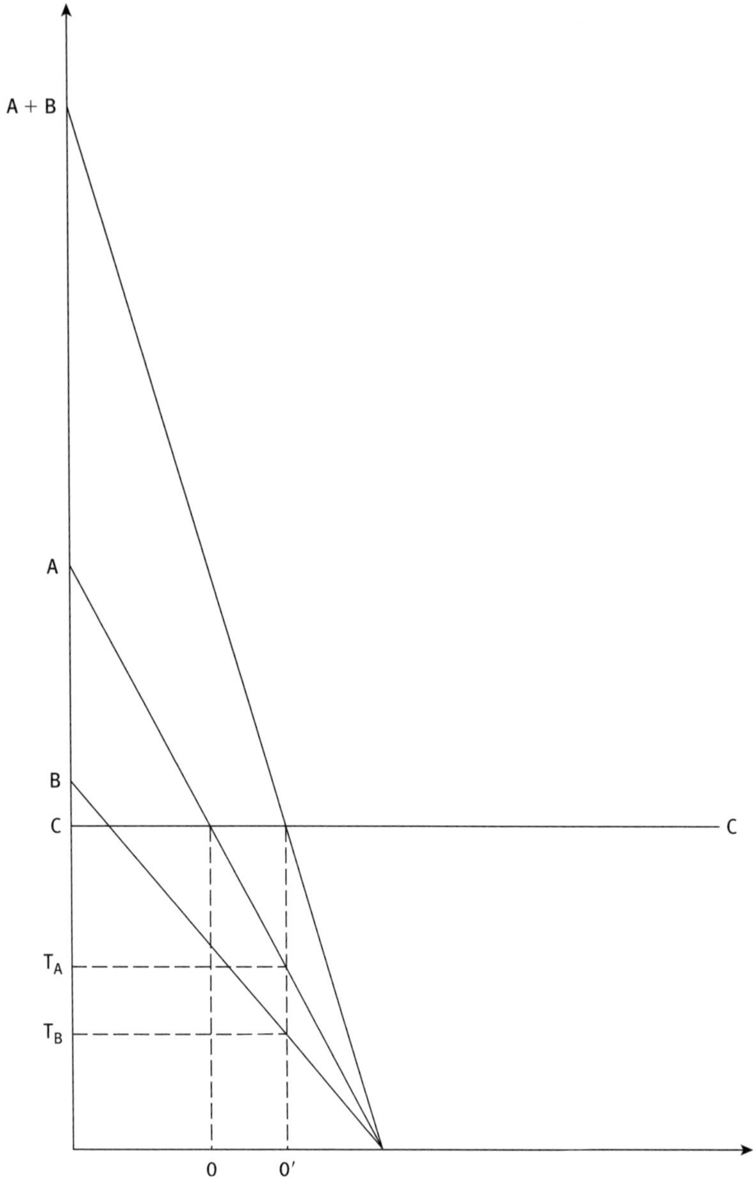

FIGURE 1

Situation where recipient is not permitted to influence the outcome

happy with the amount of transfer, which comes out at 0′. Thus we have a clear-cut Pareto optimal move. *C* benefits because he receives more money, and *A* and *B* benefit by buying what is the optimum amount for them at an appropriate price.

Note, however, that even at this level we are not totally in an unselfish world. *A* and *B* want to help *C*, but there is no reason to believe that either of them particularly wants to help the other; i.e., they would be delighted if they could shove off the cost on the other. Suppose, for example, that *A* feels that an even division of the cost of the charitable gift between the two parties is the only fair way of aiding *C*. The situation is now shown in Figure 2. Note that neither of the two parties now will voluntarily choose the amount 0′ as the size of their gifts. *A*, confronted with a lower tax price than in Figure 1, prefers 0_A, and *B*, confronted with the higher, prefers 0_B. We are back in the strategic maneuvering of the independent gift problem. Further, with only two voters, there is no way in which we can deal with it by simple voting. If we let *C* vote, we would not only contaminate our problem, but we would guarantee that the amount would be 0_A or even further to the right.

The problem here is a very general one. In distributional matters, there is very little we can do to provide a definite outcome if the parties are in favor of keeping their own money and taking the money of other people. The charitable gift to *C*, with *C* not voting, does not raise this problem with respect to *C* but does raise it with respect to the people making the gift.

In general, we will drop this problem here and pick it up later when we have a more complicated model in which the recipient of charity also can vote. It should perhaps be said, however, that in my opinion a good deal of the difficulty involved in getting popular support for various forms of aid to the poor comes from this particular problem. Since the taxes are not Lindahl taxes, then it follows that individuals do not all want exactly the same amount, and the debates among potential donors are exacerbated by the desire of individual donors to make large gifts to the poor but to shift the cost off on someone else. People who are not willing to make gifts to the poor, and/or who may have to pay a high percentage of the cost, are apt to argue for reduced gifts to the poor rather than a shift in taxes.

We did not mention this problem earlier when we were talking about transfers to people simply because they want to receive them. It is undeniably true that in that case also, within every coalition that is seeking money from the public treasury, there is a difference of opinion as to how that money shall be distributed. Further, there is in general, as we shall demonstrate below, no

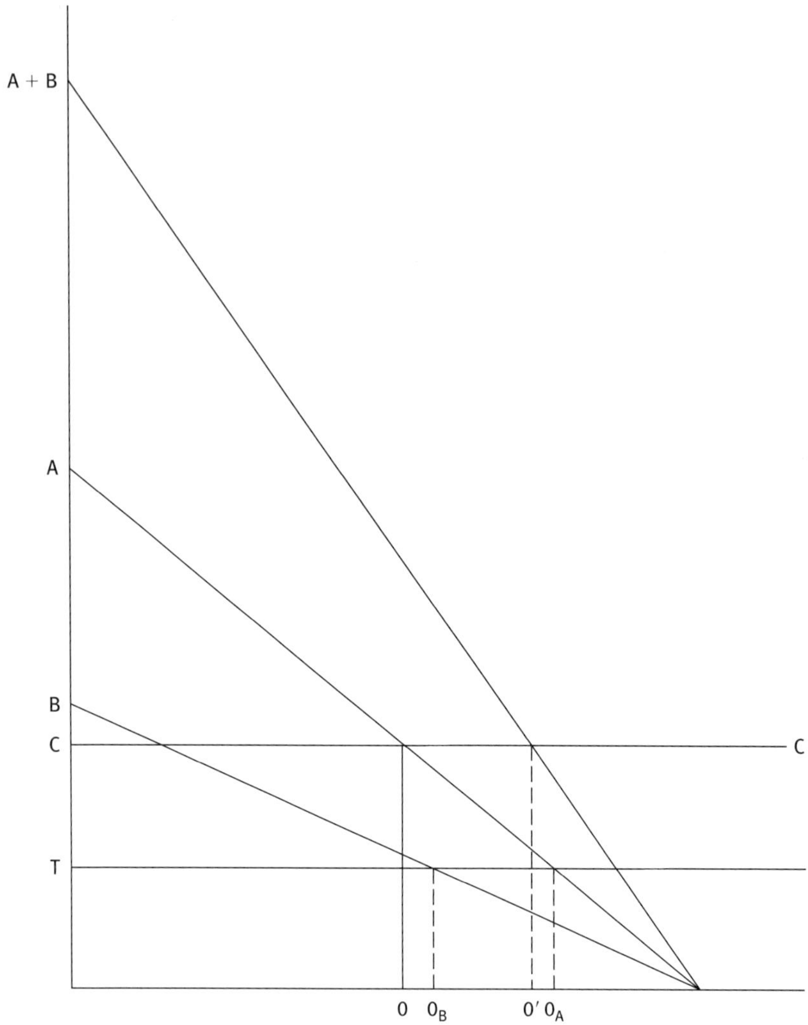

FIGURE 2
Variation of situation where recipient is not permitted to influence the outcome

straightforward voting solution to the problem.[7] It seems likely that most of the pressure groups who are successful have one way or another succeeded in suppressing this conflict. It may be, however, that the continuous threat of such conflict has great effect on the structure of pressure groups, and it may

7. See Benjamin Ward, "Majority Rule and Allocation," *Journal of Conflict Resolution* (1961): 379–89.

be one of the reasons that there are not far more pressure groups than we observe. Normally, we see a squabble between the pressure group and society as a whole, but within the pressure group there are also differences of opinion as to who should make the largest gain.

We should point out that in practice there is no longer any reason to believe that Lindahl prices cannot be obtained for public goods, including charitable gifts. The demand-revealing process provides a mechanism that permits us to approximate such prices. We have no empirical knowledge at the moment as to how close the approximation could be, but certainly it would be far better than any other known system for determining the Lindahl tax. Unfortunately, it is not obvious that we really want Lindahl taxation. Public finance scholars, for many years, tended to talk about Lindahl taxation as the optimum type for everything except income transfers, and I think they would have agreed that it was optimal there also if one considered only the people making the transfer, not the recipients. I shared this point of view, but since the demand-revealing process was invented and I began to realize that Lindahl taxes could possibly be used in the real world, I began to doubt whether Lindahl taxes are really a good thing. They are certainly elegant—at the margin they are ideal—but there does not seem to be any argument for the use of the same tax rate intramarginally as at the margin.

To return, however, to the situation in which transfers are made because of the desire of the donor, there are several basic problems. One of these, of course, is the form in which the gift shall be given. We have not talked about this so far, but it is an obvious fact from the real world that such gifts are made in many forms. Indeed, payment in kind is common. Economists have tended to criticize payment in kind because, from the standpoint of the recipient, a cash payment would always permit one to do better than payment in kind. Suppose, for example, that it is proposed to give someone a house instead of an allowance in cash that permitted him to rent it. He could, if he received the rental payment, rent the same house. Thus, the rental payment would always be superior from his standpoint because if what he wants is the house, he can rent it, and if what he wants is something else, he can use the money for some other purpose. The direct imposition of the house reduces the flexibility with which he can adjust his income to his desires. The reducing of flexibility lowers his utility if we assume that he knows what he is doing. A great many people concerned with charitable gifts apparently do not make that assumption. It might be thought, for example, that the receiver is systematically improvident and will promptly drink up his entire monthly allowance, with the result that he and his children will starve through the latter part of the month. An economist might say that the receiver's utility is best maximized by drinking it up, because that is what he does. This is obviously a judgment that the receiver is competent to judge his own utility. This judgment is not shared by everyone.

Thus, one possible reason for not giving the individual straightforward cash payments is distrust of the receiver's ability to judge his own utility. A second is lack of interest in his utility. We might want to do what is good for him rather than what will give him utility. Suppose a medieval churchman feels that it is of great importance that all people get up at 5 A.M. and go fasting to mass. He knows that most of the peasants would rather not do it, and they regard it as a serious chore. This would not stop him from imposing it on them if he had the power, because he feels his judgment of what is good for them is better than their judgment. This attitude is not confined to medieval churchmen and will, in fact, be found in a great many people.

Economists tend to refer to such people as busybodies, which, in a way, shows that economists themselves are busybodies. After all, if one busybody gets pleasure out of forcing someone else to reduce his consumption of whiskey and increase his consumption of whole wheat bread, the economist is acting as a busybody by complaining of that method of acquiring utility. I should say here that my own personal sympathies are with the busybody economist. I would prefer simply to give the money away as cash, but I have to concede that I am not by any means certain that this is more than a personal preference.

Another reason why we might choose to give in kind rather than in cash is that we really are not attempting to benefit the recipient of our charity as much as we are trying to change the environment in which we live. For example, we may feel that a group of rundown houses is unaesthetic and want to see these houses improved, at least in their external appearance.[8] Similarly, we may want children to be well washed and look healthy in preference to letting them play in the mud and eat candy. This is an example of the kind of motive that we may observe in charitable activities, and it can, of course, be mixed with a desire to raise utility, and, for that matter, to see to it that what we think is good is done. All of these motives are compatible with each other. An individual cannot maximize any one of the three if he holds one or more of the others, but it is quite possible for a person to maximize some function

8. See James M. Buchanan, "What Kind of Redistribution Do We Want?" *Economica* 35 (May 1968), for a discussion of this point.

of which all three are arguments. It is my impression that most people engaged in relief activity in fact are doing just that.

There is a fourth somewhat more sinister motive. The book by Guido Calabresi and Philip Bobbitt, *Tragic Choices*,[9] raises a new and quite profound problem.[10] Let us turn to the particular problem that they deal with—the provision of kidney machines for people who will die if not given such treatment regularly. Further, let us go back to the early period of such machines.

The machines were expensive, but the number of people with the appropriate kidney problems was not large enough that it would be impossible to provide such treatment for everyone and, indeed, that is the eventual outcome of the tale which we will discuss below. In the early days, however, the machines were not very numerous and were provided essentially by charitable procedures. There was a problem of deciding who got the machines. Some people were going to die and some people were not. The original solution was the God Committee in Seattle and similar committees in other parts of the world. These committees rationed the use of the machines to people who they thought were particularly deserving. The system eventually broke down because it became obvious that they were tending to consider the most wealthy people as the most deserving. When Congress discovered this, additional money was paid out to make the machines available to everyone, although, as we shall see below, this also raised problems.

Let us, in any event, stick to the period before the machines were made available to everyone. Any economist would say that this was an inefficient system. It would have been far superior to simply rent out the machines to whoever could pay and to give the poor people who otherwise could not have the machines enough money so that they could buy medical insurance. They could buy the kind of medical insurance that would give them the machines at a high price or the kind that would not at a lower price. Why was this solution not adopted? Calabresi and Bobbitt argue, in essence, that the reason this was not done was that some people would choose not to buy the kind of insurance that gave them the kidney machines, and thus a small minority

9. Guido Calabresi and Philip Bobbitt, *Tragic Choices* (New York: W. W. Norton & Co., 1978).

10. In some ways, it is easier to understand the problem I am now raising, not by reading the book but by reading my review of it, "Avoiding Difficult Decisions," *New York University Law Review* 54, no. 1 (April 1979): 267–79. That this review is acceptable to Calabresi, I know, because he has made some favorable remarks to me about it, personally.

would die. Economists would say that this was an efficient arrangement if they had chosen *ex ante* to take this unfavorable gamble and their utility *ex ante* was better than it otherwise would be, and Calabresi and Bobbitt do not contest this reasoning. They point out, however, that if this were done, the individuals would have it brought to their attention that the amount of money they had put up for the poor was an amount under which the poor might consciously choose risk of death under these circumstances. If Calabresi and Bobbitt are correct, and it should be pointed out that Calabresi and Bobbitt received very widespread and favorable notice, people in fact have a limit on the amount they are willing to give away, but they do not like to have the consequence of this limit brought forcefully to their attention.

The God Committee allocating kidney machines to "the most deserving" is less bothersome than the thought that someone to whom you were giving a cash transfer may consciously decide that the cash transfers you are giving him are small enough so that he would prefer to run the risk of death from kidney malfunction than buy an appropriate type of insurance.

Congress felt the same way. They originally appropriated only enough money for treating some kidney patients. To repeat, any economist would have said they could have helped the poor more by providing the funds for the poor and letting the insurance companies take care of the exceptional cases by way of higher premiums and higher benefits. They chose not to. Further, eventually—as I mentioned above—they discovered that the God Committee was using income as a standard of deservingness and decided that they would have to provide enough money for all people who needed kidney machines to get them.[11]

Congress then provided enough money to make kidney machines reasonably available to everyone who needed them. However, as Calabresi and Bobbitt point out, this also involved an implicit and not very obvious rationing device. There are a number of other quite expensive procedures that occasionally are needed to prevent death. The heart shunt is an obvious example. The same amount of money, if distributed across patients in terms of cost-benefits analysis, would have permitted the saving of more lives. Heart

11. This, by the way, seems to have sharply retarded technology in the area. There are, for some cases, special home type kidney machines, and these are normally privately purchased. They unfortunately cannot treat everyone. Granted the provision of full financing for everyone else, the development of these small home machines seems to have been less rapid than it otherwise would have been.

shunts, in general, are as necessary to maintain life and cheaper than kidney machine maintenance. Congress decided to provide a subsidy in kind, i.e., kidney machines rather than cash.[12] With cash they would have had to admit that the amount of money that they were appropriating was an amount that would lead people to choose to die.

The problem here is a subtle one, and I am not sure that Calabresi and Bobbitt are right. It seems to me, however, that we should give very careful thought to it. We are, almost all of us, charitable to some extent, but there are limits to the amount we are willing to give away. We do not like to think about these limits, and, in particular, we do not like to give away money in forms that bring these limits to our attention. Cash transfers are obviously and directly measurable. Gifts in kind cannot provide such an obvious direct measure of the benefit per person.

Let us consider the same problem in connection with our foreign aid program. The American people, generally, think that they have been generous in their aid to India, and, indeed, by the standards of current foreign aid programs, I think that is true. Suppose that we had chosen as our technique of aid to India simply making direct per capita payments to citizens of India. This could have been done by sending checks to them through the banking system, a project which would have been administratively complex but by no means impossible or even terribly expensive. Another method would have been to make a direct payment to the government of India on the condition that the government of India lowered certain of its taxes so that the money was suitably dispersed. We chose instead to undertake a large number of rather badly specified and designed economic projects. American aid money, today, comes in a package with bad economic advice from the Department of State.

It should be said that this bad economic advice, although it is indeed bad, is not necessarily a detriment to the countries concerned. Probably they would have done something foolish with the money anyway. Further, the controls that we put in certainly make it more difficult for politicians and intellectuals in these countries to steal the aid money. Whether the latter is a sensible objective or not is uncertain, since politicians and intellectuals very likely steal other money from their governments, and it is not clear that permitting them to steal from the American aid money would increase the total

12. The cash would not necessarily have had to be the complete income support. It could have been simply special payments to anyone who required any one of a number of very expensive but life-sustaining procedures.

amount they stole. Further, if our objectives are to acquire friends abroad, the people whom we prevent from stealing are a particularly conspicuous group of potential friends.[13]

But regardless of these issues, the fact remains that if we had chosen to make direct cash payments in our foreign aid program, the payments would have looked pretty small. The proposal to, let us say, build a steel mill at $100,000,000 cost in an underdeveloped country looks much more impressive than a proposal to give each citizen of the country $2.25. If the steel mill project will take five years, then it is roughly equivalent to giving each citizen in the country $0.45 a year. I would be willing to argue that citizens of the country are probably better off with the $0.45 a year than with a steel mill. After all, if this country is a good place to make steel, the international capital market will no doubt be interested in providing loans for the steel mill, and the individuals who receive the $0.45 a year can, if they so choose, invest the money in a steel mill. Presumably, they would not do so.

The actual situation, however, is not that the steel mill is better, although the bureaucrats in the Department of State, whose jobs would vanish if direct cash payments were made, are prepared to argue that it is. Nor is it that the steel mill could not be built without aid.[14] The view that somehow a large capital investment in a country is better than just giving the capital is widely held. Perhaps it reflects a puritan feeling that they should not consume but should save. I think, however, one of the more important reasons is quite simply that it permits us not to think about how small our aid program is on a per capita basis.

Although the Calabresi-Bobbitt hypothesis about human behavior is not certainly true, I find it, intuitively, very plausible, and I suspect that many of my readers will, too. The hypothesis I have given in essence says that we are not as charitable as we would like to think and that we adopt a method to conceal this lack of charitableness from ourselves.

13. I have a former college friend who was ambassador in an African country and suddenly discovered himself persona non grata, with the local dictator making loud noises about how he, as a spy of the CIA, had been trying to overturn the local government. What he had actually done was suggest that the government accounting system be revised in a way that would have made it somewhat more difficult for the dictator and his friends to build up their Swiss bank accounts.

14. It may, of course, be true that the steel mill would not be built there because it is not a very good place to put the steel mill. Under these circumstances, the $100,000,000 spent on building the steel mill is the equivalent of not $2.25 per head for the country, but perhaps $1.75 per head.

Offhand, I cannot think of any specific empirical tests that could be used to determine whether the Calabresi-Bobbitt hypothesis is correct. If it is correct, it carries with it a number of rather unpleasant conclusions. The first of these is that we cannot carefully think over, in an objective way, charitable gifts of this sort. The decision, at a conscious level, to use a method of charity that conceals from us the limits on the amount we are willing to give is a decision that in itself tears the concealment away. It is essential in this case, in other words, that we use an inept and inefficient way of making charitable gifts in order to conceal from ourselves that these charitable gifts are limited. In order for this concealment to be successful, we have to not think about the technique. Thus, the end product is that we will, of necessity, make errors, not because we as humans are bound to make errors, but because we are, without careful thought, selecting a technique, the purpose of which is to avoid careful thought because the result of the careful thought would be painful to us.

Note that all of the problems of charity that I have described so far, although I have been discussing them in the context of government charity because that is the subject of this book, also apply to private charity. Some of them are more severe in government charity. For example, the lack of motive to become well informed about the output[15] is magnified when we are dealing with public charity, because the individual's decision has much less effect on the outcome than it does in private charity. In other words, one voting decision is diluted by other voting decisions.

On the other hand, some problems are stronger in the private field than in the public. The dispute between the different contributors to a public charity, i.e., about who is to pay the tax cost, is essentially an effort by individuals to put the cost of public goods off on other persons. The voting process is clearly not an efficient way of dealing with this problem, but the procedure used in the private market, which is to let each person freely make his contribution or not, gives the free-rider optimal opportunity to avoid payment altogether. Thus, we would expect this problem to be more severe in the private market than in the public.

One minor problem with public charity is the use of the coercive tax process, which makes it possible, at least theoretically, to victimize one of the payers—a possibility that is not available in the private market. Because we are all to some extent charitable and because the total amounts given to the

15. I first discussed this in an article, "Information without Profit," *Papers on Non-Market Decision Making* I (1966): 141–59, which dealt with private charity.

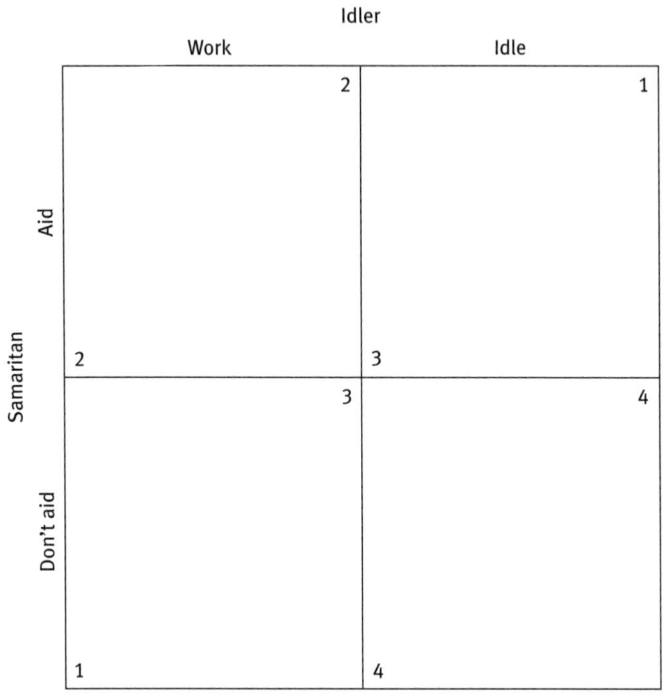

FIGURE 3
Two-person society consisting of a samaritan and an idler

poor by government are really quite restricted, I doubt that this is important. Taxpayers may perhaps be victimized by being compelled to pay large sums of money for things they do not want, but I doubt that the charitable activities of the government are a good example.

But we have not exhausted the economic problems involved in charity. Let me now turn to another one of these, the samaritan's dilemma, which was first discussed in terms of a purely private gift, but which I think its originator, James Buchanan, actually intended to be a governmental problem.[16] Whether it is more important for government or private charity will be discussed after the problem itself has been explained.

In Figure 3 we show a two-person society, one of whom is a well-off good samaritan and another of whom is a poor idler. The idler can, of course, get a job, but if he does not, he will starve to death unless the samaritan aids him.

16. James M. Buchanan, "The Samaritan's Dilemma," in E. S. Phelps (ed.), *Altruism, Morality and Economic Theory* (New York: The Russell Sage Foundation, 1975), 71–85.

The ordinal preferences of the samaritan are shown in the lower left-hand corner of each square. His optimal situation is one in which the idler works and the samaritan does not have to give him any aid. His second choice is that in which the idler works, but the samaritan nevertheless gives him a little supplementary aid. The third is where the idler is idle, and the samaritan supports him full-time, and the fourth is that in which the idler remains idle, the samaritan does not aid him, and the idler dies of starvation. This seems to me not an unreasonable ordering of preferences on the part of someone who has charitable impulses toward someone else whom he knows to be naturally lazy.

The idler has as his first preference the square where he receives aid from the samaritan and does not work. His second preference is where he receives aid from the samaritan and does work, the third where he works and does not get any aid, and the fourth where he is idle and dies of starvation. Once again, this seems not unreasonable. The strategic position here is fairly simple and straightforward: if the samaritan is a tough-minded character, he will not provide any aid to the idler, who will therefore be given the choice between the two bottom squares and will choose to work. It would, of course, be possible for the samaritan to be a little more charitable than I have assumed him to be and prefer the aid-plus-work square to the no aid–work square, perhaps because he feels the idler should have a higher living standard than he can earn on his own. This more charitable samaritan could simply say that he will aid the idler but only on condition that he works.

The idler, on the other hand, if he announces that he will under no circumstances work, confronts the samaritan with a choice between the two squares in the right vertical column. Since the samaritan prefers the aid–no work square to the no aid–no work square because he does not want to see the idler die of starvation, he would proceed to aid the idler.

This is a clear-cut case in which what counts is psychological determination. If the samaritan is a tough but charitable person, he will get the idler to work. If the samaritan is soft-hearted and the idler is firm, the end product will be that the idler will not work and will receive payments.

The problem is a real one, at least in the United States. It is clear that a great many of our idlers have succeeded in taking advantage of their strategic position; i.e., they are, in essence, voluntarily idle.[17] It seems likely that the phenomenon is much worse under government control than it would be under private charity. The reason for this is not that private charity persons are tougher than the same persons would be as taxpayers. Indeed, I presume

17. They never admit this but it is nevertheless true.

the reverse is true, since some of the voters are relatively uncharitable when we come to the tax-supported activity and, hence, have to be tougher under these circumstances than the average donor to a private charity.

The reason the private charity is likely to have few idlers taking advantage of their position is simply that there is competition on both sides of the market. Individual private charities normally can handle only a very small part of the total poverty problem, and we would need a large number of separate charities, church groups, etc., if poverty were handled by private gifts as it used to be in certain parts of the world. Thus, if the idler threatens to starve to death rather than work, the individual private charity can simply turn to someone else and give him aid. Indeed, they would be able, presumably, to supplement the income of five or six poor people who are working but not very productive at the same cost as supporting the idler.

The government, having in essence a monopoly on this kind of charity, does not have this simple, easy ability to change from one person to another. The private charity that decides to let Mr. Smith remain idle if he wishes can salve its conscience by the thought that some other private charity will take him up if he is "deserving." The government knows there is no one else to take up the burden if they drop it.

This problem is magnified by the fact that the professional civil servants who operate government programs are normally very reluctant to let the size of their programs fall by taking people off. My own reading in this area, together with a very small amount of personal experience, seems to indicate that the average social worker almost hates his clients, but nevertheless fights hard to provide further resources for them. I presume this comes, partly, from a tendency to feel that the poor should be helped and that the civil servant, personally, happens to have gotten a bad collection of the poor, which is a charitable motive, together with a completely selfish desire to expand the size of one's division. It should be said in passing that there is really no evidence that the training that social workers get in college, which is today pretty much a requirement for the job, has any beneficial effect on their activities as social workers. The more traditional "Lady Bountiful" or, for that matter, the clerk who has just been put in this job, probably would do just as well as trained social workers. Trained social workers will no doubt take this as an expression of prejudice on my part, and I will take their objection to it as an expression of prejudice on their part.

If this last problem area is much more severe in publicly sponsored aid to the poor than in privately sponsored aid, it is unique among our collection in being so. As a general rule all of the things that we have described here are problems not just of government provision of aid to the poor, but of provision of aid to the poor in general. The last few pages, which may have been considered by some incautious readers as an attack on government provision of aid to the poor, are simply a discussion of the problems of aid to the poor with special reference to the government. There is no reason to believe that these problems are more severe when the source of the charity is government rather than private charity.

These problems are severe and have attracted relatively little research attention, but it should be emphasized that their severity is in part counterbalanced by the super-Pareto efficiency of charity that we mentioned above. To repeat, a voluntarily charitable gift to the poor of $1 benefits the donor by $1 and the recipient by $1; i.e., it counts double in generating utility. This is true even if the gift is passed through government channels—if the gift is basically voluntary.[18] Thus, the problem is not a problem of getting rid of charity, or for that matter of enlarging it, but rather a problem of improving efficiency.

Let us then turn to discussions of the efficient ways of aiding the poor. First, I will talk only about aid to the poor and not aid to people who for one reason or another are thought to deserve aid even if they are not poor. For example, the sick sometimes are also poor. Nevertheless, the programs designed to aid them are different from programs designed to aid the poor, per se. A sick person who is also poor is apt to come under two programs instead of one. We shall temporarily confine ourselves to aiding the poor.

Any type of aid to people just because they are poor leads to what the insurance industry calls *adverse selection* and *moral risk*. Consider a private insurance company that offers an insurance policy under which you must pay fair amounts of money to the insurance company if your income is high, and the insurance company will supplement your income if your income falls below a certain amount. There would be two problems. The first (adverse selection) is that those people who feel that their income is apt to be high over their

18. In government charity it is unlikely that many of the voter donors approve of the exact amount transferred. They think of themselves as giving a little too much, or perhaps a little too little, to charity; but the dissatisfaction obtained from that is presumably much less than the satisfaction obtained from making the gift as a whole, together with the knowledge that you are buying your charity in a cheap market because of the collectivization technique mentioned above.

lifetime would be reluctant to enter the program, and those who feel that their income is likely to be low over their lifetime would be delighted to take it on. The result would be an unfavorable selection of clients. The second problem (moral risk) would be that once people did have this kind of insurance they would be motivated, at least to some extent, to work less hard than they had worked before they got the insurance, because the effect on their income would be less severe.

Note that this second effect is asymmetrical. Suppose, for example, that the contract the insurance company offers is one under which the insurance company will pay half of the difference between your income and the average income if your income is less than the average income in society, and it will pay for this by taxing you half of the difference between your income and the average income, if your income is above average. Consider first the people whose income is above average. As a result of this institution, the marginal return on their labor is only half as great as it would be without this kind of insurance. This should lead to them working less hard. On the other hand their total income is less than it otherwise would be, and in general, people with less wealth work harder. The two effects are offsetting, and there is no a priori reason to argue which one would be the larger. Empirical research in this area is very difficult, but insofar as it shows anything, it seems to indicate that the two effects roughly balance each other.

Note here that we have a very simple tax structure and not one that is highly progressive. If income tax structure was so arranged that the marginal return on work of upper-income groups declined very sharply while their inframarginal income was not heavily taxed so that their total wealth remained quite high, one would predict a significant reduction in work effort. This is the situation in many parts of the world. Once again, the a priori expectations of reduced work under these circumstances are hard to test, and as far as I know have not been successfully validated.

When we turn to people below the average income—those whose income will be supplemented under the scheme—the theoretical proposition is much clearer, and the empirical evidence confirms it very neatly. For people below the average income, the scheme we have described increases their total wealth, which should reduce the amount that they work, and lowers their marginal return on effort, which also should reduce the amount they work. In other words, the wealth effect and the marginal income effect work in the same direction instead of in an opposite direction as they do in the upper-income brackets. Under the circumstances, we have a clear-cut prediction that their work effort will go down.

This prediction is very strongly confirmed, first, by the actual practical experience—practically every relief program in history—and second, by a set of rather well designed experiments that were intended to test the effect of a negative income tax. It is a little hard to say exactly how much work effort would be reduced, and the negative income tax experiments do not give an exact figure because the people subject to the negative income tax experiment could also, if they wished, go on the ordinary relief program, and, hence, the disincentive effect of the negative income tax program is less than it would be if the experiment had run in a society in which ordinary relief payments did not exist. Nevertheless, it was significant; so clearly this is a real problem.[19]

The first type of moral hazard, the situation in which people who are particularly likely to be poor join the program, and people who are particularly unlikely to be poor do not, can in part—but to a very limited extent—be avoided by the government. If everybody is put in, then there is no possibility of adverse selection. In a way, it is rather like a company that can buy medical insurance more cheaply than an individual because it puts in all of its employees; whereas individuals buying the insurance not only have to pay a higher administrative cost but also have to pay an additional premium because people who take up insurance individually are more likely to be sickly than people who choose not to.

Unfortunately, government programs are not as immune to this effect as one might think. There are a great many people who would like to move to areas where there is large income redistribution. For many years in the United States, the state and local authorities had various ways of preventing people from moving into their district for the purpose of gaining such redistribution. The Supreme Court has declared this unconstitutional but has not taken any stand on the much more vigorous program of the same sort by the federal government to keep foreigners out.[20] The welfare state, under

19. Alfred Tella, Dorothy Tella, and Christopher Green, *The Hours of Work and Family Income Response to Negative Income Tax Plans: The Impact on the Working Poor* (The W. E. Upjohn Institute for Employment Research, 1971). The negative income tax experiments also indicated that this kind of insurance program sharply increases the divorce rate. Whether this is a genuine discovery or an artifact, I do not know.

20. The actual origin of American immigration controls was essentially the desire of laborers organized in the unions to prevent the arrival of large numbers of poor foreigners whose presence would lead to a fall in the marginal product of labor and wages. It is probable that this is still a stronger motive than the desire to prevent foreigners from taking up the various benefits of the welfare state, but the benefits of the welfare state are large enough now so that preventing people from taking them is an additional strong reason for restricting immigration.

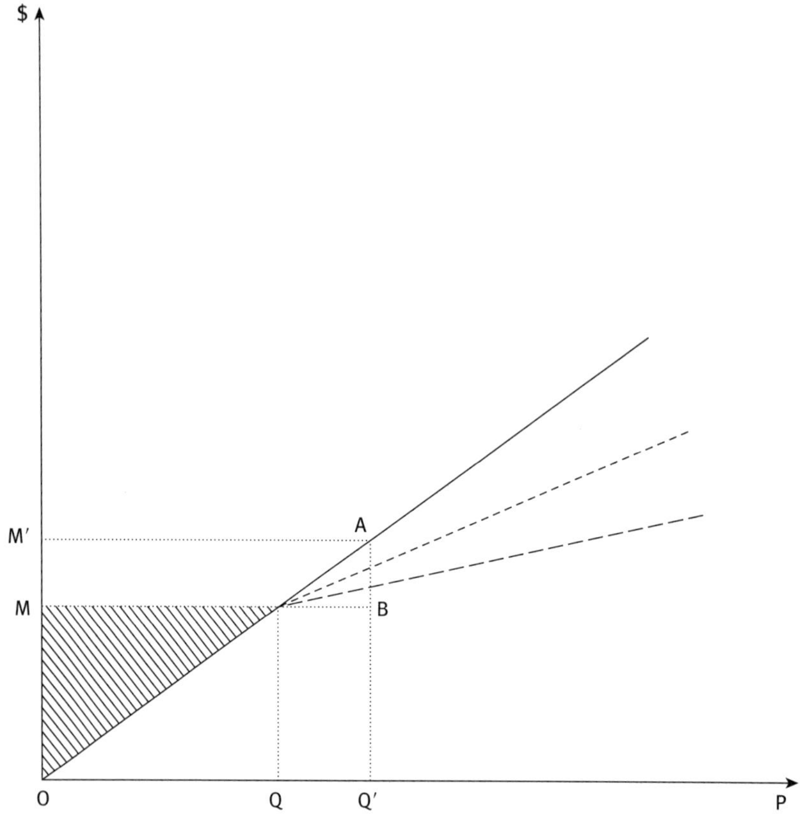

FIGURE 4
Transfer programs

modern circumstances, must run a continuous and very expensive and difficult program to keep the poor people of the world, who live in places like Africa, India, and China, from migrating in and upsetting the actuarial characteristics of the basic transfer program. It should always be kept in mind that the existing transfer program, whatever we may think about an ideal transfer program, is basically transfers back and forth between people who are in the top 10 to 20 percent of the world's population. The really poor of the world do not benefit from existing transfer programs.[21]

Let us look at the theory a little more carefully (see Figure 4). On the vertical axis, I have put incomes, in this case incomes of individuals, and on the

21. See Gordon Tullock, "The Rhetoric and Reality of Redistribution," *Southern Economic Journal* 47, no. 4 (April 1981): 895–907.

horizontal axis, people are arranged from left to right according to how high their income is, assuming no charitable distribution. The line running out from the origin at roughly a 45-degree angle is simply an indication of the income of these individuals. It shows that at Q there is some individual whose income is M and at Q', some individual has an income of M'.

Note that if we actually got empirical data and drew such a diagram, the incomes would not form such a nice straight line. The straight line is, however, easier to work with, and the actual shape of the line makes no difference for any of the reasoning that we will undertake. If the reader wishes, he can get a piece of paper, draw an accurate line, and duplicate the reasoning on his figure.

Suppose then that the citizens in our society feel that the income of members of that society should not fall below M. What they would like to do is have all the people who are located left of Q continue producing what little they can produce, and supplement their incomes by the shaded triangle. This would require a tax on people whose incomes are above Q's income, and I have shown this tax by the dotted line that shows the after-tax income.

Although this should be the objective of a relief program, administratively it is quite difficult. It is possible that small government units and private charities do succeed in carrying it out. The first problem is that the individual guaranteed a minimum income of M is apt to stop working totally if his productivity is such that he would receive less than M; and hence, instead of a transfer to him of the shaded triangle, in order to keep his income up to M, it is necessary to transfer to him the entire rectangle under the line M and left of the line Q.

We will temporarily ignore the administrative problems of getting people to work even while on relief, and just talk about the consequences of permitting those on relief to become idle. The first thing that occurs, of course, is a sharp increase in the amount of money that is necessary to keep him on the minimum income level. The second thing, however, is that individuals whose earnings are somewhat above M (people to the right of Q in our diagram) begin realizing that if they stop work their income will fall but that they will also avoid work. Leisure is a good and work is, in general, a bad.[22]

22. Work is particularly apt to be bad if we consider the type of work that the less productive members of our society are required to do. An architect may get a real pleasure out of his daily work; the garbage man does not.

As a result, a number of people whose incomes are above M cease work, and we show this on our diagram by the line M'. In practice, of course, there is no clear-cut cutoff in this way, and there is sort of a tendency for people whose incomes are close to M to stop work in large numbers, while people whose incomes are farther away have less likelihood of stopping work, but using a sharp cutoff like M' will do no harm. If, then, people below the line M' quit work, the total amount that must be paid by the taxpayer in order to keep everybody at an income level of M becomes the rectangle under the line M and left of the line Q'. The area between M and M' represents the value of leisure for those people whose income if they were working would be greater than M but less than M'. The necessary tax is shown by the dashed line.

Note that two basic costs are incurred because everybody whose income falls below M' is now not working. First, they would, if they were working, have produced something even if not very much. This production is shown by the triangle $OQ'A$. Society, as a whole, is less well off as a result of the absence of this production, which is probably not a gigantic amount but nevertheless something we would like to pick up. The second cost is, of course, that the whole rectangle $OMBQ'$ must be paid out to people who are now not working, in order to maintain their incomes above M, and the cost of this will have to be borne by the upper-income groups.

As I have said before, if this is collected from the upper-income groups by a proportional income tax, it is not obvious that it will lower measured national product. Of course, it makes the upper-income group worse off, but the purpose of any income redistribution is to make one group of people worse off and another better off, so we need not concern ourselves about this. The basic problem when people stop work, particularly when they stop work even if their earned income would be somewhat higher than their relief payments because they value leisure, is not the actual cost that it imposes on society if we have a modest level of income support, but the fact that it makes it very hard to be generous to the poor. If you move M up to a fairly high level, say half the average income, then the line M' is moved up proportionately, and the total product generated by society may be very materially lowered.[23]

23. In making calculations on the subject of this particular topic, one should take into account that relief payments are not subject to tax, and that income of people who are working is normally taxed. These payments should always be compared with after-tax income not before-tax income if you want to make a sensible policy decision.

In discussing this issue with the kind of person that I refer to as the soppy liberal,[24] I find that they frequently take the view that I am insulting the poor by implying that they will not always work as hard as they can even if they are on relief, or even if stopping work will lower their income a little bit and hence make them eligible for relief. I do not think this is in any way insulting. How many people would continue working if they were promised 90 percent of their present income on the condition that they stop work? Note that this means stopping true work. There is no reason you cannot pursue your hobby or pick up small sums of money in the underground economy even though you are on relief.[25] We should not expect the poorer part of the population, which normally have unattractive jobs, to be any more energetic than we are.

There are a number of ways of avoiding this problem. The first, and the one that seems officially simplest, is to tell the relief administrators that they must see to it that their clients work as hard as they can. It is not obvious that this very simple, straightforward technique would not work provided we had a different kind of relief administrator than we now have; however, the standard American social worker is not capable of applying this kind of coercion. Further, it is not obvious that society wants him to. We referred earlier to the samaritan's dilemma, and it may well be that society, in general, would be offended at threatening people with death by starvation if they did not work harder.

Not very long ago I read an account of an English reporter who, as part of the Singapore government's efforts to build up its image, had been flown to Singapore on the Concorde and was then given a very luxurious tour of Singapore. In the course of the tour, he had dinner with a high-level administrator and he asked him, "Do you mean then that if somebody in Singapore refuses to work you would let him starve to death?" The Chinese administrator, speaking apparently not very good English, hissed, "Yes." There is no doubt that the reporter thought that this showed a most undesirable adherence to dispassionate rationality on the part of the Singapore government. I think that the reporter in this case reflected the general American, and for that matter European, opinion. We would like to get these welfare loafers to

24. I am sometimes referred to as an ironbound reactionary by soppy liberals.

25. It would appear that in Washington, D.C., a sizable portion of the females who are receiving aid for dependent children are, in fact, employed full-time as prostitutes. The aid for dependent children income provides them with a base, but for the more attractive of them it is a minor part of their income.

work, but we are, in general, not willing to simply say, with Lenin, work or die. This would be particularly true for those people whose work is not worth very much anyway, i.e., the people left of *Q*.

Nevertheless, it seems to me that we should be open-minded about experiments for the purpose of inducing people to work while giving them some kind of minimum income. The fact that most American welfare administrators cannot do it does not indicate that it is impossible. It may simply indicate that our current welfare administrators are incompetent, that they are not adequately motivated by their superiors, or that new techniques are needed. It seems to me desirable to continue to look for such techniques.

There are, basically, two proposals to deal with this problem. The first is a very old one presented by Jeremy Bentham and then modernized by Armen Alchian.[26] Bentham suggested that the procedure problem could be solved by simply providing an infinite quantity of very easily supervised work and then paying people only if they did it. He specifically suggested that they walk on a treadmill. It should be said that in Bentham's days, although the treadmill was a rather obsolete form of energy, it was still in some use as a genuine energy form, and hence the work was not totally wasted. Unfortunately, this last characteristic is not true of the Alchian improvements.

Let us suppose then the following scheme. We have a set of treadmills at various but convenient places. Anyone is free to go and walk on the treadmill at any time he wishes, and as he does so quarters periodically fall out of the machine. The rate at which the quarters fall out can be so adjusted that the minimum income to be obtained by an 8-hour working day is whatever is desired. Although this procedure sacrifices the production of people whose total output is lower than *M* on our diagram, because the electricity generated by walking the treadmill is of very nearly zero value, it does deprive them of leisure. Therefore, the people between line *M* and line *M′* on the diagram will choose not to go on relief. The social savings could be quite significant.

In a way this involves deliberately throwing away any prospect of getting the labor of the relatively unproductive people, i.e., the labor left of *Q* and below the 45-degree line. In return, we are eliminating the incentive for "welfare loafers." This clearly is dominated by simply having everybody work by good supervision if that is, in fact, possible. On the other hand, it is equally

26. I have been interested enough in the problem so I have made some minor improvements on the Alchian version. What we will get here is my improved version of Alchian's improved version of Bentham's procedure.

clearly better than permitting all the people whose incomes are below M' on our diagram to quit work and be paid by the government.

It should be said that the system, as here described, can be improved a bit by various means. The treadmill is, of course, not the only way of making people work. In particular, a good many poor people are in bad health. Indeed, in some cases that is the reason they are poor. Hard physical labor is frequently impossible for these people. It is, unfortunately, difficult for doctors to tell with any degree of certainty whether a person who claims to be ill is really ill. The Tullock improvement on Bentham and Alchian is a device to deal with this problem. I shan't explain it here, but it is an electronic device that substantially anybody can operate without much physical strength but that requires concentration on a dull task. It, of course, generates absolutely nothing in the way of desirable output, not even the very small amount of electric power that would be generated by the treadmill.

All this sounds rather sadistic. Devices are developed, whether they are the treadmill or the Tullock clerical simulator, that do not produce anything but require an input of work. They exist wholly for the purpose of depriving people of the alternative of going on relief for leisure. They make certain that although a minimum will be provided, no one will be attracted to that income unless their productivity in a regular job is lower than that. In other words, there will be no people who could produce more than a minimum income but who prefer the minimum income plus leisure to working.

A great many people would regard this as morally undesirable, and I, of course, shall not quarrel with anyone's statements of his own moral code. I am only saying that this system would provide the possibility of obtaining a fairly high minimum income without very difficult supervision procedures and without people, whose productivity was above the minimum income by a small margin, choosing the minimum income plus leisure over regular work. Whether this system is of great enough advantage to offset the rather unpleasant appearance of the apparatus is not a matter upon which I can offer any kind of definitive opinion. The individual will have to decide that in terms of his own preference system.

A former graduate student of mine, Daniel Newlon, while he was studying under me became interested in this system. He had, before he became a graduate student, done considerable work with poor people in inner ghetto areas of several cities. He thought that it would be possible to modify the scheme so that the poor people, although compelled to work a full 8-hour day for their money, would in fact be picking up skills that would make them more readily employable later. He thought that among the poor there were a certain number of people who could be taught quite skilled activities, and proposed that "one who went on relief" would spend the first two or three days taking a series of fairly complicated computer-administered tests, the purpose of which was to separate out those with enough talent for training in skilled labor. Those who were thought suitably talented would then be put to work on teaching machines which would be as hard to use as the treadmills but which would end up with the poor having useful skills. Those who the tests showed did not have any great talent would also be put on teaching machines, but in this case the teaching machines would be devoted to teaching them such things as punctuality, working steadily through the day, etc.—in other words, good work habits. He thought that to a large extent the difficulty people he had met in the inner cities had in getting employment came from their bad work habits rather than from their absolute inability to engage in reasonably productive albeit unskilled work. It is certainly worth looking into.

The other basic way of dealing with the incentive problem is the negative income tax. This concept seems to be very hard for the average voter to understand, but it basically is a very simple idea. On Figure 5, we show the income of people in society by the solid line. Suppose that there is some minimum income that we do not wish people to fall below, and that is point *M*. Every citizen is guaranteed this income, but instead of a simple guarantee, once you have that income each dollar that you earn leads to at least some increase in your income. Suppose, for example, the minimum income is $5,000 a year, and every time you earn a dollar the result is that your income goes up by fifty cents. The easiest way of thinking about this is to assume that you simply give everyone in society $5,000 and then enact a 50 percent income tax for the purpose of financing that demogrant. This is the platform[27] that had so much to do with George McGovern's political difficulties in 1972. The fact that it is hard to sell to the voter, however, does not mean that it is not a basically good idea.

The post-tax distribution of income is shown by the dashed line. Note that taxes for other purposes, such as maintaining the police force, are not included in this tax. The exact shape of the dashed line is subject to various adjustments, but the area between the basic income line and the dashed line on the left, which is the amount in net which is paid out to lower-income people,

27. Except for the $5,000.

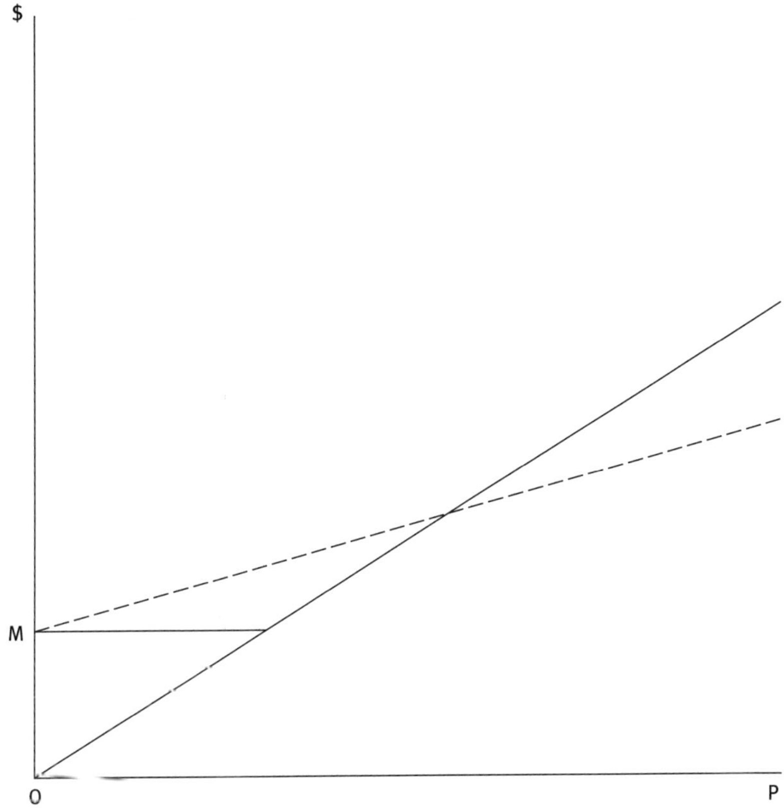

FIGURE 5
Negative income tax

must be equal to the area under the solid line and above the dashed line to the right. Note that it is not essential that the line be straight or that it, strictly speaking, intersect the base income line. It could, for example, reach the income line at some point, then there could be a space in which no one is taxed at all, and then a higher tax above that point, giving a sort of S-shaped line.

This system, which attracts a lot of economists, does not provide any particular incentive for complete leisure as does the current system in which one can get relief by simply stopping working or being willing to tell a few lies to the social workers. It does, however, offer considerable disincentives for hard work in the lower ranges, and the negative income tax experiments indicate that the cost of these could be quite significant. Further, if *M* is set at a reasonably high level, total cost of the scheme is likely to be very high. Lastly, the whole system is likely to have enough progressive characteristics so that the disincentives to work are not confined to the poor people who are helped but, to some extent, fall on the upper-income groups, too. Of course, this is the traditional income redistribution measure of efficiency in which we consider measured product. It is quite conceivable that the total utility generated by such a system would be greater than without it, even though measured product went down.

I believe that these three possible methods of dealing with the tendency of people to go on relief because they appreciate leisure are more or less exhaustive, although various combinations or variants on them can quite easily be developed. The problem here is simply a special application of the samaritan's dilemma. People at the bottom level of the income pattern have obviously strong reasons for not wanting to work and for taking advantage of any apparatus set up. Most upper-income people are not willing to simply threaten them with starvation if they do not work hard. The problem is a real and difficult one. My view that small-scale, private charities usually avoid this problem may or may not be true. In any event, the samaritan might feel that avoiding the problem, the way private charities do, is not desirable because the total amount available from private charity was less than he thought should be provided.

This chapter has been devoted to the problem of government income redistribution with two restrictions. The first is that the motive for the restriction be desire on the part of the donors to help the recipients, and the second, which comes from that, is simply that it be done democratically but with the recipients not permitted to vote. I trust that the reader by now has come to the conclusion that this is not an easy problem. To say that it is not an easy problem is, of course, not to say that it is impossible to solve or that we should not work on it. The next chapter will be devoted to the situation in which we are attempting to aid the poor but the poor are permitted to vote; i.e., there is a mix of motives—the upper-income people are interested in helping the poor and the poor are interested in maximizing their own incomes. The first group are charitably inclined; the second are an example of our people who want the transfer because they want the money. It will, of necessity, be even more difficult than the case we have discussed in this chapter.

LOCAL REDISTRIBUTION

As a rule of thumb, economists normally justify government intervention in any part of the economy by the existence of externalities there. The desirable scope of the government agency which then deals with the externality is normally calculated from the geographic scope of the externality. Thus, fire departments are normally local, because the direct externality of an uncontrolled fire is only a few hundred yards, and the somewhat indirect externality of having a large enough fire department to be efficient, normally can be obtained in quite a restricted area. Air pollution, on the other hand, in general, could not be controlled locally and hence is rationally allocated to higher government agencies.

There is, however, an exception to this rule, which is aid to the poor. The normal argument against having income redistribution allocated to local governments is not that the externalities are broad, but simply that migration would make it impossible for local governments to accomplish much income redistribution. If one particular local government had a higher relief payment than others, the poor would migrate into it. Upper-income people would conversely migrate away from areas where the taxes to help the poor were higher. As a consequence there would be a continuous competition to lower payments.

The theme of this chapter will be that this last position is a mistake. It is a mistake which is made by many economists, including myself, but is nevertheless a mistake. This mistake was, in fact, noticed some time ago by Pauly,[1] and further commented on by Buchanan,[2] but both their articles seem to have been largely forgotten. Further, they mainly dealt with the theoretical possibility. The point of this chapter is both to recall their basic idea and to examine the practical problems and possibilities of actually applying them.

Reprinted, with permission, from *The Economics of Wealth and Poverty* (New York: New York University Press, 1986), 113–27.

1. Mark Pauly, "Income Distribution as a Local Public Good," *Journal of Public Economics* 2 (February 1973): 35–58.

2. James M. Buchanan, "Who Should Distribute What in a Federal System?" in *Redistribution Through Public Choice*, ed. H. Hochman and G. Peterson (New York: Columbia, 1974).

Before dealing with this matter, however, I should briefly discuss the true externalities that do exist in connection with aid to the poor. These externalities first discussed by Milton Friedman in *Capitalism and Freedom*,[3] and elaborated on by myself in *The Economics of Income Redistribution*,[4] are essentially production externalities rather than consumption externalities. To take an example from purely private charity: my university is currently soliciting funds from all of its alumni. It has made arrangements with one particular wealthy donor to match all funds produced by the alumni on a one-for-one basis. Thus, they tell the alumni that each dollar they put up will in fact increase the income of the university by 2 dollars. They no doubt told the wealthy donor the same thing.

Superficially, this looks like fraud, but as a matter of fact, it is perfectly correct. If my gift to some person or institution is to be matched by 1 or 10 million other gifts of the same size, then in deciding, either voluntarily as in this case of the university, or through voting on a level of aid which will be compulsory on all donors, I should in fact take into account the cost to me and the total benefit. Thus, for example, if I am voting on the level of aid to the poor, and do not feel that most of my upper-income neighbours would lose greatly by transferring some of their income to the poor, then I should select that total transfer in which that transfer and my tax payment, which is a small fraction of the transfer, are in marginal adjustment by my preference function. Characteristically, I will give more by this method than I would by making an independent gift.

Note that there is another externality, but one which does not require any particular centralisation of charity. Currently, there is drought in much of Africa, and the Ethiopian government has succeeded in making the drought much more deadly in Ethiopia than in the other parts of the African continent, and at the same time getting a great deal of publicity about the bad conditions of its citizens.[5] International relief agencies are trying, not very successfully, to feed the perfectly genuine starving citizens while not assisting the Ethiopian government in its political objectives.

It is clear that many American citizens feel an externality here in the sense that they are affected by the suffering of the Ethiopian citizens. This,

3. Chicago: University of Chicago Press, 1962.

4. Boston, The Hague, London: Kluwer-Nijhoff, 1983.

5. There is no doubt that the citizens are in a very bad condition, and there's no doubt that the Ethiopian government is taking advantage of this opportunity to maximise a number of its domestic goals such as suppressing guerrilla warfare by its domestic opponents.

however, does not require from the American standpoint that a government agency be set up, whose jurisdiction involves both the United States and Ethiopia. The American citizens can, both through private charity and through government programmes, transfer whatever amount of funds they wish to Ethiopia. The production externality mentioned above is, as far as the American citizens are concerned, internalised by the use of the American government.

In any event, it would appear that the externality generated on people by the suffering of others at considerable distances from them is much lower than that which they suffer from people close in. The amount that the United States is willing to contribute, both through private charity and through government aid, to save the genuinely starving people in Ethiopia is a trifle compared with the amounts which are transferred domestically. Further, even domestically, there are large differences between the actual levels of relief from state to state. Although there are complaints about this, they are not strongly enough felt so that the majority of the American citizens choose to do something about it.

Traditionally, in the United States, this latter kind of externality, that is, the domestic externality, was dealt with not by a central government programme, but by allocating responsibility for the poor in each community to that community. Before the 1930s the states sometimes did, and sometimes did not, enact standards for the local communities. Sometimes these standards were actually expenditure standards, but more normally they simply indicated which community had to take care of which person.

The system apparently worked reasonably well, because the feeling of sympathy for the poor, although perfectly genuine and worldwide, in fact falls off as you move away from the sympathising person. The amount that he will give to the poor in his own county is greater than the amount that he would give, on a per capita basis, to the people in the next county. In general, with everyone feeling this way, the citizens of each county give to their poor enough so that the residents of neighbouring counties do not feel it necessary to supplement it. There is, of course, no reason why they could not do so if they wished, and historically, through private charity, they have occasionally done so. There is no legal restriction here.

I read in Washington newspapers denunciations of southern states, such as Mississippi, for having very low relief payments. There is absolutely no feeling that the citizens of Washington and its environments have any responsibility to do anything more about it. They could, of course, tax themselves and send the money to Mississippi. Indeed, since the Washington area has the highest income in the United States, and Mississippi a much lower one, if they were genuinely charitably concerned, I suppose they would do this. I feel confident that their actual attitude on this matter, however, is that they wish the payments to the Mississippi citizens were higher than they are, but the benefit they would see from having a dollar added to the Mississippi budget is less than the cost of 1 dollar to them.

The production externality listed above, however, would appear to fit here also. Relief to Ethiopia is currently being given by a large number of governments. In each case, the government of the donor country, let us say, Sweden, itself makes up its mind as to how much it is to give. If we were to establish some kind of collective organisations in which the citizens of all of these states jointly voted on how much they would transfer to Ethiopia, the production externality argument indicates that they would choose to transfer more than they do now. The Swedes would do more under matching conditions. Nevertheless, once one gets up to numbers of 100 or so, further gains in increasing the total number of donors who are making the collective decision are relatively minor. The gain comes in the early part of the process when you move from 1 to 10 to 100 and to 1000 donors voting on their decision as a block.

But all of this is theoretical. Let us turn a little bit to empirical data, and here I am going to survey briefly what empirical data we have on decentralisation of aid to the poor. The first, and in some ways most astonishing, is the English system just before the welfare reform associated with Bentham. The statute of Elizabeth second[6] provided that the poor would be taken care of by the local parishes in England, which had a Board of Commissioners for this purpose. The problem that disturbed Bentham, and apparently all the other people at that time, was that under the so-called Speenhamland system, the amount going to the poor was excessive and was causing severe financial problems.[7] The point of the reform was to prevent the parishes from wasting the taxpayers' substance. Surely, this does not look as if the production externalities argument that I gave above was an important factor here. The new system was, in fact, considerably less generous to the poor than the old one had been. It is, of course, true that this change was in part total reorganisation rather than centralisation, but the change was a matter of an Act of Parliament and not of the parishes deciding to take action on their own.

6. That is, the second year of Elizabeth I, not Elizabeth II.

7. "One-sixth of the population was in receipt of parish relief of one kind or another." Gertrude Himmelfarb, *Manhattan Report*, vol. 5, no. 1, p. 3.

As a second example of the same kind of thing, Lebergott[8] has collected data on the relative payment to the poor from 1850 well into the era of the modern welfare state. The data come from the census and are organised by state, but in many states the actual payments and organisation of the whole programme were local rather than state government responsibilities. The amount, which was, in essence, the minimum income which a poor person could receive under these circumstances, fluctuated, but Lebergott's general conclusion is that relatively the poor did about as well in the 1850s as in the 1950s—or, for that matter, in the 1980s. Centralisation of aid to the poor has not greatly benefited them.

As a last item, I am a citizen of the Washington area and read *The Washington Post*, a typical bleeding-heart journal. I find a steady scattering of articles about the very poor in Washington; they used to be called the grating people, and are now referred to as the homeless. These people are far worse off than anyone else in the area and, interestingly enough, are primarily being taken care of privately. I don't want to oversimplify. Many of the people concerned in aiding these poor are themselves civil servants, or, for that matter, politicians, and they're quite expert at, rather indirectly, getting federal government money. Further, just before the last presidential election, one of the leaders of this poor movement started a fast, wanting further federal government money. Fearing that bad publicity would come if the leader died[9] before the election, the Reagan government made a sizeable grant to the particular private organisation with which he was associated. Nevertheless, basically, the welfare state is not helping these very poor people particularly.

This is not a unique characteristic of Washington or the United States. One of the results of the severe winter in Europe in 1984/85 was the discovery that there were about 5000 people in Paris quite literally sleeping under bridges. The police rounded up most of them before the cold killed them, but some died. They were also found in London and elsewhere.

I don't read the newspapers of Paris or Rome, but I do read *The Washington Post*. It is notable that the *Post* is very disturbed about these poor people,

8. Stanley Lebergott, *Wealth and Want* (Princeton, N.J.: Princeton University Press, 1975); the data below are drawn from his chapter "A Century of Guaranteed Income in the US," 53–68.

9. I do not think that he was running a complete and total fast, however, since he seemed to have lived too long for that.

and some of its reporters, if their stories are to be believed, regularly make small cash contributions, but they do not suggest that the welfare state be discommoded by being rearranged so that these people are taken care of by regularly appointed civil servants.

Currently, their basic problem is that they have great difficulty dealing with civil servants, forms, etc., and the welfare bureaucracy doesn't want to inconvenience itself for them. The actual private charity made available in Washington for these very poor, in spite of the existence of the welfare state, is a rather strong indication of what I might call the normal state. In the nineteenth century, in addition to the governmental programme whose data were collected by Lebergott, there was a great deal of private charity.

Today, once again, there is a great deal of private charity, but the private charity today almost uniformly takes the form of gifts to research, universities, etc. One of the results of the development of the welfare state was that most citizens came to the conclusion that the poor were being taken care of, and hence that their charitable instincts should be directed elsewhere. With the development of various specialised bureaucracies to take care of this money made available by charitably inclined citizens, all of which are devoted to something other than helping the poor, it is quite hard to get the money back to helping those poor whom the welfare state does not help. I should say, however, that in Washington, private agencies now exist for the purpose of collecting money and using it for the benefit of these grating people. Such agencies are in fact developing rapidly, so one can predict that they will be better off in the future. For the reasons given above, however, it would be far better if the government took up their care, and there are some movements in that direction.

How, then, do we have what appears to be a radical difference between theory and practice? Further, if theory has influenced practice, a great many programmes have been shifted to the central government on the grounds that they're impractical at the local level. This was the rationalisation for making social security a national instead of local programme, and, in that particular case, this was probably sensible. It would not have been feasible to deal with it in a disaggregated way because it involved an intergenerational transfer rather than a transfer to the poor. Transfer to the poor, on the other hand, I believe could be dealt with locally.

This automatically raises the general problem of what can and cannot be done in the way of local government transfers. One can use the above history as a sort of a guide for the future. Apparently, local governments can indeed take care of the poor as well as they're taken care of now. In general, they cannot engage in the very large transfers which are so characteristic of modern welfare states, back and forth within the middle class. It is probable that they can operate minor transfers away from the wealthy to the rest of the society, but they cannot organise very large transfers of this sort. Since there is some doubt as to whether democracies in general have, in practice, made large transfers from the wealthy to the rest of us, it is not obvious whether this is a disadvantage of local government as opposed to national government. There are, of course, many people who would say that if it could not make large transfers of this sort, this would be an advantage.

These are general conclusions. Let us go through my reasoning, and let me begin with the transfers away from the wealthy, then the transfers back and forth in the middle class, and end up with the transfers to the poor.

If we look at traditional American society, we observe that the wealthy, one way or another, normally made more or less voluntary transfers to the citizens of the area where they operated. In a way, these transfers were not transfers, but the purchase of respect and admiration from their fellow citizens. When it was completely voluntary, there were, of course, individuals who did not participate in this activity, but most wealthy people did. If we return to the Washington environment, the Wolf Trap auditorium was originally a private gift, and when it burned down, various wealthy people, mainly Mrs Filene, paid to have it rebuilt. Needless to say, the opening of the new Wolf Trap auditorium consisted of a large, "We like Mrs Filene" ceremony.

In general, upper-income people who are willing to make gifts of this sort have no particular objection to having these gifts collected by way of a progressive tax, provided progression is not too severe. Those particular upper-income people who don't want to make gifts object; but they're probably outnumbered by their colleagues.

It should be said, however, that all of this permits only relatively modest transfers from the wealthy. Since it is not obvious whether we make large or small transfers now, whether this indicates that local governments could do more, or could do less, is not clear. With a local government, individuals obviously can simply move out, and wealthy people might do so. It should be pointed out, however, that if the wealthy people earn their living in one particular city or are wealthy because they own property in it, then they cannot move. One would anticipate that any given level of tax would lead to some equilibrium with presumably at least some people who needed to give immediate direct supervision to the sources of their wealth, feeling that paying the graduated income tax was less of a sacrifice than living somewhere else. The higher the tax, the fewer such people.

There is an interesting example of this in Switzerland, where graduated income taxes are in fact collected by the extremely small Swiss cantons. There are limits to the amounts that can be extracted this way without encouraging migration as the Stadt of Basel discovered. In general, they are able to charge a graduated income tax, with the wealthy citizens who pay these taxes apparently regarding it as something of a matter of pride and getting a great deal of local respect because they do pay them.

Somewhat of the same effect will be found in the United States, where many individuals pay state and federal taxes.[10]

There is no doubt that Connecticut has a good many people who otherwise would live in other parts of the watershed of New York City because it has no income tax. You do find wealthy people, however, living in New York City itself, upstate New York, or New Jersey, in all of which cases they pay other taxes which are somewhat higher. Apparently, as long as the degree of progression is moderate, wealthy people do not object too loudly.

All of this would indicate that upper-income people have some charitable impulses like the rest of us. The problem with graduated taxation is that you can't collect from them more than a rather modest amount before they begin seriously thinking of moving. Whether this modest amount is greater or less than is in fact collected by the big centralised governments is an open question, but, in my opinion, it is considerably less.

Those people who feel that we should transfer as much or more away from the wealthy as we now do would object to this aspect of redistribution being transferred to local governments. Note once again, however, that it is not immediately obvious how much is transferred away from the wealthy. A great many income redistribution schemes which fall heavily on the wealthy lead not to transfers away from them, but to their losing considerable sums of money because they invest their funds in areas where the return is low before taxes, but after taxes higher than it would be had they chosen more productive investments. This is a net social waste, which does have the effect of making the wealthy poorer, but does not involve any transfer to the rest of us. Indeed, the rest of us are worse off because these investments are less

10. This is a little misleading for foreigners. The federal government permits the local government tax to be subtracted from the income upon which the federal government tax is calculated. Thus, the real effect of that state tax is less than its normal effect. It is nevertheless real.

productive than the alternatives which would be adopted were the taxes lower. In fact, many scholars think that the actual taxes collected from the wealthy would be higher if we lowered the nominal rate, with the result that they switched out of such tax-saving or tax-sheltered investments.

Nevertheless, I think we have to concede that local governments would have difficulty extracting large sums of money from the wealthy. They could no doubt extract some money; in other words, their tax system could be progressive to some extent, but not to an extreme degree. Perhaps, in this case I am simply reflecting my initial training in economics, because Henry Simons was firmly in favour of centralising a graduated income tax on exactly these grounds. He was, of course, thinking of a tax, the upper brackets of which were very much lower than the upper brackets are now.

The second category is the very extensive transfers that now go on in the modern welfare state back and forth within the middle class. Subsidies for farmers, paid for usually by the poorer parts of the population who eat the lower-quality foods; transfers from the economically active to the retired, regardless of whether the retired are poor or not; transfers to workers in the car industry and owners of stock in American car firms by way of restrictions on imports: all of these and innumerable other activities by modern governments, in net, are simply transfers back and forth in the middle class.[11] Some of these programmes, of course, do indeed benefit the poor as well as other people. Elderly poor people collect their social security pensions[12] as do elderly wealthy people.

In general, however, most modern welfare states have certain special programmes that deal with the poor. In the United States this is supplementary security income. A poor person who is old will receive a pension from the social security system, but if that person has been poor all his life and hence the accumulated taxes he paid in were not enough to give him an adequate pension, he will be given supplementary security income. Since he will receive the same sum total of a social security payment and supplementary security income, regardless of the size of his social security pension (provided, of course, it is not greater than the supplementary security income), in essence, from his standpoint, all the taxes he has paid are wasted. He receives two cheques instead of one, but they total to the same amount;[13] that is, he receives the same

11. There may be a certain small part of this which is financed by the taxes on the wealthy.

12. And, in fact, on a proportional basis, do better.

13. This is an administrative matter; he could have the two payments given in one cheque.

as he would have received if he had paid no social security taxes at any time in his life. The basic transfer component of the social security is simply from the young to the old, rather than from the well-off to the poor.

Anyone who knows anything at all about American local governments realises that local governments also engage in middle-class transfers, but on a very small scale. If permitted by the higher-level governments, particularly the federal courts, they will establish local monopolies for such craftsmen as electricians and barbers. They use their zoning regulations to change the value of land in various parts of the city, and in most places there are continuous rumours—true or false, I do not know—that this is a relatively corrupt activity. They also relatively rarely pay their own employees the marginal value of their services. To take one particularly obvious case, the Washington bus drivers are clearly paid more than the marginal value of their services. We find a number of cases in other cities where this kind of thing is done. On the other hand, where the city or local or state government has significant monopsony power and its employees are not well organised, there may be underpayment.[14] All of this involves transfers back and forth within the local middle class.

But although these transfers are clearly possible and do exist in local governments, they are completely trivial compared with the transfers made by the national government. One of the original arguments for having the Social Security Administration national rather than local was that people would move. I don't think it occurred to most of the people who offered this argument that it implied that, really, over their lifetime, most people preferred not to have such a programme. They may, however, not have realised that it was possible to vest the pension right.

The last may not be intelligible to non-Americans, but a great many private pensions, and for that matter government pensions, for their employees are "vested." This means simply that if you move or change your job, you retain the appropriate actuarial value of your pension rights, with the pension being paid at retirement. To explain how this could have worked locally, suppose that I am born, brought up in Rockford, and employed by Woodward Governor, as in fact I was, and then left Rockford and, indeed, Illinois. I would have acquired certain rather restricted pension rights, and they would remain with me. If I die, they would be extinguished, but if I did retire at the age of 65 living in Hawaii, I would receive pension from the state of Illinois, or from the city of Rockford, depending on how this had been organised.

14. This leads to underqualified personnel.

Clearly, the structure that I've just described would have been quite possible if the pension rights were actuarially accurate. Indeed, at the moment, such vested pensions are regularly offered as an additional employment incentive by private companies all over the United States. There is no reason to believe that local governments could not have done so also.

The problem with the social security is that it is not actuarially sound. Almost everybody in the United States who is under the age of 45 would be better off if they could somehow get out of the programme. On the other hand, if that group did get out of the programme, there wouldn't be enough money left to pay the pensions of the people who are now drawing them, and the people over the age of 45 who still stand to gain from the programme, and hence would stay in. The basic problem, of course, is that although a private pension scheme invests the money that you pay into the pension fund, so that when you retire you get the initial amount plus the interest on it, the social security system doesn't. It is true that as the total size of American labour payment increases, partly through increasing productivity and partly, in the past, due to rising population, the pension can be increased. But it can't be increased enough to compensate for the lack of the interest payments.[15] Thus, the young have a very substantial incentive to move out, and, if they do, either the old will not be paid, or the tax will have to be raised on the young, which would give them a stronger incentive to move out. The problem is, of course, particularly severe because younger people are highly migratory anyway. Further, none of them would tend to feel there was some prestige in being marked out as wealthy members of the society as the payers of moderately graduated income tax might. Thus the system simply could not be implemented.

The same, of course, would be true with respect to the farm subsidies which are such an important part of the governmental distortion of the income distribution in most modern welfare states. Local governments simply couldn't do them. Indeed, most of this back and forth in the middle-class income transfer would be impossible if redistribution was made a local government activity.

In my opinion and, I think, in the opinion of most economists who thought about the matter, this is an argument, although not necessarily a decisive argument, for moving these functions to local government, insofar as

15. See my *Economics of Income Redistribution* (Boston: Kluwer-Nijhoff, 1983), chapters 7 and 8.

these activities can be regarded as simply government-sponsored insurance. For example, the old-age pensions or medical insurance—if they are actuarily sound, there is no reason why the local governments cannot carry them out. Vesting provisions equivalent to those now used for people who move from one employer to another could be developed without any great technical difficulty, for people who moved from one area to another. These, of course, are not true transfers, unlike such government programmes as the present American social security system. Once again, I think most economists who thought about the matter would prefer the actuarily sound schemes, which local governments would be forced to adopt, to the kind of tax on the young for the benefit of the old which seems generally attractive to politicians. It is not obvious what the average citizen would think about this. One of the reasons it is not obvious, of course, is that, at the moment, he doesn't understand the issue and hence has no fixed opinion.

Let us now turn to our final area: aid to the poor. The first thing to be said here is that most people are in favour of aiding the poor and that there are perfectly good reasons for collectivising this aid. Collectivisation, however, does not need to go very much beyond the local area in order to obtain most of its advantages. There is no reason to believe that this would cause any great difficulty if the various local government units were of roughly the same wealth and charitable deposition. It is, on the whole, unlikely that this will turn out to be true in most modern states, unfortunately.

Let us then consider a nation composed of two local communities, one of which we will call New York, and one of which we will call Mississippi. Average per capita income in New York we will assume is $10,000 per year, and in Mississippi, $5000 per year. New Yorkers establish a welfare programme which guarantees that the income of individuals who are unemployed, etc., will not fall below $2500 per capita, and the citizens of Mississippi, who have relatively exactly the same charitable instincts, set up a programme where the income will not fall below $1250 per capita.

The first thing to note is that it is clear that the citizens of New York are more charitable towards other citizens of New York than they are towards citizens of Mississippi. There is no legal or constitutional barrier preventing them from supplementing the Mississippi payments to the Mississippi poor by adding on their payments. Let us suppose that for the same budgetary cost they're now using for their $2500 payments they could pay enough to the people in Mississippi so that the poor in both states received $2000 per year per capita. There is no reason why this is not feasible, but we do not observe it.

Why not? The answer, I think, is simple and straightforward. Charitable impulses fall off rather rapidly as you move away from your current location. Those New Yorkers who think about the poor of Mississippi are apt to feel either that the other citizens of Mississippi should tax themselves more vigorously in order to subsidise them, or that other states than New York should be taxed to help the people in Mississippi.

I had, rather by accident, a rather striking example of this while interviewing a candidate for an assistant professor's job in my department. He was from New York and doing a doctoral dissertation on welfare payments to the poor. The theme of the doctoral dissertation was that we should have a national system rather than a set of state systems. The reason that he gave for this—obviously a rationalisation—was that we didn't want people migrating from state to state in terms of the size of their welfare payments. We want them migrating in terms of opportunities for jobs. Thus, a national system would eliminate one possible reason for people moving to places where they are not really needed.

I suggested that his native New York could deal with the problem by simply reducing their payments, and he indignantly rejected this. I then pointed out that almost certainly a national system would pay everybody, including the poor in New York, less than New York was now paying them, and it was clear that he didn't want to talk about the matter further. Note that he was seeking a job and hence trying to make a good impression on me, but he was not capable of saying directly that he thought New York's payments were too high, granted the current institutional system.

In any event, the expectation with this kind of a system would be that a large number of the poor would move to New York. Indeed, people who could obtain jobs in Mississippi and who would prefer a Mississippi job to the Mississippi welfare payment might decide to go to New York because they prefer the New York welfare payment to the Mississippi job.

The solution to this problem, traditionally, has been simply to return the citizen of Mississippi who becomes unemployed in New York to Mississippi. In New England, in the 1820s and 1830s, for example, a recent immigrant into a local town who, in the opinion of the supervisors, was in danger of becoming a candidate for public charity, would be told that he should return to his native town. If he chose not to, he would not be eligible for relief if he later needed it.[16] With this system, a wealthy community could offer higher

16. Samuel Colt, as a young man, came very close to receiving such a warning. Indeed, he would have had he not on the evening of the relevant meeting of the city council saved the life of the daughter of a prominent local man. He later married the girl and, of course, became one

payments to its poor than a poor community could without there being any tendency of people to migrate to the wealthy community in order to collect the payments.

In more recent years, the standard situation has been a little more humane. We are now wealthier and can now afford to give better treatment. Thus, a person who came from Mississippi and who shortly[17] after applied for relief would simply be given a one-way bus ticket back to Mississippi.

Interestingly enough, this system is today still maintained at international levels. The United States spends a good deal of time and effort trying to prevent non-Americans from benefiting from the American welfare scheme. They are either prohibited entry or physically deported.

This scheme permitted different communities to pay different amounts of support to their poor, depending on local preferences. Presumably the wealthier communities paid more and the poorer communities paid less than would a national scheme.

The Supreme Court, not very long ago, in one of its more muddle-headed decisions ruled this unconstitutional. It said that all Americans have a constitutional right (nowhere specified in the Constitution but nevertheless something we would on the whole like to have) to travel, and that denying them relief payments violated that right. I refer to this as muddle-headed. One of my reasons for this is that states are still permitted to prevent outsiders (i.e., immigrants) from earning a living. Suppose, for example, that I am an electrician living in Mississippi, and New York has organised a licensing scheme for electricians controlled by the existing electricians who quite naturally don't like competition. The Supreme Court takes the view that I do not have a constitutional right to move to New York and practise my trade as an electrician, but I do have a constitutional right to go there and go on relief.

But regardless of the muddled nature of the Supreme Court's views, the current situation in the United States is that local governments cannot pay a higher than average benefit to the poor and confine that to people who have resided in the local area for some time. This does not mean that such aid cannot be given by the local governments, and indeed it is a local function in the United States today. It does mean, however, that there are considerable

---

of the wealthiest men in New England. We can see that the local government's judgement as to who was likely to become poor was decidedly defective.

17. I emphasise shortly.

difficulties for various local governments, particularly those that wish to be generous to their own citizens.

A return to the earlier system in which they returned the unemployed to their place of origin, would, in my opinion, be an improvement, but we now live in the computer age, and a more sophisticated system is possible. The right to unemployment payments could, in a sense, be vested just like pensions. Suppose, for example, that I have been a citizen in Mississippi for 25 years and then move to New York, where I am employed for one year before I become needful of government aid. I could be given 25/26 of my Mississippi payment and 1/26 of my New York payment, either partly by the Mississippi government and partly by the New York government, or entirely by the New York government. This would be treating the charitable provisions as rather like an insurance policy supported by the taxpayer on the analogy of vested pension rights. We could call it vested unemployment insurance rights.

It might be argued that the base for such a scheme should be only years after the age of 18 or only years employed. It is also not necessary that the actuarial accounting be as simple as in the example above. Any good economist or actuary could work out several thousand variants on the basic idea, but there is no need to go through them now.

Thus, it seems to me that there is no obvious reason that aid to the poor should not be made locally, as indeed it was during most of the history of the United States. This requires, of course, that the upper-income citizens of the locality are not likely to move out because of the taxes to aid the poor. Granted what a small portion of the budget that aid to the poor is everywhere, however, that seems fairly secure. Further, as I have said before, helping the poor is something most of us want to do, and most of us do not have any great objection to paying moderate amounts of money to that end.

The centralisation of aid to the poor in the United States is a hangover from the Great Depression. The immense increase in the number of people to be helped put a severe strain on both private charity and local relief organisations. That they would like to be helped is obvious, but it's not obvious why the federal government stepped in. Probably that had something to do with the political mystique of the period.[18] As a general rule, emergencies

18. In another fiscal crisis, the Civil War, the federal government, by way of providing the states with quotas of enlistments that had to be met either by volunteers or by conscription, led the states to enact gigantic enlistment bonus programmes. Thus, the fiscal difficulty of the federal government was in part taken care of by hiving off a large part of the payments to the soldiers in the federal army onto the states.

frequently lead simply to reorganisation without much thought as to what that reorganisation is. We may be observing an example here.

The general theme of this chapter has been that it is not obviously impossible to get a good deal of income redistribution with local government organisation rather than national. It is true that transfers of large amounts of money away from the wealthy are difficult locally, but modest amounts can be transferred away. It is not obvious that our present system actually does transfer more than the modest amounts which could be obtained by state and local governments. Transfers back and forth within the middle class would be much harder, although not impossible, if carried out by state and local governments, but most economists would regard that as a decided advantage. Aid to the poor would work as well locally as at a national level; in fact it could be argued that it would work better. The amount of aid paid would vary from community to community in terms of local preferences and resources. Those who believe that all Americans should receive a particular minimum income which is higher than that which some of our communities would choose to pay[19] may find this offensive. We should keep in mind, however, that a national system will not only raise the amount paid in the poorer communities, it will lower the amount paid in the wealthier communities.

All in all, it seems to me that the very simple straightforward line of reasoning which is so common among economists in this area is wrong. I say that even though I am one of the economists who has frequently used it. Most of our income redistribution could be done locally. The fact that transfers back and forth within the middle class would be harder locally than nationally is obviously an advantage. Those who feel that the upper-income group should be despoiled of more money than local government could undertake would be in favour of a national tax on the upper-income brackets. Granted how little we transfer away from these people now, however, such a tax would be quite an inconspicuous feature of our national revenue accounts.

It would appear that the United States had a better system on these grounds before 1930, when there was a graduated income tax on the upper brackets, than it has had since. The change was a by-product of the Great Depression, and, like many other things that came out of the Great Depression, it was a mistake.

19. And who of course also believe that other human beings, non-Americans, should be given only trivial payments.

AID IN KIND

In many cases, instead of simply giving the poor money to spend as they wish, aid has taken the form of providing gifts in kind, usually with some provision by which the recipient may not resell. It is obvious that such provisions are not maximising from the standpoint of the recipient who would prefer cash. After all, if he wants whatever is provided in kind, he can purchase it on the open market.[1] Analysis of redistribution in kind by economists has, to an overwhelming extent, simply taken the form of pointing out that it is less beneficial to the recipient than direct cash payments. I will not quarrel with this point, but I nevertheless feel that redistribution in kind deserves more analysis. What analysis has been done on redistribution in kind normally begins by assuming that there is an altruist and a poor beneficiary and that the altruist is interested in the consumption by the beneficiary of only one good. The utility function of the altruist takes the form:

$$V_B = V(X_B, Y_B, Y_A)$$

while the utility function of the recipient takes the form:

$$V_A = V(X_A, Y_A)$$

As can be seen, the recipient is uninterested in the consumption of the altruist, and the altruist's interest with respect to the recipient concerns only one good of a two-good universe.

This is an incorrect representation of the situation. In practice, altruists are not simply interested in the consumption of one good by whomever they are attempting to benefit. The person who is strongly concerned about the housing of the poor would be most unhappy if they starved to death in mansions. What he is objecting to is the mix of goods which they consume. He thinks they consume the goods in improper proportions, but he does not concern himself solely with the consumption of one good.

Reprinted, with permission, from *The Economics of Wealth and Poverty* (New York: New York University Press, 1986), 128–35.

1. It might be that the government is capable of providing the gift in kind at a lower cost than its market provision. Under these circumstances, a gift in kind could be argued for as benefiting the recipient. So far as I know there are no examples of this in current redistribution programmes.

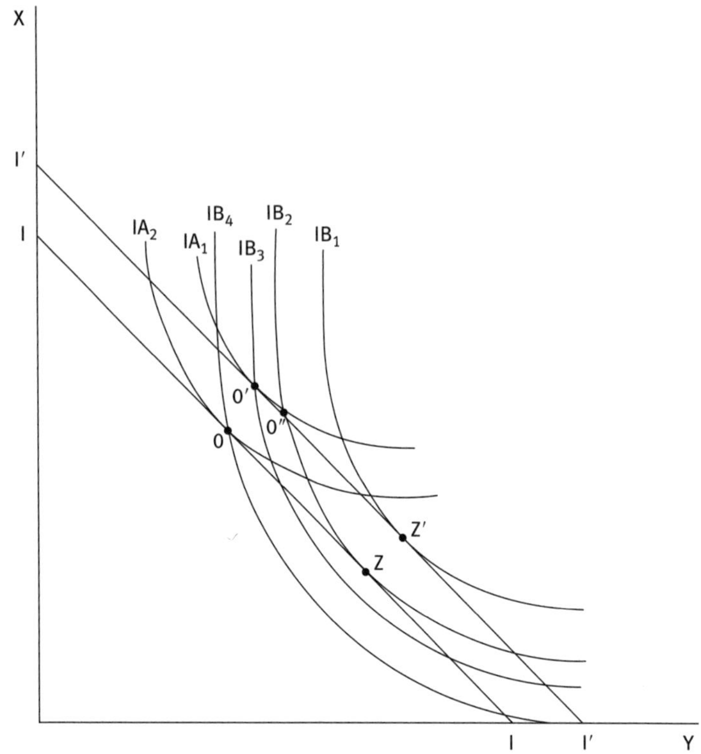

FIGURE 1

Look at Figure 1. We show there a two-good, X and Y, universe and start with a budget constraint for the potential recipient of charity, line I-I. Granted the indifference curves for the potential recipient, $IA_{1,2}$ he chooses to consume at 0. There is also in this world another person, Mr B, who is concerned about the well-being of Mr A. He feels that A is both too poor and expending his income improperly. His indifference curves for consumption of X and Y by A are shown by $IB_{1,2,3,4}$. He feels that given the income restraint I-I, A should be consuming the bundle Z instead of bundle 0. He could, of course, in some societies, simply order A to consume the appropriate bundle, and we will indeed discuss that situation below. For the moment, however, we will talk about circumstances in which he cannot simply order A to change his consumption.

Suppose then that a transfer is made to I so that his new income constraint is I′-I′. Left to himself, I, the beneficiary, would choose 0′, which from the standpoint of the altruist is better, but still not very good. The altruist would

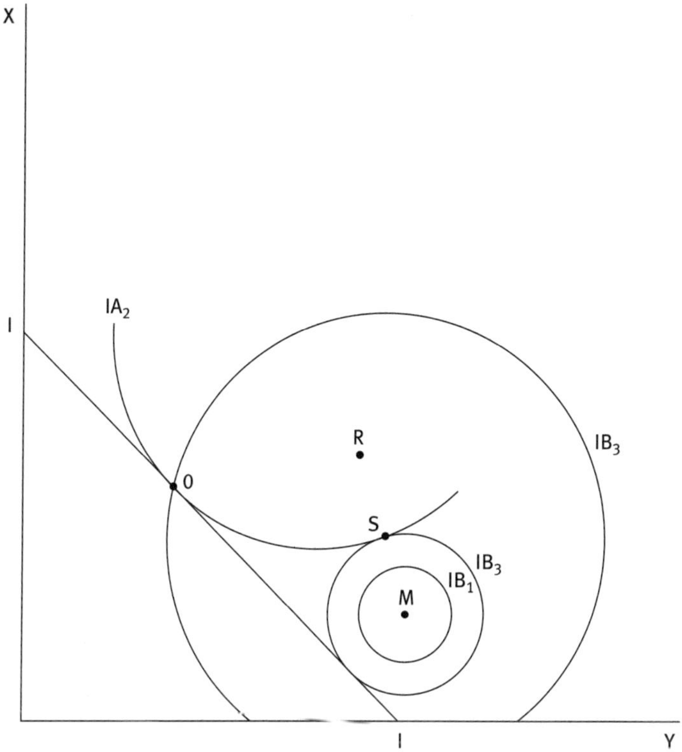

FIGURE 2

much prefer I to choose 0″. Further, if the gift is made conditional upon his changing his consumption bundle to 0″, A will indeed regard that as better than 0. In essence, he has been bribed, but the bribe is conditional on I's changing his consumption pattern.

The indifference curves in Figure 1 for B are his preferences for the expenditures of A. They do not include any element of cost to him. Suppose, however, that we introduce a possibility of B making a gift to A. The gift is, of course, a cost to him. Under these circumstances, we can draw a new set of indifference curves for him as we do in Figure 2.[2] We show his preferences for various consumption bundles by A, granted that if A consumes more than I-I, the difference will have to be paid by B. Under these circumstances we would

2. In essence we have moved to a three-dimensional diagram in which expenditure by the altruist is the third dimension. Figure 1 is the base plane of this diagram, and Figure 2 a plane cutting the figure at an angle so that the altruist's expenditure rises to the right.

expect that the indifference curves would be closed in the way that they are shown by $IB_{1,2,3}$ in Figure 2. There would be an optimum for B which is shown by M. Reaching M, however, can only be by direct orders and not by bribery. The best that our altruist can do is to choose that point where his highest feasible indifference curve is tangent to the indifference curve of A at the *status quo*, or S. Note that S is Pareto-optimal, and under the circumstances there is no change which will benefit both parties.

It is, of course, not necessary for us to seek this kind of tangency. It might be that the optimum of B for A's consumption, together with B's subsidy, would be a point which lies within the indifference curve for A which passed through the *status quo*, a point like R. In this circumstance he would simply provide the gift in kind at R without concerning himself about other parts of his indifference surface. Once again, this outcome is Pareto-optimal.

This assumes, of course, that it is possible for the altruist to provide the gift in a form which prevents A from retrading it and reaching some other location. For many governmental subsidies in kind this is fairly easy. For example, subsidised housing, where housing is actually literally provided by the government. In others, for example, food stamps, it is probably possible but not quite so easy. In fact, the government has not made any very serious effort to achieve that goal. Reselling raises quite complicated issues which will be discussed below.

Meanwhile, let us turn to another form of subsidy which occurs when the altruist, instead of providing a mixed bundle which is to him optimum, subsidises the consumption of whatever good he thinks is ranked too low in A's preference function.[3] The situation can be analysed by Figure 3. In this case the then-poor person is consuming at 0 where his indifference curve IA_1 is tangent to the budget constraint. If the altruist begins to subsidise consumption of Y, then the budget constraint will swing out, pivoting on the point where I-I intersects the X axis. This will increase A's consumption of good I as he adjusts to his continuing changing budget constraint, and the line labelled TL shows the locus of his consumption bundle as the subsidy grows.

3. He could, of course, tax the other good, the one in which he wishes to have the volume reduced, but we are assuming that he is attempting to raise A's total consumption. The mix of a tax on one good consumed by the aided person and a subsidy on the other which ends with A better off is, as far as we know, not used in the real world and is rather complicated, and hence we shall not discuss it here.

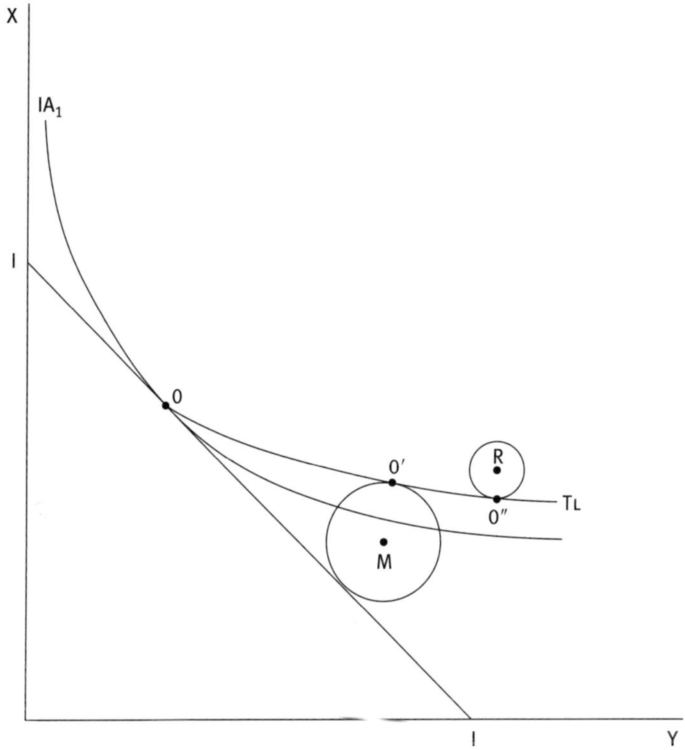

FIGURE 3

We have drawn in two different sets of indifference curves for the donor. In one case the optimal is at M, and he would try to select that subsidy which puts his highest possible indifference curve tangent to the purchase curve of I, i.e., at 0′.

This is, of course, perfectly standard. The second possibility, shown by R and the indifference curve drawn around it, is somewhat more surprising. It is possible, but not likely, for the altruist in this case to have this kind of indifference curve and optimal relation to the performance curve, because there is no way of guaranteeing by subsidy that the performance curve passes through the optimum. In any event, this would lead to 0″ as the outcome.

It should be noted that neither of these points is Pareto-optimal. This is simply because the donor has restricted himself to an inappropriate way of making his gift. If we assumed that this restriction is somehow a fact of nature or, alternatively, that the individual values this particular method

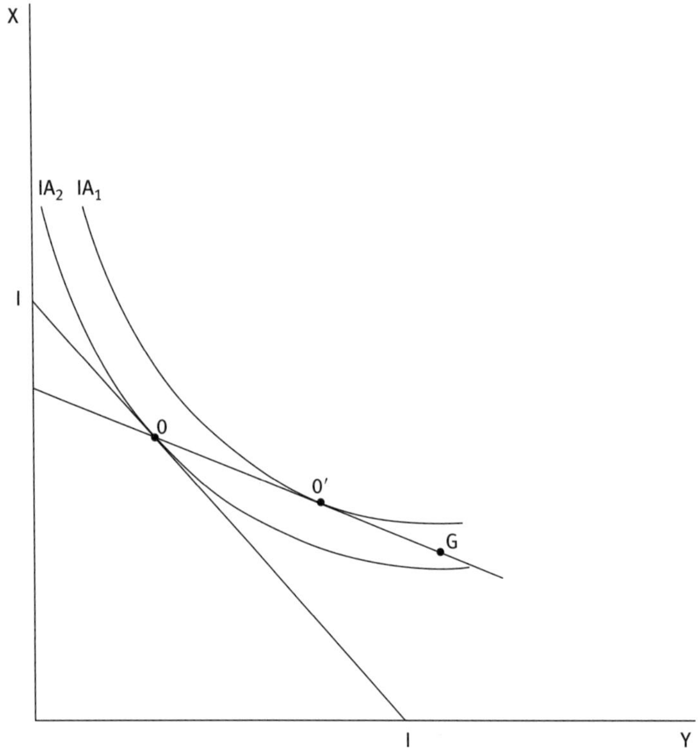

FIGURE 4

so highly that he is willing to take inefficiency in other areas, then 0′ and 0″ would indeed be Pareto-optimal.

It may be sensible here to pause briefly and make a few remarks about Pareto optimality in charitable transfers. In general, bargaining between the two parties is impossible except insofar as pure transfers of information may be helpful. The problem is that any sacrifice made by the donee in order to make the donor better off is equivalent to simply a different gift from the donor than the one he has chosen. Thus, if there is a point which is superior to the current donor choice of policy and gift, and which is favoured by the donee, the donor can always move to it without the donee's permission. Hence, bargaining cannot reach Pareto-optimal locations.

When the donor makes his gift in kind in order to change the consumption of the donee, it is sometimes possible for the donee to resell the goods and use the money obtained to purchase other goods. This situation is analysed with the aid of Figure 4.

As is customary, we show the initial income constraint I-I and two indifference curves for the recipient. We assume that the donee makes a gift to G, which together with a cost he charges, puts the donee initially at G. Since this is superior to 0, where he started, he will agree to go along with it. He can now, however, sell the product Y to whatever extent he wishes. He will not, however, when selling it, receive the same price that he would have paid if he were buying it, because this market functions like most markets do. Thus, he faces the line G-0′as his sale line and sells enough of product Y to move to 0′, which in his view is superior to both 0 and G.

It would be possible to draw a set of such reactions to various gifts from the donor, and then the donor could choose which reaction was highest on his indifference curve and make the gift which led to that. Note the complexity of this problem, however. The donor has to make guesses as to how much it will cost him in gift at G to get the recipient to 0′. This involves not only a knowledge of how much of the stuff 0′ will sell, but also a rather complex geometry. I have not chosen to attempt to present this on the diagram, but I suspect that this difficulty may be one of the reasons why there are fairly extensive efforts to prevent donees from reselling various gifts in kind which they receive. In the case of food stamps, these efforts have not been either very heavily enforced or very successful, but in the case of subsidised housing they are usually applied pretty strictly. The difference may reflect the differential difficulties of policing the two areas. Note that if we were capable of preventing the individual from reselling, then the donor could achieve a Pareto-optimal point. If he cannot prevent resale then the outcome will not be Pareto-optimal.

So far I have talked solely about direct charitable payments in which the charitably inclined person has no power to compel the recipient of his charity to do anything; he must bribe him. It is true that in the real world we observe that there is a good deal of use of the police power to change other people's consumption patterns. For example, altruistically inclined Mr B may think it is bad for Mr A to consume cocaine, copies of *Penthouse*, or the services of a gambling casino. One way of dealing with this is simply to make it illegal. Further, in general, desires of this sort are not directly connected with efforts to benefit A by other means, although as we shall see in a moment, sometimes they are.

This situation is shown very simply on Figure 5. Assume that commodity X is a commodity which the individual is not supposed to consume, and that he is currently consuming it at level 0. Our altruist or meddler, depending on what the readers of this paper prefer, would like to have him consume less and

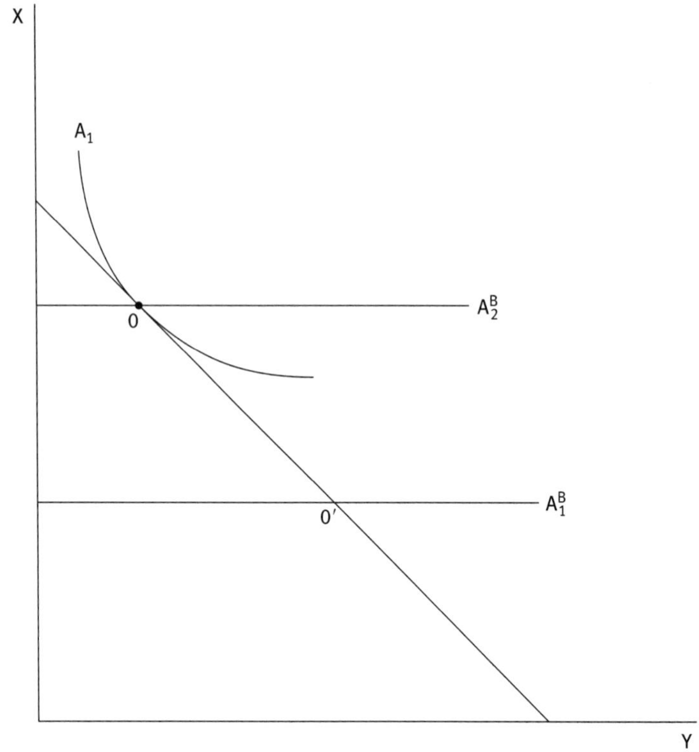

FIGURE 5

is willing to use police power to do so. He has a set of indifference "curves" such as $A_1^B A_2^B$. Once again, pushing A downward on this table consumes resources, and hence his optimal situation is not the horizontal axis but some point slightly off the horizontal axis where the expenditure on police force resources exactly balances his disutility from observing A consuming X in Figure 5 at 0′. Once again, this is a Pareto-optimal point because no bargain between the two parties is possible as long as B controls the police force and has preferences we have specified.

Strictly speaking, this analysis has little to do with charitable provision, but as a matter of practical fact a great many people seem to think that if we are making charitable provisions for someone or other, we should have further control over his expenditures. We don't want him to drink them up, gamble them away, or use them entirely to consume drugs. Thus, a libertarian who would be totally unwilling to enforce laws against drug consumption on the population in general may nevertheless feel that an object of charity can reasonably be required not to consume drugs as a condition of receiving his charity. Granted that the recipient of the charity can always turn down the charitable offer, however, it would not be possible to push A down below the indifference curve A_1 at which he can attain the monies through his own efforts. All that really can be done in this case is that the police power can be augmented with respect to people on charity so that they have less possibility of cheating than does the ordinary citizen.

DEMAND REVEALING, TRANSFERS, AND RENT SEEKING[1]

Several new and radical methods of aggregating preferences, i.e., voting, have been proposed essentially by mathematically inclined economists in recent years. One of these, "Demand Revealing," is, in my opinion, far superior to the others or for that matter to our current methods.[2] This system involves the "Clarke tax," a (usually minuscule) tax on the voter which has the bizarre characteristic of improving the quality of the vote.

Let us begin with a simple situation: one group of people, let us say, the farmers, wish, via the government, to obtain transfers from another group, let us say, all taxpayers. This is, of course, characteristic of substantially every modern democratic country.[3] Figure 1 shows the net social cost of the transfer (per dollar transferred) by the line CC, and the benefit the farmers receive by the line BB. It is assumed that the demand by the farmers for their transfer is literally its dollar value. This seems reasonable.

Line BB, or the social benefit of retransfer, must of necessity lie below line CC if there is any administrative cost of making the transfer at all. Since there always is, the demand-revealing process which would sum the demand of the farmers, together with a zero demand of the non-farmers for this particular procedure, would show its appropriate size as zero.[4]

Reprinted, with permission, from *The Economics of Wealth and Poverty* (New York: New York University Press, 1986), 136–42.

1. The author benefited from very helpful comments by T. Nicolaus Tideman and Ed Clarke.

2. For a simple explanation, see T. Nicolaus Tideman and Gordon Tullock, "A New and Superior Process for Making Social Decisions," *Journal of Political Economy* 84 (October 1976): 225–73.

3. In this example, and in all others in this chapter, we will assume that the amount is a continuous variable. Adjustment of the models to deal with discontinuous outcomes is simple.

4. This same result can be obtained by two other ways. We could assume that the transfer is intrinsically inefficient, as all farm transfer programmes in fact are, with the result that line BB lies much further below CC than it does in Figure 1 of the previous chapter. Secondly, we could assume (probably correctly) that the donors of this gift not only do not want to pay their taxes at the value of those taxes, but actually were somewhat annoyed by the whole procedure. Under these circumstances their demand curve, instead of lying along the horizontal axis, would lie somewhat below it, and when we summed the demand curves, line BB would be once again moved down.

FIGURE 1

The Clarke tax here is probably non-existent. The reason for this is that it seems likely in any realistic case that the costs of administering a transfer, and, hence, the distance between line CC and BB, would be greater than the taxes paid by any individual taxpayer. Under these circumstances the removal of any individual, for the purpose of computing the Clarke tax, would make no change in the outcome, and, hence, there would be no Clarke tax. If this were not true—that is, some individuals' tax burdens were larger than the entire cost of administering the transfer—then the outcome is indeed strange. No transfer would be made to the farmers, but every taxpayer whose potential tax burden exceeded the administrative cost would pay a Clarke tax equivalent to the amount that he would have paid had the transfer proposed by the farmers gone through. In theory, although not probably in any realistic case, the sum of these Clarke taxes paid by the various objecting taxpayers could be equal to the total transfer which would otherwise have been made. The farmers would not receive any benefit from this, however, and it seems very dubious that they would even propose the transfer unless we were in a society with a really ferocious class struggle.

Farm aid programmes frequently, however, take the form of administrative rules which implicitly transfer resources from the general citizenry to the

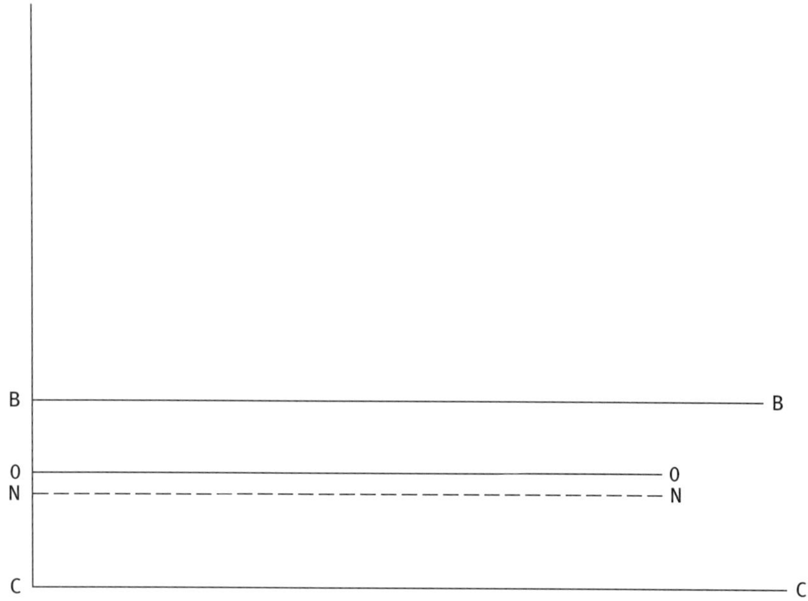

FIGURE 2

farmers. The American system, for example, consists both of a tax subsidy and a price support programme.[5] There is, insofar as it is a simple administrative rule, no direct tax cost.

Such administrative regulations can be dealt with by the expedients shown on Figure 2. The individuals are permitted to indicate the loss that they receive through the administrative rules. Thus, line BB is the benefit the farmers receive, line 0 is of course zero, and the victims suffer the cost shown by line CC. When we add these lines together, we get the dashed line marked NN, which is below zero, and hence, once again, there is no programme. This figure could be made a little more complicated by drawing another line which shows the administrative cost slightly above the zero line. Here again, rent seeking is eliminated.

Once again, there is at least a theoretical chance of significant Clarke taxes falling on the potential victims, but there would be no transfer.

The general policy of permitting people to cast such negative votes through the demand-revealing process seems to be a desirable one. After all,

5. The system is even more complicated than that. The bulk of the tax subsidy is used to fund the price support programme.

we can be damaged by things other than taxes. The alternative, of course, would be to compute the implicit tax involved, but that would require a government bureaucracy making decisions as to how much things cost people, and it's better to let the people make the decisions themselves.

There would, however, be a small problem of education here. One can readily understand an individual who objects to a particular government policy solely because it will cost him some tax money, mistakenly feeling that he should cast a negative vote instead of a zero vote. This would be unwise because it increases his chances of paying a Clarke tax. There is, of course, no reason why the demand-revealing system could not be converted so that the tax always showed itself as a negative amount below zero, but the system would be less elegant.

So far we have been dealing with pure transfers in which the victim is injured and the beneficiaries gain less than the injury. Most economists do not like such transfers, but there are some cases in which at least some economists would be in favour of such a transfer. If the majority of the voters wish to tax a particular minority—millionaires or Jews, to take two groups of which this apparently was true in certain countries in recent times—then the result of the demand-revealing process would be radically different from that of majority voting. There is, of course, no reason why, if we have two different ways of making decisions, one of them majority voting and the other the demand-revealing process,[6] they should lead to the same conclusion always. The decision between them must be made on extrinsic grounds.

Let us now turn to cases in which there is a genuine public good involved. In Figure 3, we show the situation which would arise if it were proposed to put a bridge across part of the Puget Sound, with A and B being people who would benefit from that bridge, and C being a resident in New York who never intends to visit the Far West. I assume that A and B have exactly identical demands for the bridge, for simplicity. Their demands are then shown by the line A and B. The man living in New York, C, has a zero demand, and this is shown by the horizontal axis. The sum of the three is shown by A + B + C and is, of course, identical to the line which could be shown A + B. A socially optimum amount of bridge building is O. If we use Lindahl pricing, and one of the advantages of the demand-revealing process is that it permits close approximation of Lindahl pricing,[7] the cost of the bridge

6. Or any other way which insures that only Pareto-optimal decisions are made.

7. See Tideman and Tullock, "A New and Superior Process for Making Social Decisions."

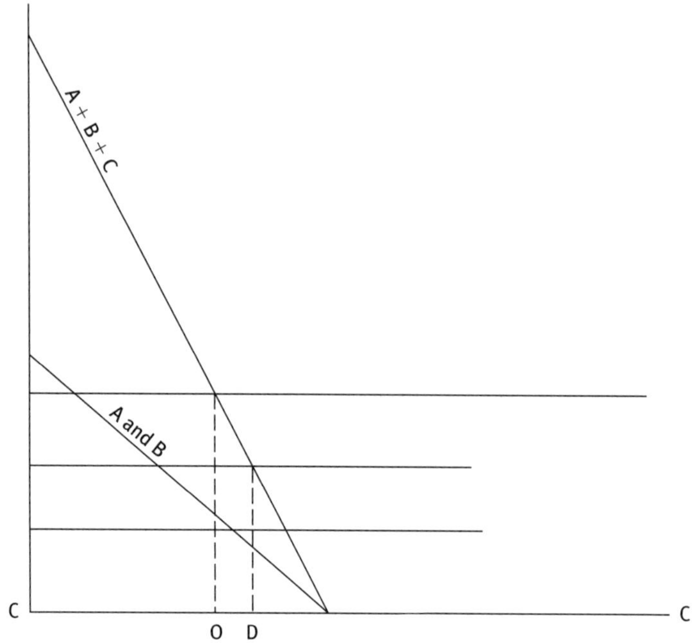

FIGURE 3

would be evenly split between A and B: C would pay nothing. Indeed, with Lindahl pricing, simple majority voting, which in this case might well be unanimous, would show as much bridge purchased as the demand-revealing process.

If we assume that A and B, making up the majority, would like to exploit C a bit, and hence decide that the cost of the bridge should be evenly divided among the three of them, then they would choose to purchase D bridge. If they decided to use their majority to exploit him even further and put the entire cost of the bridge on him, they would, of course, buy out to the point where their two demand curves reached the horizontal axis.

Here again, majority voting, with the majority also permitted to vote on the tax, leads to an outcome which is different from the demand-revealing process. I have difficulty believing that there will be many economists who, in this particular case, prefer the majority voting outcome.

I have not drawn in the mechanism for determining the Clarke tax, because in real-world situations there are many more voters. The total size of the Clarke tax shrinks as the number of voters rises, and in fact becomes very

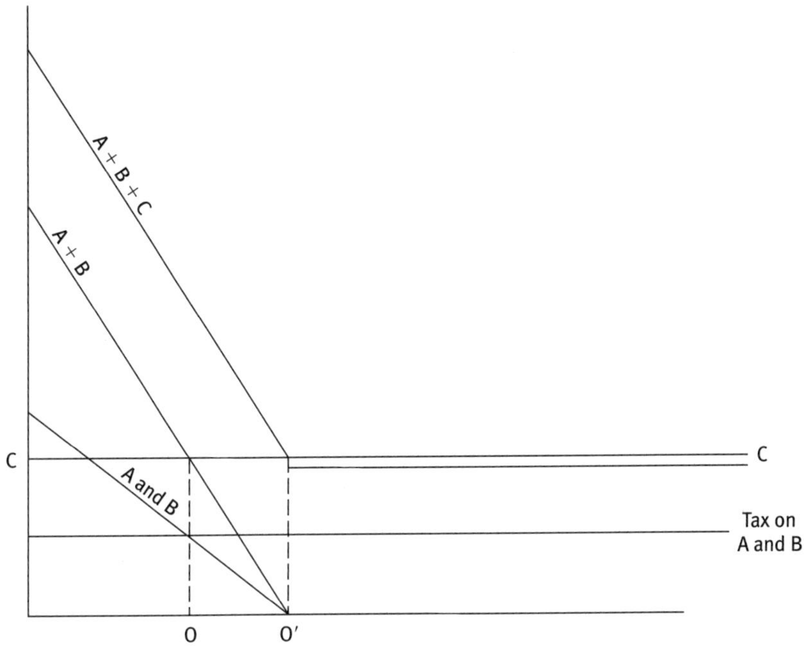

FIGURE 4

small eventually. It will always be larger than it would be, however, if C's interests were not strictly opposed to A's and B's.

There is another case in which the interests of the two parties are opposed, but where there is at least some desire to produce the good on the part of all of them. Suppose A and B are well-off, and C is poor. A and B have a demand for aid to C as shown by the line A and B in Figure 4. C's demand is, of course, the line CC, showing what he will receive. Adding the two well-off demands, we get the line A + B, and O shows what could be argued was the social optimum. C, however, has a demand for the transfer, which is exactly the same as the transfer itself. If we add C to A + B, we get the line A + B + C, which I have shown falling below the cost line at O′ on the theory, once again, that there is at least some administrative cost. It can easily be argued O′ is the social optimum.

Note that in this case a simple majority vote, with A and B splitting the cost of the transfer between them, which is, of course, the Lindahl tax price, would generate O. This is, however, merely an artefact of this particular example. With a larger number of voters, and the poor making up a minority of the voters, the demand-revealing process would normally lead to more redistribution than simple majority voting. The exact amount would, of course, depend upon whether the poor did or did not vote.

The problem here, as can be seen, is one of the franchise. If we look at the real world, we find that sometimes beneficiaries of charitable activities are permitted to vote and sometimes not. At the moment, the ones who are not permitted to vote are mainly those foreigners to whom we give aid, but historically it has not been particularly uncommon for domestic recipients of charity to be automatically deprived of their vote. Dicey, in fact, was quite upset when England, breaking a precedent, provided that certain old-age pensioners should retain the vote while receiving their pensions.[8] If you look at the real world, it is not obvious that it makes much difference whether the poor are permitted to vote or not. *A priori,* one would assume that the poor would do better when they vote on the amount they will receive. What little empirical evidence we have, however, seems to indicate it makes little difference.[9] In any event, if the recipients of charity are not permitted to contribute their vote, the demand-revealing process should transfer to them somewhat more than they would obtain under simple majority vote. If they are permitted to cast their vote, it should transfer more.

In sum, my initial feeling that the demand-revealing process would not work very well in transfer cases turns out to be largely misplaced. The Clarke tax prevents a number of transfers where the transfer itself is not welfare-enhancing, and in other cases, where it doesn't actually prevent such transfers, it at least reduces them. In those cases where the transfers are welfare-enhancing—that is, charitable transfers where the donors obtain at least some benefit from the charity—the demand-revealing process will lead to somewhat more transfers than simple majority vote, and quite possibly considerably more. It depends on franchise.

Thus, what I think has been the most important argument against demand revealing is, in actuality, a result of comparing the demand revealing with perfection. When you compare it with other realistic voting methods, it works better in transfers as well as in other areas.

8. A. V. Dicey, *Law and Public Opinion in England* (London: Macmillan, 1962), xxxv.

9. This subject is discussed at great length in my *The Economics of Income Redistribution* (Boston: Kluwer-Nijhoff, 1983).

EPILOGUE—THE GRATING PEOPLE

Washington is the capital of the world's largest welfare state. It is also a place where the poorest people in the city are taken care of not by the welfare state, but by private charity. The same situation will be found to exist in the capitals of most other welfare states and, for that matter, in other cities in the United States, but I propose to confine myself to Washington because I know more about the situation here.

The exact number of "homeless" or "hungry" is not known.[1] This is particularly true because whenever anything is done which improves the status of such people, their numbers increase. This is not intended in any sense as a criticism of them. It is, however, obvious that if you set up a soup kitchen which provides free, if rather bad, meals, you must expect that not only people who have nothing to eat will turn up at that soup kitchen, but a certain number of people who before it opened were feeding themselves badly, and doing badly in most other aspects of life, will decide to take the free food and use their small income for other things. The same is, of course, true of free shelter.

This has been a problem with charitable provisions from earliest times. Further, it is a problem which I do not know any way of curing and which doesn't bother me particularly. Those people whose incomes are so low that they patronise the church groups which provide free meals and free shelter in Washington seem to me people who are in need of help. I would, in general, prefer that the help be given in a more efficient way than providing them with free meals or shelter, but that does not mean that I resent their taking advantage of the meals and shelter. The problem that I am concerned with is why this condition persists. Why doesn't the welfare state take care of these people?

It is not that they are inconspicuous. *The Washington Post*, a couple of winters ago, published a picture on its front page of one of these people lying on

Reprinted, with permission, from *The Economics of Wealth and Poverty* (New York: New York University Press, 1986), 205–6.

1. After an exhaustive and careful study, the government department of Housing and Urban Development found that the number of homeless was between 192,000 and 586,000. *A Report to the Secretary on the Homeless and Emergency Shelters*, HUD Office for Policy Development and Research, 1 May 1984.

a grating and literally covered with snow. He was directly across the road from the White House, and it was clear they thought this was a terrible situation. Indeed, they may have exaggerated the desperation of his position. I don't think he was cold, as the snow was on the outside of a sort of tent that he had constructed. They had, however, no suggestions whatsoever as to what should be done about him. They simply took the view that it was a bad idea, and vaguely implied that President Reagan was responsible. They did not suggest that their readers send in contributions which they could use to take care of the matter; Mrs Graham, the owner of the *Post*, who is wealthy enough easily to take care of all of the present numbers of grating people in Washington, did not offer to do so; and, last but not least, and most mysteriously, they did not criticise the government welfare agencies for not rescuing this man.

It has to be said that most of these people are indeed somewhat difficult to deal with. They are often mental cases, who have difficulty making any kind of social contact with other people; they have difficulty negotiating even with civil servants; and they tend to fight with each other if brought together in aid shelters. Still, it is possible to help them, and, indeed, there are a number of voluntary charities in Washington which do so. Further, these voluntary charities are quite skilful at coercing the federal and local governments into giving them funds which they use to supplement their private charity.

Why, however, do we observe this matter simply being left to these private charities? To put the matter at its crassest and most imperialistic, why do the welfare state bureaucracies not take advantage of this opportunity to expand their appropriations and scope of activity by asking Congress to fund a special programme for this purpose? Why doesn't *The Washington Post* suggest it? I understand why the current voluntary agencies don't directly demand a government programme. After all, this would lead to unemployment for their own personnel. But I would think they would at least be pushing for government grants large enough to permit them massively to improve their current charitable activities.

None of these things is happening. And frankly, I don't understand why not. Well-intentioned, charitable people should be trying to get government aid for these people. Crass selfish bureaucrats should be trying to get aid for these people and well-intentioned intellectuals or, for that matter, imperialistic intellectuals, such as the staff of *The Washington Post*, should be pushing for such government programmes, yet we observe that none of these things are happening.

There are, of course, individuals, including a certain number of people from all of the categories I've listed above, who are making charitable gifts to help these people, sometimes making considerable personal sacrifice. Nobody seems to feel that a major government programme, or, for that matter, even a major charitable drive, to help them is justifiable. In keeping with what was said above, I don't understand why not.

One of the themes of this book has been that we have a lot of puzzles in the field of charitable activity. From my standpoint, this is the most recent one that I have encountered, and in many ways the most puzzling. Possibly one of the readers can solve the problem.

PART 3

REDISTRIBUTIVE POLITICS

THE MACHIAVELLIANS AND THE WELL-INTENTIONED

This chapter is devoted to a topic which many of my readers may think is a complete waste of time. I propose to demonstrate that programs which are designed with a means test, i.e., in which the money goes only to the poor, benefit the poor more than the Bismarckian programs in which the payment goes to substantially everyone. If the reader feels that this is obvious, he is free to skip the chapter, but I believe that this discussion is necessary because there is a great deal of literature which argues the contrary.

When I first studied this subject, almost all government aid to the poor was administered only to the poor, and there was a means test to see to it that no one got welfare who wasn't poor. The generosity of the means test can perhaps be criticized. At that time, in the mid-part of the New Deal, proposals to extend them generally following Bismarck—e.g., making such things as aid to the old and the sick apply to all old and sick, not just the poor ones—were much canvassed. The standard argument was essentially one of being nice to people.

It was argued that the poor would feel insulted if you compelled them to prove they were poor. If the program were generalized, offered to everyone, then the poor would not have to prove that they were indeed poor. To make this argument a little more intelligible for modern readers, I should point out that at that time only a small portion of the population actually filled out an income tax form. Today, when almost anybody with an income is compelled to reveal that income to government officials, the argument would not appear to have much validity.

In any case, the argument is an example of Hamlet without the Prince of Denmark. The poor may indeed regret having to prove they are poor in order to receive, let us say, an old-age pension, but the person who is really not poor and who hence does not receive an old-age pension is much more likely to be benefited by the abolition of the means test than is the poor person. This argument will be worked out in more detail later in the chapter, but, once again, it seems to me fairly obvious, and I regret indeed having to go

Reprinted, with permission, from *Welfare for the Well-to-Do* (Dallas: Fisher Institute, 1983), 31–50.

through the details of the argument. It is only the existing state of the literature in this area which makes it necessary for me to do so.

Today, fashionable proponents of generalizing government income transfer programs, free medicine, old-age pensions, etc., instead of confining them to the poor, use another argument. This argument is that the middle class will in fact not vote enough money to provide, let us say, good medical attention to the poor if the poor are the only recipients of government medical attention. If, on the other hand, everyone receives government medical attention, the middle class will vote enough money to provide good medical attention, because middle-classers want it themselves, and the poor will benefit from it.

This argument is what I call well-intentioned Machiavellianism. It is argued, in essence, that we must fool the middle class into providing better medical attention for the poor by connecting it to better medical attention for the middle class itself. Personally, I do not believe that the middle class is so stupid that this trick will work. If people do not want to help the poor, they have many ways to avoid it.

In practice, complicated government programs, such as free medical aid or free old-age pensions which are distributed to everyone, normally involve a certain amount of filling out of forms and dealing with the bureaucracy, and the middle class is better at that than the poor. All of the statistics on the point indicate that, as a matter of fact, middle-classers are more successful in getting good medical attention and schools out of the government than are the poor, even when the program is nominally open to everyone. This should not surprise us. Once again, the poor, in general, are poor because they are not terribly competent in various things, and dealing with the government is one of them. A man who is capable of making \$35,000 a year at some private occupation is far more likely to be successful in negotiating with a bureaucrat than is the man whose earned income is \$5,000 a year.

There is another problem. If we are attempting to fool the middle class into voting more money for the poor than it really wants to by attaching aid for the poor to a program which directly benefits the middle class, we should keep in mind that we are not necessarily the only Machiavellians around. I do not doubt that there are well-intentioned people who are interested in reaching good ends by rather dishonest means. Indeed, one can find many such types scattered throughout history. But, although such people do exist, there are far more people who find it desirable to cover essentially selfish goals under slogans of public good, such as aiding the poor.

The Machiavellian, in this case the man who proposes generalizing government aid and claims the reason is that he wants to help the poor, and who thinks that the middle class will vote more for them if it is also on the same program, must realize that he is putting a low evaluation on the charitable desires of the middle class. He is also assuming its members aren't very bright.

He may be right about both of these things, but we should always keep in mind that he may also be wrong. Further, many of the people who argue this way may have quite selfish motives. They may be bureaucrats (or people who would like to be bureaucrats) simply interested in expanding the program so that there will be more high-ranking positions. They may be middle-class types themselves, whose real concern is that they think it is unfair for the poor to receive "benefits" which they do not. In my private discussions I've found that advocates of generalizing our current medical program to cover everyone usually start by talking about the desirability of benefiting people whose income is above the present cut-off point but below their own, which indicates they are trying to benefit some people who aren't poor. Normally, however, they then go on to talk about their own situation and remark about how unfair it is that they would have to pay themselves if some kind of catastrophic illness not covered by their current insurance strikes them.

In dealing with these people I cannot say I have been effective. Aid to the poor, in my mind, raises quite different problems than providing general medical attention to everyone. The particular argument that the upper-income groups are not protected against catastrophic illness is normally true, but insurance covering such illness is available, albeit expensive. There is, however, no reason why it will be cheaper if provided by the government than if provided privately. Somehow, though, I never succeed in making these points convincing.

There is here, however, another and more important point, which is that as a matter of fact catastrophic illnesses which do strike people normally are dealt with by the public sector in any event. Characteristically, if someone contracts a disease which requires hospitalization and which leaves him unable to earn an income for many years, he or his family first deplete their own resources and then turn to the state, which maintains specialized hospitals for this purpose. I do not wish to argue that these hospitals are particularly well run or luxurious, but they apparently do represent the popular view of what should be done with such cases, and certainly they are not private. Only the wealthy deal with those members of their family who have catastrophic diseases through the private marketplace. Most of us do, in fact, turn to special state programs for such diseases. Once again, I have never been successful in pressing this point on people who are interested in general public medical care.

Now it may be that my inability to succeed with these arguments indicates that I am not good at disputation or that the arguments themselves are basically poor. I do not believe so. I think the reason I am unable to convince people in these areas is that they believe that whether they receive aid under these programs or not does not much affect their tax payments. In other words, they are hoping to transfer expenses to other people. They are not charitably trying to generalize, but are attempting to obtain a private profit out of government. My arguments do not have much effect because they are addressed to the overt arguments used by my interlocutors and not to their actual motives. But here, again, I may be totally wrong. I am in essence implying a Machiavellian approach to the argument to the people I talk to, and this may be erroneous.

There is, however, one very clear-cut characteristic of this type of well-intentioned Machiavellianism, and that is that it is necessary for proponents to use arguments which are not their real arguments. They hope to get the bulk of the people to vote for something they don't really want—e.g., greater medical attention for the poor—by attaching it to greater medical attention for themselves. The trick requires deception, and it is by no means obvious that the well-intentioned Machiavellian will be the only person attempting to deceive. And in a way, the well-intentioned Machiavellian is at a disadvantage compared with the more conventional Machiavellian, who is not attempting to achieve a charitable goal.

Thus, we probably have alliances between well-intentioned people who are attempting to do good by deceiving the average voter, and the people who are not particularly well-intentioned and who are attempting to benefit by the same deception. Further, in this case it is not clear what the average voter's position is. If the average voter, for example, is interested in benefiting himself and doesn't care much about the poor, there is an effective method for achieving that selfish objective, a transfer to himself rather than to the poor. I propose to demonstrate a little later in the chapter that a means-tested program to cover the entire population attains the selfish objective. If you feel it is necessary to continually talk about helping the poor but don't really care about them, you should, in general, be in favor of generalized programs. If you are seriously interested in helping the poor, then you would want to generalize the program only if you were convinced that the majority of the people didn't feel that way and you could trick them by generalization.[1] This is, I think, unlikely, but in any event you would find yourself aligning with the genuine Machiavellians, and you would not be able to tell them from the well-intentioned Machiavellians.

Once we go in for political trickery, we may well accomplish things that we could not accomplish without that trickery, but we may also be tricked. The con men say you can't cheat an honest man. I do not think that is entirely true, but it is certainly true that the man engaged in a devious plot is frequently misled, with the result that the devious plot produces something that was no part of his intention.

Let me discuss two examples. In England, the institution of the National Health Service generalized what had previously been a rather elaborate free medical service for the poor into a medical service for everyone. It happened to occur at the same time as the antibiotic revolution, the greatest medical advance in history. In spite of this tremendous improvement in medical technology, the death rate of the poorest fifth of the English population actually rose at that time. The apparent explanation is fairly simple and straightforward. There was a shift of medical resources from the poor to the middle class, and the poor suffered from it.

My second example comes from the United States. The passage of the Medicare-Medicaid programs did two things. They somewhat expanded and improved the medical aid to the poor. It should be said that this is a normal routine. We do not normally keep our various charitable programs at a continuously rising level as society gets wealthier. There are periods in which the level remains stable, then a sharp rise occurs, and then another period of stability and a sharp rise. It goes up in steps. One of these steps in medical aid to the poor occurred at this time.

The other thing that happened was the extension of free medical care to all the old, not just the poor old who had had it before. The net result of the change was, of course, a sharp increase in the incomes of doctors,[2] an increase

1. There is another argument sometimes used here which is that the poor do not know the present programs and, hence, do not apply for them; whereas with generalized programs they would be well-informed and would apply for them. I don't believe this is a truthful statement about the information status of the poor, but if it is, surely this is the most expensive conceivable kind of advertising program.

2. It is intriguing that the free medical attention used to be a direct charity by the doctors themselves who did not charge for poor patients. They have now succeeded in getting the government to cover this expenditure, in fact cover it with very good fees. The benefit to the doctors is probably greater than the benefit to the poor, although it is likely that medical attention for the poor has also improved.

which I suppose with time will eventually disappear but is still having its effects, and a sharp increase in the well-being of older people who had enough money so that they were not eligible for means-tested free medical attention. The poor whose medical attention increased did, of course, gain to some extent, but it is almost certain that the additional subsidy to older people who were not poor caused, for a period, a switch of medical resources away from the older poor towards these older well-off people.

Of course, those citizens of the United States who were neither old nor poor also suffered a reduction in medical attention because of the increased resources available for the older non-poor. The cost clearly fell, to a large extent, on the non-old, non-poor. Whether the poor, old or young, gained or lost from the whole thing is not clear. I would say that they gained, but not as much as they would have gained had the upward step not also been extended to the older non-poor. The gainers clearly were the old non-poor and the doctors. This is the kind of result that one rather anticipates from well-intentioned Machiavellians. The well-intentioned Machiavellian, in order to conceal his actual plans from the potential victims, has to refrain from public discussion of his real motives and plans. Since he has to refrain from talking about his actual motives and plans in public, he does not get the benefit of public discussion in drawing them up and may well end up as he did in this case, primarily benefiting a group of people who were most assuredly not poor.

Let us now turn to a little more formal analysis, and for this purpose I will have to use some diagrams. Let me assure the reader who is unaccustomed to economics that these diagrams are simple and easy to follow. For the more sophisticated, who find these perhaps too simple, a more conventional set of diagrams may be found in my *Economics of Income Redistribution*.

In Figure 1, on the vertical axis, I show a simple dollar measure, and on the horizontal axis, people are arranged from left to right according to income. People who have no income at all, except government aid of some sort, are at 0, and I have rather arbitrarily stopped the table at $100,000 on the right, but there is no intrinsic reason that the diagram could not be continued out to any income desired.

I assume that there is already in existence a government-sponsored aid program for medicine for the poor. This program, of course, like all medical aid, actually aids different people to a different degree, but this, over large numbers, works out to so much per head. If the reader wishes, he can assume that the government simply gives each poor person a medical insurance policy, and this policy cost is shown by the solid line marked "medical aid." I as-

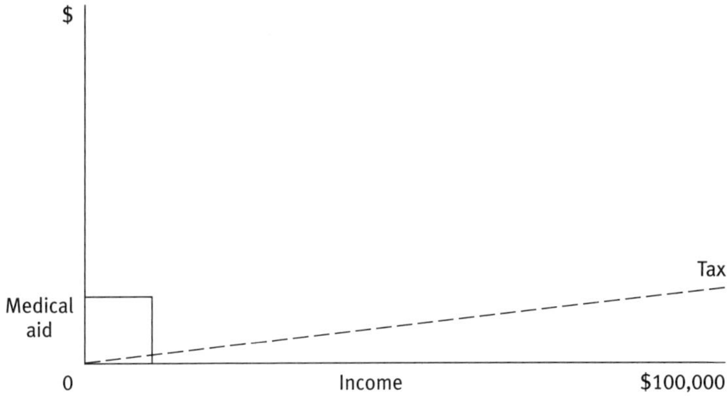

FIGURE 1

sume that this is available only to the poor, which we will assume is roughly the bottom 10 percent of the population, so that all poor people receive the aid marked "medical aid," and this drops to zero as you get beyond the level of poverty.

In general this last assumption is not true of means-tested American aid programs. As a general rule, instead of dropping off abruptly at some point, they fall off gradually as incomes rise. Adjusting my diagram to take care of this gradual change instead of the abrupt cut-off at a given income makes it more complicated but does not change the principle. Once again, if the reader is interested in the more accurate representation of the present system, he will find it in *Economics of Income Redistribution*, but I can assure him that it makes no difference in principle, only in the details.

This medical aid, since it is government provided, must of course be paid for in taxes, and I have assumed that the taxes rise as income rises, with people with low income paying some taxes, which they do, and people with higher incomes paying higher taxes. For simplicity in drafting, a straight line is used to indicate this increase, but once again, there is nothing in the reasoning that follows which requires a straight line. If the reader is interested, he can draw various other shapes, providing only that they continue to rise as income goes up.

How does this leave various citizens? The answer is shown in Figure 2. The solid line in Figure 2 is the net outcome for any citizen of the combination of the aid, if he is eligible for it, and the taxes for whom everyone is eligible. The poor person now receives his insurance policy paid for by the gov-

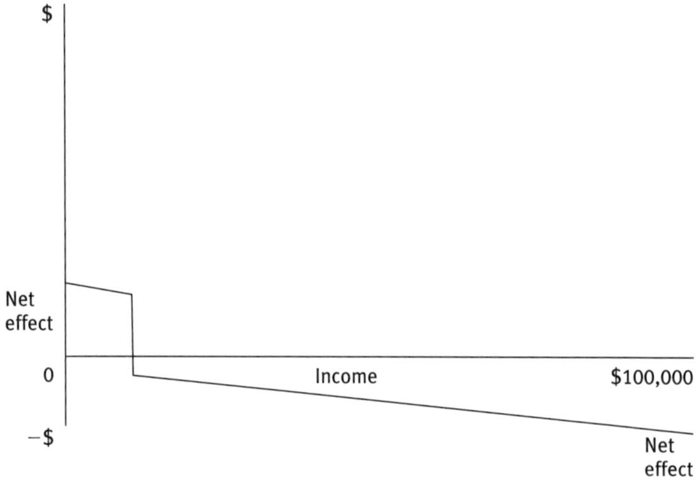

FIGURE 2

ernment but also pays in taxes, with these taxes increasing as he becomes less poor. Hence, instead of having a straight line for medical aid, this net aid (medical aid minus tax cost) slants downward slightly. As soon as one passes the point where the means test cuts off the medical aid, he, of course, receives no more medical aid but continues to pay taxes. Hence, the citizens who are well-off enough to fail the means test have a net loss on the project, shown by the line slanting downward below zero, indicating that as you get wealthier the program inflicts greater cost on you.

It is not obvious from the fact that the upper-income people face a net cost in monetary terms that they would be unhappy about the program. They might have genuinely charitable feelings and be interested in helping the poor through the program. The line does not show their utility, but the objectively calculated tax cost to them. In fact, Figure 2 is simply calculated by subtracting the dashed tax line of Figure 1 from medical aid, with medical aid for those people who flunked the means test, of course, having a zero value.

In Figure 3, we show a universal medical program which provides for each citizen the same medical insurance policy, once again shown by the "medical aid" line but, of course, going all the way to the right. As pointed out above, this is a little unrealistic, because when the government does provide medical aid and assistance, upper-income people do somewhat better than lower-

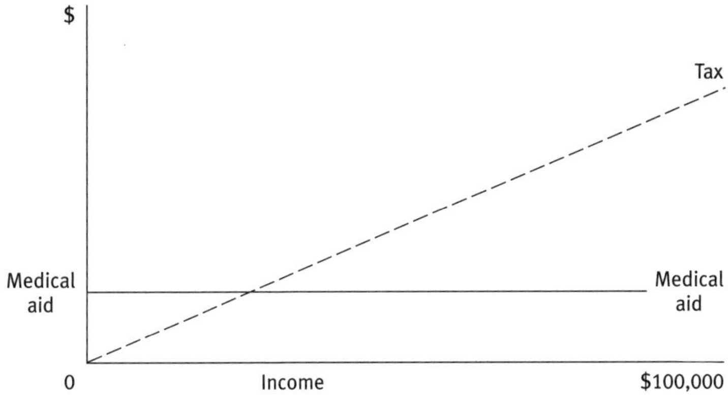

FIGURE 3

income people, but we will leave that out here. Further, this diagram doesn't really deal with the argument that if you give the middle class free medical aid, it will vote for more medical aid and, hence, benefit the poor indirectly. In this case the middle class is voting for the same amount of medical aid. We will deal with the well-intentioned Machiavellian argument below.

There are two differences between Figure 1 and Figure 3. The first is that medical aid is now universal, and the second is that the tax is now higher. Once again, in Figure 4 we show the net effect. It will be noted that the poor receive the same medical attention they did before but pay higher taxes. A number of people who had not received free medical attention before but now receive it will pay higher taxes. For some of them this is a good bargain, but for some the increase in taxes is more than the improved medical aid. In any event, the very wealthy probably will not take advantage of the government's free medical aid. From their standpoint the only effect is the increase in taxes.

Figure 5 shows the difference between the effects on different parts of the population as shown in Figure 2 and in Figure 4. I should add that these diagrams are not geometrically completely accurate. One of the problems of drawing diagrams of this sort is that it is essential that they be intelligible, i.e., that you don't put the lines too close together. The problem can be eliminated by using algebra instead of diagrams, but the diagrams are simpler. Even though they are not exactly to scale, they are not in any way misleading. Some of the effects are smaller than shown on the diagram. The diagram shows them larger simply because if I made them small enough the printer would find two lines running together.

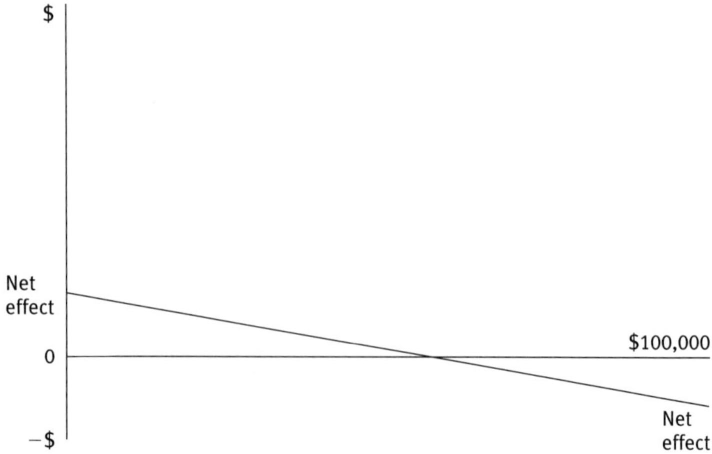

FIGURE 4

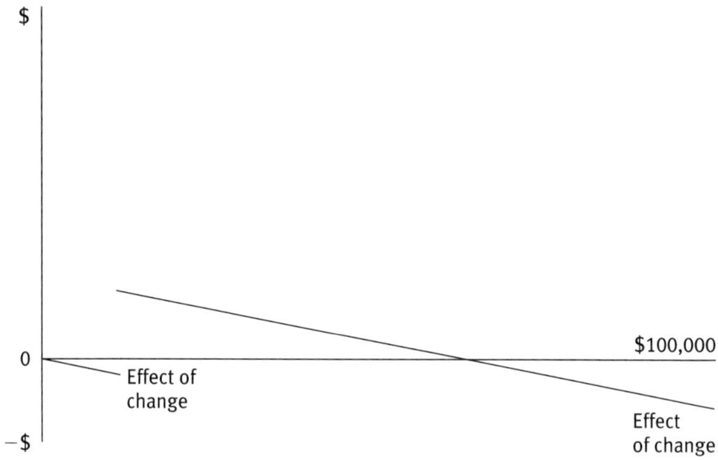

FIGURE 5

In any event, it is clear that the universalization of the program has hurt the poor, benefited a large group of people called the middle class, and then injured the very well off. The reason for this is simple. Members of the middle class now receive free medical attention, and, although their taxes have gone up, the tax increase is less than the value of the medical attention. The poor are receiving the same medical attention they received before but are now paying more taxes. The wealthy are paying taxes which are higher than the medical aid they now receive.

Here we see the basic problem with the Machiavellian approach to these matters. There is a large group of people who have a perfectly sound selfish reason for wanting the program to be universalized. This group of people, in general, is not only much larger than the poor but also politically better organized. That they favor the change is not surprising.

The Machiavellian has to believe that the people who accept the change, which in its present form will actually injure the poor, will now proceed to vote higher taxes upon themselves, thus increasing their own medical aid and, as a by-product, aid the poor more than the increase in taxes which universalization of the program brought about. This, of course, is possible.

But suppose that the middle-class types who in fact gain by the program are not easily fooled. There is nothing to prevent them from maintaining the previous government aid program at the level it was before, when it was aid for the poor only, and also providing that people who wish can purchase additional services. From the middle-class standpoint, if they do not really want to increase aid to the poor, this would be more efficient. As a matter of fact, all medical systems which are purportedly universal do have this characteristic, although in some cases, for example, Sweden and Russia, there is a little concealment of the phenomenon.

Members of the middle class can, however, actually gain. They can provide exactly the same medical aid for everyone that they provided before for the poor and supplement that aid out of their own pockets for their own benefit. The result will be a small but real transfer of funds from the poor to the middle class, because the poor's taxes have gone up. The universalization of medical attention is certain to transfer some money from the wealthy to the middle class. It will also transfer some funds from the poor to the middle class. Only if the universalization is combined with a rise in the level of medical aid can the poor gain. Even then the poor can be injured if the increase in aid is largely concentrated in areas which are politically influential—for example, in the suburbs rather than the central cities.

As mentioned before, in England the generalization of medical care led to an actual rise in the death rate of the poor. To be considered here is the probable phenomenon that will occur whenever you generalize aid. It should be noted that it is essentially a temporary development, not permanent. Still, "temporary" in this case may mean 20 years. What happens is fairly simple.

Let us take England in the 1930s. The wealthy could well afford excellent medical care and got it. The poor benefited from an elaborate government-sponsored program of free medical aid. The middle class had to pay for its own medical attention and consequently economized on it. By this, I do not mean that its members ran serious medical risks but merely that they calculated the desirability of a doctor's visit against the desirability of some other expenditure in their budgets.

With the generalization of medical aid to all persons, the middle class now got its medical attention free and increased the amount of medical attention it received. Consumers characteristically increase consumption of goods when the price goes down.

The total number of doctors, hospitals, etc., in England, however, was the same the day after the generalization of the program as it had been before. The middle-class individuals, with their larger demand, were able to divert a good deal of medical attention from the poor to themselves because of their greater ability to handle forms and because the doctors in practice preferred to deal with them rather than the poor, since there was no monetary difference. Thus, the death rate among the poor actually rose at the time the medical service was universalized.

This was an extreme example of the injury of the poor by the generalization of the free medical attention they were already using, but something milder can be expected in every other such extension. General government-run medical programs are not a good way of helping the poor. If you are convinced that the middle class will not vote enough money to give the poor adequate medical attention, the Machiavellian technique of generalizing medical attention so that the middle class also gets it, with the objective of helping the poor, is unwise. There may be other reasons for universal medical provision by the government.

Suppose, however, that we do want to have universal medical provision by the government, and we do not want to hurt the poor who already receive such free medical attention. The universalization of the program will increase the demand for medicine by the middle class, and a certain amount of medical resources will likely be transferred from the poor, who have not increased their demand, to the middle class, with the result that the poor get not only higher taxes but poorer medical attention. Is there anything that we can do about this?

Yes. There is a program which could be put into effect which would prevent the poor from being injured by the universalization of the program. I am going to describe such a program here. My reason for describing it is not that I wish to urge its adoption but to point out that none of the people who advocate generalization of medical care have ever talked about the matter and certainly have not made any effort to solve the problem. From this I deduce that the well-intentioned Machiavellians, who actually are attempting to help the poor by this indirect means, are outnumbered by the true Machiavellians in the middle class, who will themselves gain by the program and who are not particularly concerned about the poor.

If we want to help the poor, there are two basic problems: the increased tax burden on the poor, which is pretty much unavoidable, because general taxes do hit them, even if not hard, and the fact that they would now have a smaller part of the total medical demand than they had before. These problems can be counterbalanced by another means-tested program. Under such a program, the poor not only receive the general program for the country as a whole, but receive an additional means-tested program. The purpose of it is (a) to compensate them for the increased taxes, and (b) to see to it that their relative demand for medical services remains as high as it was before. In other words, in the past they received free medical services, and the middle class paid the bill. Since the middle class is now receiving free medical service and, hence, are in a position to pull services away from the poor, the poor should be given some additional resources to offset that pull.

This program sounds and is bizarre. But to universalize medical attention and not injure the poor, something like this is necessary. The well-intentioned Machiavellians should be in favor of it, and, indeed, it is a test to tell the well-intentioned from the not-so-well-intentioned.

Such a program could be put on a more or less temporary basis. A crash program could be introduced at the same time to increase total medical resources in society so that the total amount of resources would rise enough to compensate for the increased demand from the middle class. It would probably still be true that the middle-class members would do better than the poor because of their superior ability to handle forms and bureaucrats, but with a combination of my temporary and rather bizarre program and a long-run increase in resources, the poor could still be guaranteed the same medical treatment as they had before.

As a matter of fact, no programs of either of these types have been tried by those countries which have universalized medical attention. What normally happens is, first, the incomes of doctors go up sharply because of the increase in demand, and there is a shift of resources away from the poor. Secondly, the state becomes concerned about its high expenses and begins to take advantage of its monopsony power to force the returns of doctors down. The end product is, in England, that the total amount of resources used for treatment of illness is much lower as a percentage of G.N.P. than in the United States, and you have the immense delays before medical treatment, which have excited so much comment. Indeed, private medical insurance has developed in England for people who want to get high-quality and immediate medical service instead of having to depend on the state system.

But, to emphasize, all of this should not be taken as a conclusive argument against something like the British Health Plan. I am personally opposed to such a program, but I realize that there are arguments for it other than helping the poor. The fact that it is unlikely to help the poor is not a conclusive argument against it, because it does not deal with the other possible reasons for establishing such a program. I would be willing to debate the issue on those other grounds, but not here.

In the discussion of a universal medical program in the United States, none of its proponents have dealt at all with the problems it is likely to inflict on the poor. The argument that it will benefit the poor is frequently made, but the reasons given are the ones that I believe I have discounted earlier in the chapter.

For purely selfish reasons, people in certain income brackets should favor it—in those brackets where they are now not eligible for free medical aid but where the taxes they would have to pay if the medical aid were made universal would be less than the benefit of the medical aid to them. Once again, this is a purely selfish drive, and as far as I can see, the basic support for universalization of medical service comes from that group together with certain political and bureaucratic entities in which the expansion would increase employment opportunities. In a democracy we expect people will, to a large extent, vote for those things which will benefit them. If everyone votes for things that benefit himself, then things that benefit the majority will get through. This is surely not a bad thing. But to say that this program is actually aimed at benefiting a specific group of non-poor people, a very large group, is quite different from saying that it will help the poor.

Why then do we observe people arguing for the program on the grounds that it will help the poor? The answer, I think, is fairly simple. Most of us like to think of ourselves as helping the poor and doing other good things, and we like also to have our own income and real well-being improved. The politician who argues that you should do something which will benefit you, not because it will benefit you but because it is abstractly good and just, gets more votes than the politician who points out the difficulties with that line of reasoning. All of us like to think that we are better, more altruistic, more charitable, than we actually are. But, although we have this desire, we don't want to pay for it. We are willing to make a sacrifice of perhaps 5 percent of our real income in charitable aid to others. We would like to think of ourselves, however, as making much larger transfers without actually making them. One of the functions of the politician in our society is to meet this demand—the demand I suppose one can call a demand for hypocrisy but nevertheless a very human demand. He provides arguments that programs which benefit us personally are actually aimed at helping the poor, the national interest, a cure of cancer, etc.

Note that I am not criticizing people who have these particular motives. I have them myself. And the "well-intentioned" cover for programs whose actual motives are mainly selfish is endemic not only in democratic politics but in politics everywhere. We also find it in the market. The businessman, changing his product line to make more money, is apt to refer to the change as "serving the customer." In fact, if he makes more money, he probably will, but his motives are somewhat more crass.

Bismarck obviously knew of this, and he was one of the more successful politicians of modern times. The changes he made in Germany when he invented what we now call the welfare state both directly benefit a large group of people and could be argued for on charitable grounds. That political trick has continued.

That the proponents of most generalized plans are not really particularly interested in helping the poor seems to me fairly certain, mainly because in reading their works I never find discussions of the actual probability that their programs will hurt the poor. In general, as I demonstrated above, the program can be altered in such a way that it does not hurt the poor, but that is never part of the real-life political proposal. From this, I deduce that the actual motive of most of these generalization programs is not to help the poor but to help people who are well above the poverty level.

Once again, I am not criticizing people for trying to benefit themselves through use of the political process. We all do it, some more successfully than others. What I am saying is that we should have intellectual clarity in dealing with these problems. We may not particularly want to help the poor, but if we do want to help the poor, the effective methods, in general, are means-tested, direct-aid programs. Free medical aid for the poor, pensions for the elderly poor, college scholarships for the children of the poor (probably with arrangements so that if the children of the poor later become wealthy they will repay the state for this investment)—all are better ways of helping the poor than general programs which provide services to everyone.

The point of this chapter has been that means-tested, direct aid for the poor, rather than the Bismarckian generalization of programs for everyone, is more likely to help the poor, if that be the objective. As I said at the beginning, this seems obvious, and it is hard to see why people argue on the other side, but the fact remains they do.

HELPING THE POOR VS. HELPING THE WELL-ORGANIZED

Discussion of government income redistribution usually turns on the problem of whether we should try to equalize incomes. I hope that I have convinced the reader by now that this is only a minor aspect of the problem. Most government income redistribution goes not to the poor but to people who for one reason or another have sufficient political influence to get it. The poor are normally not among this group, although they certainly do receive considerable amounts of funds from the government, probably mainly because people are charitable.

Why the basic discussion has tended to deal only with helping the poor is not clear. Let me go back to a piece of not-so-ancient history: the gasoline price controls which were installed after the organization of the oil cartel in 1973. The average person remembers this as a period in which the newspapers denounced the large oil companies and in which he had to spend long periods of time in gasoline lines. He may also remember that gasoline prices were lower then than they are now, although, interestingly, if you allow for inflation they were not very much lower.

Let us look at this as a political example of redistribution. It was talked about at the time as something which was necessary to prevent the poor from having to pay too high prices for their gasoline. In a way it was slightly pro-poor, because the time of the poor is worth less than the time of other people, and, hence, sitting in gas lines was less costly to them than it was to others. Indeed, some of the poor actually got jobs[1] taking other people's cars through gas lines. But this was a minor effect.

What, then, were the major effects of price controls other than long gas lines? The price controls held the price of gasoline at a price so low that it was not possible for someone to import Arab oil at the cartel price and sell it. There was a control on the wellhead price of American oil which was kept much below the Arab price. This would have meant that those American oil companies with a lot of domestic capacity would have made a lot of money,

Reprinted, with permission, from *Welfare for the Well-to-Do* (Dallas: Fisher Institute, 1983), 63–72.

1. Which they did not report to their relief supervisor.

and those that did not have domestic capacity would have gone bankrupt if nothing else had been done. The government, therefore, set up an elaborate scheme under which, in essence, domestic oil-well owners were required to subsidize the import of oil from the Arabs. Sending in the Marines is no longer fashionable, and the only price, therefore, that could be kept down was the American oil-well price.[2]

What were the results? First, American car owners bought gasoline at a lower price than they otherwise would have. Of course, they had to sit in lines, and that is a costly activity. It seems likely, however, that the average driver benefited in net, even if not much, from the combination of lower prices and long gas lines. This gain presumably was roughly proportional to the amount of gasoline consumed, which means, of course, that it was to some extent larger for upper-income people than for lower-income people.

The other big gainers here were those extremely wealthy people, the Arab sheikhs. Without the subsidy for imported oil, the amounts purchased by the United States would have fallen off considerably. This was, of course, the program that was implemented in Europe. I made some calculations on this, based on the existing data on elasticity, and concluded that for every dollar saved by American gasoline consumers, the members of OPEC made an additional two dollars. Of course, the domestic consumer had a good deal of the dollar he saved offset by having to sit in gas lines and rearrange his life to meet the shortage. (It is possible that if the United States had not put on the price controls the drop in demand for Arab oil would have been large enough that the cartel would have collapsed. The last is only a possibility, but we should not have been offering the Arabs a guarantee against the risk of breaking their cartel, even if that risk was not gigantic.)

Here, then, we see a program which was argued for in terms of helping the poor and which helped them only slightly if at all. It did help almost all Americans who didn't own oil wells, although the help was probably modest. There was a very large gain from the program for a group of people who most Americans don't think are particularly meritorious and certainly are not poor, the Arab sheikhs.

I should say that there is no evidence whatsoever that the Arabs lobbied for the program. They apparently did not understand it either. Indeed, it is astonishing that ever since the original cartel, the American government has

2. I am simplifying this system. Some of my readers may think oversimplifying, but the full details are too lengthy to elaborate here.

carried out a number of policies which indirectly tend to stabilize the cartel. As far as I know, in no case has Arab political influence been behind these policies. They are usually intended for something else and just accidentally benefit the cartel. They have, however, cost the American taxpayer and gasoline purchaser a great deal of money.

My point here has been that a good many programs which purport to help the poor actually do not, and "helping the poor" is in a way simply a cover for other motives. Clearly, the American voter who talked about the need to keep price controls on gasoline to help the poor was primarily concerned with price controls to help himself. He did not understand economics enough to realize that this was not a good way of helping himself, even though that was his objective. The aid to the poor was a political cover story.

We find this commonly in the redistribution which goes on in our society. A great many programs purport to be aimed at helping the poor, but actually are aimed at helping someone else—someone who is politically more influential. It should be said, of course, that there are programs that do help the poor, and some of the programs which actually aim at benefiting the upper middle class have as a by-product some aid to the poor.

But, many government programs which are announced in terms of helping the poor simply injure them. Most of our agricultural programs make food more expensive, and these programs tend to concentrate on the types of foods that the poor consume. Luxury foods are seldom produced under acreage restrictions, but wheat is.

What I am suggesting, then, is that the basic argument on income redistribution has been miscast. One can be interested in helping the poor and against our present income redistribution policies.[3] On the other hand, one can be interested in getting some special government benefit and totally uninterested in the poor.

This is the reason, I suspect, why the means-tested programs are unpopular now. They help the poor and no one else. The politically powerful groups who would like to use the government to increase their wealth cannot generally benefit from means-tested programs. But if we want to help the poor, that's the way to go.

How did we get into this situation? Most people learn in their high school civics courses that the government exists to serve the public interest and to

3. When I say "our" here, I really mean the whole civilized world, not just the United States. Our programs are very similar to those in other countries.

equalize incomes. It should be frankly said that as a matter of fact the government does many things which serve the public interest, and it is quite possible to argue that it also equalizes income. Furthermore, if we look through history, most governments have done some things to benefit the public interest, maintaining police and defense forces, building roads, etc., and have put heavy taxes on those wealthy people who are not government officials while making charitable gifts to the poor. They still do so today.

Throughout history, however, governments have also been used as a means of increasing the wealth of people who are by no means poor. The various royal palaces scattered across Europe are evidence that at least one group of wealthy people found the government a source of more wealth. But the kings and noblemen who lived in those palaces were not the only people who used the government to augment their wealth. From earliest times, governments have been used as a source of revenue. We should not be surprised about this. Most human beings are interested in improving their incomes and are willing to use a wide variety of methods to do so. If I can raise my income by lobbying in Congress for something or other, I will do so.

This whole subject—the use of the government as a way of increasing wealth—was rather ignored by social scientists for the last century. Recently, a great deal of interest, particularly among economists, has been focused on the problem. It has the undescriptive title of "rent-seeking."[4] Lurking behind this poor title is simply the study of the way in which the government is used to raise people's income.

The subject of this study is complicated in detail, but its general lines are simple, and indeed many of my readers may regard them as obvious. I would not quarrel with the view that the main outlines are obvious, but would point out that they are not normally talked about in discussions of income redistribution. Normally, income redistribution is discussed in terms of helping the poor and not in terms of helping those who want to be helped.

In a democracy, the way it works is fairly simple and straightforward. A great many, probably most, voters tend to vote in terms of what they think will benefit them. The Tombigbee Canal, for example, will indeed benefit people living along its course, mainly because its construction activity will raise their wealth and not because of the canal itself. We should expect them

4. See "Toward a Theory of the Rent-Seeking Society," edited by James M. Buchanan, Robert D. Tollison, and Gordon Tullock, Texas A&M University Press, 1980, for a collection of articles on the topic.

and the political representatives they have in Washington to favor it. Similarly, farmers benefit from our farm program and vote for people who favor it.

We do not want to oversimplify here. Most of the residents along the Tombigbee, and most farmers, are not solely interested in their own wealth, but they are interested in it. Thus, most people running for Congress talk about the public good, helping the poor, etc., but also give great emphasis to various things which they know will directly benefit special interest groups in their constituency.

Once a matter has reached Congress, various bills dealing with the special interests are passed by a combination of logrolling and lobbying. Logrolling, in which congressmen trade votes on issues, is the foundation of democratic politics, although not discussed much in the high school civics courses. Lobbying is also important, not only in democratic politics but in all other kinds of politics that we know of. It does get discussed in high school civic classes, mainly being denounced as wicked.

I don't wish to quarrel with anyone who believes lobbying is wicked, but I should point out that we can hardly expect people to stop doing it as long as it is profitable to the lobbyist. If we organize ourselves and hire a lobbyist, and he tells congressmen that we are going to vote the next election in terms of how successfully the congressmen get our interests supported, we can expect that the congressmen will make a good college try and that we will get a reasonable return on our resources. Looked at from the standpoint of the person contributing to the lobby or voting in favor of his special interests, the situation is just like any other investment or act intended to increase his income. This is what is called "rent-seeking," and it is an unfortunate characteristic of our modern society that this is immensely important.

If we look over the world's history we find most of the time that this kind of rent-seeking has been immensely important. During a period in the 19th century it was relatively unimportant. It was not that the governments did not engage in rent-seeking, but they were small enough that rent-seeking was a rather small percentage of the gross national product. By now, the second half of the 20th century, governments all over the world have gone back to the historic norm. They are once more quite large, and once more rent-seeking has become a large percentage of the G.N.P.

Rent-seeking is economically important, not because the various special interest groups distort the economy, although this does occur, but because the resources invested in attempting to obtain these special privileges could have been invested in more productive activities. Rent-seeking and the use of government to obtain wealth is, from the standpoint of society as a whole, a completely wasteful activity. Somebody gains and somebody loses. Further, it is always true that the person who loses loses much more than the person who gains. This is different from the market activity where the gain of Mr. A may lead to no loss but to a gain to all other members of society. If it does lead to a loss of other members of society, then those losses will be smaller than Mr. A's gain, so that there is a net gain for society as a whole.[5]

To a considerable extent, income redistribution is the result of rent-seeking. To a considerable extent, however, it is rationalized in terms of helping the poor even if it doesn't. The reason for this apparently is simply that information conditions in politics are poor.

Once again, we are turning to an area which, for many generations, was largely ignored by social scientists but has now become quite important. This is the economics of information. Scholars of this area study the question of whether people will acquire information or won't, usually with the assumption that they only acquire information which is worth as much to them as the cost of getting it. This assumption is a simplifying one. All of us have a good deal of information we have acquired because we were simply interested in it or we thought we had a duty to acquire it. If the system is to operate well, however, we should have more information.

The basic problem with democratic politics is that, for most voters, acquiring politically relevant information is not worth more than it costs. Consider, for example, a citizen voter who during the time of the first establishment of the oil cartel, 1973–74, decided that he would become well-informed about the actual effect of the price controls in the United States. The average citizen is not accustomed to doing that kind of research, is not familiar with the type of libraries which carry the data, and doesn't have the necessary training to understand a good deal of the material he would find if he looked. If he actually wanted to be well-informed, he would have to put a great deal of time and effort into studying the problem.

But once he had become well-informed what effect would it have? The only result would be that he could cast an informed vote in the next election and perhaps write a letter to his congressman. The payoff to him in the sense of changing American policy would be so small as to be quite invisible. Thus,

5. I am simplifying fairly drastically here. In particular, there are, of course, the cases where there are large externalities in which the market does not work. Fortunately, these do not seem to be overwhelmingly common.

he would have spent a great deal of time and energy in searching for information which actually did not benefit him. He would have raised his income considerably more had he looked for some information directly concerning his private business.

This line of reasoning frequently makes people indignant. The argument that we all have a duty to be well-informed is repeated frequently by teachers and preachers. I do not want to quarrel with it. I simply would point out that most people do not have any material motive for becoming well-informed about politics. They do know something about politics because they find it an interesting topic. As far as we can tell, however, their knowledge of politics tends to be rather superficial and concentrated on exciting rather than important matters. Public opinion polls invariably show that the voters are badly informed about complex topics. Since the bulk of income redistribution matters are complex, they are badly informed about them.

Here it should be said that the special interest groups normally have an interest in diminishing the information of the average voter. If they can sell him some false tale which supports their particular effort to rob the treasury, it pays. They have resources and normally make efforts to produce this kind of misinformation. But that would not work if the voter had a strong motive to learn the truth. There is not much point in trying to convince housewives that the canned tomatoes you are selling are much better quality than they are. She may buy one can, but as soon as she opens it she finds it is of low quality and doesn't go back. In politics, unfortunately, this rule does not exist, because the voter never has the opportunity to open the can.

The problem, then, appears to be a serious one. The government, in addition to generating various public goods and to some extent helping the poor, is being used to a large extent to transfer income back and forth in our society in a highly wasteful manner. Further, if we look over history, this has been a characteristic role of government throughout almost all of recorded time. It is true that the 19th and early 20th centuries, in the area around the North Atlantic Ocean, this activity was rather minor, but that was the historical exception. The normal fate is a rent-seeking government.

What can we do? We should turn to the experience of the 19th century, the great exception. In England, from about 1775 to about 1850, a general climate of opinion was built up under which the government was confined to those activities which it could actually perform reasonably well. This climate of opinion developed partly as the result of clear and unrelenting propaganda by the people who understood the problem and who were interested in benefiting both themselves and the country. This was a period in which a large number of intellectuals argued not for larger slices of the pie but for a larger pie.

Unfortunately, the situation changed. Today the government is engaged in many activities, most of which are rationalized in terms of either improving the national product or helping the poor. In fact, the government's major activity is redistribution.

What is needed today to curb government overextension is to duplicate the intellectual accomplishments of the early 19th century. Voters must be given accurate information about the true nature, purposes, and effects of government redistribution programs as they affect them. Without it, they will remain unable to evaluate redistribution on the basis of actual results rather than alleged intentions, and unable to know if they really want to pay the price.

The proponents of redistribution claim that their programs help the poor. They do help the poor—which they also help to create—but not much. Basically, the modern redistributive state transfers money back and forth within the middle class on the basis of the power of political organization and public misinformation. This political power is not easily overcome, but we should see to it that the truth is known. Until it is, the government will continue to serve the interests of political factions in the middle class, using money appropriated under the guise of helping the poor.

HORIZONTAL TRANSFERS

This chapter and the one immediately thereafter will be devoted to the rather simple model in which transfers are made from *A* to *B* solely because *B* wants them and not because *A* has any desire to make the transfers. That such activities are common in the modern world is, I take it, obvious. It is also obvious that such transfers have always been part of government activities. We should not be surprised that profit-making individuals should seek profit out of the use of the coercive power of the state to obtain funds from other people. It is reported that when Alexander the Great had a pirate chief brought before him, the pirate said, "The only difference between us is that you have more men and ships." This was, in fact, a correct evaluation of the situation, although it did not save the pirate chief's life.

Indeed, although Alexander probably had other motives, such as spreading Greek civilization, there seems no doubt that his principal motive in his successful war with the Persian Empire was to convert himself from the hereditary chief of a small kingdom north of Greece into a world emperor. It certainly raised his personal living standard, and, indeed, it is now thought that his death came because he took too much advantage of the luxuries which his conquests made available to him.

Alexander is not the only example of this sort of thing. Not very long ago, the owner of some real estate in Blacksburg, Virginia, asked the zoning board for a zone change. The owner's motive was simple and straightforward: the land was worth $500,000 more in a new zoning category than in the old. His proposed change was objected to by a number of surrounding householders, all of whom would have found the value of their houses falling if he received his variance. Once again, their motives were fairly straightforward, although it should be said that both parties to this dispute spent some time arguing that their particular view as to what the zoning category should be was in accord with truth, justice, and beauty.

All of this should not surprise us and is not intended as a criticism of

Reprinted, with kind permission of Kluwer Academic Publishers, from *Economics of Income Redistribution*, Kluwer-Nijhoff Studies in Human Issues: An International Series in the Social Sciences (Boston: Kluwer-Nijhoff, 1983), 17–31.

Alexander the Great, the pirate, or my neighbors in Blacksburg. All of them behaved as we expect human beings to do. Indeed, if the pirate had been a little more successful and had been able to found a kingdom in some of the islands in the Mediterranean, no doubt everyone would have quietly forgotten that he was originally a pirate.

The discussion of government that one normally finds in the literature in democratic countries is actually a discussion from the standpoint of an atypical historical experience. The world today is largely controlled by despots of one sort or another. Further, throughout history, democracy has been quite a rare form of government. Limited franchise democracies spread over much of the Mediterranean world during the period of the efflorescence of Greece and early Rome, a number of limited franchise democracies developed as city-states during the Middle Ages, and full-fledged democracies of the sort we know began developing essentially in England, and then spread throughout much of the world. The high point of that development was in 1914, with democracy having been, on the whole, in retreat since then. Today, democratic governments are largely, although not entirely, confined to the North Atlantic Basin.

The first governments of which we have historical knowledge were not democracies but despotisms, and so far as we know, historically, democracy has always developed out of despotism rather than being founded itself. The myth of a group of people getting together to collectively decide on an organization to generate public goods is a myth,[1] but a myth that is of great value for certain types of political and social analysis.

If you look at the real world, however, it seems highly probable that the state did not originate as people voluntarily cooperating, but rather as someone with a comparative advantage in violence conquering his neighbors for the specific purpose of taxing them.[2] Tribal or village organizations very likely are much older than man himself; that is, we probably moved across the line from ape to man already organized in hunting bands. Larger organizations,

1. Something a little different than this has happened occasionally. People who already have democracy have had constitutional conventions to provide improved democratic institutions. Our own example in Philadelphia, in my opinion, fully deserves the praise it has received.

2. For a summary of the anthropological literature on the origin of the state, see Robert H. Bates, "The Centralization of African Societies," Social Science Working Paper 400, California Institute of Technology, and Fred H. Willhoite, Jr., "Reciprocity, Political Origins, and Legitimacy," Coe College. In the Willhoite paper, the first few pages, which are devoted to biology, can reasonably be skipped.

however, had to be invented, and from what little we know about the early period, they apparently were invented by a simple conquest. Conquest, of course, always remained important in the development of government. The reason that the founding fathers were able to meet at Philadelphia was previous conquests, and the importance of their work there was immensely increased by a steady policy of conquests of the American continent carried out by the citizens of the United States. We are all much wealthier as a result of this action than we would be had our ancestors not used forceful methods to create a very considerable transfer.

But the objective of this chapter is not forceful transfers by governments through international action, although making or preventing such transfers has always been a major government action, but internal transfers—transfers not like those of Alexander the Great but like my neighbor who wanted a zoning variance. Further, although administrative action, like the decision on the zoning category, is certainly of great importance to the wealth of many people, we shall begin with programs in which *A* is actually taxed, and the money is used in some way for the benefit of *B*. Normally, as we shall see, the benefit for *B* is rather indirect, and the tax may also be rather indirect, but that is, in general, necessary for the enacting of the transfer.

The tax on *A*, let us say, a head tax used to make a direct, specific payment to *B*, is usually regarded by economists as efficient. They will say that the tax simply moves from one point on the Pareto optimal frontier to another. At best, economists will discuss whether the change in incentives caused by the prospect of such a tax in the future leads to less physical production.

The other type of efficiency, i.e., a greater total utility from the change, even if it has no effect or perhaps a negative effect on production, is seldom if ever discussed by economists except in the one special case of transfers to the poor. Put more generally, if for some reason we believe that $1 in the hands of *B* will generate more utility for *B* than it would for *A* if it were still in *A*'s hands, then we can increase total utility by the transfer. Unfortunately, we will very rarely have any direct evidence of this sort on utility, although rough judgments can sometimes be made. Once again, some more formal analysis will be undertaken a little later.

It should be said that in this chapter and the next we will not discuss transfers from upper-income groups to lower-income groups. That subject will be deferred. Here, we will assume that the transfer is horizontal, i.e., goes to people in roughly the same income class. There will be some discussion of the tendency of the upper-income groups to lose in such transfers, but, basically, we will think of the transfer as among people regardless of their comparative incomes. The transfer is as likely to go from *A* to *B* regardless of who between *A* and *B* has more money.

The reason for this restriction is that it is analytically much easier to discuss separately transfers motivated by the desire of the recipient to receive them and charitable transfers. Unfortunately, in the real world the two tend to be mixed, and after having dealt with the two separately, it will be necessary to consider them jointly in later chapters. I must ask the reader, however, to put aside temporarily his desire to look at the real-world situation and instead to consider only some simplified models. I hope that the result of this procedure will be greater clarity and understanding.

It is now time to introduce some formal analytical apparatus. In this apparatus, I will assume that we know the demand of various parties for income transfers. Since the invention of the demand-revealing process,[3] we have realized that we can operationally produce such demand curves, and, hence, it is legitimate to use them. I should say, however, that, although their general shape is correct, the demand curves used in this book are simply assumed rather than the result of empirical research.

In Figure 1, we show the size of the transfer from *A* to *B* on the horizontal axis, and the transfer cost in the customary $1 unit on the vertical axis. Thus, line *BB* represents continuous identical units of transfer from left to right; the larger the transfer made, the farther it would go in that direction. The demand-revealing process permits us to draw in the demand curves of the parties for any government action. In this case, however, there is no complication. *A* has a zero demand for all units of the transfer because he gets no benefits out of them, and *B*'s demand for each unit of the transfer is the horizontal line *BB*, which is also the total demand. It is clear that the lines do not intersect, and if we just stopped here, we could not say anything about an optimal transfer except that it could be zero. As a matter of fact, however, there are at least some slight administrative costs in taxing *A* and delivering the money to *B*, and these are shown by drawing a line *CC*, the cost of the transfer, slightly above *BB*, the benefit of the transfer. Since the demand for the transfer (line *BB*) lies everywhere below the cost of the transfer (line *CC*), under the demand-revealing rule, the optimal transfer is zero, which will not surprise many people. However, if the status quo from which we started was

3. See Gordon Tullock and T. Nicolaus Tideman for a basic explanation. "A New and Superior Process for Making Social Choices," *Journal of Political Economy* (October 1976): 1145–59.

FIGURE 1
Transfer costs according to size of transfer

the one in which the transfer was being made, then the opposite situation would exist. The cost of terminating the transfer would be line *BB*, for what *B* was getting, and the benefit would be line *CC*, which would be the amount that the transfer was injuring *A*. Since line *CC* is everywhere above line *BB*, this reverse transfer would be efficient in our present very simple model. Once again, there are no surprises here. It may be that the reason we never observe this simple, direct kind of transfer, in which *A* is taxed for the benefit of *B* unless *A* happened to be much wealthier than *B*, is the obviousness of the above line of reasoning.

The demand-revealing process reveals demand (how much people would pay for something) and not the utility obtained from it. It is certainly possible that *B* would gain much more utility out of the transfer than *A*. Suppose, for example, that *B* is a well-known bon vivant who is likely to enjoy almost anything, while *A* is a very inefficient generator of utility. Under these circumstances, if we redrew the diagram to show utility, the *BB* line would lie far above the *CC* line.

Unfortunately, we have little reliable information about people's efficiency in generating utility, so we cannot do this. *B* may be a more efficient generator of utility than *A*, but he may also be less efficient. The principle of sufficient reason leads us to assume that the distribution recipients and beneficiaries of such transfers, in terms of their efficiency in generating utility, are probably about the same in most cases.

There are certain things we can say about utility generation, however. First, we are talking about a monetary transfer, and almost everyone has agreed that above a very low point monetary income is subject to a declining margin of returns. If that is so, whatever the utility that *B* gets, it would decline consistently from left to right. Similarly, the declining margin of utility on the part of *A*, the taxpayer, indicates that the cost line, if drawn in utility terms, would rise steadily from left to right. If we did know the utility of the two parties and drew in their demand lines in those terms, then even if *B* were a more efficient generator of utility than *A*, the two lines might intersect.

As I remarked earlier, a rather odd definition of efficiency is often used when discussing income transfers, i.e., the actual effect on total physical or measured product. What effect would this transfer have on efficiency measured in that way? The assumption a priori is none, because there has been no change in any of the margins, and the transfer from *A* to *B*, which increases the wealth of one and lowers it for the other, should have wealth effects that cancel out. Once again, all of this assumes that we do not know a great deal about the two parties, because it might be that one or the other was particularly sensitive to changes in wealth.

We rarely find this simple cash transfer in the real world. What we find are much more complex transfers which have definite economic effects. Why these dominate will be discussed later, but it may be good to stop and consider a particular type of realistic transfer and look at its efficiency effects.

Suppose that the government puts a tax on the sale of fluid milk and uses this to subsidize the sale of cheese. This may seem absurd, but as a matter of fact, an arrangement that has this net effect is part of the American government's regulation of the dairy industry.[4] It should be said that, as far as I know, this arrangement was not originally put in to injure the sellers of whole milk and benefit the sellers of cheese but to profit the dairy farmers. Further, it is only a small part of the total package of controls on dairy farming that were intended to aid the return of dairy farming. Nevertheless, it is a nice simple case from our standpoint, and the transfer effects I am going to describe do, indeed, occur.[5]

4. Note that all of this is really of more historical interest than current. The arrangement still exists but is now completely dominated by other aspects of the program.

5. The following discussion will tend to separate the purveyors of whole milk from purveyors of cheese. As a matter of fact, there is a substantial overlap in the two industries with the same enterprises frequently being involved in both.

The first thing to be said about this particular tax is that the benefit to the cheese manufacturers and the harm to the sellers of whole milk are fairly modest. Both use the same raw material, milk from dairies, and the net effect of this arrangement was intended, to some extent, to raise the price of milk as it was sold by the dairy farmer. This increase was, however, small if it ever really existed. The benefit to the producers of cheese was simply that they could sell their cheese at lower prices and, hence, could sell more of it.[6] The cost was partly borne by consumers, who, facing an artificially lowered price for cheese and an artificially raised price for milk, allocated their consumption budget in a way that was optimal from their standpoint but that gave them less satisfaction than they could have obtained from the same funds had the government not introduced this program.

The manufacturers of cheese, however, had a certain number of facilities for cheese, and with this subsidy the demand for their plants was now higher than it had been before. They would, therefore, for a while, earn scarcity rents on their cheese-making capacity, and this in essence would be the entire transfer they received. Contrariwise, the milk sales organizations would find that they had some excess capacity because the rise in the cost of milk meant that they could sell less of it, and hence they would, for a time, face an industry depression in which they received less than a normal return on their capital investment.

With time, we would anticipate that these factors would be adjusted by capital market flows. More money would flow into manufacturing cheese until the return of resources there was normal, and at the same time, resources would flow out of the fluid milk industry until once again resources received normal returns. The end product then would be a situation in which both the milk and cheese-making industries were technically efficient and earning normal returns. Society as a whole would be injured to some extent because of the inefficient division of the consumer's budget between cheese and milk, and there might be a gain in the price of whole milk as sold by the dairy-farming industry.

Here we have what is very clearly an inefficient transfer and, furthermore, an inefficient transfer from which at the end of the process no one is gaining.[7]

6. Now they sell a large part of it to the government, which is competing with the economic community in Europe for the honor of being the largest owner of elderly cheese and butter.

7. If the dairy farming industry gained from the transfer, presumably resources would move in until these gains had been dissipated.

Unfortunately, the second part of our reasoning, the demonstration that the termination of the transfer would be optimal, is not so clear here. If the tax and subsidy were abolished, then there would be a period in which there would be an excess of resources in the cheese-making industry and a shortage in the milk industry. This would lead to a situation in which the resources used in both of those industries were used in less than their optimal way, and in a strict technical sense, both industries would remain somewhat inefficient until the necessary capital adjustments had, with time, been made.

There is no law of nature that says that the gain to the owners of the milk sales organization would be greater than the loss to the producers of cheese. Indeed, I think that the opposite is true because the capital adjusts in the milk industry much more rapidly than in the cheese industry, and the temporary gains to the owners of milk sales organizations would be less than the temporary losses to the owners of the cheese factories. Needless to say, I do not conclude by arguing that the subsidy arrangement should be retained. It is, however, a more complicated situation.

As we shall see below, this is rather typical of the transfers that are motivated by the desire of the recipients to receive them. There are some cases in which the transfer remains permanent—a medieval baron who seizes Monaco and is able to successfully pass it on to his descendants, for example. But more normally, the transfer is dissipated rather quickly. Capital and other resources flow into the subsidized industry and out of the taxed industry (which may be the whole economy) until the returns are normal.

Once the capital adjustment has occurred, no one is making any profit out of the new arrangement, but we could expect that the cheese makers would fight hard to retain it because of the losses they would suffer if it is cancelled. In this case, the owners of the dairies would be fighting on the side of the general public, since they would gain from the termination.

The general inefficiency of this transfer is obviously great. The adjustment in the prices of cheese and milk does not lead, even in the short run, to pure profits equivalent to the change in prices. Production will rise in the cheese industry and fall in the milk industry, but the net change in profits will be considerably smaller than the total change in receipts in the two industries. The present value of the total change at the time the tax and subsidy are introduced is that of a declining profit and loss, which, even in the first year, will be considerably smaller than the change in receipts. The change in prices will be more or less permanent, although the shift in resources will lead to some change over time.

But this is by no means the only total cost here. Normally, such transfers do not simply come out of the blue; they are lobbied for by the beneficiaries and lobbied against by the victims.[8] This whole subject, which goes under the name of *rent-seeking*, will be discussed later, but it should be said that the total amount of resources used by potential beneficiaries of government transfer advocating the transfer, and by potential victims of such transfers opposing it, may well be of the same order of magnitude as the net transfer itself. Thus, it is quite possible that this inefficient transfer will, in net, generate substantially no benefit for anyone, although the harm imposed is considerable.

But if the transfers are hard on everyone, as I have argued, why do we see so many of them? Indeed, making transfers of this sort is surely the largest single activity of the modern state. The answer is the nature of the political process, which makes such transfers politically desirable even if, *sub specie aeternitatis*, they are clearly undesirable.

Let me then begin discussing the politics of these transfers. I shall begin with a simple model, which the reader may think unrealistic. I agree with the reader, but the model is much discussed in the relevant public choice literature, and there are certain aspects of the model that can be observed in the real world. In Figure 2, we show a polity with five citizens, *A*, *B*, *C*, *D*, and *E*. At situation 1, they have an income that is $10 for *A*, *B*, *C*, and *D*, and $20 for *E*. This particular polity makes its decisions by simple majority voting, and, therefore, it is at least theoretically possible for a coalition of *C*, *D*, and *E* to put confiscatory taxes on *A* and *B* and divide the money evenly among them, as is shown in situation 2.

This is, of course, not the only coalition of three that could exist for redistributive purposes. In situation 3, I show another coalition of three people, in this case *B*, *C*, and *D*, who through their majority vote have deprived *A* and *E* of all of their funds. Note that *B*, *C*, and *D* are better off in this coalition than in situation 2. Again, there are many other coalitions that could beat situation 2 or situation 1 or, for that matter, situation 3.

Situation 4 is a coalition that beats the income distribution in situation 3, although not that in situation 1. It is more or less a theoretical example of how unegalitarian majority voting could get by a series of votes. If situation 2 were put against situation 1, a majority would be obtained. If situation 3

8. In this particular case, the basic cause of the provision was lobbying by the dairy farmers, not by the cheese industry, but it may be that the cheese industry had something to do with the particular form of the regulations.

	A	B	C	D	E
1	10	10	10	10	20
2	0	0	$16\frac{2}{3}$	$16\frac{2}{3}$	$26\frac{2}{3}$
3	0	20	20	20	0
4	1	0	0	21	38
5	0	1	1	0	58
6	0	0	20	20	20
7	15	30	0	0	15

FIGURE 2
Polity of five whose decisions are made by simple majority voting

were put against situation 2, a majority for situation 3 would be obtained, and if situation 4 were put against situation 3, once again a majority would be obtained. In practice, of course, nothing remotely like situation 4 could be obtained in any voting body, because no one has the kind of agenda control necessary to carry out the series of votes that would lead to it. Further, if it were obtained, it would be abolished in the next round. Another extremely inegalitarian coalition in which they that have shall receive is demonstrated in situation 5. It could beat situation 4, once again under the assumption that individuals simply always vote for a change that benefits them. In the real world nothing like this is probable, but situation 5 does indicate that it is not inconceivable that the wealthier member of the group, in this case *E*, will do very well out of the voting process.

In practice, of course, the coalition in which the three parties end about equal is a bit more likely than the inegalitarian coalition shown in situations 2, 4, and 5. The fact that *E* starts with more income does not really have any great effect on the ultimate outcome, because by majority voting all of the money can be shared in any way one desires, and that includes his $20 as well as the $10 possessed by each of the other four. There is $60 to distribute by majority vote; the fact that *E* started with $20 of it is simply irrelevant. This is the one element of this model that I think may have some application to the real world. Wealthy people may indeed be members of coalitions, but the coalition is apt to be egalitarian. For situation 6, which is the same as situation 3 except that *E* is now a member of the winning coalition and surely much better off than he was in situation 3 even though he simply retained his original wealth and gained nothing. A potential high-tax payer is an inconvenient person to put into the winning coalition unless he is willing to agree that the ultimate outcome is taxes and payments that leave him more or less as well-off as the other members of the coalition. If he wants more, it is unlikely he will get it.

This is merely a special application of the general view going back to von Neumann and Morgenstern that voting coalitions tend to be egalitarian, not in the sense that the whole society is equally treated but that the members of the winning coalition are relatively equal among themselves. The argument for this is simply that *D* in situation 4 and *E* in situations 4 and 5 are in extremely dangerous positions. They are likely to find that another coalition has been constructed in which they are left out.

The distinction does not have to be that extreme. In situation 7, we show a coalition which would beat situation 3 if everyone simply voted their direct self-interest. Suppose, however, that *A* and *E* approach *B* with the offer of this coalition. Unless *B* has some kind of legal way of binding them, he arguably should reject the offer on the grounds that once he has broken the coalition of situation 3, it is highly likely that *A* and *E* will then form a more egalitarian coalition with either *C* or *D*. Thus, in a way, this kind of pure transfer coalition has a tendency toward egalitarianism among the winners and among the losers, but not between the winners and the losers.

As a matter of fact, we do not see this kind of transfer very much in the real world. Not only do we not see direct cash transfers enacted in this way, if we look at the various government benefits that are distributed through society in noncash forms, we do not find that they all accrue to the voters for whatever party happens to be in power. This is incidentally true in England, where there are no constitutional restrictions, just as in the United States.

What keeps this kind of income redistribution from being carried to an extreme level? There are, I think, three explanations, two of which are not particularly technical but are also weak. The first explanation is simply that people feel that it is immoral to make this kind of transfer. Granted the other transfers that they vote for, I find this very dubious. Another variant of this same argument—if they do it, other people will later do it to them—is simply a rational argument for an essentially moral position.

We do find a great many transfers in society enacted by other means and in other circumstances, so I do not believe that these moral principles are very strong. Moral principles do have one political effect: they create a market for rationalizations. People apparently do feel at least vaguely guilty if they use the state to plunder their neighbor, so there is a steady, continuous demand for arguments to prove that one is not plundering one's neighbor, that he originally got his money by theft, that he is a wicked man, that the gods of history are on your side, etc. The number of special interest groups who have invented proofs so that direct transfers to them are in the public interest is legend. There does seem to be a market for this kind of thing, and a great many intellectuals are engaged in filling the demand.

The second nontechnical explanation for what keeps extreme kinds of income distribution from happening is simply that the incentive effects would be monstrously undesirable. If simple cash transfers by majority voting were a major function of government, then it is likely that the principal activity of society would become arranging or resisting such transfers. Production would be unwise, because you could have the money transferred away from you. It would be much like a society in which private theft would be legal, except that in this case you would not even be able to protect yourself against the negative transfer. The reduction in total production would be immense.[9] It could be argued then that no one would want to get into the game.[10] It would always be to your interest to organize such a coalition, because whether you organize one or do not has relatively little effect on whether other people do. It is better to be a member of the first such winning coalition than to be a loser on the first coalition.

Nevertheless, as I have said before, we do not observe this kind of coalition in politics in the real world. Further, we do not even observe coalitions that concentrate all of their benefits on their winners when the transfer is not

9. Transfers from the wealthy to the poor also have incentive effects, but they are much milder.

10. This assumes that the constitution permits this kind of transfer. The British constitution and many other constitutions do. It is not clear whether such transfers would be constitutional in the United States. They would certainly require careful draftsmanship. We do not observe them in England.

cash. Most transfers in modern society take the form of such things as public works projects, taxes on competing goods, regulations, etc. There are straightforward cash transfers to certain groups (those connected with the social security system are large), but these fundamentally are quite different from what we are talking about now.

To take an example of what does not happen, when the Labour Party wins in England it normally enacts various pieces of legislation that will to some extent benefit its members and injure those who voted Conservative. The degree to which it transfers funds in this way is, however, decidedly limited. Take one obvious example. Districts that vote for Labour do not seem to do any better in public works projects than districts that vote Conservative. Indeed, districts that do best seem to be the marginal districts whose vote might possibly go the other way next election. The strong position of the marginal districts is, of course, obviously politically sensible, but why spend any money at all in safely Conservative districts?

The answer to these questions is not absolutely clear. One answer is that large transfer coalitions of the sort which we have been discussing are intrinsically highly unstable.[11] Briefly, the internal dynamics of the coalition are under continuous, severe strain because the losers always have to offer at least marginal improvements to a few members of the winning coalition as incentives to switch. Since in the real world these transfers are handled mainly in the form of special projects and not direct cash, exact equality is not possible. Under the circumstances, the organizational problem of coalitions of this sort is just too great.

But we do observe a great many transfers carried through by democratic voting bodies. How is this done? The answer is that a different type of vote trading is used. This is called *explicit logrolling*.[12] Turning once again to Figure 1, suppose on Monday, *A* goes to *B* and *C* and tells them that he is putting up for vote on that day a bill in which everybody will be taxed $2 in order to pay *A* $10, or a net gain to *A* of $8. *A* suggests that *B* and *C* enter similar bills to their advantage and agrees to vote for them when the bills come up. This will give *A* a net profit of $4. *B* and *C* agree, and the bill is passed. On Tuesday, *B*, who already has an agreement with *A*, approaches *D*, suggesting that he will in the future vote for a similar bill for *D*. The bill

11. See my "Why So Much Stability," *Public Choice* 37, no. 2, pp. 189–202.

12. For an exhaustive analysis of logrolling and its efficiency effects, see James M. Buchanan and Gordon Tullock, *The Calculus of Consent*, Ann Arbor: Univ. of Michigan Press, 1962.

is then passed with the votes of *A*, *B*, and *D*. On Wednesday, *C* enters such a bill. He already has *A*'s promise to vote, and so he approaches *E* and suggests that he will vote for a similar bill for *E* if *E* votes for the bill for *C*. He agrees, and the bill passes with the votes of *A*, *C*, and *E*. On Thursday, *D* approaches *E* and offers to vote for *E*'s bill if *E* will vote for *D*'s bill. The agreement is made, and the bill benefiting *D* passes with the votes of *B*, *D*, and *E*, and on the following day the bill benefiting *E* passes with the votes of *C*, *D*, and *E*.

The net result of this is, of course, that everybody has the same amount of money that they entered with. As we shall see below, this is not too bad a description of what happens in actual government transfers except that government transfers normally involve at least some dissipation of resources so everybody, in fact, is worse off at the end of the game.

Of course the kind of highly symmetrical structure that I have assumed here would not be expected with only five voters. With a larger number of voters it is not unrealistic, but let us leave that problem, together with the problem of inefficiency in the process, for later discussion and confine ourselves simply to the present model. First, note that if one of the parties refused to enter into these bargains, it would injure him and benefit the others. For example, suppose that *E* was unwilling to enter into such a bargain. The only result would have been that the four bills passed (together with their appropriate majorities) would be *A* (*A*,*B*,*C*), *B* (*A*,*B*,*D*), *C* (*A*,*C*,*D*), and *D* (*B*,*C*,*D*). *E* would pay out $8 and get nothing in return; the others would all pay a total tax of $8 and get a return of $10. As before, the individual among those who vote for the logrolling bill would gain a net of $8 on the bill that was passed in his favor, and in return he would be compelled to vote for taxes for two bills, each of which lost him $2, with the result that his net profit would be $4 on the bills for which he voted, and he would lose $2 on the bill which he voted against. *E* would lose $2 on each of the bills he voted against, for a total loss of $8.

One possible objection to this scheme is simply that a solid coalition of, say, *A*, *B*, and *C* could obviously do better than *A*, *B*, and *C* can do with this kind of logrolling. This is true but does not happen often because of the difficulties of maintaining such a coalition. More important, however, granted that the bills take place through time and that individuals have a strong motive for wanting to be seen as reliable for future bargains, there is no real opportunity for such a bill to be put before the house. It is much easier for *A* to simply approach *B* and *C* with his simple little proposal that they vote for him and he votes for each one of them individually than it is for him to organize a comprehensive coalition for *A*, *B*, and *C*. The difference is, of course, very small if we are dealing with only five people as we are here, but the House of Representatives has 435 members, and getting a constitutional majority of them together in one coalition is a great deal more difficult than simply going out and making reciprocal promises on one specific bill with half of them.[13]

If we consider this kind of bargaining, with a large number of participants, as there are in most legislative bodies, it is fairly obvious why no one gets left out. In essence, there is a market, and anybody can sell his vote by the simple expedient of lowering his price a little bit. With bargaining and information being reasonably good, one would anticipate roughly a standard price. This is indeed what happens. The payoff to each constituency is much like that to any other, although the particular form the payoff takes may vary. Members of the Agriculture Committee, for example, get special privileges in agricultural bills, which they pay for by getting less than even treatment in other areas. On the whole, however, this expenditure by constituencies is rather egalitarian.

The reader will, however, have already noticed a severe problem with this type of voting. It may be the equilibrium state in a legislature, but it would normally lead to all the members of the legislature being voted out. There are inevitably at least some administrative costs in transferring money from one constituency to another. That being so, the total amount that any constituency wins must be less than it loses. If these payments were in cash, that would be obvious, and the voters would be motivated to throw those rascals out with great frequency. It is probably this fact that explains the fact that transfers are almost never in cash.

If we look over the traditional collection of activities undertaken by government, it is immediately obvious that many of them can be quite profitable, in the sense that the total benefit is markedly in excess of the total cost. An obvious case is the police department, which in most cities is a small part of the total budget, but which confers immense benefits upon the citizenry.

13. Candor compels me to tell the reader that this is my explanation of the absence of general coalitions making large direct cash transfers. It is not unanimously held by students of public choice. Indeed, the journal *Public Choice* is currently holding a discussion on the point. In any event, we must agree that the kind of coalition in which the majority transfers large sums in cash to itself from the minority is unknown in democratic societies except insofar as the wealthy are regarded as a particular minority. Even there, they are a very small minority, and they do not suffer too badly.

We would, then, want the government to carry out a considerable number of activities in which it taxes the citizenry in order to provide some services that are worth more than the taxes.

We must be careful here because this may be used as an excuse for taking over private activities. There are many things done by governments that could just as well be handled by private market; i.e., individuals could directly purchase whatever is provided by the government activity, and the consumer surplus would be the same or, in all probability, much greater. Nevertheless, although we have to be careful, there is no doubt that there are many government activities in which the citizenry achieve a large profit. Indeed, it is my opinion that government, as a whole, has been an agency that profited its subjects, even such an apparently exploitative government as that of Louis XIV.

Given the opportunities for this kind of investment of the taxpayers' money, if the investments were all pure public goods, it would be possible to pass them without any vote trading. Every constituency would gain. Although this does happen, the overwhelming majority of government activities are either the provision of private goods, which could be better provided by the private market, or the provision of goods that generate benefits for a large number of people, but not the entire polity.[14]

Consider, for example, the road net. The net as a whole is of immense benefit to any country, but individual segments of it frequently are of only very modest benefit to most of the citizens and of great benefit locally. Consider the part of Tom's Creek Road that goes by my house: almost everyone benefits to a trivial extent from the fact that transportation to and from this area is easier than it would be otherwise, with the result that whatever is produced in the area will be sold outside at a somewhat lower price, and residents in the area will be willing to pay a somewhat higher price for things that they import than they would if the road net were not there.

The main benefit, however, clearly falls on those people who frequently make use of the road. This is quite a wide range of people, with the amount of utilization depending very much on the specific circumstances of each householder or enterprise.[15] Theoretically, it would be possible to set up a

14. There are also some government goods, the benefit of which spreads well beyond the country in which they are generated. In these cases foreign countries can be free-riders as NATO has free-ridden on the American military establishment.

15. The only enterprises are farms.

special collective organization that dealt with that particular road, with all the individuals being taxed and having their votes weighted in terms of the importance of the road to them.[16] Obviously, the administrative costs for this project would be greater than its benefit. Further, if all cases in the United States where government generates externalities were set up with separate agencies dealing with them, the individual voter would face an immense collection of different administrative agencies for which he had to vote. The burden would be excessive, he would probably not bother to vote in most elections, and he certainly would not cast informed votes.

What we need is another system in which the government is fairly simple and deals with all of these possible benefits.[17] Unfortunately, the benefits fall on different people: I am a member of the group who will benefit by improving Tom's Creek Road and also a member of those who would benefit by various improvements around the university, but less than one-third of the people who live on Tom's Creek Road fall in the second category, and less than 2 or 3 percent of the people who would benefit from improvements around the university would benefit in a major way with improvements of Tom's Creek Road. The solution is to have a set of government units (a limited number because of the voting problem), each of which deals with a number of different problems, the externalities of which are overlapping and not identical. Logrolling is one solution, although I do not claim it is the only or the ideal way of dealing with this problem.[18]

Unfortunately, once we set up a system of this sort, the prospect of considerable cost being imposed on the voter is real, and the prospect of using it for straightforward transfers is also real. Turn back to Figure 1. Assume that

16. As a matter of fact, the demand-revealing process makes this quite feasible. See Tideman and Tullock, "A New and Superior Process for Making Social Choices," and the special issue of *Public Choice* for an appropriate explanation. T. Nicolaus Tideman and Gordon Tullock, "Coalitions under Demand Revealing," *Public Choice* 38 (1981): 323–38.

17. The reasoning here follows primarily my "Federalism, Problems of Scale," *Public Choice* 11 (Spring 1969): 19–31.

18. In addition to the demand-revealing process discussed above, there is E. T. Hæfele's "General Purpose Representative." This would be a representative elected by each small district who would be a member of quite a number of different small governments dealing with specialized activities. These small governments would characteristically have different geographic scope, but all would include the district in which he was elected. The individual representative of a given area would then make trades with other representatives in which the benefit or cost to his area on a given bill is taken into account.

instead of direct transfers there are five road repair projects, one for each of our citizens, and that the benefit from completing these road repair projects is, in each case, $8 for the citizen who lives on that road and $1 apiece for the other citizens who benefit to some extent from improved access to the citizen living on the road. The net benefit, then, is $12. Assume once again that the road improvement can be carried out at a cost of $10, and a bill is put up to tax everyone $2 for repairing the road. Clearly, looked at socially, this is a desirable bill, and if we assume that similar bills will be passed for the roads of the other individuals, society as a whole gains from the passage of these bills. Without logrolling, however, each of the five bills would fail. Further, if we try to put the whole thing together in one bill, it would always be subject to being beaten by a bill for repairing only three of the five roads.

The failure of combination bills does not seem to be true of Congress, but the combining of a whole series of such projects into one big bill is done apparently only to save time. The type of coalition that produces benefits for a majority only is administratively impossible, and hence a combined bill, with the same outcome as if the bills came in one at a time, is enacted after committee hearings.

Unfortunately, there are not only clear-cut cases of social benefit from logrolling. A social loss can be generated by logrolling, too. Suppose that we change our example above in only one way: we lower the direct benefit that each person gets for having his road repaired to $5. Under these circumstances, repairing the road will benefit the citizen who lives on the road $5 and the others $1 apiece, or a total of $9, while the cost will be $10. It is socially undesirable that this road be repaired.

Unfortunately, logrolling would lead to the road being repaired. If *A* asks *B* and *C* to vote for repairing his road in return for agreeing to vote for repairing their roads, he must assume that he will be paying out $6 in taxes on this bargain, but the benefit that he will get back is $5 for his own repaired road and $2 as an externality on the repair of roads for *B* and *C*, or a total of $7. It is a profitable bargain from his standpoint and from *B*'s and *C*'s standpoints. The logrolling circle, which gets all of the roads repaired, can occur under these circumstances, too.

As a general rule, simple logrolling of the sort we have described can be used to pass through Congress any bill, the net benefit of which is greater than one-half the net cost. Indeed, the situation is even worse than that. If we have single member constituencies, as we do in the United States, the benefit to a majority of the congressmen's constituents in a majority of districts could get a bill through Congress. Thus, a bill, the net benefit of which was only 26 percent of the net cost, could theoretically pass, if the distribution of the benefit was right.[19]

Before we can go further with this line of reasoning, however, it is necessary to look into both the actual welfare effects of differential provisions of special projects to different groups in society and the information conditions for voting. As we shall see, these permit transfers, concealed within the government voting project, from some members of society to others. It seems likely that these transfers are immense in most modern societies, although actually measuring them is difficult. We can, however, say for certain that they are much larger than the transfers to the poor.

19. Once again this matter is discussed with much greater thoroughness in *The Calculus of Consent.*

INFORMATION AND LOGROLLING

The main purpose of this chapter is to examine the problems of information in a democracy and their effect on logrolling and particular logrolling transfers. It is necessary first, however, to look a little more carefully into the welfare implications of logrolling. I should say here, for the benefit of those interested in income transfers who are not accustomed to economic reasoning and to particular economic applications in political problems, that we always use examples with a very small number of people simply because such examples are easier to deal with. These examples are intended to be small-scale models of real-world situations. In our very small models of only a few people, however, negotiations between the parties would probably eliminate the problems that lead to the outcomes we predict. Thus, the small-scale model is in this respect unrealistic. In essence, we assume that no negotiations or bargaining takes place among the very small number of people that could not take place within a group of 100,000. All of this makes the reasoning easier to follow and does not affect the conclusion, but it does give a certain aura of unreality to the discussion.

Given this caveat, Figure 1 shows a project, let us say, road repairing, that is contemplated in a three-person nation. The vertical axis shows cost in dollars, and the horizontal axis shows the quantity of road repairing to be done. If we assume that the road repairing can be measured in $1 units, then the line *CC* shows the cost of each quantity of road repairing. In our little society there are three people: *A*, whose demand for road repairing is quite high (line *A*); *B*, whose demand is comparatively low (line *B*); and *C*, whose demand for road repairing is absolutely zero (horizontal axis). If we add these demands vertically, we get the line $A + B$ together with the demand of *C*, which is zero. The social optimum is at *O*, where the total social demand for road repairing crosses the total cost. This will maximize the net social benefit after the costs are paid for.

Reprinted, with kind permission of Kluwer Academic Publishers, from *Economics of Income Redistribution*, Kluwer-Nijhoff Studies in Human Issues: An International Series in the Social Sciences (Boston: Kluwer-Nijhoff, 1983), 33–48.

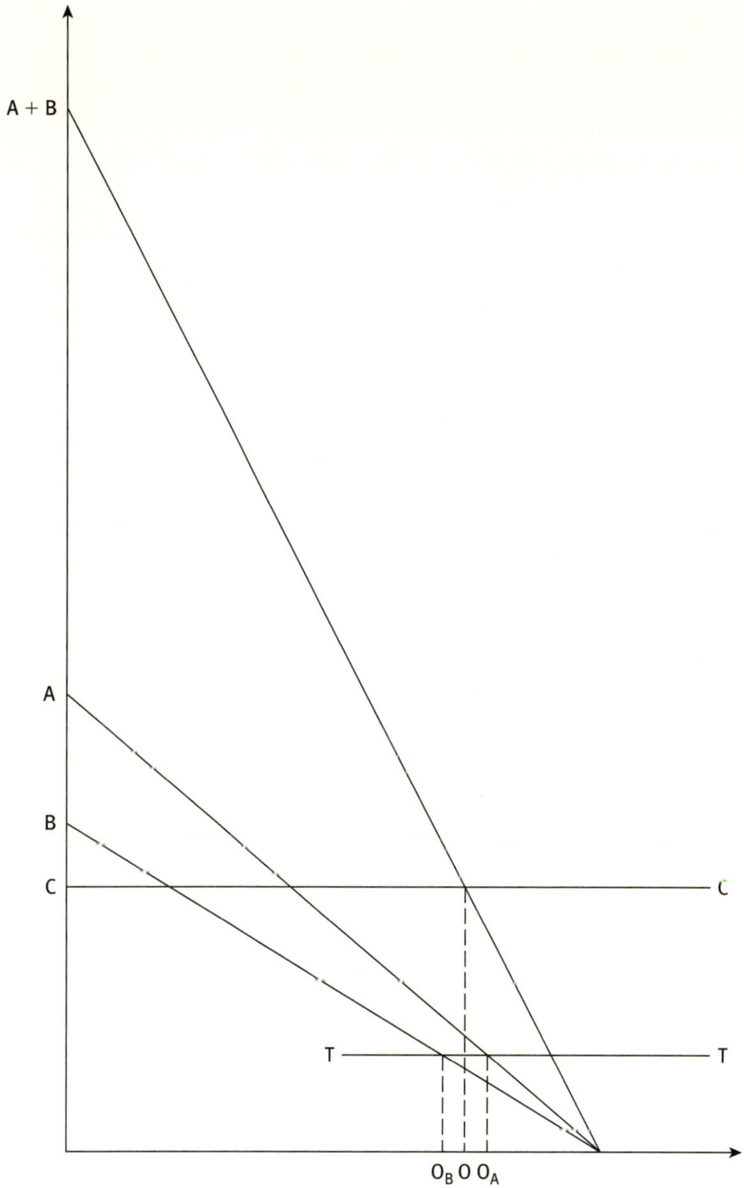

FIGURE 1

Project contemplated in a three-person nation

Paying for it must, however, be done by taxes. Lindahl taxes charge each of the parties an amount that is equal to the area whose height is the point of intersection between their personal demand curve and the line *O* and whose width is the distance from the origin to *O*. The sum of such Lindahl taxes will always be exactly equal to the total cost of the provided good, and each individual will find himself paying his marginal evaluation of the public good for each unit.

It is an interesting fact that the demand-revealing process provides a method of approximating such Lindahl taxes;[1] however, they are not used anywhere in the real world. Their use would eliminate a very large number of what might be called by-product transfers; i.e., situations in which some public benefit is purchased by government for perfectly good reasons, but the costs and the benefits are distributed quite differently, with the result that there is, effectively, a transfer from part of the population to the rest.

But, assuming we will not be using Lindahl taxes, let us consider a very simple system where each of the three members of this society pays an equal tax, which is one-third of the total cost. This is shown by line *TT*. In this tax arrangement *C* would prefer none of the road repairing, *B* would prefer the amount O_B, and *A* the amount O_A. With majority voting, the median voter, *B*, would prevail, and O_B road repairing would be done, which is socially a suboptimal amount.

Suppose, however, that logrolling takes place. Obviously, no logrolling is possible just between *A*, *B*, and *C*. Suppose there is a much larger society, and they are only three citizens of it. In Figure 2, we have collapsed *A* and *B* into a group, which we shall call the high demanders for some government service. Their demand for the service is shown by the line *A*. The social cost of the service per unit is *CC* as usual, and the optimum from society's standpoint is *O*. There are, however, a large number of other people in the society who are totally uninterested in this particular project but who have to pay the bulk of the tax support. Once again we are assuming that the tax (*TT*) is evenly distributed over the citizenry.

We put the matter to a majority vote. If the people without the demand are much more numerous than the high-demand group, the outcome would be a zero provision. With logrolling, however, that is not so. The high-demanders have a demand shown by the intersection of their demand curve

1. T. Nicolaus Tideman and Gordon Tullock, "A New and Superior Process for Making Social Choices," *Journal of Political Economy* (October 1976): 1145–59.

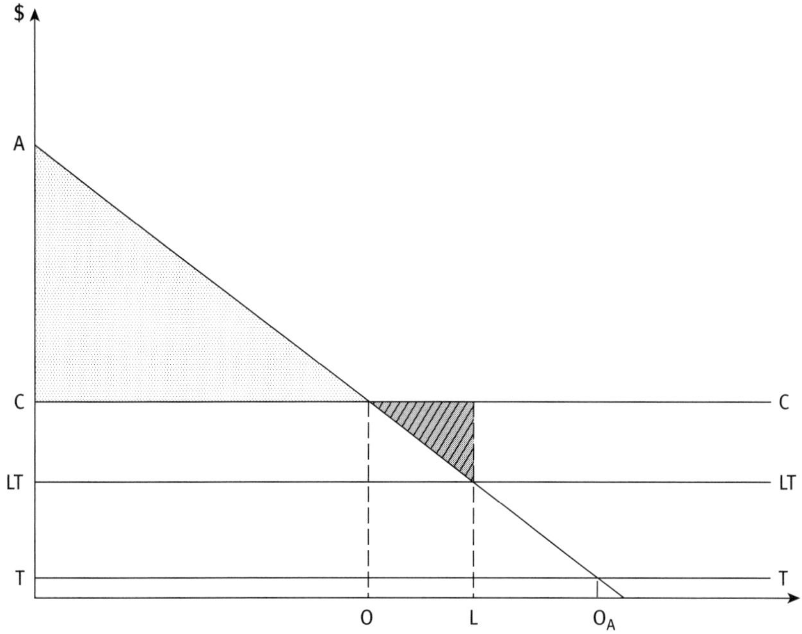

FIGURE 2
Project contemplated in a nation of more than three people

with their cost curve. Their cost curve is the line TT, and this optimum is O_A. Since they will not be able to get that, they have to make deals with other people in which they vote for other projects in return for people voting for theirs. The high-demanders have to buy only half the legislature, however, so their cost will not be the total cost, or line CC, but the lobbying cost, or line $LTLT$. The total amount provided will be L, which is well above the social optimum. There is a social cost of this overprovision shown by the shaded triangle. Note that in this particular diagram, the consumer benefit from providing the first units (shown by the stippled triangle) is much larger than the shaded triangle. This is, of course, simply an artifact of the way I have drawn the diagram. The relationship between the two triangles could be anything. There could, for example, be no stippled triangle at all.

Note the distribution of benefits and costs from this project. High-demanders achieve a gain equivalent to the triangle bounded by the vertical axis, line LT, and line A. Those low-demanders, who were bought by the logrolling agreement to vote for the project, were presumably compensated elsewhere, so we can ignore them temporarily. They may do as well as the high-demanders on this project as on other projects in which they are high-demanders. Those who are not members of the particular set of bargainers that passed this bill will pay a cost equivalent to the rectangle bounded by the vertical axis, line *L*, line *LT*, and line *C*. Since everyone is going to be a winner on some logrolling deals and a loser on others, the net effect can be quite a significant reduction in total output, and with a little less symmetry, very considerable transfers within society.

Granted that each member of Congress may choose to benefit only a majority of his constituents, the total social loss can be quite great. Further, as we shall see when we discuss the information conditions, all of this is, in a real sense, an underestimate of the degree to which overexpenditure on government projects can occur.

Before we turn to these information problems, there are some general considerations. First, although I do think that logrolling leads in many cases to an overprovision of government services, it should be said that in other cases it leads to a provision of desirable government services that would not occur otherwise, and, hence, society is better off. I am not arguing that government or logrolling should be abolished or that the net cost of logrolling is negative. Looking at government as a whole, I think the situation is somewhat like Figure 2; that is, the consumer's surplus on the earlier units of government provision exceeds the cost of producing the later units. Government unambiguously dominates the no-government situation, but a selectively trimmed government would dominate the government we now have.

The general inefficiency which I perceive in government and which we will be discussing later does not necessarily involve transfers. Inefficient projects are not obviously transfers, but they may have strong transfer components. First, there are many projects undertaken by the government that are fairly straightforward transfers, with no positive product produced. The obvious case of this is the agricultural program, whether it takes the form of subsidies for the production of crops that we do not want or restrictions on the production of crops that could be sold. Both of these techniques lead to the value of farmland going up or being kept at an artificially inflated value, and the citizenry paying, through taxes or restrictions or both, higher prices for farm products. Nothing is here except a transfer, and, further, the transfer is hideously inefficient in that total cost to the citizens is much greater than the benefit to the owners of agricultural land. There are many other programs of this sort.

Dominantly, however, government activity consists of producing something that does indeed have some social benefit even if the social benefit is much less than the cost. Let us consider my favorite pork barrel project, the conversion of Tulsa, Oklahoma, into a deep-water port[2] at the expense of taxpayers. There can be no doubt that there are economic advantages to this, but there also can be no doubt that these economic advantages are immensely smaller than the total cost.

Should we count this as a transfer? The first thing to note is that, if it is a transfer, most of the funds used to deepen the river were not really transferred to anyone but were dissipated in the act of deepening. The contractors who did the work presumably made no higher profits than contractors in other parts of the United States, but the existence of this project, which increased the demand for certain types of engineering activities, presumably raised the return on engineering all over the United States. I imagine this increase was very small and very dispersed. Those particular contractors who got the contract for deepening the canal were no doubt grateful for them, but they got them by a bidding process and probably did not make immense amounts of money.

The principal beneficiaries were people who owned real estate at locations where its value would be increased by the canal, who seemed to have been rather disappointed by the size of the increase, which was smaller than anticipated, and various citizens living in Tulsa and other parts of Oklahoma, who found that things they sold got a slightly higher price and things they bought came at a slightly lower price because of this improved transportation facility. It is fairly certain that the total benefit to these people was only a small fraction of the cost to taxpayers all over the United States. Probably, even the citizens of Tulsa paid more in taxes for the construction of this canal than its benefit to them. The explanation for the completion of the canal has to be put on not simple logrolling but logrolling augmented by the information problems that will be discussed in the latter part of this chapter.

Nevertheless, the question comes, "Is there a transfer?" This is a matter of definition, and it is not obvious that reaching an agreed definition here is a matter of great importance. If you want to call the Tulsa Oklahoma Ship Canal a specialized transfer to Tulsa from the rest of us, or if you want to say that it was a ferociously inefficient product of logrolling that, among other things, raised the wealth of some citizens of Tulsa a little bit and lowered the

2. Twelve feet.

wealth of the rest of us quite a large amount, I shall not quarrel. We should keep in mind, however, that projects of this sort are normally implemented because the recipients want them, and the recipients are expecting a specific narrow benefit. Thus, the motivation behind them is, to a very large extent, the desire to receive transfers, and those who oppose them, insofar as they do, are normally objecting to paying the taxes; i.e., they are defending themselves against the transfers. In the Tulsa, Oklahoma, case the result was inefficient, but there are no doubt cases in which similar logrolling leads to the construction of projects whose value is greater than their cost. I suspect, for example, that that is true of much of our road net.

In any event, I leave to the reader the decision as to whether such activity is a transfer or not. There are, in essence, three categories of transfers. An activity of the government that raises the wealth of some citizens for producing nothing of economic value or, as in many cases, actually lowering total production. Much of the farm program falls in this category. The second category would be those cases in which the government act does indeed produce something that has economic value, but the value is less (usually much less) than the cost. The third case would be where the government produces something, the economic value of which is in excess of the cost. In all three of these cases the gain may be concentrated in a minority, and a majority may be paying the cost. Politically, they all look much the same. They are all examples of logrolling, and the congressperson and congressional district that benefits probably do not bother to distinguish among these three categories. It is, however, sensible for us to keep them distinct.

Let us now turn to information problems. Unfortunately, the information problems in democratic voting are extreme. Basically, there is no reason why the voter should be particularly well informed about anything. He presumably has some information about the world, and if he casts a vote it is only sensible to make use of this information,[3] but there is little or no motive for his acquiring more information. Further, if the information that he has is, in fact, false (i.e., misinformation), there is nothing much to be gained on his part from correcting the error. The reason why this is so can be seen from the following equations:

(1) Payoff $= B \cdot A \cdot D - C_v$
(2) Payoff′ $= B \cdot (A + \Delta A) \cdot D - C_v - C_i$

3. It is not necessarily sensible to think hard about it.

$$(3)\ \text{Payoff}'' = B \cdot \Delta A \cdot D - C_i$$

$$(4)\quad = \$10{,}000 \cdot \tfrac{1}{4} \cdot \frac{1}{10{,}000{,}000} - \$100$$

$$= \frac{1}{4000} - \$100$$

$$= -99.75$$

where

Payoff $=$ payoff from vote without special information.
Payoff$'$ $=$ payoff after the voter has taken the trouble to inform himself.
Payoff$''$ $=$ payoff to the act of acquiring information.
B $=$ the benefit the voter expects if his party wins.
A $=$ the likelihood that the voter's judgment is accurate.
ΔA $=$ the change in A as a result of becoming informed.
D $=$ Difference the vote will make.
C_v $=$ Cost of voting.
C_i $=$ Cost of obtaining information.

Equation 1 shows the payoff to a vote, assuming the voter simply takes advantage of whatever information he has and acquires no further information to improve his vote. He starts with some information, and this will surely affect his vote. He could, however, acquire further information in order to cast a better informed vote as is shown by equation 2.

Let us, however, examine equation 1 with some care. The first three items are his estimate of the benefit he will get from his party winning, or from the proposition which he favors winning. Note that this includes any subjective benefit he may receive because he wants the world as a whole to benefit. A is his estimate of the accuracy of his own judgment. This is an unusual thing to put in an equation, but the only certain effect of improving your information is that you feel a greater confidence that you are right. A is also unusual in that the probability runs from zero, for a feeling that you are about as likely to be right as wrong, to one, at a feeling that you are certainly correct. This rather unusual way of presenting the estimate simply makes the mathematics easier. D is the likelihood that the individual's vote will make a difference, and C_v is the cost to the voter. It should be pointed out that C_v is not necessarily a positive quantity. It could be that the voter gets positive pleasure out of voting, which is greater than the cost of going to the polls, or that failing to vote would make him feel guilty, and the subjective cost of this guilt would be greater than the cost of going to the polls. In both of these cases his estimate of the cost of voting would be negative, and, in consequence, he would be motivated to vote regardless of the values of B, A, and D.

Equation 2 shows the effect of acquiring information in order to improve the vote. Improving your information will not necessarily increase or reduce the benefit that you feel you will get from the outcome. It could do either one. It could, of course, also lead you to decide to vote in the opposite direction. That again, however, is not certain to increase or decrease the benefit you get out of your side winning. Thus, B remains the same in the equation. Your certainty of being correct, however, should be increased by improved information. This could be incorrect only if you had a totally false estimate of your own accuracy before, and the improved information led you to reach a more just estimate that was lower. This seems unlikely.

D is the probability that your vote will affect the outcome and is not changed. The cost of voting is not changed (remember it could be negative), but there is the cost of obtaining information. Normally, this cost will not be in the form of direct cash outlay, but the use of your time, such as going to the library, watching television programs that you would not get any entertainment out of, asking questions for which you do not get any entertainment value, etc. You, presumably, would watch all the television programs you want to, read what you want to in the newspapers, etc., without running cost, under equation 1. Equation 2 only deals with that information you might pick up in order to improve your vote, not that information you acquired for other reasons.

In order to find the net payoff, we subtract equation 1 from equation 2 and obtain equation 3. Its meaning is, of course, very simple: the increase in accuracy of your vote times the benefit and the probability that your vote will have an effect is the first term, and the cost of obtaining information is the second. In equation 4, we insert some reasonable numbers. I assume that your personal evaluation of the benefit that you will achieve from your party winning is \$10,000. The exact number here makes very little difference. As far as A is concerned, I once again assume that you felt that you had a three out of four chance of being correct before, which in our system gives you a value of one-half, and that the result of collecting further information is that you now feel you have a seven out of eight chance of being right, which again gives you three-quarters, and the difference between these is one-quarter.

The probability of affecting the outcome used is a very rough figure, but probably not particularly inaccurate in the average American presidential election. In practice, of course, one would have to look carefully at the polls and make an estimate, which in 1964 or 1972 would have been much smaller than 1/10,000,000, but in 1968 or 1976 would have been larger. I then assume that the cost in making the increase in your information was $100. Once again, I think this is a very modest number, but almost any reasonable number will have roughly the same outcome. The calculations are then carried out, and it will be noted that the net effect of acquiring this information is that you are $99.75 worse off. The careful, well-informed voter will come to the conclusion that being careful and well informed about his vote has a negative payoff, indeed a substantial one. One should acquire information about politics only if one gets positive enjoyment out of it or if it comes to you rather by accident while you are turning to the sports page.

This theoretical proposition shocked a great many people when it was first proposed by Anthony Downs,[4] but the voters themselves seem always to have known it. All efforts to determine how much voters know about various issues indicate that their ignorance is really appalling. They frequently do not know the name of their congressman even right after an election.

As a particular illustration of this, the Reagan camp was rather scientific in its approach to information and commissioned a number of polls to find out what people think. They discovered that most people thought that during the Nixon and Ford administrations, and for that matter during the Eisenhower administration, not only was the president Republican but Congress was, too. As a result of this, the Reagan camp put in hand a program to convince the voters that Congress has been Democratic since 1954. Tests run late in the presidential campaign indicated that the educational campaign had paid off, and it is possible that the change in the composition of the Senate was in part the effect of this campaign, although there were many other factors involved.

Note there has been nothing said here about voters being irrational. Also, it is not true they know nothing about politics. It is fairly impossible to live in the present-day world without knowing something about politics. Further, talking about politics is one of the standard conversational gambits, and most people learn whatever happens to be a popular subject in their particular culture in order to engage in the pleasant activity of conversation. It appears, however, that learning about politics does not in general lead to a

4. Anthony Downs, *An Economic Theory of Democracy* (New York: Harper and Row, 1957), 207–19. See also my *Toward a Mathematics of Politics* (Ann Arbor: University of Michigan Press, 1967), 100–114.

change in basic positions. Indeed, the better informed a voter is, the less likely he is to change from one party to another.[5] This is further proof that people pick up information about politics not in order to improve their vote but for various social reasons. They do not pick up information in order to change their vote. Of course, any information they do have can change their vote, but that is not the reason they get it.

All this has shocked a number of professors of political science who were accustomed to telling their students that they have a duty, not only to vote but to cast a well-informed vote. I imagine, however, that their students will continue to behave like the students of the last generation of political scientists; i.e., they will not become very well informed except for those for whom politics is a hobby.[6]

The situation had been clearly understood by the great Italian economist Vilfredo Pareto, who, almost a century ago, wrote:

> Let us suppose that in a country of thirty million inhabitants it is proposed, under some pretext or other, to get each citizen to pay out one franc a year, and to distribute the total amount amongst thirty persons. Every one of the donors will give up one franc a year; every one of the beneficiaries will receive one million francs a year. The two groups will differ very greatly in their response to this situation. Those who hope to gain a million a year will know no rest by day or night. They will win newspapers over to their interest by financial inducements and drum up support from all quarters. A discreet hand will warm the palms of needy legislators, even of ministers. . . . On the other hand, the despoiled are much less active. A great deal of money is needed to launch an electoral campaign. Now there are insuperable material difficulties militating against asking each citizen to contribute a few centimes. One has to ask a few people to make substantial contributions. But then, for such people, there is the likelihood that their individual contribution to the campaign against the spoliation will exceed the total amount they stand to lose by the measure in question. . . . When election day comes, similar difficulties are encountered. Those who hope to gain a million apiece have agents everywhere, who descend in swarms on the electorate, urging the voters that sound

5. Intellectuals characteristically are not quite totally devoted to one party. It is part of their self-image as intellectuals that they cast at least a few votes every election for the other party.

6. This last category may contain a very large number of the readers of this book and their friends.

> and enlightened patriotism calls for the success of their modest proposal. They will go further if need be, and are quite prepared to lay out cash to get the necessary votes for returning candidates in their interest. In contrast, the individual who is threatened with losing one franc a year—even if he is fully aware of what is afoot—will not for so small a thing forego a picnic in the country, or fall out with useful or congenial friends, or get on the wrong side of the mayor or the *prefet*! In these circumstances the outcome is not in doubt: the spoliators will win hands down.[7]

Basically, of course, Pareto was right—as he was on almost everything—but it should be pointed out that we do observe very few direct cash transfers of this sort. There are some, but the average transfer is disguised as something else. A civil servant may be paid more than is actually necessary to obtain suitable help, a road may be laid out in such a way as to increase the value of certain pieces of real estate, the government may give up large potential mineral royalties on land in order to keep it "unspoiled" for a very small collection of upper-income people who like to visit it, or there may be restrictions on what an optometrist may do in order to increase the income of oculists. All of these are examples of fairly straightforward transfers from a large group of people to a small group of people, but none of them do it by the direct cash method. The reason, I believe, is information. If we accept Pareto's discussion as being literally what he thought, the program would certainly attract newspaper attention, almost everyone would know that it was going to cost them one franc, and the only beneficiaries would be a small group of people who were going to get the money, and it would fail. It is true that Pareto refers to the act as taking place "under some pretext or other," but what we normally observe is that the pretext has to be fairly complicated, and characteristically the result is that both parties, the taxpayers and the recipients, could be better off if a direct cash payment had been arranged.

Consider the list of transfers I gave above: suppose that the civil servant is being paid $5,000 more than is necessary to get his services. Note that this is as close to a direct transfer as any of these examples will provide. He would presumably be better off if we gave him $4,995 as a straightforward pension. We could then pay to whoever occupied his job, which might be him, the

7. V. Pareto, *Cours d'Economie Politique*, 1896, in *Sociological Writings*, trans. Derick Mirfin, ed. S. E. Finer (London: Pall Mall Press, 1966), as quoted in *The Years of Economists*, 1980–81, comp. George J. Stigler and Claire Friedland (Chicago: University of Chicago Press, 1980).

true economic value of the activity. This would mean that he would have greater freedom and that he could easily change jobs if an opportunity came up, and the government would also have the additional freedom of being able to change employees in terms of relative competence. Attaching the pension to the job lowers the total social product unlike the direct cash payment, but the cash payment would be too obvious and would not get through in a democracy.

That a direct cash payment would be less costly to the economy as a whole is even clearer in the other cases. Laying out the road at its optimal location and then levying a special tax on those who gained from this layout, and using this to transfer to the politically influential person who wanted it laid out in another way, would surely be better for the economy as a whole. The Audubon Foundation not only campaigns vigorously to keep government lands unspoiled, it owns a certain amount of wilderness land of its own. It grants mineral leases on these lands while opposing similar grants by the government. I doubt that this is an effort on their part to increase the value of their own mineral resources by reducing competition, but it does indicate that to the Audubon Foundation, the value of unspoiled nature is less than the value of the mineral lease. In the case of government land, however, the members of the Audubon Foundation can enjoy the unspoiled nature of the land, but the general taxpayer will benefit from the lease payments. In this case, they prefer the land to be left unspoiled. Surely there is some cash payment to users of these lands, which is less than their mineral-leasing value, that would fully compensate them for having them leased.[8]

With respect to the oculist-optometrist problem, a simple tax on glasses could be used to pay a fee to all oculists and could be so designed as to benefit the oculist more than do the present arrangements, and at the same time permit the net price of glasses for the public to be lower. In all of these cases, we would be better off with direct cash payments, but the direct cash payments obviously would not go through in a democracy. The pressure groups find it necessary to conceal their activities under "some pretext," and this pretext normally greatly reduces the efficiency of the economy. Traditional examples are the tariff and the farm program.

8. This is particularly true since valuable minerals are, in fact, found only under a small part of the earth's surface. Specific areas would be devastated if the surface was stripped off to get to a big seam of coal, but the total land area so mined would be a very small part of the total wilderness.

A more recent, and rather sensitive, example concerns the very elaborate facilities now being put in place so that people in wheelchairs can get about relatively conveniently. It seems to me fairly certain that the net cost of all of these things is massively higher than the benefit to the wheelchair occupants who use them. The cost, however, is concealed, and the bulk of it is not a tax cost in the direct sense; it is a cost imposed on all sorts of people, such as proprietors of restaurants, by a government regulation. Most people are, indeed, sorry for those among us who have to use wheelchairs and are quite willing to help them. It would appear, however, that the people who are organizing the pressure group for these people feel that this desire to help would not actually lead to large cash gifts. Suppose, for example, that the net value of all of these special resources[9] is $80,000 per wheelchair occupant per year.[10] We would not be willing to vote that amount in cash, but if the actual cost is concealed we are able to do so. Thus, the potential Pareto optimal bargain in which we stop all of these activities and pay each wheelchair occupant, let us say, $20,000 a year would be impractical because the citizenry would, in fact, not be willing to make that large a sacrifice if they realized that was the cost.

This is a particular case in which everyone, including myself, feels sorry for the people aided and is willing to aid them. It would appear, however, that they can get more aid if they conceal the actual cost than if they take it directly. One could go on with other examples. Traditionally, the tariff and the farm program have been used by economists as examples of this kind of non–Pareto optimal transfer.

Still, the basic phenomenon pointed out by Pareto is clearly real. The individual whom we represented in the set of equations is far more likely to know about something that concerns him to a considerable extent than about something that affects him very little. Traditionally, this has been discussed under the title of special interest groups, and there has been a feeling that, basically, most special interest groups are people who are employed in some profession and therefore know a good deal about it. The exploited groups are their customers. There is no doubt there are many such cases, but

9. The rental value of the space occupied by such things as larger washroom compartments, special parking, etc., is probably very considerable, looking over the country as a whole.

10. The amount is an oral estimate, not based on very much research, by a senior government economist.

there are a number of other cases in which special interest groups are not professionally involved.

The Audubon Foundation, mentioned above, is a group of people who know a great deal more about the wilderness that they wish preserved than the average taxpayer knows about its cost. An even better group are those people who fly private airplanes. In net, there are very large government expenditures to provide airports and other facilities for this group of upper-income Americans at much less than cost. What is needed is a politically influential group that can, one way or another, be organized with a pretext under which the transfer to them can be concealed and the cost can be spread out widely enough so that most people will not notice it. Unfortunately, these conditions are often met.

The organization of the group is probably the crucial characteristic here. A pretext can be found almost anywhere, and any relatively small group of people can receive benefits that are to them, individually, sizable without the amount growing large enough so that the general taxpayer will notice it. Organization, however, is a different matter. Here, we have a case in which the public good externality paradigm, which so frequently causes difficulty, actually gives us a net gain by making it less likely that pressure groups will get large amounts of money out of the government.

Suppose that I am a dry cleaner, and the dry cleaners of my state decide to organize for the purpose of raising the standards of dry cleaning by not permitting anyone else to enter into the dry cleaning business and perhaps by providing a minimum price for dry cleaning by law. If I join with them in this organization, I will have to expend resources on what is clearly an uncertain investment. It will pay off very well, of course, if they get it through, but they are not certain to do so. On the other hand, if I do not join them, I reduce the amount of resources available to the pressure group only to a very small extent, and hence reduce the likelihood that these bills, which are very much to my interest, will be passed only to a very small extent. Thus, normally, if I calculate the odds carefully, I will decide that the reduction in my benefit from investing is less than the cost of the investment, and I will not invest. My fellow dry cleaners will make the same calculation and the pressure group will not be organized.

The problem is the main theme of Mancur Olson's famous *The Logic of Collective Action*. Unfortunately, there are ways of getting around the public good difficulty in the organization of a great many pressure groups. Still, the public good argument is probably the explanation for there not being many more than there are.

There are two ways in which pressure groups can be organized in spite of the above problem.[11] The first of these is the one emphasized by Olson, the possibility that the pressure group will be organized for some purpose other than engaging in political activity and then engage in that activity. He points out that the farm pressure groups are essentially organized around cooperatives of various sorts, particularly insurance. The American Automobile Association, which used to be very influential, was organized around the provision of a number of services to people driving in the United States, but nevertheless maintained active lobbies both in Washington and in the states in favor of various things that motorists would like.

There is no doubt that there are many cases in which pressure groups are organized this way, but this kind of pressure group always lives a somewhat dangerous life. For example, consider the American Automobile Association (AAA). It occurred to some of the major oil companies that they could supply the services to motorists at a lower cost than the AAA because they would not put any of their resources into the particular lobbying activities that it was undertaking. They were therefore able to charge a lower price and attract the bulk of the customers away from the AAA. The individual customer was probably better off when the AAA was strong, since his share of the lobbying cost was very small, but it was nevertheless true that the effect of his contribution of the lobbying effort was so small that he was sensible to switch to the oil company automobile service rather than stay with the AAA. This problem always exists for this kind of pressure group, but it has to be admitted that many of them nevertheless exist.

The second way in which the pressure group can be organized was first suggested by Richard Wagner and involves the politicians themselves acting as entrepreneurs.[12] Thus, a congressman may decide to take the leading role in obtaining advantage for some special group, with the theory that they will compensate him with their vote or perhaps by campaign contributions. In this case, there is much less chance of direct competition by outside agencies, but it is also true that congressmen have limited amounts of time, and the number of such entrepreneurial activities they can engage in is limited.

11. There is, in a way, a third—i.e., if the number of people in the pressure group is very small. For example, automobile manufacturers and the UAW are all pressing for restrictions on Japanese cars. The public good argument does not apply with much force to such small groups.

12. Richard E. Wagner, "Pressure Groups and Political Entrepreneurs: A Review Article," in *Papers on Non-Market Decision Making*, ed. Gordon Tullock (Charlottesville: Thomas Jefferson Center for Political Economy, University Press of Virginia, 1966), 162–70.

But if organizing a pressure group is going to be difficult, there certainly are plenty of them in the United States and, for that matter, in all modern countries, and we observe their product on every hand. The investment of resources in organizing pressure groups and protecting yourself against the activities of pressure groups are costs. Thus, not only does the pressure group transfer funds from, let us say, the general taxpayer to people flying private airplanes, but there are resources invested by the private aircraft owner in organizing this transfer. This phenomenon goes under the name of *rent-seeking*, and, in many circumstances, the amount invested in obtaining the transfer is as large as the transfer.[13] In the case of the type of pressure group we are discussing here, it is unlikely that this is so. The free-rider characteristic of the pressure organizations, i.e., the fact that individuals who decide not to join or who pay only a small amount to them, means that the investment in organizing political pressure on Congress is considerably less than the benefit. It may be that in the type of pressure group mentioned above (the one where a small group of large operators are joined together) the total cost is close to the total benefit.

But if the total cost to private persons of this kind of lobbying activity is probably not on the average as great as the benefit they will achieve, it is nevertheless very large. About a year ago, I was called upon to testify before a Senate committee and then later to read a paper at an FTC meeting in connection with a bill that had attracted a good deal of interest from both large corporations and large labor unions. I was astonished at the number of people crowded into the hearing room and later filling a large auditorium at the FTC meeting. Further, these people were not casual visitors. The bulk of them were extremely expensive special representatives who, in my opinion, fully earned their high fees from the private standpoint of the people who employed them. From the standpoint of society as a whole, however, their activity was almost entirely wasteful.

It is not only this kind of very expensive, specialized representation of large corporations that wastes funds in these areas. Some time ago a small corporation that I am associated with found that one of its minor products was in danger of being banned by the Consumer Product Safety Agency. The product, although small, was quite profitable, and the corporation did not want it banned. On the other hand, the total return on the product was only

13. See James M. Buchanan, Robert D. Tollison, and Gordon Tullock, eds., *Toward a Theory of the Rent-Seeking Society* (College Station: Texas A&M University Press, 1980).

about $30,000 or $40,000 a year. The company was too small to maintain a Washington representative, but it turned out that there is a market in this kind of thing. The company hired, on a piecework basis, a representative in Washington who knew the right people, arranged for the president and chairman of the board to talk to the appropriate civil servants, and the product was not banned.[14]

Any visitor to Washington these days is surprised at seeing the people who go to the Kennedy Center.[15] The expensive restaurants that now dot Washington and that add so much attraction for the casual visitors are largely new and did not exist when the government itself was small enough so that influence in Washington was not a major matter for large-scale rent-seeking.

We can now draw this chapter to a close. The costs imposed on society by these transfers are indeed very large. The benefits from the social standpoint are substantially nil. Indeed, if we are interested in helping the poor, it is likely that these transfers actually lower the income of the poor as well as that of almost everyone else. It is a case of the prisoner's dilemma. All of us would be better off if this kind of activity did not go on, but all of us are better off individually if we engage in it.

Let me here summarize the various costs by going through an invented example. Suppose that special interest group A was well enough organized to get some money out of the government and the money will take the form of a subsidy on some product that they regularly produce. Ten million dollars is to be raised from the general taxpayers and paid to this group, and the program is to be a continuing one. The benefit to this group in the first year is, however, a good deal less than $10 million. The price of their product to the consumer goes down because of the subsidy, and hence they sell more units, but the profit to them is not anywhere near $10 million. Let us, for simplicity, assume that they make $5 million in the first year.

With each succeeding year, however, their profit declines. Partly this is because new resources are attracted into the industry by these superior profits, and partly because of the fact that specialized resources now in the industry

14. In my opinion, in this case it was indeed proper to leave our product on the market and, in fact, they would never have taken the matter up at all had it not been for another equally minor special interest that wanted it banned. Nevertheless, the resources invested here by the two sides were, in net, socially wasteful.

15. Notably, here, the pressure group representatives are subsidized since although the costs of their seats, and the seats of the congressmen who are their guests, are very high they are nowhere near the cost of maintaining the Kennedy Center.

have their value capitalized and are then sold. Twenty years after the program began, there may be nobody in the industry who is making more than a normal return, although the product they produce is being sold to the consumer at a subsidized price. This means, of course, that other products are being sold to the consumer at prices that are slightly above their cost of production.

At this stage, we have a system that imposes very considerable deadweight losses on society because of the inefficient pattern of production but apparently does not seem to benefit anyone. If we consider withdrawing the subsidy, we realize that although none of these people are obtaining increases in income above what they could earn in other occupations, the withdrawal of the subsidy would mean a rise in the price of the ultimate product and fewer sold. This would result in too many resources in the industry, and for a considerable period of time resources in this industry will receive less than average returns. Once again, the eventual result, of course, will be that everything will return to the equilibrium price. Under the circumstances, the people in the industry will continue to invest resources in Washington to see to it that the subsidy is continued, not to make a profit but to avoid loss.

So far we have simply talked about the economic loss. Let us consider the political losses. The first are the resources put into obtaining a transfer. Let us assume that this was $1 million originally, and then as time goes by the people maintain an office in Washington to watch Congress and defend their special privilege, which costs $100,000 per year. Thus, in the first year they made a net of $4 million, and then their returns gradually fell until they were zero. Of course, the zero return includes $100,000 for an office in Washington.

But this does not exhaust the political losses. In addition, the political process as a whole has been affected. Congressmen have been pulled away from other activities which, at least theoretically, might have benefit to the country as a whole. The large offices that congressmen maintain are devoted to this kind of special interest work, frequently for much smaller groups than our example, i.e., the social security applicant who wants to get a better pension. All of this means that less time is available to consider public interest matters. The cost is not at all clear but possibly large.

The net effect of all this is that after a while society is distorting production by a tax subsidy program that no longer benefits anybody, but which costs quite a bit to maintain. Any dispassionate student of democracy would have to admit that this kind of thing is certainly very common. The bulk of all transfers are of this sort. Fortunately, in the next chapter we will take up a more cheerful subject—transfers to help the poor.

THE MIXED CASE

In this and the following chapters, we will be dealing with more realistic cases in which motives of the voters are mixed. In this chapter, we have mainly a theoretical discussion of what I think is a fairly simple case, a case in which the only issue for voters is a transfer to the poorer part of the population and where the upper-income groups have genuinely charitable motives and hence want to make at least some transfer. It differs from the last chapter in that the poor people will be permitted to vote, too. The situation can be seen in Figure 1. Once again we have *A* and *B*, who have genuinely charitable intentions with respect to *C*. The cost of the transfers is shown by a horizontal straight line in the usual way. The transfer demands of both *A* and *B* are shown by the appropriate demand curves, and we note that with private provision, *C* would receive at least B_0. The social optimum from the standpoint of *A* and *B* only is shown by the sum of lines *A* and *B*, or line $A + B$. This would lead to a transfer of *O*. All of this is reminiscent of the last chapter.

We now turn to a new point. *C* is now permitted to vote, and his demand for the transfer is, as a first approximation, simply the full value of the transfer, in other words the line *C-C*.

Before going further with the analysis of this problem, it might be wise to stop briefly and talk about the operational meaning of the demand curves on this figure. Lines *A* and *B* raise no particular difficulty, because they show what *A* and *B* would be willing to pay in order to generate a given transfer for *C*. It is, indeed, possible to "sell" transfers to *B*, let us say, at more than $1 per $1 of effective transfer, and most charities do that because of their administrative costs. It is also possible to "sell" charity to people at less than $1 per $1 by the simple expedient of offering contingency contracts. This is also very common in charitable organizations. A wealthy person will put up a large sum of money that is to be made available only if it is matched on, let us say, a 50-50 basis. This permits him to purchase the charity at half-price, and those people who make the matching contributions also do so.

Reprinted, with kind permission of Kluwer Academic Publishers, from *Economics of Income Redistribution*, Kluwer-Nijhoff Studies in Human Issues: An International Series in the Social Sciences (Boston: Kluwer-Nijhoff, 1983), 73–96.

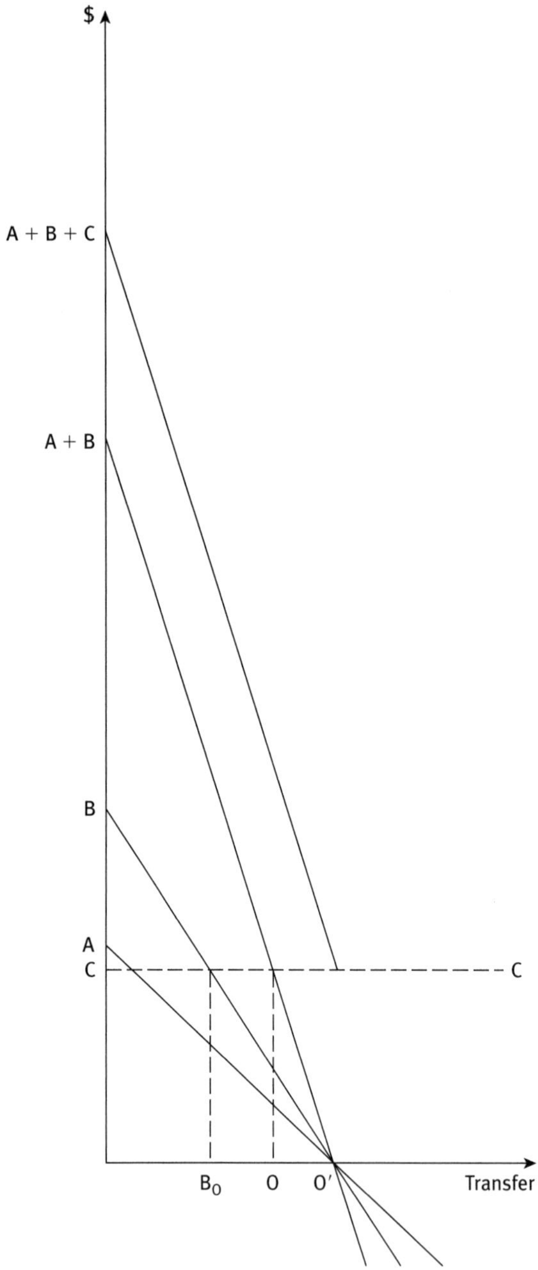

FIGURE 1

Situation where recipients are permitted to influence the outcome

When we come to *C*, however, life is more difficult. If we assume that he is actuated by envy—i.e., he actually likes to get the money for himself from *A* and *B* because he wants to impoverish them—then he would presumably be willing to pay somewhat more than $1 for the receipt of $1. We thus have a demand curve that is slanted upward to the right. Our assumption that he is an impecunious person, however, means that he would not be able to do this, and hence the horizontal line seems to dominate. In essence, the horizontal line showing that *C* will pay $1 in order to receive $1 seems reasonable. It might be, however, that *C*, like everyone else, has some charitable feelings and feels slightly embarrassed as the amount of money transferred to him gets larger and larger. In this case his demand curve would slant slightly downward from the point where *C* intersects the vertical axis.

To give such a curve operational meaning, let us assume that *C* has to suffer the administrations of a social worker in order to receive his money. This social worker asks him to go to her own office, sit in a hard chair while waiting, and then answer questions and listen to lectures on industry. We would predict that as the amount of money that he was receiving increased, the amount of time he would be willing to wait in a hard chair and the patience with which he would listen to lectures for the marginal $1 would decline. This would give us an operational meaning of the downward slant.

Nevertheless, for present purposes, we assume that *C*'s demand for charity to himself is simply the amount that he gets, and hence line *C*. This, however, raises a couple of other minor points. Firstly, there will, of course, be some administrative cost in transferring the money from *A* and *B* to *C*, and hence the amount that *C* receives will be slightly less than the amount *A* and *B* pay. This is important, because if we add *C*'s demand onto the demand of *A* and *B*, and assume that the demands of *A* and *B* are straight lines that at O′ on the horizontal axis drop to zero and then remain zero from then on, the outcome would be indeterminant if *C*'s receipts were exactly the same as *A*'s and *B*'s payments. It could, in fact, be any point on the line *CC* to the right of O′. If we assume realistically that there is a slight administrative cost, however, the line $A + B + C$ would actually cross line *CC*, and then turn sharply to the right at a point where the $A + B$ line reaches the horizontal axis. To avoid cluttering the diagram, I have not drawn this additional line. It would, presumably, be only a very slight distance below *CC*, and hence an accurate drawing might make it necessary for the reader to use a microscope to read the diagram.

All of this, however, assumes that *A*'s and *B*'s demand for charity to *C* is zero from O′ right. It is an ordinary observation of modern life that people who engage in making transfers to the poor tend to become positively annoyed when these transfers get above what they think is a reasonable amount. Under these circumstances, lines *A* and *B* would continue downward below the horizontal axis as in Figure 1. This also would give us a definite solution to the problem even if there were no administrative costs. The drop below this line would indicate that *A* and *B* would actually be willing to pay something more than $1 between them to avoid payment to *C* of $1.

The reader can conceive of his emotions if a tax were imposed on him for the purpose of making a gift to David Rockefeller on his next birthday.[1] I suspect that most readers, even though they do not personally dislike Mr. Rockefeller, would be delighted to pay an amount 1 percent greater than their tax to some organization that would excuse them from the tax.

There are a number of problems here. For example, if instead of using these straight lines for demand, we used a curve that approached but did not reach the horizontal axis, then assuming that administrative costs were zero or very close to zero, the difference between points O and O′ would be very large indeed. Without empirical evidence, we do not actually know what the shape of the curve would be.

But this is not the only problem. It is not at all obvious that the point at which the demand crosses the cost is the amount of charitable distribution to the poor that "ought" to be made. To take one obvious alternative, we might argue that the distribution that will maximize utility is the right amount. Another distribution would be the one that tends to equalize utility. These two would presumably be very different, with people who are subject to severe handicaps that lower their utility receiving very large payments under the second system and very low payments under the first.

One of the things that I have discovered is that most problems of this sort have not been thought through. Most people with whom I discussed the matter, or authors who have written about it, seem to have some vague idea that there is a right amount of redistribution. Almost any proposal that I make which is a specific target for income redistribution makes them unhappy, but when I ask what is the right amount, I get very little enlightenment. This is not particularly surprising. Most of us are taught to talk about

1. When Princess Anne was married, the Army decided to collect a voluntary gift from its members for her. As is rather characteristic in drives like this (the reader may consider the United Fund as an example), a good deal of pressure was in fact put on, and some of the privates resented it.

charitable redistribution and make remarks about how we would like to help the poor. On the other hand, we are just as well trained to make rather modest redistributions of income outside the family.

All of this may sound hypocritical, and I suppose it does meet the formal meaning of that term, but I do not think there is any conscious hypocrisy. We live in a society in which everyone talks as if they want to redistribute a great deal, but in which people, in fact, redistribute very little to the poor. Further, a great deal of redistribution is redistribution to the person who arranged it, i.e., redistribution to the politically powerful. Most of it is rationalized as redistribution to the poor even if the person who is doing the rationalization is a millionaire. He will rarely say that his own gain is the reason he is in favor of redistribution. Normally he will point out that somewhere in the world there is some poor person who may conceivably benefit from the transfer.

It may be that I have overlooked some new literature. It may be that those people who argue for income transfers have reached some kind of a general agreement of how much should be transferred. There are occasional cases of individuals who produce arbitrary numbers that they say are the right amount of transfers.[2] In general, however, they do not say how much, and when they do say how much, the amounts differ a great deal from author to author. Further, there is little argument for any given amount.

If we observe the real world, we observe modest charitable distributions by private gift and modest charitable distributions by way of the government. In both cases, the amounts are comparatively small. Indeed, among the private gift market, gifts to churches that presumably are intended to benefit the person who makes the gift by keeping him out of hell are considerably larger than gifts to more genuinely charitable objects. In the political realm, the same is true. We transfer far more money to special interest groups than we do to the poor. All of this, however, is normally discussed under the rubric of charitable transfers.

This discussion may sound extremely critical. In a way it is critical, but I am merely trying to defend myself against an attack that I am sure will be made. I feel almost certain that any proposal I have for actually determining the optimal amount of income redistribution, no matter how theoretical it may be, will be subject to criticism on the grounds that it does not give the right amount, though the person criticizing will not tell me what is the right

2. Thurow, for example, feels that the highest income an American should receive is no more than five times as much as that of the lowest income American.

amount. Further, there will be a general implication that my numbers, whatever they are, or my method of calculation, whatever it is, does not produce enough transfer. At the same time, people are likely to point out that it is politically impractical to give even that much.

All of this is most inconvenient to the student, but I think it also reflects the generally undeveloped state of knowledge in the field. The reader may have noticed that I have not endorsed any particular amount of redistribution. Since I am not prominently known as an egalitarian, this may be taken as an illustration of my views, but I do not think that anyone else has given us a way of determining the right amount of redistribution. Where people suggested methods, it invariably turns out that they do not really believe in them.

May I here cite a personal example. Anthony Downs,[3] in his book *An Economic Theory of Democracy*, argues that democracy is desirable because it permits the poor to use the power of their votes to take money from the rich and thus redistribute income. I know Downs, and so I asked him why he thought this was the right amount, pointing out that we could very easily change the voting franchise in such a way as to either increase or reduce the amount. He immediately responded that the change in the voting franchise, producing different amounts, would produce the wrong amount. I then asked him how he knew that this existing amount was the right amount, and he said that it was because it came out of the current method of voting.

Clearly, the argument is circular. Equally clearly, Anthony Downs is an extremely intelligent man who feels strongly on these issues. He simply has not found it necessary ever to really carefully go through his ideas in the area. Further, I suspect that he would find it very painful if he did, because he, like almost everyone else, talks much more charitably than he acts and does not, in fact, want to change his manner of behavior to fit his talk.

I am not suggesting that people act in accordance with what they say, but that they say in accordance with what they do. In other words, I am suggesting we amend our language and not our behavior. Like most economists, I tend to think how people act is a better representation of their real thoughts than what they say.

But this particular suggestion for moral reform is not my main point here. My main point is that I, of necessity, in writing this book, have to talk about some kind of optimum redistribution. It seems to me that taking that

3. Anthony Downs, *An Economic Theory of Democracy* (New York: Harper and Row, 1957), 207–19.

optimal redistribution from what people say would be very unwise. Hence, I am more interested in how people actually act on redistribution than in what they say about it.

If we consider how people actually act about redistribution, we fairly soon come to the conclusion that they are charitable, but not very. This is the position I am going to take. I shall discuss what is the likely outcome of various courses of action, not what people say they think they should do. The reader is then permitted to make up his own mind as to what should happen, and I would like to suggest that he consider what he is likely to do, not what he would like to think that he is likely to do. Having chosen his optimum, he can then consider institutional changes that might lead to that outcome.

For example, if the reader feels that charity by government should be greater than it now is, he could seek a constitutional amendment that simply says that it shall be some particular amount. I doubt that such an amendment would be adopted unless people actually favored that amount, but it certainly would be true that the offering of such an amendment would lead to a lot of quite amusing discussion as people explained that while they, of course, wanted to give away 10 percent of their income to the poor, for various reasons it just was not practical.

A second, more indirect method would be to change the weighting of our votes. Currently, all democratic governments use a very simple weighting system in which an individual's vote is either weighted at one or at zero. For example, I have a vote weight of one in Montgomery County where my home is and zero in Blacksburg where I work. I have a single vote in the affairs of the State of Virginia as a whole, but zero in either West Virginia or North Carolina, both states that are within a short distance of my home and where affairs do affect me in various ways. I, of course, have one vote in the national elections but none in the elections of Canada or Mexico.

This system is so customary in democracies that I think most people do not realize just how special it is. The argument for government activity is the internalizing of externalities and provision of public goods. Almost never are externalities or public goods so constituted that they fit the existing boundaries neatly. As a rough rule of thumb, most externalities have their greatest effect at some point, or small area, and then gradually fall off as you move away from them. In some cases, of course, the movement away is not geographic but along some other dimension. I, for example, am totally uninterested in tennis except that I rather resent having to pay taxes to maintain public tennis courts, and, hence, giving me one vote on this issue, where a man who is fanatically interested in tennis also receives one, seems odd. Similarly, with respect to geographic boundaries, the citizens of India have a very considerable interest in the American aid program for India and various American foreign policy decisions. They are given no vote in them at all. There surely are some Americans for whom this is of much less importance than it is to the average citizen of India, but the Americans are given a one rather than a zero weighting.

It is an interesting characteristic of demand-revealing[4] that this problem vanishes under it. It is not necessary to assign preliminary weights of zero or one to the voters, they will assign their own weights themselves. Thus, if the citizens of North Carolina are interested in something that is going on in Virginia, they will assign themselves weights that are equivalent to their actual demand for whatever government services are in Virginia. Presumably, these would normally be lower than the weights that would be self-assigned by the citizens of Virginia, and, hence, they would have less influence than the citizens of Virginia, but everyone would have an influence that was proportional to his demand for the public services rather than the arbitrary zero-one weighting that is our current system.

Leaving aside demand-revealing, there does not really seem to be any reason for the zero-one weighting system. Further, it seems to be particularly hard to argue for in connection with income redistribution. Note that when I say it is hard to argue for, I am not alleging it is easy to argue against. It would appear, if we were talking about income redistribution, that there simply is no reason for any particular weighting. Different weightings would give different amounts in income redistribution, and we have no way of determining what is the correct amount.

If we are interested in raising the demand, then presumably we would try to give more votes to those who have the greatest demand for the charity and fewer votes for those who have a lower demand. This probably would mean some kind of weighting system under which people eligible for relief receive fairly high weightings, and also, perhaps, for people in upper-income brackets who are characteristically more charitable in absolute terms, although perhaps not in relative terms, than people in the lower-income brackets. We have no idea what the appropriate structure would be, but we can say the present system is not obviously correct.

4. T. Nicolaus Tideman and Gordon Tullock, "A New and Superior Process for Making Social Choices," *Journal of Political Economy* (October 1976): 1145–59.

Suppose, for example, that we feel that the poor do not benefit by our present society and that they should receive more. The simple way of arranging for this would be to see to it that everyone's vote in elections was the reciprocal of his income. If, on the other hand, we felt that the poor on the whole are doing better than they should, then weighting the ballots so that, let us say, each person is permitted to cast as many votes as his dollar income for that year would no doubt lead to some change. Probably a proposal that each person be permitted to cast as many votes as his dollar income, up to some fairly low maximum so that the tendency of the wealthy to be very charitable would be eliminated from the weighting system, would be even better from this standpoint. Of course, we could either increase or reduce these effects by such devices as squaring the income or taking the square root, and so on.

All of this may seem bizarre, but I think if the reader considers it a little bit he will realize that by bizarre, in this case, he simply means something he has not thought about before. There are, as far as I know, no very good arguments for these different weightings that I have proposed, but I also know of no arguments except tradition for the weighting we characteristically use.

Demand-revealing, in income redistribution, unfortunately also has a very severe problem. That problem is that what is revealed is the demand. Demand, as all economists know, is not the same as need. It is need plus effective ability to make one's need felt in the market by having adequate purchasing power. Most people who are interested in income redistribution feel that need should be measured in a direct way without purchasing power being thrown in. If we had a way of measuring individual utilities, this might well be possible, but at the moment we do not have such a method. We are stuck with either some kind of arbitrary weighting of votes or demand-revealing, which does not reveal exactly what most people think should be revealed. It is clear that neither is very well adapted to the problem, but it seems likely that in that minority of the world where democratic voting is still retained, the zero-one weighting will be the foundation of most income redistribution, and I shall confine myself to that from now on.

It should perhaps be said, as another digression, that it is customary both in practice and in theoretical discussions to skip this whole problem by simply assuming that we know what "need" is. There is wide disagreement about it, but social workers will tell you that need is a certain amount. Different social workers specify different amounts. Politicians will tell you that the need is other amounts, with, once again, different politicians differing. The same variance applies to the opinions of the rest of the population.

The "need" in this case characteristically is, in fact, a political compromise between a desire to be nice to the poor and a feeling that you do not want to give them your entire income. It is, of course, obvious that need, in any real meaning of the term, is not a national matter; i.e., it is not any more expensive to stay alive in the United States than it is in those parts of China that have a similar climate to the United States. Nevertheless, we usually pretend that they need less than we do.

A good many writers have taken the view that need is essentially a psychological rather than a physical matter and that the important point is to have a particular relationship of your income with that of other people. In other words, the poor mother in the Sahel watching her child starve to death is not really made terribly unhappy about it, because it is a very common event there, and she does not feel discriminated against. The black in Harlem who does not have a color TV, on the other hand, is very unhappy because he observes that community standards involve a color TV. I have invented an unkind, if accurate, aphorism for this: "if everybody in the village has a toothache it does not really hurt."

The main function of this argument is that it makes the people in rich countries happy about largely confining their charity to other members of their nation instead of feeling guilty about not helping the poor people in places like Bangladesh, Africa, and China. If we really thought all human beings were alike, we would not discriminate in favor of the poor in the United States. In fact, we propose to discriminate in favor of the poor in the United States, and we require some kind of rationalization other than simply admitting we are more interested in American poor people than others. This relative deprivation hypothesis provides such a rationalization.

One argument for the relative deprivation hypothesis is that our charity is controlled by the votes of poor Americans. If that is so, they are likely to want the money to go to themselves and not to the poor Indians. This would account, in part, for the fact that much more money does go to poor Americans than to poor Africans, even if the poor Africans are much poorer.

But, in any event, we do observe this concentration of aid on people who by world standards are quite well-off, while people who by world standards are badly off do not receive very much. Whether it comes from a voting procedure under which the poor in upper-income areas are permitted to partly control the local charity or whether it reflects nationalistic feelings in a more direct way, I do not know. But one should not talk about existing aid programs for the poor as if they were efforts to treat all people alike or make payments in terms of need. They are heavily national in their orientation, and poor people who happen to be born in the wrong nation receive little aid.

There is one rather temporary argument that can be used for providing somewhat higher aid amounts to people in upper-income areas like Harlem, as opposed to lower-income areas like the Sahel. This is not that the necessities of life are more expensive in Harlem than they are in the Sahel, but that it is almost impossible to buy the absolute bare minimum subsistence diet and minimum subsistence shelter in Harlem because material of the Sahel level of quality is not available. One could predict that if one dropped relief payments in Harlem to the Sahel level, merchants in Harlem would begin stocking this kind of product at the kind of prices one would pay for it in the Sahel. Temporarily, however, it would be impossible to purchase a Sahel-quality diet or Sahel-quality shelter and clothing. Of course, if we dropped relief to the Sahel level, there would be a very sharp change in the number of people who were attempting to get aid anyway. I am not arguing that we should do this, but simply pointing out that the normal language that we use to talk about aid to the poor does not describe accurately what we in fact do.

Let us return to the more technical problem of what we can expect a democratic society to do for the poor, granted that the poor are permitted to participate in the voting process. The first thing to be said is that there is no reason to believe that the outcome will be equivalent to the point where the sum of the demand curves crosses the cost line in Figure 1. Indeed, there does not seem to be any reason to believe that the outcome of such a voting procedure will meet any other criterion than simply being the outcome of that procedure. A devoted democrat, of course, will regard this as proof that it is the right amount.

The problem here is that we are now confronted with a game without a core. This is characteristic of almost all cases of income redistribution, with individuals interested in the income redistribution for purely or partially selfish, as opposed to purely charitable, motives. We mentioned this problem briefly in passing in Chapter 4 when we pointed out the desire of the two potential donors of charity to each work off as much of the cost on the other as possible.

In the real world, of course, societies are very large. For simplicity, I want to confine myself right now to a society of three persons, *A* and *B*, who are charitably inclined toward *C*, who is a poor person and a potential recipient for charity. Let us assume *A* is more charitable than *B*. Let us further assume that decisions are to be made by simple majority voting. For simplicity, I will assume that *A* has an income of $100 a year, *B* has an income of $50 per year, and *C* has nothing—if we ignore what he gets from relief. Let us further assume that if we added demand curves, adding only the curves of *A* and *B*, that *C* would get $15 a year, which with Lindahl taxation would be raised by a tax of $10 for *A* and $5 for *B*. If we add in *C*'s own demand for charity to get the demand by all three, the amount that *C* would get would be $20. Here we cannot, strictly speaking, produce a Lindahl tax, but we can introduce a tax that is equally disliked or, in essence, requires an equal overpayment by both *A* and *B*, and this tax would be $12.50 for *A* and $7.50 for *B*. As I said above, there is no reason to believe democratic voting will in any way approach this goal.

Let us assume that by an act of God, or some other method, our society starts in a situation in which *A*, through a private charity, is making a $6 contribution to *C*, and *B* is contributing nothing. *C*, of course, would prefer to get more. This is shown by the first line in Figure 2, where the $6 paid out by *A* is marked as −6. Note that I indicated payouts by minus numbers and receipts by positive numbers, but in this particular case *A*, presumably, is not unhappy about making the $6 payment. In the current situation, $6 in charity to *C* meets *A*'s preferences.

Now let us suppose that *C*, who would like more money, approaches *A* and suggests to him that the charity be collectivized, specifically that a tax system be established under which both *A* and *B* would pay in $7.50, and *C* would get $15.00. This benefits both *A* and *C* and injures *B*. *A* is benefitted because, although he pays more, the increase in payments to *C* is $9.00, and that is a bargain for him at $1.50. This coalition is therefore a majority. The situation is shown in the second line.

A	B	C
−6	0	6
−7.50	−7.50	15
−15	−5	20
−10	−20	30
−30	−15	45
0	0	0
−5	−10	15

FIGURE 2

Society of three persons, of which A and B are charitably inclined toward C

With this new status quo, let us assume that *B* decides to approach *C* with another proposal, specifically that *B* contribute $5, and *A* be taxed $15, with the result that *C* gets $20. Once again, there is a two-voter majority for change. The process may go on indefinitely, and I have put below the first three lines in Figure 2 a number of other lines, each of which is a two-party coalition that beats the one above and which wanders vaguely across the conceivable issue space. Note that substantially anything can happen in this model.

Clearly, this is not what we see in the real world. We do not observe rotating coalitions of this sort in democratic governments. Indeed, democratic governments tend, if anything, to be rather stodgy and likely to stick to given policies long after the motives behind them have disappeared. Certainly, basic institutional structures stay in existence for very long periods of time, and that includes redistribution of income.

Further, we do not, in the real world, observe the kind of situation we show here in which there is blatant unfairness toward one group. It should be said that we do occasionally see this. There may be situations in which one area, one type of political position, or one group is permanently barred from power, causing considerable discrimination. Let us take what in many ways was the most extreme example of this: Northern Ireland, before the British government intervened, upset the previous Protestant supremacy, and inaugurated the current blood bath.

The Catholics were in a permanent minority and, because of gerrymandering, normally had less than one-third of the legislature, although they had one-third of the votes. Fair districting, of course, would have left them still in a minority, and this was clearly a permanent condition. Northern Ireland, like the rest of the United Kingdom, was a welfare state with large-scale government investments in housing and other services. There is no doubt at all that the Catholics did worse on these dimensions than the Protestants.

But although there is no doubt that the Protestant supremacy discriminated against the Catholics, the discrimination was not gigantic. You could not tell, for example, by simply walking through a government-owned housing development whether it was Catholic or Protestant, and, indeed, there was a good deal of intermixture of the two groups in the period before the British government's destruction of the old regime. The current completely partitioned nature of the Belfast population comes from the recent unpleasantness rather than from the long period of stable but rather oppressive government by the Protestants.

The Catholics were undeniably severely annoyed by the previous system, which did discriminate against them, but it was more a matter of annoyance over a number of minor discriminations that did not greatly damage the Catholics than it was the outcome of a true persecution. That this is so can easily be seen from population movements. Northern Ireland is a rather small spot on a rather small island. There are almost no restrictions of any sort at the borders of Northern Ireland and the Republic of Ireland. Under the circumstances, the Irish citizenry of Belfast could have without the slightest difficulty moved across the border. They chose not to, and, in fact, the net flow of Catholic migration was to some extent in the other direction.

Admittedly, the disasters inflicted on the economy of Ireland by the early de Valera government were probably, to a considerable extent, responsible. The British government does not run its economy well, but compared with de Valera in the early part of his presidency, they were economic geniuses. Still, it is clear that the average Catholic Irishman living in Belfast preferred to put up with the numerous minor discriminations rather than move to Eire.[5]

But although I am not attempting to excuse the situation in Northern Ireland, which I think is very likely the most extreme case of a democracy discriminating against a block of its voters, it is clear that the discrimination was not very severe. Note here that when I talk about discrimination I am not using the word in the normal meaning. As a general rule, the individual who talks about discrimination begins by having some idea in his mind as to what is the proper distribution of power, good manners, money, etc. He then notes that this distribution is not the one in use and says that this represents discrimination. This is not what I mean.

My view of discrimination here is simply that the individual voters do not get roughly equal treatment. Thus, with my definition, the fact that upper-income people pay somewhat higher taxes and do not get that back in government services[6] is an example of discrimination against them. If I understand the popular literature on this matter, the average person would say that the fact that they do not pay more taxes than they do indicates discrimination in their favor.

5. There were also minor discriminations against the Protestants in the Catholic Republic of Ireland. Indeed, the Protestant population of the Republic has declined sharply.

6. Except insofar as police and national defense services probably protect people in proportion to their wealth.

I am not trying to change the common use of the word "discrimination," but I do have to have some technical term here and I am using discrimination. A priori, one would think that a vote is a vote is a vote, i.e., that everyone would get about the same amount of return on a vote in terms of government satisfaction. True, it does seem to fit the real world fairly closely.[7] In democracies the government boodle is passed out in a moderately egalitarian manner throughout the society, although at any given point some particular pressure groups are doing better than others.

Indeed, the money is almost always passed out by methods which, in detail, are highly discriminatory. Subsidies to farmers, for example, do not go to anyone else, but the general picture is that almost anybody who chooses to organize a little bit will get some kind of favor. This is the kind of "nondiscriminatory" approach that one expects in a democracy. The point is that this is what we observe in democracy, not the extremely discriminatory and rapidly changing pattern of the model in Table 1 later in this chapter.

The model in which the outcome is pretty much indeterminant and rapidly shifting, but always has the characteristic that discriminates against some transitory minority in favor of an equally transitory majority, does not fit the world. Is there a model that does? Is there a model that fits the world better and that is equally well developed? The answer is yes, it is the logrolling model first outlined in "Problems of Majority Voting"[8] and then greatly developed in *The Calculus of Consent*.[9] Although the stability of this model has been questioned, the questioning comes from not fully understanding the time path that is followed by the voting procedure in most representative bodies.[10]

If we observe a functioning democratic legislature in the United States, we see that it runs by the logrolling process. Logrolling also dominates the procedure of legislatures around the world. The basic difference is that it is carried on in a much more overt way in the American legislatures than elsewhere. In any event, the relatively stable model that explains redistribution of income is based on logrolling.

7. Which might explain the fact that the wealthier people pay higher taxes and get fewer services.

8. Gordon Tullock, "Problems of Majority Voting," *Journal of Political Economy* 67 (December 1959): 571–79.

9. Gordon Tullock and James M. Buchanan, *The Calculus of Consent: Logical Foundations of Constitutional Democracy* (Ann Arbor: University of Michigan Press, 1962).

10. See debate in *Public Choice*, beginning with Tullock's "Why So Much Stability," vol. 37, no. 2 (1981): 189–202.

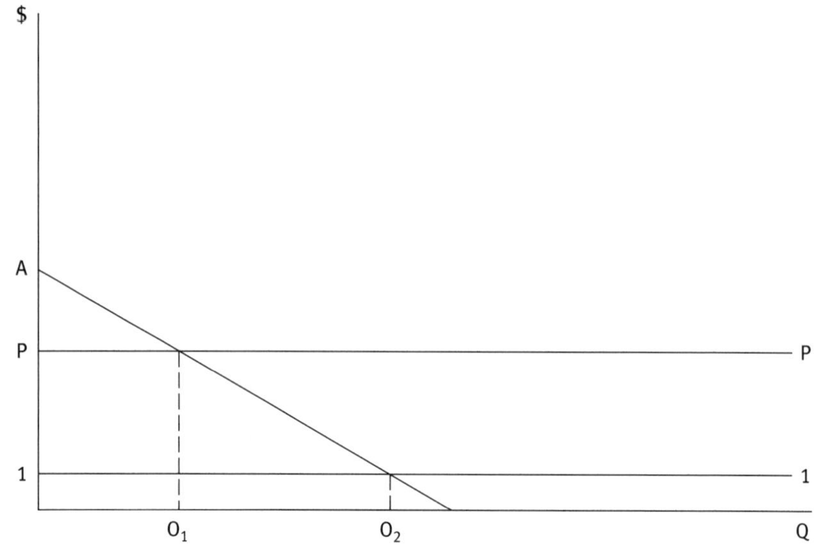

FIGURE 3
Society of five persons, of which A, B, C, and D are charitably inclined toward P

Before dealing with the complexities of logrolling, however, let us look at Figure 3. Here I have shown a society of five people, four of whom, *A*, *B*, *C*, and *D*, are charitable and have the same demand curve for charity, shown by the line *A*. There is a fifth member of the society, *P*, who is poor and wants to receive charity, and his demand curve is shown by the line *AA*, which represents the cost of giving him each dollar. Suppose that one charitable person, *A*, is in fact giving O_1 to *P*. We noted that under these circumstances, *B*, *C*, and *D* have no motive for taking any action at all. *A* would presumably prefer to have somebody else pay the charity to support *P*, and hence he has some motive for action, and *P* would, of course, like more charity. There is a Pareto optimal move here, essentially because I drew the diagram with that intent. If *A*, *B*, *C*, and *D* all decide jointly to give O_2 to *P*, then distribution of costs will be as shown on line 1 of the figure, and all four of them are happy because their demands for charity are met because $O_{2/4}$ is what they would be willing to pay for an O_2 payment to *P*, and that is what he is getting. *P*, of course, is better off, and *A* is particularly benefitted. His payment has fallen while at the same time his charitable instincts are more thoroughly fulfilled.

Let us pause briefly here and consider the situation of all of these people when bargaining with the others. *A*, *B*, *C*, and *D* can reasonably assume that

P will take as much as he can get. No one, however, knows the actual demand for charity that each of our charitable individuals has. If, for example, *D* announced that he had no desire to help *P* at all, there would be no way of demonstrating that this was not true. He might, therefore, be able to enter into a bargain with other people under which he receives some sort of compensation for agreeing to make the charitable contribution to *P* which he wants to make anyway.

Thus, *P* is at a bargaining disadvantage. The others know his demand curve, but he does not know theirs. Further, the various potential donors do not know each other's demand curves, and hence their bargaining also suffers from the same difficulty. It is only if some kind of collective provision were made to aid *P*, which was less than some individual[11] thought was adequate and inadequate enough so that he was willing to supplement it out of his own pocket, that we could discover actual demands. In the more normal situation, in which collective provision is greater than individuals would be willing to provide, there is no way of estimating the demand curve of the individuals for charity to *P*.

This being so, the situation here of *P* is no different from the situation of any citizen of a country who has a special project that will benefit him and that is to be funded out of the general costs. Whether *P* wants a direct relief payment while *D* is interested in having a harbor dredged is a matter of formal indifference.

Here I must briefly disgress to discuss logrolling in some detail. The reason for the detailed discussion is that I must explain both why there is a fairly stable solution and why the poor may not do very well under it. Briefly, the reason the poor will not necessarily do very well under it is the extreme ease of concealing charitable desires. Logrolling involves a trading of political favors—you vote for my bill and I vote for yours.

To put the matter very simply in a sort of introduction of the more complicated explanation that will follow, if I am a charitable person and *P* is a poor person, I may conceal from *P* my charitable instincts and offer to trade a vote by me on a bill to transfer funds to *P* for his voting for a bill to dredge the New River and make Radford a deep-water port. *P* can, without too much difficulty, judge the intensity of my desire for the Radford port, and I can assume that he is opposed to it to the full extent of any tax that he might have to pay. When it comes to my voting for charity to him, however, it might well be that I am selling him something that I would really be willing

11. Or group of individuals, through some organized charity.

to give. From my standpoint, this is ideal, since he gets exactly the charitable gift that I think he should receive while I get his vote.

Note, of course, that we would not expect anything this perfect. Presumably I would be reluctant to enter into an agreement under which he received less than I would voluntarily give him without compensation.[12] But, on the other hand, he might work me into making a payment larger than my own desires as a voluntary gift. Still, there is no reason to believe that the outcome would be that I would give him, in the logrolling bargain, an amount that was much larger than my (secret) personal desire to help him.

That is, however, very simple. Let us look at the matter more carefully, and for that purpose consider Figure 4. The three panels of Figure 4 represent three possible logrolling situations with our little five-member legislature, *A*, *B*, *C*, and *D*, who are charitable toward *P* but who have other things they would like to get, and, of course, *P* himself. We assume in each case that the constitutional provision involves a series of specific projects, each of which will cost $10, and that the tax will be evenly divided so that each party pays $2 on each of these projects. In the top left panel, for each of the projects there is a gain to the person who receives the logrolling benefit, whatever it is, of $12 so he nets $10. For all these projects, socially there is a net gain of $2, and we would like to have a system that produced them.

In the second panel, each individual receives a gain of $9 on his project, or a net of $7 after he has paid the $2 tax. These projects are clearly undesirable, since the social gain is less than the social cost, but unfortunately logrolling, even with perfect information, would permit them. The third panel is the same as the second except that *P*, in this case, receives only the same amount that he puts in, i.e., $2, and hence, in net, makes no gain at all. It is quite possible that in real terms the poor in our society are in that situation; i.e., the gain that they get over what they would get from voluntary charity is no larger than the tax amount they pay. The real point of this panel, however, is not to indicate that that is true, but to simply illustrate that it is possible for an individual to do very badly indeed in logrolling.

Let us consider the logrolling process a little more carefully, and for this purpose we will use the top left panel, although in my opinion the other two panels are no less realistic. Suppose then that *A*, *B*, *C*, and *D* each want the harbor of their city dredged, and *P* would like a charitable payment above and beyond what *A*, *B*, *C*, and *D* would voluntarily give him. We here assume

12. As part of bargaining maneuvers for future transactions, however, I might accept this arrangement once.

	A	B	C	D	P
A′	10	−2	−2	−2	−2
B′	−2	10	−2	−2	−2
C′	−2	−2	10	−2	−2
D′	−2	−2	−2	10	−2
P′	−2	−2	−2	−2	10

	A	B	C	D	P
A′	7	−2	−2	−2	−2
B′	−2	7	−2	−2	−2
C′	−2	−2	7	−2	−2
D′	−2	−2	−2	7	−2
P′	−2	−2	−2	−2	7

	A	B	C	D	P
A′	7	−2	−2	−2	−2
B′	−2	7	−2	−2	−2
C′	−2	−2	7	−2	−2
D′	−2	−2	−2	7	−2
P′	−2	−2	−2	−2	ϵ

FIGURE 4
Three possible logrolling situations

for this panel that *P* somehow knows what *A*, *B*, *C*, and *D* would give him voluntarily and hence is bargaining for more.

On Monday, *A* approaches *B* and *C* and suggests that they vote for a bill providing project *A*′, and *A* agrees in return to vote for projects *B*′ and *C*′. The bill is thus passed. On Tuesday, *B*, who already has the promise of *A*'s vote, approaches D and suggests that D vote for B' because B will then vote for D'. D agrees, and project B' is implemented. On Wednesday, C approaches P and suggests that P agree to vote for C' in return for C's voting for the charitable payment to P labeled P'. P agrees, and C' is then voted through with the votes of A, C, and P. On Thursday, D approaches P and suggests that he will vote for P' if P votes for D'. P agrees, and D' is then passed with the votes of B, D, and P. On Friday, the P' project is passed with the votes of C, D, and P. Thus, all of these projects have passed.

It has been argued that this project procedure is unstable; in other words, each bargain could always be dominated by another. This is not necessarily true, but let me temporarily turn to a discussion of the second and third panels. On the second panel, the project itself is not socially desirable. Since when one considers such projects as the Tulsa deep-water port or the Tombigbee Canal—the first of which, to my distress, to have been completed, and the second of which may be completed—it is obvious that such things do occur. Indeed, granted that information is usually very imperfect, such projects occur on a much more wasteful scale than is shown in the second panel.[13]

The third panel represents a situation in which P, for one reason or another, simply does not have an adequate project available that will lead to his receiving a large payoff. He makes the best of a bad bargain and accepts an agreement that pays him 2 + epsilon, at a cost of a \$2 tax payment, with a result that he ends up with epsilon. If he refused to vote for the first four projects, he would be worse off. In practice, granted the fact that he does not know how much A, B, C, and D would be willing to give him voluntarily, it is certainly possible that he will end up with a negative result from his logrolling, although one would anticipate that in the long run A, B, C, and D would voluntarily raise his grant to whatever their voluntary gift level is.

But, basically, the problem faced by the poor person is that faced by the others. He has to engage in bargaining in order to get his special aid under a logrolling system. The only disadvantage he has is that it is not easy for him to deduce what other people's actual preference functions are. If they are totally selfish, then he will do about as well as other people out of the logrolling deal. On the other hand, if in fact they are altruistic and he is assuming that they are totally selfish, he may be selling his vote for little or nothing.

13. All this is discussed in great detail in Tullock and Buchanan, *The Calculus of Consent*. See also my "Why So Much Stability."

Still, an assumption that they are altruistic, and hence that he should get for his vote an amount above and beyond what they would give him altruistically, is risky. It is particularly risky since the individuals who are altruistic may well feel a positive moral aversion for giving him more than what they think is a suitable amount. They may feel, for example, that an object of charity such as he is should not have more than a certain living standard, and their aversion to his having more than that living standard may be considerably stronger than their aversion to the tax cost.

As far as I know this particular possibility has not been canvassed in the literature, but it seems to me quite in accord with what I observe around me. A great many people are indeed charitable, but tend to get very indignant when an object of charity receives more than they think is just. This is true even if they, themselves, are not the sources of that additional payment. Logically, we should always be happy at the good fortune of someone else unless that good fortune injures us, or unless it is great enough so that it perhaps arouses envy on our part. As far as I can see, however, this is not the normal attitude toward poor people who are on charity. There is a positive feeling that they should be prevented from suffering any real hardship, but also that they should not have "luxuries." All of this can be rationalized quite easily under prevailing moral codes, but I see no point in doing so now. The only point I wish to make is that this attitude may make logrolling for amounts above the voluntary gift level more expensive than it would appear.

Once we get away from the simple, selfishness model and begin admitting interdependent utility functions, we not only make our model more realistic but we also make it more complicated. Suppose *A* has an income of $10,000 a year and *B* has zero income. *A* may feel that it will be desirable for *B* to have an income of $2,000 a year and be willing to even make the necessary sacrifice himself. This is, of course, interdependence of utility. *A* may also feel that, since *B* is not actually earning his income but is an object of charity, he should not have an income above $2,000, and *A* might even be willing to make some sacrifices himself in order to see to it that *B* does not have that higher income. This is another interdependence and just as reasonable as the first. Further, as far as I can see, both interdependences are in accord with human behavior.

There is, however, another and more delicate reason why the poor may not do too well out of the logrolling process. Here I must be very careful and begin by warning the reader that I am not imputing any moral fault to the poor. The fact is, however, that the poor are generally not highly competent people. That, indeed, is why they are poor. The man who is not capable of holding down a good job is probably equally incapable of efficiently selling his vote in the best market. In other words, he is likely to do badly in the political marketplace as well as in the economic. The fact that they are rather inadequate may reflect their heredity, the environment in which they are brought up,[14] or some disabling disease, but the point is that one of the reasons the poor do not seem to do very well in modern welfare states is they are bad at manipulating the welfare state. The fact that they are, in general, bad at manipulating may also account for the fact that they are not very well off.

The average attitude of the average American toward the people who are on relief is usually one of indignation at the large amounts of money they get. Normally, I find that when I explain to the average American how little the poor actually get, they suddenly say that the amount is, in fact, inadequate.[15] The average citizen is aware of how expensive the welfare state is and mistakenly thinks that the reason it is expensive is that a large amount goes to the poor. He is, however, normally in favor of giving to the poor larger amounts in base income than they now have.

We must here be a little careful. The poor in our society who are under the care of the welfare establishment frequently have calculated incomes that are quite high. This is because they are given by the welfare establishment a large number of special benefits that they probably value very little. A welfare mother who has four children, all undergoing compensatory education, may easily have calculated real income, including the cost of that compensatory education, of $20,000 a year, while her cash income may be as low as $5,000 or $6,000 a year. The taxpayer sees the $20,000 a year, but she would probably be delighted to trade that for $8,000 or $9,000 in cash. Indeed, working families who are making $8,000 to $9,000 a year in cash and who have problem children whom they do not send to expensive special schools could reasonably both feel annoyed at how much is being spent on her and at the same time feel sorry for her poverty.

Here, it appears, the problem is simply bad administration of the relief program rather than either over- or underinvestment of resources. The standard middle-class social worker is apt to have a set of attitudes toward the

14. At the moment, it is fashionable to refer to the absence of suitable role models. I do not doubt that this is true in many cases, but there are other problems in the educational environment than that.

15. This, of course, involves nationalism, since the amount is much higher than the average world income.

clients with whom he or she works that leads to an extremely bad allocation of resources. In a way, social work training is training in spending money to help the poor inefficiently. Further, the various categorical programs that have been enacted, to a large extent under the advice of the welfare workers, also involve basically inefficient expenditures. All of this seems to indicate that the poor are politically inept, and I believe that is indeed true. Once again, this may be the reason that they do so badly in our modern society.

I must now discuss why the logrolling equilibrium I have described above is stable, but why coalition equilibrium is not. Consider again the top left panel of Figure 4. I discussed how a logrolling coalition could develop with everyone getting his project enacted. It clearly would be to the advantage of *A*, *B*, and *C*, however, to form a permanent coalition in which A', B', and C' are enacted and D' and P' are not. This coalition would appear to dominate the logrolling arrangement. The reason that it does not is simply that it is, itself, unstable. There are no stable majority coalitions in this group, because each is dominated by another. This point is a little concealed in Figure 4 because we assume that each particular project has a specific cost and a specific payoff and that there is only one for each person. In the real world, although it is undeniably true that most of the projects have a specific cost and a specific payoff,[16] there are a great number of them, and hence the number that any individual gets can be varied. Assume a society in which there are not only all three panels of Figure 4 available but ten duplicates of each. Let us assume that the projects have declining marginal utility. Under these circumstances, normally one could anticipate that a grand total of ten of the projects would be implemented, and the others not, under the logrolling equilibrium. This equilibrium would be dominated by a coalition system in which only three of the parties received the full value of nine projects themselves, and the other two receive none. The coalition, however, would be dominated by another, in which the two left out in the first coalition formed an agreement with *C* under which he received four of his projects, and each of the others, *D* and *P*, received only two of theirs. We could go on and on as was pointed out in connection with Figure 1. There is, thus, no single coalition that dominates the logrolling equilibrium.

In most modern countries all transfer arrangements are made in such a way that the return on the marginal unit of labor is considerably less than the average return on a unit of labor; i.e., they are progressive. This is true, not

16. Some of them are expandable or contractable.

only with the wealthy who pay positive taxes but also with the poor who receive transfers that decline as income rises.

Thus, the effect of this situation is to lower the total incentive for work by making the marginal effect greater than the intramarginal effect. There seems no way this can be avoided, however, if income equalization is part of the objectives of the scheme.[17] The basic problem here is that we do not know how much the poor would receive in the form of voluntary gifts from the upper-income people. Conceptually, we can consider a situation—which was the law in 19th-century England and more or less enforced although not formally the law in many American states in the 19th century—in which those who are in receipt of transfers do not vote. Would the poor do better or worse under those institutions than they do now?

The a priori expectation would be that the poor would do worse, because the power of the poorest vote is added on to the charitable expectation when they can vote. The bargaining problems that we have described above, however, may make this uncertain. The poor may end up with roughly the same amount as they would have received by voluntary charity—even less under some circumstances.

The problem here is empirical, since theory does not seem to lead to any definite conclusion. Unfortunately, empirical data are very sparse. So far as I know, the only evidence on the amount that the poor received as a percentage of average income in the 19th century is Lebergott's tiny study.[18] It seems to me extremely desirable that further research be done on this subject, and, indeed, it would seem to be a suitable topic for a large number of doctoral dissertations. It would be a difficult but probably not impossible task that would require plowing through many detailed ancient records. For what it may be worth, Lebergott's study shows that the poor in the 1850s and 1860s were doing roughly as well as they do now on a relative basis.

The second problem in making such a comparison is that we do not have very good data on transfers to the poor now. The various experts on the subject disagree greatly on the size of these transfers. I suppose that is not surprising on an issue in which both ideology and sizable policy considerations are involved, but it does make the situation somewhat obscure. One thing that is

17. For a striking illustration of this effect, see Edgar K. Browning and William R. Johnson, *The Distribution of the Tax Burden*, American Enterprise Institute for Public Policy Research, 1979.

18. Stanley Lebergott, *The American Economy* (Princeton: Princeton University Press, 1976), 57.

TABLE 1 ***Taxes and Net Transfers per Household in Dollars***

INCOME DECILE	AVERAGE BEFORE-TAX, AFTER-TRANSFER INCOME PER HOUSEHOLD	AVERAGE TAX PAYMENT PER HOUSEHOLD	AVERAGE NET TRANSFER PER HOUSEHOLD
1	$ 3,022	$ 353	$ 1,454
2	6,503	811	2,748
3	9,054	1,479	2,184
4	11,723	2,368	851
5	14,602	3,388	− 693
6	17,664	4,501	−2,264
7	20,973	5,599	−3,624
8	25,579	7,183	−5,155
9	32,370	9,747	−7,628
10	64,138	24,624	−21,876
Top 1 percent	$166,037	$79,420	−$76,019

SOURCE: E. K. Browning and W. R. Johnson, *The Distribution of the Tax Burden*, American Enterprise Institute for Public Policy Research, 1979. Reprinted with the permission of The American Enterprise Institute for Public Policy Research, Washington, D.C.

certain, however, is that under modern circumstances, the poor do not do terribly well. Bismarck's invention, the welfare state, engages in immense amounts of transfer of income, but not very much of this transfer goes to the poor.

To illustrate this point, I will draw my data from the above-cited paper by Browning and Johnson, mainly because they show the largest post-tax and -transfer degree of equality of any modern students. If their estimates show that only small amounts may go to the poor, then the reader can rest assured that other estimates show even less.[19] Let us therefore consider their results. For this purpose, look at Table 1.[20] You will note that households that end up in the bottom decile receive a net transfer of only $1,454. Interestingly enough, the next two deciles above receive larger transfers in net than the bottom decile.[21] This is partially accounted for by the fact that we are taking

19. Sheldon Danziger, Robert Haveman, and Robert Plotnick, "How Income Transfers Affect Work, Savings and the Income Redistribution," *Journal of Economic Literature* 19, no. 3 (September 1981): 975–1028.

20. Browning and Johnson, *The Distribution of the Tax Burden*.

21. This is partially offset by the fact that households get larger as you move up the income ladder.

the families by their after-transfer decile. Thus, one of the reasons why households are in the second and third decile from the bottom is that they have received larger transfers. Still, the average household's income from sources other than transfer, in the second and third decile, is larger than that in the bottom decile. All of this is exaggerated when we remember that the transfers here do not contain the bulk of those transfers that are intended to benefit special interest groups, such as the farm program. Once again, this emphasizes that the modern Bismarckian welfare state is not really terribly concerned about the well-being of the poor.

Browning's figures are based on 1976 data, and he shows the total transfer income in the United States as $200,000,000. Rough calculations show that the new effect of this on the bottom decile are transfers of about $8 billion from which should be subtracted about $3 billion in taxes. The second decile up receives twice that amount, with a good deal larger tax burden, and the third decile up, which is still receiving more in net than the bottom decile, does even better. In other words, the poorest 10 percent of the households receive considerably less than 10 percent of the total transfers in our society, even calculating them entirely as welfare state transfers and not including special interest group transfers, and the bottom 20 percent receive less than 20 percent of these transfers.

Let us now turn to Table 2, which shows the source of income by deciles. You will note that the bottom 10 percent includes substantial payments as "capital." This is one of the peculiarities of our methods of calculating income in which older people who may have quite consciously planned to have a small before-transfer income, since they can depend on social security payments, are considered as poor. Many of these families own their own homes, and the imputed capital value is shown here. Others have various other minor capital sources of income.

Nevertheless, it is obvious that for people in this bottom category, the bulk of their income comes from transfers, and the extremely low level of the income described before indicates how little they net. It is notable also that the top 10 percent of the population actually receive considerable cash transfers. Indeed, it is quite probable that the actual total amount of transfer that they receive in the cash transfer column is greater than the amount received by people in the bottom decile. Once again, the welfare state is not particularly kind to the poor.

I do not want to go further into the data here. Anyone who wishes to examine them will reach roughly the same conclusion I have, that is, that the

TABLE 2 ***Source of Income by Deciles of Before-Tax, After-Transfer (BTAT) Income***

	PERCENTAGE OF DECILE BTAT INCOME			
DECILE	LABOR	CAPITAL	CASH TRANSFERS	IN-KIND TRANSFERS
1	26.0	14.0	47.2	12.5
2	34.3	10.9	36.9	17.9
3	48.0	11.6	28.2	12.3
4	61.0	11.5	20.7	6.8
5	70.9	10.7	14.6	3.8
6	77.2	10.2	10.5	2.1
7	80.7	9.9	8.1	1.3
8	81.5	10.6	7.0	0.9
9	79.8	13.7	5.8	0.7
10	55.7	40.0	3.9	0.4

SOURCE: E. K. Browning and W. R. Johnson, *The Distribution of the Tax Burden*, American Enterprise Institute for Public Policy Research, 1979. Reprinted with the permission of The American Enterprise Institute for Public Policy Research, Washington, D.C.

welfare state is an immense apparatus for transferring income, but the bulk of it is not devoted to aiding the very poor. If we take the bottom one-half of the population, it is clear that on the whole they do much better out of the system than the upper one-half. In other words, there are transfers away from the upper part of the population, but the transfers are not particularly concentrated on the poor. Envy or the use of political power to transfer funds to oneself is a better explanation for the transfer than is a desire to aid the poor. Nevertheless, the poor are aided. The only question is whether they are aided more than they would be by completely voluntary charity or by a voting system in which the recipients of transfers would not be permitted to vote.[22]

This is particularly surprising given the fact that the standard justification for the welfare state is that it helps the poor. It is not at all obvious that it

22. Obviously, if the recipients of transfers were not permitted to vote, the very large transfers to the middle and upper classes would not exist. This would lower the total tax burden and very likely benefit the poor. Another comparison would be one in which the poor are not permitted to vote but everyone else is, and hence the transfers back and forth in the upper 80 percent of the population continued.

helps the poor more by direct transfers than it would under a more traditional regime, and it certainly leads to a lower rate of economic growth, with the result that in the long run the poor—like everybody else—are worse off. We must seek some explanation for the welfare state other than aiding the poor. The obvious explanation is simply that people have made use of the government to transfer funds to themselves. This should surprise no one. The average profit-seeking individual will seek his profits where he can find them, and there is no reason why he should be more reluctant to use the government for profit seeking than the market.

By sheer accident the first draft of this chapter was written in Hong Kong on July 25, 1981, and the morning paper had on the front page an article describing a desire on the part of the Hong Kong government to increase the number of taxi permits (the new permits to be auctioned) and the complaint of the taxi owners against this plan. The entire discussion was in terms of essentially selfish desires, although the individuals seemed to think that these were morally desirable. The motivation of the government apparently was solely to get the revenue, and the motivation of the taxi owners who owned the existing permits[23] was simply that the value of their property not be degraded. I am sure the reader of this book will be able to put his finger on several dozen similar incidents if he simply reads the *Washington Post* or the *New York Times* for a few days.

This is typical and should not surprise us. The government is, in part, an apparatus for generating public goods, but the modern welfare state is even more an apparatus for generating transfers to people who happen for one reason or another to have political power. The actual mechanism of these transfers, however, is quite complex, and I believe that most of the people who are involved in the activity partially conceal their real motives from themselves. More accurately, I suppose, they have two motives: a weak motive to help people and a strong motive to help themselves. They find no need for distinguishing these motives when they make decisions. Further, they normally talk about their desire to help other people, although they will, of course, on occasion talk about their desire to help themselves. The same is true of the poor who receive transfers; i.e., they frequently talk about the desire to help other people rather than themselves. The reason they do not do better, I believe, is their weak bargaining position.

23. Worth about $60,000 U.S.

GENERAL WELFARE OR WELFARE FOR THE POOR ONLY

There is a rough rule of thumb by which we can detect which projects are designed to help the poor and which are not designed to help them. This rule of thumb is that if there is a means test, i.e., if the aid is so arranged that it cuts off at a reasonably low level, then it is designed to help the poor. If there is no such test, then it is not designed to help the poor, although it may, in fact, do so to some extent. This rule of thumb is undeniably rough, but it seems to fit the world fairly well. I have found, however, that the matter seems to be highly controversial, so I will explain in some detail why the switch from a means-tested program to a general aid program would, in all probability, hurt the poor.

When I first became interested in this subject, the standard explanation used for switching from aid to the poor only to some kind of general program was always that the poor would feel insulted by the need to prove that they were poor. They were being distinguished from the rest of the population in this way. It is, of course, true that a means-tested program that requires the poor to prove that they are poor is less convenient for the poor than a general program. The main people who are injured, however, are not the poor but the people who are directly above them in the income scale and who are deprived of the aid by the means test. Further, I have frequently found that people who talk about the poor being insulted by the means test will then go on and say that they think it is just plain unfair that they, themselves, or perhaps some of their relatives, have been barred from the program because they have too much income.

Recently, in the social welfare community, another argument for abolishing the means test has surfaced. It is argued that the middle class will not vote for adequate medical care, old-age pensions, etc., if they go only to the poor. If these pensions and aid go to the middle class, however, they will regard themselves as beneficiaries and hence vote large enough amounts to be of in-

Reprinted, with kind permission of Kluwer Academic Publishers, from *Economics of Income Redistribution*, Kluwer-Nijhoff Studies in Human Issues: An International Series in the Social Sciences (Boston: Kluwer-Nijhoff, 1983), 97–110.

terest to themselves. The poor would then free ride on these large gifts that the middle class are giving to themselves.

This description, of course, begins by taking a very uncharitable view of the middle-class attitude toward charity. Further, it implies that the middle class are not very bright. I note, by the way, that many of the people who make this particular proposal are themselves either administrators of the program, who gain in other ways from its expansion, or middle-class types who, in essence, are saying that they are nobler than the other middle-class types. This is an example of what I call "well-intentioned Machiavellianism." One favors a program for a motive that is moral and good. For political reasons, however, simple, direct action is not regarded as feasible. An indirect and Machiavellian technique is then adopted for the purpose of maneuvering around the political obstacle. The people who talk this way are not in any sense immoral, although their approach to their desired goal is frequently quite unscrupulous.

There are three problems with well-intentioned Machiavellianism. The first of these is simply that the political judgment may not be good—i.e., the aid to the poor or other object could be attained directly as well as by this indirect means, and, indeed, the indirect means may hinder achievement of the goal. With respect to this problem, nothing much can be said of a general nature; the individual situation should be examined very carefully. It should perhaps be said, however, that a great many of these programs have turned out not to achieve what the enthusiasts wanted for the poor.

The second problem, and this is far more complex and difficult, is that Machiavellians are, after all, Machiavellians. The person who tells you that he is advocating a program—which incidentally will help him—because it is an indirect way of helping the poor is, first, indicating that he thinks the average voter does not really want to help the poor that much. In other words, he is consciously attempting to avoid the results of the democratic process. This does not necessarily rule out the program, since you may favor the outcome more than the means. It does, however, indicate that the motives may not be exactly clear-cut and simple. Further, he may be concealing, not only from other people but from himself, a stronger selfish drive that he does not want to admit.

The third problem raised by well-intentioned Machiavellianism is simply that it requires concealment and deception, and it is not obvious that the well-intentioned will win at this game. If we look over the very large list of programs that have been advocated at one time or another on the grounds that they help the poor, we will find that the overwhelming bulk of them do not help the poor but do indeed help certain well-organized groups. Members of well-organized groups normally do not consciously want to injure the poor, and, indeed, they may want to help them, but it is very easy to think that something that helps you will help the poor as well.

The history of means tests as opposed to universal programs illustrates this. Universal programs were made important political realities by Bismarck, who was not exactly noted for his desire to help the poor. His invention has been copied throughout the world by groups of people who say they are helping the poor when it is not at all obvious that they are.

Before discussing the standard welfare programs in later chapters, however, let us now consider with some care the effects on the poor of the change from a means-tested program to a universal program. There are, roughly speaking, two kinds of means tests. Income testing normally means that income must be under a certain level, not above it, although a certain number of programs of the latter type do exist. In one type, full service is provided below a certain income, and no service is provided above. The other type is what we may call a negative income tax type in which services are provided on a graduated scale. For example, in the first type we might have programs under which everyone whose income is under a particular amount gets free medical attention from the state, and anyone whose income is above that amount gets no attention. The sliding scale type of program would provide state assistance in catastrophic illness cases at some fairly high income, and as income fell, the program would gradually add additional services until the very poor found even routine dentistry paid for. We take up these two procedures in series with the sharp cut-off first because it is simpler.

The universal programs would involve providing the service to everyone. For an example, consider the British National Health Service. It should be kept in mind, however, that in the countries in which services of this sort are provided (education in the United States, medicine in England, etc.) there is also privately provided supplementary service for the upper-income groups. The private schools in the United States, or the small but growing part of the population in England who carry health insurance in order to get services of doctors as private patients rather than as state patients, are examples. This is also true in Russia, although in Russia there is, in addition, a program to provide special medical facilities free to upper-ranking members of the hierarchy. Indeed, the special medical facilities for Brezhnev seem to be quite unprecedented. In his recent visit to Germany, it was revealed not only that he is always accompanied by a crew of doctors, nurses, etc., but that they have a special van that is in essence a custom-designed intensive care room for his particular collection of illnesses.

We will, however, mainly ignore these supplements that upper-income groups normally purchase for themselves under "universal" programs largely for convenience of analysis. Our basic objective will be to compare income-tested programs with universal programs, and for illustrative purposes we will use medicine.

There are three different ways in which medical provisions could be distributed. Firstly, everyone could provide their own. In practice, no doubt, this would be accompanied by a good deal of private charity, but we will ignore this, not because it is unimportant but because it complicates the analysis and is not vital to our subject. The second way of providing medical treatment is to have a tax-supported system that provides to the poorest part of the population a specified quantity of medical aid. In the third case, the state provides full medical care for everyone.

It could be assumed in both the second and third cases that the state-provided aid is (at least by intent) all of the medical services that the individual will receive. Our main objective will be considering the likely outcome in the second and third cases, with the first case present only for logical completeness.

Note that the poor person would normally in voting count the value of the medical care to him at his price, i.e., at his rather modest tax cost. Presumably this would lead him to favor in the voting process a different amount of medicine than that favored by the rest of the community. This should be true whether he was voting on a specific program only for the poor or for the general program for the community as a whole. Further, in both cases the poor person would presumably prefer a direct cash transfer rather than the payment in kind. It could then be used for anything. Payment in kind has to be justified on the grounds that the poor person is not very competent in investing his own money or on *Tragic Choices* explanation offered above. In neither case is it a decision the poor person is apt to be very happy with. Still, there is a saying about not looking gift horses in the mouth.

In all real societies, the providers of services have considerable influence on how much is provided, and the providers of the services in this case are the medical professions. They may be able to push the total provision high enough so that the indigents are receiving considerably more medical attention than is the average citizen. The reason this is possible is simply that the doctors, etc., are themselves likely to vote for increased provision to the poor, not because they feel sorry for the poor, but because they want their own incomes raised. They will characteristically already have incomes well above average, and hence they become the median voter, with the result that the poor, the doctors, and, let us say, the top 30 percent of the population may jointly make up the voting block that passes these high expenditures.

We should pause briefly here to mention two aspects of the real world. One of them is that the transfer from an income-tested system to a system of general provision does not increase the number of hospitals or doctors in society in the short run. At best it will lead to a rearrangement of the current medical resources, with some people getting more and some people getting less. In the case of the British National Health Service, for example, its installation led to a very pronounced reduction in the resources available to the poor, with the result that during the period in which medicine was being revolutionized by the introduction of antibiotics, the death rate of the poorest part of the English population actually rose.[1]

The second characteristic of the real world is that always, and under all systems, the incurably ill requiring custodial care tend to get relatively poor treatment. The reason is that they are very expensive, very discouraging, and tend to be unable to do very much in the way of exerting pressure for themselves. As an example of this poor care, the British Health Care Service actually has standards for maintenance of such people that are not intended to provide them with the best available medical attention on the grounds that, on the whole, it is better if some of them die. This group of people are normally poor not necessarily because they were originally poor, but because their illness makes them poor.

Under any system, then, people who are sympathetic with poor medical patients are apt to look at this particular category and decide that the current system, whatever it is, is inadequate. It should be said that this judgment, given the right values, is perfectly correct. Anyone who feels we should put very large resources into dealing with those people who have either physical or mental illnesses of a chronic or incurable nature, and who require custodial care, is apt to be disappointed with any medical system in the world. There is no reason, of course, why society could not decide to do such things as improving our current state hospitals or the equivalent institutions in

1. Gordon Tullock, "The Charity of the Uncharitable," *Western Economic Journal* 9 (December 1971): 379–92, and Julian Le Grand, *The Strategy of Equality* (London: George Allen & Unwin, 1981), 38.

England.[2] The decision to increase the transfer of funds to these people, however, has little or nothing to do with the choice between income-tested systems and universal care systems, since chronic or incurable patients, in either event, are almost certain to be in the hands of the state. Hence their treatment is essentially dependent on charity by the voters.

But leaving this special category aside, the benefits, if any, that the poor receive from universalization depend on what we might call the degree of inadequacy of the medical attention that the poor received before the change. In this case "inadequacy" cannot be defined technically, because it depends on the total resources available. The real question is, are the poor getting less than their per capita share of medical attention? Even that is not quite fair, because all of the empirical studies of national health services indicate that the poor, because of their difficulty in filling out forms, poor motivation, and sometimes their difficulty in dealing with officials, get rather less than their share on a per capita basis of the medical resource of the society.[3] Let us say they get 90 percent of what a middle-class or upper-class person would receive dealing with the same legal apparatus.

In order to make the problem clear, let me simply invent some numbers. Let us assume that some individual poor person has an income of $1,000 and was paying 1 percent of that, or $10, as his share of the support of the income-tested health scheme. He was receiving under this income-tested scheme $80 a year worth of medical attention. The government program is now adopted, which provides $100 of medical attention for every citizen in the country. This means the total taxes used to pay for medicine will rise, shall we say, five times, and if he is still paying his same allocated share of the cost, he finds himself paying $50 in taxes. Even if he got the full $100 worth of treatment, he would be worse off than he was before.[4] If we assume that he actually only gets 90 percent of the national standard because of his difficulties in handling the system, of course, he would be even worse off.

2. These remarks are of a general nature. Both systems have individual institutions that are markedly better at least than their average and others, of course, that are markedly worse.

3. Julian Le Grand's study shows that in England the poor do in fact get more medical attention per capita than the well-off. This is, however, because they have a poor state of health and are ill more. Their attention per illness is less than that of the upper-income brackets. (Le Grand, *The Strategy of Equality*.)

4. Some people would say this might not be true because the expenditure of the additional $20 on medicine for him would be of more value to him than the $50 which they would allege he would waste on something else, like drink or the numbers game. I do not regard this as a truthful description of the behavior of the poor, but there are people who believe this.

In the particular case that we have assumed, he would become better off only if the increase in medical attention he received nearly doubled the amount he had before, i.e., if the charitably provided medical care was only a little over one-half of the national standard. Further, this would be true only if, to him, the marginal unit of medicine that he received was worth more than the taxes he paid on that marginal unit. Note that all of this depends on the exact numbers I have chosen, but I invite the reader to experiment a little bit with realistic numbers.

The specific empirical evidence is that the pressure for universal medical programs does not seem to come from the poor but from the lower middle class. Indeed, there is a very high correlation between pressure groups pushing for universal medical care and pressure groups pushing for raising the minimum wage. Since the minimum wage act clearly hurts the poor, one has to deduce that these groups do not have the interests of the poor very strongly at heart.

This does not mean that no one else is in favor of it. In the upper-income groups are a number of people who favor it, partly, I suspect, through miscalculation of its effects on them and partly through genuinely charitable motives. There are also people among the poor who favor it. The real push, however, comes from organizations like the AFL-CIO, whose members might well benefit. Of course, I would like to have better empirical evidence, and note that all this empirical evidence indicates is that the principal beneficiaries of universal medical treatment will be the people who are just above the cutoff line on income-tested medical provision for the poor. It does not prove that the poor do not, in fact, still gain.

Turn now to Figure 1. Here I have arranged the population from left to right according to income, with the poor at the left and the wealthy at the right. On the vertical axis, I have the loss and gain from universalization of a previous income-tested scheme. Since the effects on the poor are ambiguous, I have not drawn them in, but I have shown the situation of the middle class and wealthy by the slanting line. Those members of the middle class who are only just above the cutoff point make quite large gains, and the gains then fall until they reach the individual who has exactly the same increase in tax payments as his medical costs. He is, of course, the individual who divides the "middle class" from the "wealthy" (by our special definition). Above this point the "wealthy" suffer increasing losses.

It is clear that the exact location of the net payoff line depends, in part, on whether the program, in net, transfers funds from the poor or does not. If it transfers funds from the poor, then the payoff line will be higher than if the

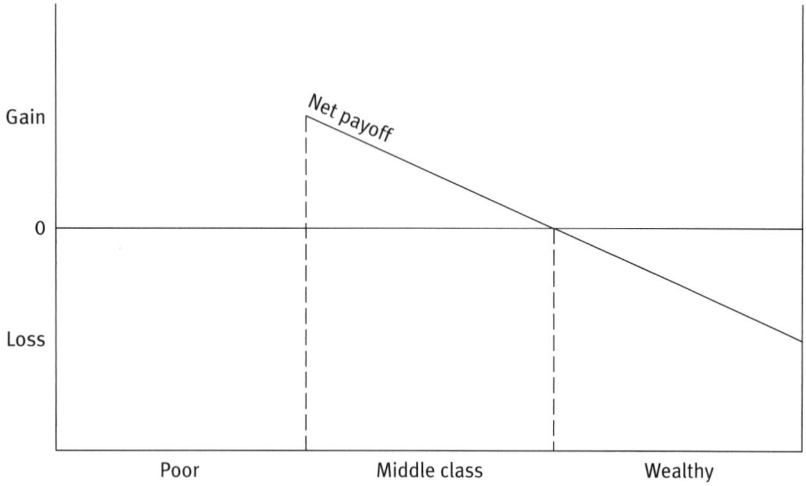

FIGURE 1
Net payoff according to income

switch to universal medical attention leads to more resources being spent on the poor. When this line is shifted, the dividing line between the wealthy and the middle class also shifts. If we assume that the people vote in accordance with their interests, this shift changes the number of people voting for universalization.

In general, if universalization actually transfers funds away from the poor, the category we have referred to as middle class will be larger, and hence there will be more votes for the program; if it transfers funds to the poor, the category we call middle class will be smaller and the wealthy category will be larger, and hence there will be fewer votes for the program. Of course, it is not only the middle class and wealthy who vote on the issue; the poor do also. If the poor favor universalization, then the loss of some of the voters from the middle class to the wealthy class by lowering the net payoff line would make no great difference. The poor are about 10 percent of the population; thus, they only need to have 41 percent of the remainder on their side to win.

The second way in which a system can be income tested is if it is introduced in a graduated, rather than a sharp-notch, method. In other words, as your income rises, the amount you get falls. For example, a medical program in which the amount of medical attention paid for by the state falls as your family income rises, or the present arrangement with food stamps, under which the number you can buy changes in such a way as to reduce the real subsidy as

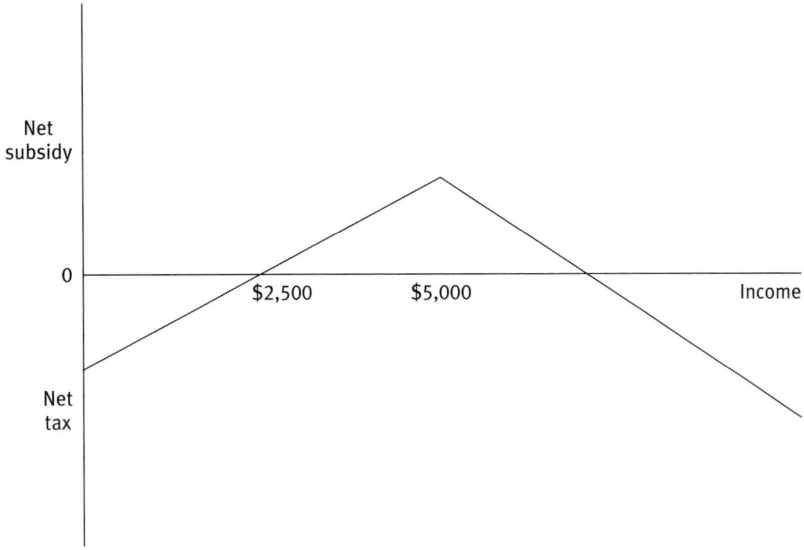

FIGURE 2
Effect of a universal medical program

your income rises. If medical programs were converted to a universal program under which everyone received the full cost of their medical attention paid for by taxes, then the net effect would be to make the people at the very bottom of the distribution worse-off because they now pay at least some taxes which they did not pay before and receive the same or fewer services.[5]

It seems likely, as shown in Figure 2, that the increase in medical services will begin to offset the rise in taxes at some fairly low income (I have arbitrarily chosen $2,500) and then remain above taxes to reach a maximum improvement at $5,000, with a gradual fall as the increased taxes come closer and closer to, and eventually pass, the benefits from free medical attention. The wealthy are injured, and there is a gain, part of which falls in the group that we may arbitrarily refer to as poor, but the upper end of the poor group, and part of which falls in the group that I call middle class.

Occasionally, universalization of programs is urged on the grounds that income-tested programs in fact do not reach all of the poor. It is implied,

5. People who actually had no income before, if they were to stay alive, must at any event have consumed food. Presumably this would be slightly more expensive because of the tax increase.

although as far as I can see there is no strong argument for this being so, that making the program available to the upper-income brackets will increase the number of poor people who use it. Even if this were true, it would be an extraordinarily expensive way of increasing the number of poor people in the program.

The poor people who are not in the program are presumably out partly because they really do not like the program, partly because they have difficulty with filling out government forms, dealing with civil servants, etc., and partly through mere ignorance. The first is not a problem, since people who voluntarily and with full knowledge choose not to enter the program are presumably better off outside it. The second would not in any way be affected by universalizing the program, since the red tape would probably be more severe in a large program than in a small program. The third calls for an advertising campaign, and such a campaign would surely be immensely cheaper than extending the program to the whole population.

The situation of the poor is ambiguous. Firstly, we have pointed out they certainly gain considerably less than the people in the lower end of the middle class from the universalization. Secondly, it is not improbable they will lose. Thirdly, it is extremely difficult to calculate exactly whether they will gain or lose. The calculation problem is made even more difficult by the fact that almost all of the people who are experts in the field will be in favor of universalization because almost all the people who are experts in the field will in one way or another gain if the service is universalized. The experts are apt to be either employees of the welfare service, potential employees, or people who expect research grants from the welfare service, etc. There are occasional specialists in this field whose income does not either directly or indirectly originate in the welfare program itself, but their number is very small compared with the number of specialists whose income will actually increase whenever the welfare programs are expanded.

Thus, the possibility that the poor will lose from the program is not apt to be much emphasized even if it is true. The poor are apt to be told they will gain, whether they do or do not. They do not face an easy calculation problem like the lower middle class and must depend on experts or learn to do rather complicated calculations themselves, and hence are apt to be deceived. In this respect, we have here another example of a general problem of the poor in a democracy. People, in general, are poor for reasons that not only make them inept in a private marketplace, but also make them inept in the political marketplace. In consequence, they tend to not do very well in the distribution of pork, which is an important part of politics. Perhaps as a result of their low general motivation or perhaps because they understand this situation, they tend to abstain from voting in any event. In general, what they get out of democracy reflects not their potential voting power, which tends to be wasted, but essentially charitable motives on the part of upper-income voters.

Anthony Downs has attempted to refute the above argument by pointing out that it would always be possible to expand the aid to the poor at the same time as a given program was universalized, and, hence, the poor would not necessarily lose. This, of course, is true. Universalization plus something else does not lead to the same results as universalization alone. We could always offset the bad effect of one program with another program. This does not change the fact that universalization, taken by itself, injures the poor.[6]

It would appear, however, that all this is not actually too relevant to the type of social welfare activity under discussion. What we now think of as a welfare state was invented by Bismarck for the specific purpose of providing a politically viable way of beating off socialism. The early programs in Germany (the programs that everyone else has copied over the years)[7] had rather diffuse and complicated redistributional effects. It is certain, however, that they were not intended to transfer funds from the middle class to the poor. The point is particularly important because in general there is not all that much money among the wealthy if we define them the way they are normally defined, and hence any large transfer to the poor has to come out of middle-class pockets.

The transfer of funds from the wealthy, even though it is not large-scale in absolute quantity, benefits mainly the middle class. When the poor are given special privileges (and they are in all societies), this reflects charity on the part of the middle class and wealthy rather than their political power. In any event, if we look at the actual history of the development of social security and other universal programs in the United States, it is fairly obvious that redistribution to the poor was not one of the major objectives.[8]

6. My basic paper and Downs's comment on it are in the process of being published in a special proceedings volume to be issued by the Institute for the Study of Poverty, University of Wisconsin, Madison, Wisconsin.

7. David Collier and Richard E. Messick, "Prerequisites versus Diffusion: Testing Alternative Explanations of Social Security Adoption," *American Political Science Review* 69, no. 4 (December 1975): 1299–1350.

8. Carolyn Weaver, "The Emergence, Growth, and Redirection of Social Security: An Interpretive History from a Public Choice Perspective." Dissertation, Virginia Polytechnic Institute and State University, 1977.

Medicare, a general program for all of the old, could be predicted to lead to a very sharp increase in the incomes of doctors and civil servants rather than to lower-income groups. It should also lead to a rearrangement of American medical resources in which the principal beneficiaries are older people who are not particularly poor. The older poor were, of course, already receiving free medical attention. This increased demand for medical services, combined with no increase in the number of doctors or hospitals, in the short run surely meant that everyone else, including the poor, had a reduction in their medical care.

At the same time Medicare was passed, Medicaid, an income-tested program that provided resources only for the poor, was also enacted. It seems likely that Medicaid counteracted the effect of Medicare for the non-elderly poor. The net effect of the two programs was surely to benefit doctors and the older non-poor. Whether the poor benefitted or not is something that cannot be said for certain, but if they did benefit, it was because of the existence of the income-tested program.

I would like to say that this phenomenon occurred not only in these two cases in the United States, where they are the two most significant examples of recent expansion in social welfare activity, but always and everywhere. Unfortunately, I cannot, because I simply do not know enough. Here again, empirical research is called for, and unfortunately it is an extremely difficult type of empirical research. Substantially, each social welfare program in each country must be looked at in great detail, with great care, and with a good deal of skepticism for mistakes that were made by its apologists to see whether this is a general phenomenon or not.

As a start on this empirical research, I should like to discuss a few studies that I have succeeded in turning up. The first of these concerns Germany in the period 1969 through 1975, which was the initial period of the governing Social Democrat–Liberal coalition government. This government passed a considerable number of redistributional laws and increased the size of the transfer sector quite considerably. Martin Pfaff's study of this period[9] shows a net increase in inequality during this period. The increased transfers, even though enacted by a basically left-wing government, benefitted the middle and upper classes rather than the poor. This study is particularly notable because Professor Pfaff's predilections are quite in the other direction.

9. Martin Pfaff, "Patterns of Inequality in Income: Selected Determinance, Countries, and Policy Issues for the 1980s," 30–35. The paper was prepared for the ASSA meeting in 1978, but it is to be part of a book to be published in Germany.

That the same phenomenon occurred in Britain under its former Labour government was indicated by an article in the London *Economist*.[10] Between 1974 and 1976, a period in which once again a new left-wing (Labour) government was enacting very large increases and rearrangements in the social welfare programs, the number of poor almost doubled.

My third bit of evidence comes from Switzerland, where there are direct public votes on many issues. Werner Pommerehne has chosen a number of communes in Basel and examined the redistributional effect of direct popular voting on budgets.[11] These votes were not all specifically on social welfare programs, but they did have considerable distributional impact. Pommerehne's study raises a certain number of difficulties with respect to the definition of transfer or nontransfer patterns of taxation and expenditure. It is, however, clear from the results of his study that there is at the very least no strong tendency to transfer funds to the poor when the populace is permitted to vote directly on such issues.

If we go to the underdeveloped world, two Indian scholars[12] calculated the Gini coefficient for government employees and then for the pensioners, i.e., retired government employees. They found that the Gini coefficient for the actual employees was much lower than for the pensioners.[13] The apparent explanation is that inflation has tended to lower pensions, and the existing powerholders in India, whether they are the civil servants or legislatures, have raised the wages and improved the pension prospects of active civil servants while letting the pensions of the already retired personnel deteriorate. This is not directly relevant to the income-testing hypothesis, but it is in general accord with Professor Pommerehne's results. The legislature and civil service of India are much more concerned with their own well-being and with middle-income groups than with the poor and elderly pensioners.

As my last, and by all odds best, example Julian Le Grand has examined carefully a number of aspects of the British welfare state.[14] His study regularly shows these programs are not radically egalitarian; i.e., they do not provide perfect equality in the benefits distributed. They do, in general, increase the

10. September 8, 1978, p. 108.

11. Werner W. Pommerehne, "Public Choice Approaches to Explaining Fiscal Redistribution." The paper was presented at the 34th Conference of the International Institute of Public Finance, Hamburg, September 4–8, 1978, and will be published in the proceedings volume.

12. V. Jagannadham and C. M. Palvia, *Problems of Pensioners*, New Delhi: Bhanurha, 1978.

13. Ibid., 92.

14. Le Grand, *The Strategy of Equality*.

degree of equality in the state; i.e., they are egalitarian in tendency but not strongly so. Further, Le Grand based his work on the statistics that were available but that are not ideal for our purposes. The tax burden on the poor from universalization is, for example, not a visible part of these statistics. Thus, it is possible that the poor benefitted even less than he shows. I began this section on empirical data by saying we need further studies. It seems to me that the Le Grand project is an almost ideal example of the kind of work that should be done. I hope Le Grand will continue to expand on his present work and that many other people will follow in his footsteps.

Of course, these are merely a set of samples. They are, however, the only ones I could find in which the subject had been discussed at all. I cannot say on the basis of this evidence that the phenomenon is general, but I suspect it is.

It is not generally realized that the expansion of one government program to aid the poor normally leads to the reduction of other such programs. There are two basic reasons. The first is simply that the government cannot spend an infinite amount of money, and an increase in budget on one item is likely to lead to at least some reduction in budgetary provision for other items. The second reason is that the reduction is particularly likely to occur in related items because congressmen are likely to feel that if HEW is doing very well on program A it is only fair that part of the cost be taken from HEW's program B.

The only empirical study of this effect that I know of, Lindsay and Zycher's examination of distributional effects of the Canadian health plan, finds that "most of the cost of the Canadian National Health Insurance was borne by the economically disadvantaged."[15] There are a number of statistical problems with the Lindsay and Zycher paper, which is a pioneering exploration of a completely new field, and we should not put too much dependence on it until the work has been repeated by other scholars in other areas. Nevertheless, it is the only empirical evidence on the point at the moment.

If this is very general, it is not difficult to explain, particularly in the case of the United States. People who are interested in expanding social welfare systems from income-tested to universal programs are characteristically interested in the expansion rather than in helping the poor. Establishing the program requires political support, which almost of necessity has to come

15. Cotton M. Lindsay and Benjamin Zycher, "More Evidence on Director's Law," 1978, unpublished, p. 3.

from the group that we have referred to as the middle class, since it is the only group that makes an unambiguous gain. This group will be smaller and less enthusiastic about a program so designed that the poor will benefit considerably, because there is simply that much less left for them.

Hence, people trying to introduce some kind of general health insurance are not likely to propose a program that will transfer funds from the middle class to the poor. There is another alternative, however, which is to finance the program in such a way as to transfer funds from the wealthy—preferably the truly wealthy and not just the people whom we have nominated wealthy in our somewhat arbitrary category. The trouble with this is that this is probably the best informed, most politically influential group in the electorate. Further, it is a fairly small group and hence able to organize much more efficiently than large groups.

In general, to try to get anything through Congress you should try to avoid antagonizing any sector of the population. Now, of course, there are things put through Congress despite disadvantage to specific groups—our whole energy program, for example—but on the whole this is something to be avoided. The national health program would be easier to put through Congress if the cost does not fall too conspicuously on the wealthy. On the other hand, if the cost does not fall too conspicuously on the wealthy, then it must fall on the middle class or on the poor. The proponents of the program then are likely to set up financing methods that lead to the whole program being mildly regressive.

It should be noted that insofar as the middle-class voters can succeed in getting funds from the wealthy, there is no obvious reason why they should pass them on to the poor. Thus, even if we do have a scheme that raises the cost to the upper-income groups, there is no reason to believe that the poor rather than the lower middle class will benefit.

While I find this line of reasoning persuasive, it is clearly much less rigorous than the models I have used before. I have difficulty imagining how it could be tested. Detailed historical research of the sort that Carolyn Weaver did on the origins of the Social Security Act[16] would be called for, and unfortunately, this type of historical investigation has the characteristic that it is always possible for historians to disagree. So we end what has unfortunately been a largely theoretical discussion of the topic. I have been able to enliven the theory a little bit by calling attention to some empirical evidence, but it

16. Carolyn Weaver, "The Emergence, Growth, and Redirection of Social Security."

is hardly ideal. I have found a little statistical work and have been compelled to refer to matters that are public knowledge to support my point of view. Since these illustrations are not exhaustive, the possibility of contrary observations is always real.

Any extension of social welfare activity provides a direct benefit to those who receive it and a direct cost to those who are paying for it. Those who are paying for it may be the recipients, but we have to net out the two sides of the budget. This is, of course, particularly important when we are contrasting an income-tested program with a non-income-tested program, because the improvement in the quality (if there is such an improvement at all) for the people who have previously been receiving the income-tested service is apt to be much less than the gain obtained by people who were previously not receiving it because the income test barred them.

The third item that has to be netted out is the cost to the former recipients of the income-tested service, in that the additional budgetary cost of spreading the service over the population as a whole probably will mean that various other services that they would be entitled to are either contracted or at least not expanded as rapidly as they otherwise would be. Only when we have completed this rather difficult computation can we tell whether the people who previously received the income-tested service benefit from or are injured by the expansion to society as a whole.

Fortunately, the calculations for the rest of the society are a good deal easier, although here again all three of these items are present. The rest of society will receive a benefit, pay taxes, and the existence of the program will have effects elsewhere in the government budget, which will benefit or injure them. In either case, however, it is usually fairly easy to work out the direction of the effects. With the poor, the problem is much more difficult. This involves simply the measurement of effects. When we consider the political forces that may lead to the expansion of a program, it is generally clear that if the people who are interested in expanding the program are trying merely to help the poor, they have chosen an inept way of doing it. It is sensible only if they can trick members of the middle and upper class by that indirect method into voting for a program to help the poor more generously than they are willing to give in a direct and open way. Politics involves misinformation and trickery, and so the possibility that this will happen cannot be totally ruled out.

PART 4

THE EXPANDING FRONTIERS OF WEALTH REDISTRIBUTION

OLD AGE PENSIONS

In Chapter 6, I pointed out that it was by no means obvious that the generalization of welfare programs from the poor to the entire population, orginally carried out by Bismarck, either does help or was intended to help the poor. In this chapter and the next I am going to discuss one particular example of this generalization: the social security system for old age pensions, which is indeed the example that is most relevant to most Americans because it is the only one that we have adopted in full. In order to discuss it in an orderly way, I am going to start with a very simple model invented by Paul Samuelson[1] and then gradually complicate this simple model until we reach something similar to our real-world system.

Let us begin then with a very simple society. In this society there is no growth or shrinkage. The population and the per capita income remain constant over time. There is no interest rate, and everyone has exactly the same pattern of life. They are born and brought up to the age of 20 at which point they go to work; they work until the age of 65, when they retire; and then they die at the age of 80. We assume that children under the age of 20 are taken care of by their parents, and that the people beyond the age of 65 live on their savings.[2]

You will note that the work period for each individual is exactly three times as long as his retirement. Let us assume that our citizens characteristically save 20 percent of their income (this is rather high, but note that there is no interest rate) and, thus, are able to live on three fifths of their active income when retired. We now have a stable society that is making reasonably good use of its resources, essentially because everybody is absolutely equal.

Reprinted, with kind permission of Kluwer Academic Publishers, from *Economics of Income Redistribution*, Kluwer-Nijhoff Studies in Human Issues: An International Series in the Social Sciences (Boston: Kluwer-Nijhoff, 1983), 111–22. Copyright 1983 Kluwer Academic Publishers.

1. Paul Samuelson, "An Exact Consumption-Loan Model of Interest with or without the Social Contrivance of Money," *The Scientific Papers of Paul Samuelson*, vol. 1 (Cambridge, Mass.: The M.I.T. Press, 1966), 219. I have made a few minor changes in his model, but they do not affect his general principles.

2. If we assume that their children pay part of the support of their parents (and of course they have a legal responsibility to do so if they have adequate income), then the model would be modified somewhat but not importantly.

Suppose now that a nobleman named Bismarck appears and suggests that instead of following this system, everybody would be automatically taxed one-fifth of their income, and this amount would be paid to retired persons so that they all will get an income of 60 percent of what they are making before they retired.[3] At first glance it would appear that this is a change without substance. Everyone will, as before, spend 20 percent less than their income while working and will receive 60 percent of their working income in retirement.

But that is only in the steady state. Consider the transitional stage. The day after the program goes into effect, everyone can stop private savings because they know they will have 60 percent paid to them by the state. On the other hand, the tax would be exactly the amount that they were saving. But the amount already saved is now free for expenditure.[4] They can now begin consuming the funds that they saved, secure in the knowledge that their income will be kept at a minimum of 60 percent of their earned income when they retire. The sensible thing to do would be, of course, to set up some kind of lifetime consumption pattern to get rid of this accumulated surplus.

As a result, everybody over the age of 20 in this society is now better off than they were before, albeit the amount depends on how many years they have been working. The 21-year-old, with one year's savings in hand, benefits a little because he can now spend that saving. The man who is just turning 65 has a lifetime expenditure equivalent to 9 years' earnings that he is free now to spend, in addition to receiving his full pension, and is very much benefitted, indeed.

All of this looks like magic, since there has been a very sharp increase in the quantity of goods available for consumption without any increase in production. Everyone above the age of 20 has had his consumption increased

3. Note that for simplicity I am assuming that people already retired begin getting their pensions when a program is established. Most of the pension systems actually established did not have that feature. Only people who paid at least a little tax received pensions. My model is, however, simpler, and the point is of no practical importance.

4. There is here a certain problem, since the amount available for expenditure is larger than current production. We can assume that the saving was done in real consumer goods or that a saving in funds was somehow matched with real goods that were kept out of use. In the real world, of course, investments are normally put into producer goods, and the switch to expenditure would mean a rapid running down of the capital stock of the country. This running down of the capital stock is, I believe, a real phenomenon, but the subject is discussed later. For the time being, I suggest that the reader assume that the saving was done in the form of current consumption goods.

even though the society before was in a steady state in which the amount consumed (by both active and retired) in each period was the same as the amount produced, and the amount produced has not increased.

The explanation essentially is that a new asset has been created—something like a government bond. A debt has been laid on all future generations, counting those who are 64 years as being very slightly part of the future generation and those under the age of 20 and the unborn as being decidedly future generation types. Instead of saving from now on, each individual will be taxed, and the goods taken will be used to support the current elderly rather than held for future consumption.

Once the system reaches a stable state, which will be when the people now 20 die, so the entire population is composed of people whose working life and retired life is under the system, everyone will be, in essence, putting aside 20 percent of income while working, and living on 60 percent of income while retired. The total consumption bundle for society, and for people of each age group, will be the same as it was in our first state before the introduction of social security. There has, however, been a major gain by the people who were over 20 years during the period in which the new system was instituted. If they are the only people permitted to vote for the new system—future generations being deprived of franchise in most systems—they can well give themselves this large gift.

So far nobody has lost from the change, but that assumes that the system will last in perpetuity. If the system is ever stopped or even reduced for any one of a number of reasons—war, revolution, change in political ideas, foreign conquest, or a sharp inflation that erodes the value of the pensions—there will be a corresponding cut or elimination in the retirement income of the recipients.

Just to make this clear, let us go through what would happen under those circumstances. Suppose, then, that the country is conquered by another country that believes only in making gifts to the poor and that, being much poorer than our initial country, defines "poor" fairly harshly. Since everybody in our society is equal, there will be no poor, and we need not pay much attention to that category. Under these circumstances, everybody in the society who is over the age of 20 will lose. They will have to begin saving in order to pay for their pensions. If they save exactly 20 percent, which is what we were having them do before, then the pensions will be a declining function of their age at the time the program was stopped. The person who is 65 years or older would have no savings, and the people under the age of 65 would be able to accumulate retirement savings that gradually declined from the age of 20.

Presumably, the individuals would choose to save more, and a number of the older people would go to work rather than starve to death. The cost would, once again, be borne in one generation, and the next generation would be in the original situation. Thus, introduction of the social security system leads to a large transitional gain for all adults at the time it is introduced. Once it has reached the steady state, the situation is more or less identical to what it was without it. The termination of the system inflicts a large loss on the adult population at the time it is terminated, but, once again, after the situation reaches the steady state, it is indistinguishable from the original system.[5]

The system involves, in essence, the transfer of the burden to the future. It can only be argued for if it is assumed (and Samuelson makes this explicit assumption) that the new institution will be permanent. Of course the adults alive at the time of the start are probably not all that concerned about their distant descendants, and the gain that they make probably greatly outweighs in their minds the loss that might conceivably be suffered some time in the future.

Now let us make a slight change in our model. Let us assume that some of the citizens of our first state arrive at the age of 65 without adequate savings to live on between then and the age of 80. We need not concern ourselves as to why this is so. They may be improvident, victims of wasting diseases, or just unlucky in some way. Let us further assume that society supplements the incomes of these people so that they obtain an income of 60 percent of their employed earnings when retired. This is paid for by a tax on the entire society amounting to 1 percent. Under these circumstances, the switch from the previous arrangement, in which most individuals saved, to one in which there is a tax on everyone of 20 percent, which is used to pay a pension, would not benefit these poor people at all. They would get the same as they did before. But it would benefit the rest of society because the 1 percent special tax could be eliminated. Each individual who previously had been saving 20 percent of his income and paying 1 percent tax now pays a 20 percent tax and is not required to save. The beneficiaries are the taxpayers.

This example may seem unrealistic, but the principal respectable argument for social security, as opposed to letting people take care of their own retirement, is based on it. In the late 1930s, when we adopted our first social

5. Some scholars have suggested that the social security system could be terminated without loss to the current generation. See Peter J. Ferrara, *Social Security, The Inherent Contradiction* (Menlo Park, Calif.: Cato Institute, 1980). I doubt that these procedures will work.

security system, it was argued that we would have to pay for the retirement of the poor anyway and that making them pay their retirement income by way of a tax was desirable from the standpoint of the rest of society. Further, this argument is still frequently used.[6] There is no doubt that granted the assumption that we will make charitable provision for certain people, a tax and pension system that eliminates the need of doing so would be to the benefit of everyone except the people who previously received the charitable pension and who are now required to pay the tax. Note, however, that this is a fairly clear-cut example of a direct effort to make the middle class better off at the expense of the poor.

This may seem a little uncharitable to the middle class but consider the situation. The poor have an expectancy at the beginning of the system of an income from the charity of the well-off. This expectancy is, in reality, a property of theirs in the ordinary economic definition of property even if not in law. If there were any doubt that the middle class would make the payment, then the argument we have given above falls to the ground because the middle class could simply stop the payment rather than make it. In essence, the middle class is charitable enough so that it finds providing for the well-being, at least at a minimum level, of the poor ranks fairly high in its preference function. Making the poor provide for themselves, however, ranks higher. Thus, the major beneficiaries of socializing saving under these circumstances, and at the same time socializing the payments for the poor under a different rubric than before, are those people who are working and find themselves paying out only 20 percent in taxes instead of saving 20 percent and paying 1 percent in taxes.[7]

Let us return to our original equal society and complicate it a little. Firstly, let us assume that there is an interest rate, although the society remains stable.[8] Since the society is a stable society, this simply means that investment

6. Sherwin Rosen, "Some Arithmetics of Social Security," privately circulated, 3. Hal R. Varian, "Pensions and Public Policy," privately circulated, 1.

7. As a piece of technical economics, the failure of the poor to save in this case may or, then again, may not exert an externality on the middle class. It all depends on definition. I tried the problem of whether it was a genuine externality or not on a collection of economists with special competence in this area, and the best answer that I got was "that is the wrong question."

8. There is considerable debate, economically, on whether or not there would be an interest rate in a stable situation like this. In my opinion, those who argue for such an interest rate are correct, and the others are not, but if the reader disagrees with me on this point, may I ask him to simply suspend his criticism until later. We are going to shift from our present stable society to a growing society shortly.

does pay off up to the point that it replaces wear and tear on existing machinery. It is normally true in the United States that we do not count as investment those parts of our expenditures on capital equipment that are just designed to replace existing capital. They are characteristically regarded as part of the depreciation allotments of the company and as a cost. It is, however, quite possible to simply let the machinery deteriorate, and the decision to keep it up must be based on the view that it is a worthwhile activity. If it does not pay anything at all, then presumably we would prefer to let the machinery deteriorate. In any event, this assumption merely means that capital has a value in the sense that it not only increases capacity but wears out and must be replaced.

Let us assume that the interest rate is high enough so that if the identical members of our, once again, identical society save 10 percent of their income and invest it at the going interest rate, they can retire on a pension of 60 percent of their earnings. Really, they are better off than those of our first society, because capital is productive and savings can be rewarded. Let us now assume the same "reforms" we described before, i.e., that everybody is taxed 20 percent and that the funds derived therefrom are used to pay pensions of 60 percent of previous earnings to all people over the age of 65. There are two effects here, one of which, the decline in the total value of the capital stock, will be deferred for a moment. Let us assume that, mysteriously, the capital stock remains constant.

Under these circumstances, the individual will find that he now must make larger payments to receive the same pension as before, because the payments are spent instantly and not invested to earn interest that is then used for the pension. At first glance this might seem a fairly unlikely thing to happen, politically, but consider that it is not by any means a disaster for all members of society. Obviously, it is not a disaster for people 65 or over who suddenly receive 60 percent of their working income in addition to the 60 percent they were already spending from their investments. They benefit greatly. If we work our way down from 65 we would find that the benefit fell steadily as we took younger and younger age groups, eventually getting to zero. The group below that would receive positive detriments, the detriment rising steadily until we reach people the age of 20 or below, who, together with future generations, would have markedly lower well-being than before this institution was introduced.

It seems likely that a majority of voting adults in our society would benefit by the change and hence might be interested, politically, in this change.[9] It would be a clear-cut case of part of the present generation benefitting at the cost of the rest of the present generation and all future generations. Further, in this case as well as in the previous one, an eventual termination of the system, i.e., a stopping of the pension scheme, would inflict great transitional costs. In this case, however, there would also be transitional gains.

We have not yet fully plumbed the disadvantages of this system. With a guaranteed pension for everyone and with everyone having lower disposable income, presumably the amount the individuals would save and invest would go down; indeed, many would disave, with the consequent social costs. How much savings would go down would depend on various factors that we need not go into here, but part of the machinery would not be replaced, and the end product would be that the total output of the society, and, hence, individual incomes, would fall. Altogether, this particular change appears very clearly undesirable.

The second part of these two unfortunate effects of social security has led to a very vigorous controversy currently appearing in the economic journals, the problem being whether the social security system has or has not lowered the amount of investment in the United States. Personally, I find it very difficult to understand anyone who feels convinced that it has not lowered total investment, but it also should be said that the debate so far has been rather inconclusive. It has involved both theory and efforts to statistically measure the reduction.[10] The various methods by which this can be done lead to different results, and there does not seem to be any strong reason for selecting one.

All we can actually say is that the statistics are not very informative at the moment, although by the time the reader reads this perhaps the conundrum will have been solved. A priori, the system should have reduced savings with the result that the American GNP is lower than it otherwise would be.

9. See Edgar K. Browning's "Why the Social Security Budget Is Too Large in a Democracy," *Economic Inquiry* 13 (September 1975): 373–88. Currently, the social security system is in severe financial trouble, and hence, it is fairly certain to have either its payment or its tax schedule modified in some way. Under the circumstances, there seems no point in presenting any detailed figures on the transfers involved.

10. See M. Darby, *The Effects of Social Security on Income and the Capital Stock* (Washington: American Enterprise Institute for Public Policy Research, 1979), and R. J. Barro, *The Impact of Social Security on Private Saving* (Washington: American Enterprise Institute for Public Policy Research, 1978).

It should, however, be kept in mind that the Americans invest not only in the United States but also abroad. Perhaps the reduction of savings in the United States has lowered the world product, and as a result, the actual effect on the United States is not particularly visible. This would mean that a number of people who are much poorer than Americans had their incomes kept lower than they otherwise would be, but that Americans themselves have suffered only a modest reduction.

Let us now assume that society is, in fact, growing, although we will assume that its population is still a stable one and that growth takes the form of rising per capita incomes. This growth, we shall assume, is the result primarily of investments, although in the real world it would appear that a great deal of the growth is the result of new knowledge that does not entirely come from formal investments if we use conventional accounting techniques.

Let us begin by assuming that the rate of growth of per capita incomes is exactly the rate of interest. For example, growth is 5 percent, and that is also the rate of interest.[11] We again assume that in the starting situation individuals are saving part of their income and investing it. It is no longer possible, however, to assume that their pension will be 60 percent of a constant annual income, because the annual income will not be constant but will be rising. Further, they will have smaller incomes in the early part of their working life from which the interest accumulation will be greatest, and the higher incomes later from which the interest return will be relatively minor. Still, let us go back to our assumption that individuals saved 10 percent of their income, and with the accumulation of that saving, plus interest, at the age of 65 they characteristically purchase an annuity that will pay them a pension which they regard as optimal, granted the fact that they have to save more money to have a larger pension.

Assume, under these circumstances, that once again a reform is made, and they are taxed 20 percent of their incomes in order to pay to all people who retire a pension that will be equivalent, under these circumstances, to 60 percent of current income of employed persons in each year. In other words, the absolute value of 60 percent will rise at 5 percent a year as the income of the rest of the population rises. The individual return is considerably greater than the tax payment. Indeed, the individual will, if one looks only at his accounts, achieve a substantial return on his "investment." The only thing that has

11. Once again, I do not wish to argue that this is necessarily what would happen. The assumption will be relaxed later.

happened is that his individual payments in taxes are higher than the amount he would have saved before, but his pension will also be higher than it would have been before. Indeed, it is rather hard to see how an individual could guarantee himself this kind of increasing pension under present insurance institutions, although I suppose actuaries could work it out.

Let us then, once again, go through the question of who gains and who loses. Let us in doing so leave aside the probable decline in total savings as well as the problem of retardation of the growth rate and simply assume that the growth continues at the same rate as the rate of interest, and enough money is saved to retain that growth rate.

Under these circumstances, the people 65 years and older gain when the program is put in hand.[12] Then, once again, there would be sizable, but not quite so large, benefits for the people who are younger than 65 years and steadily shrinking benefits as we go down the age pyramid. In this case, however, it is not at all obvious that anyone who is working age at the time that the procedure was introduced would lose anything by it except that he can no longer make voluntary decisions as to how much he would save. Presumably this does lower his utility, but we will, for the time being, ignore that source of disutility.

The system would be like the system with which we started, in that the first generation makes a large gain throughout, with the gain greatest for the older people. Once the system has reached a Samuelsonian steady state it will continue to exist with nothing much in the way of gains or losses for people in the society, and when it terminates there will be a gigantic transitory cost imposed on the generation then alive. Once again, the highest termination costs are on the older, and lower costs on the younger.

In the real world, rates of growth are characteristically lower than interest rates. There are, of course, cases in which rates of growth have been higher than interest rates, particularly in countries with access to the international capital market and very good growth potential. On the whole, however, interest rates have been higher than per capita growth. Granted that this is so, then the situation we described before is not nearly as simple and straightforward. Suppose that the interest rate of the society is 5 percent and the rate of growth is 3 percent. Once again, we tax people 20 percent of their incomes in order to provide them with pensions of 60 percent. If the individuals

12. In the real world, some people over 65 may not be permitted to join the program when it is first introduced.

invest the 20 percent throughout their lives, they could obtain larger pensions, or alternatively, they could have acquired the same pensions at a lower investment.

Once again, the lowered incentive to invest should lower total per capita incomes, but we will ignore that factor in our calculations. Depending on the difference between the interest rate and the rate of growth, there would certainly be some people at the young end of the population at the time the program is adopted who would be harmed by the change to a social security type of voluntary savings way of providing for their old age. It would still be true, however, that the older people would surely gain. The exact point in the age of distribution in which one switched from gain to loss would depend on the exact difference between interest rate and the rate of growth. It is not at all improbable that a majority of the voting population at the time the program is installed would make a net gain.

Once the system has come into a stable state, i.e., once everyone receiving a pension had entered the system at the time he entered the work force, all would be losing, in the sense that they would have been better off had they not been taxed and had made voluntary investments. And, of course, if the system is terminated everyone would suffer losses, with the older people suffering the largest losses. This is a case in which there are significant transitory gains for a large part of the existing generation when the program is put into effect, but the program causes significant losses for every succeeding generation. It is an almost perfect case of a transitional gains trap.[13] It is an unfortunate characteristic of functioning democracies that future generations cannot vote, and the present generations do not necessarily take their interest completely into account. This would be a case in which they are positively injured to the benefit of part of the present generation.

Let us complicate our problem further by assuming a world in which the population and per capita incomes continuously rise. This has been descriptive of the western world as a whole over the last 200 years. Whether it can be continued indefinitely is a subject on which I do not propose to speculate. Under these circumstances, the individual contemplating the system assumes that he will actually be able to tax a larger population than the population that will be receiving the benefits. There will be a larger group of people in each age level as you go from the top to the bottom, even though in our

13. See my article "The Transitional Gains Trap," *Bell Journal of Economics* 6 (Autumn 1975): 671–78.

population everybody dies at the age of 80, because the population is steadily increasing. Thus, the system of taxing everybody some percentage amount and using that to pay pensions could provide an income in each year of 60 percent of what has been the average per capita income of working personnel at a tax cost in which both the per capita income rate of growth and the population growth are taken into account. If the rate of income growth—the total GNP growth—is greater than the interest rate, then, once again, everyone alive at the time this system began would gain.

The American economy, certainly in recent years, has not grown as rapidly as the prevailing rate of interest, at least for sophisticated investors. Historically, it also appears that the rate of growth of the population of a state is a highly irregular and unpredictable variable. The fact that it grows at a high rate at one point does not indicate that it will continue to grow. Further, the fluctuations in the population rate we observe in the real world may mean that the ratio between retired persons and persons who are of working age can change quite sharply, even when the total population is not changing very rapidly. Thus, it would not be terribly wise to depend on growth in population to support the social security system, although it must be said that for many years the American government did. Payment for this great expectation is now coming due.

In all of the systems we have discussed so far, the structure has the characteristic that in the first generation a fairly large number of people, predominantly older people, in the society gain. The younger people will gain if the rate of growth of society is greater than the rate of interest, and they will lose if it is less. In general, the latter is a more reasonable assumption. When the system is in equilibrium—i.e., when everyone now alive in society entered it at the same time he began working—no one gains from the system unless the interest rate is lower than the rate of growth, in which event everyone gains. But, though no one gains from the system, there would be large groups who would be injured by its termination. Specifically, they will be all those people who are old enough so that the termination of the system and a switch by them of their social security payments into interest-paying investments could leave them with smaller old age pensions than they would get under the old system. This would generally mean the bulk of the older population. The younger part of the population would, of course, gain from the termination of the system. The exact transition point would depend on the difference between the rate of growth and the interest rate. Nevertheless, it would obviously be, politically, very difficult to terminate such a system once it had started. In the final generation, the termination of the system would indeed be a catastrophe for a large part of the population; although if the interest rate and growth rate had the appropriate relationship, younger people would gain.

Note that in this entire discussion I have simply ignored inflation except occasionally to refer to the real value instead of the money value. The reason for this is that it is easy enough to index the social security system, and, indeed, the American system has been indexed.[14] There is one effect of inflation that should, perhaps, be mentioned here because it has been empirically important in the recent history of the social security system. The United States moved from a long-run period of money which, if not stable, at any event, had no persistent tendency to inflate into a period of fairly rapid inflation. The transition from relatively stable money to an inflationary situation is always very disturbing. Thus, there have been periods of time when the real rate of interest for many people has actually been negative.

A comparison of the effect of having saved money over the period in which most present-day pensioners are acquiring their pensions, as opposed to making the contributions that they in fact did, would indicate that even if the social security pension system had not been sharply expanded, which it has, they would probably have done as well in the social security system as on investments. This is characteristic of what we may call "new inflation," or inflation that has begun before people become adjusted. In the long run, however, it is not possible to hold the real rate of interest down by inflation. Indeed, the United States discovered this in the latter half of the 1970s.

Thus, the likely future prospect, assuming that inflation continues, is that the more customary relationship between return on savings and the rate of growth will reestablish itself. If inflation is stopped, a great many people who have saved money during the inflationary period and acquired assets whose appreciation value will be very great when inflation is stopped, will make great gains, thus making the social security payments appear to be very minor compared with them. This again, however, will be merely a transitional effect. In a steady state, with some rate of inflation, which may be zero, a social security system that is linked to the growth rate of the national product will normally pay less than the real interest rate, although it is conceivable that it might pay more.

14. In fact, it was overindexed for a while, with the result that it looked as if eventually the older people would be absorbing the entire national product. Congress has now partially corrected the error.

What has all of this to do with helping the poor? The answer is, obviously, not very much. I have been describing a system developed in the late 19th century and continued to the present in which it is very hard to argue that the poor are benefitted at all except insofar as older people are among the poor. If we look at lifetime incomes, however, there is no significant benefit to the poor.[15] I have discussed it at great length because a great many people seem to think that the social security system, per se, is part of our welfare program, and, indeed, it is the most important single government transfer.

It is, of course, true that there are many poor among the elderly population. Further, once a system such as the social security system has been running for a number of years, the number of poor in the older population, if we do not count their social security payments as income (i.e., the number who would be poor if social security were terminated), is apt to be quite large because the people do not save as much for their old age. Also, the tradition of children taking care of their parents may be greatly weakened by the social security system. My own opinion is that if the social security system were terminated, children would immediately begin taking care of their parents, with the result that there would be a voluntary intergenerational transfer. Certainly, people would begin saving more money. At the very least, people would save the same share of their after-tax income as they do now, and the after-tax income would be higher, of course. Presumably, most people would be sensible enough to realize that there is going to be no government provision for their retirement and that they should do something about it themselves. I do not know whether this would lead to enough saving to completely replace the social security pensions.[16] It might indeed lead to higher old age pensions, because the addition of the interest multiplier to savings would make it easier to build up a large pension. It should be pointed out here that the people who make the voluntary decisions to save are also the people who vote. There is no obvious reason why they should be more provident in one area than in the other. Thus, the people who were taxed 20 percent of their income in order to receive 60 percent of their working income when they retired might, if they received interest payments that in effect doubled the return on their savings, choose not to save 10 percent and get the

15. Most existing social security programs have provisions that directly benefit the poor. They are discussed later, but empirically, until very recently, they were trivial compared with the transfer from the working population to the older population.

16. In the ultimate stable state, not in the transitional state.

same pension but to save, let us say, 15 percent to guarantee themselves 90 percent of their working income when they retire.

It has never been exactly clear why people choose to retire on lower incomes than their working incomes. If we go back to the period before social security and before the significant drive on the part of the government to get retirement ages down,[17] we find that people tended to have declining incomes toward the end of their lives. Those who had some source of income other than work, whether this source of income was returns on their savings, support by children, or public charity, would, as their income declined, eventually reach the point where they preferred that other source of income, together with leisure, to working. Thus, as a general rule, people retired, their income went down, and they chose retirement at a lower income than their final working income because they preferred leisure. Thus, the custom that older people had lower incomes than people in the active phase of their lives became well established. There does not, however, seem to be any other reason for it.[18]

Why our government policy should aim at older people having lower incomes than active people is not in any way clear. The statement that they have lower demands is simply a repetition of the statement that they are accustomed in our society to have lower incomes. Apparently, this is not thought of as a social problem, although I cannot think why not.[19] But, in any event, the fact that they do have lower incomes, and would have lower incomes without social security, means that whatever measure in absolute income you use as poverty, there will be a higher percentage of the older population than of the working-age population in it. One can imagine a government's social

17. This is, of course, well before the current drive on the part of the government to get retirement ages up for the upper classes while keeping them low by means of social security for the lower classes.

18. This is assuming we are talking about real incomes. A great many elderly people, of course, are in fact owners of substantial real estate in the form of their houses, with the result that their real income is considerably higher than the calculated income normally given them. I am referring to the real income, not the calculated income.

19. It can be argued that retired people need only 65 to 80 percent of their preretirement income to avoid a drop in living standards. According to this argument, people no longer have work-related expenses such as special clothing and carfare. Also, they have Medicare, lower income taxes, no child-care expenses, and they eat less. See Alicia Munnell, "The Future of the U.S. Pension System," in Colin Campbell (ed.), *Financing Social Security* (Washington: American Enterprise Institute, 1979), 257–59.

welfare program intended to change this so that average incomes are as high in the older cadres as in the younger, but our advanced thinkers do not seem to be interested in that particular reform.

So far we have been discussing a system that is simply introduced, goes into equilibrium, and is perhaps terminated. In practice, most real-world social security systems since Bismarck's invention have tended to gradually rise in size and coverage. This means that we have always been in the first generation. A proposal, for example, to increase the social security tax by 1 percent and use the amount to increase pensions appropriately benefits all of the older people and injures the younger, just as the introduction of a new program would do the same to a smaller extent.

Recently, and this development will be discussed much later, after we have talked about the charitable aspects of social security, there has been some tendency for the social security to go down, which means that the older people are injured and the younger people benefit. The tendency to grow, which is almost 100 years old in Germany and a little over 50 years old in the United States, can hardly be projected permanently into the future, because eventually such growth would absorb the entire national income. Thus, eventually, a maximum will be reached. Of course, it is possible that the system will begin to shrink in the future.

As long as it is growing, we have what amounts to a first-generation system for at least part of the program at all times. It is only after the growth has stopped that we reach the steady state, and, of course, it would take about 50 or 60 years for that to occur. During the growth period, the primary effect of social security is to work a transfer to the members of the present generation from members of the next generation, and the members of the next generation cannot vote.[20] The fact that this procedure has received, on the whole, a very good press among intellectuals is, in my opinion, astonishing. That they should not be opposed to it does not surprise me, but that they should argue strongly for it does. Perhaps the explanation is simple: they are members of the present generation.

20. This is, of course, something of an oversimplification. For more careful statement, see Browning's "Why the Social Security Budget Is Too Large in a Democracy."

RISK, CHARITY, AND MISCELLANEOUS ASPECTS OF SOCIAL SECURITY

So far, except in the very simplest version of the Samuelsonian model, we have not talked about aiding the poor qua poor. In this chapter we will discuss the social security system as a way of aiding at least some of the poor, and also, to reinforce what was said before, as a way of making the poor "save" for their own retirement. Before doing so, however, it is necessary to look at a few special aspects of the scheme. Firstly, when the program was introduced in the United States, it did not have the direct tax transfer characteristic that it now does. The money collected from the early contributors to social security was, in fact, invested in government bonds. There was a reduction in the federal deficit in 1937 because of the new social security taxes and, as yet, no benefit payments. It has been suggested by some economists that this reduction in the federal deficit is one of the major causes of the 1937 depression.[1]

Thus, at the beginning there was an effort to set up a system in which interest would be paid on genuine investments.[2] The amounts of the tax and the amount to be paid were such that for most Americans, at that time, these investments would simply be a portion of their total portfolio. It may have appeared to many middle-level Americans that diversifying their investments to some extent by this particular form of forced saving was desirable in terms of risk reduction. In any event, this original program involved no transfer from the young to the old or from future generations to the present generation.[3]

Reprinted, with kind permission of Kluwer Academic Publishers, from *Economics of Income Redistribution*, Kluwer-Nijhoff Studies in Human Issues: An International Series in the Social Sciences (Boston: Kluwer-Nijhoff, 1983), 123–35.

1. See Kenneth D. Roose, *The Economics of Recession and Revival* (Hamden, Conn.: Archon Books, 1954).

2. It should be noted that in 1936–37 the federal debt was very small, and there was no apparent prospect of repudiating it by inflation.

3. This is a little oversimplified. The details were such that there would be some transfer but not very much. There was a sharp transfer away from working wives.

After a few years, however, the scheme was changed to its present pay-as-you-go scheme. A small reserve, originally the money that had built up the first few years of the program, was to be kept for the contingency that in some year, or perhaps a short series of years, the total expenditures would be greater than the total receipts. Thus, the scheme was changed from an investment program to a friendly society, i.e., an arrangement under which one group pays in and another group gets out. The group that paid were young, and the people that were paid were old; it was, in essence, a transfer from the young to the old and from future generations to the present generation, but, of course, the scheme sacrificed the interest payments. However, it should be pointed out that, at the time this change was made, interest rates were very low. In fact, in real terms, possibly their historic low, while recovery meant that GNP was growing very rapidly indeed.

So far as I know, no one announced any calculations on this matter at the time nor was the particular method of calculating the pensions designed to automatically increase total pensions as the amount taken in increased. Nevertheless, anyone who thought about the matter would have realized that if the interest rate and rate of growth continued at their current levels, and Congress behaved in the way one expects politicians to behave,[4] it would turn out to be quite a satisfactory investment—indeed a more satisfactory investment than any other that was reasonably secure. In any event, for the bulk of the population it would be only one part of their portfolio, and the change in the method of financing might be regarded as an improvement in diversification.

All of this implies, more or less, a "rational expectations" perspective. I do indeed feel that people cannot be readily fooled again and again by the same simple trick. They will eventually realize that inflation lowers their real income and take appropriate action, thus making inflation no longer a way of getting rid of unemployment. With complex matters of the sort I have described here, however, it is by no means obvious that people would put the time and energy into calculating the exact outcome. I would anticipate that people would make many errors. I see no reason, however, to believe that these errors would be biased in any particular way. If we thought of everybody making their own calculations, I would anticipate that the calculations

4. Here it should be remembered that social security funds are partitioned off from the rest of the budget; thus spending the social security surplus for other things would have been politically difficult for Congress, while keeping a large surplus rather than paying out to the old people the sum of money drawn in would be equally difficult.

would tend to be randomly distributed, with the mean near the correct value unless there was some reason why erroneous calculations were easier to make in one direction than in the other.

In fact, of course, people do not do very much in the way of making their own calculations and do not necessarily even read those provided by the media. There seems no reason for these to be systematically biased in any particular direction, but it is true that the media have a strong tendency to copy each other and, hence, to go one way. The media are apt to turn to "experts" for advice. In the particular case of government programs, and especially those government programs that involve expenditures in the future, this advice tends to be bad. The government civil servants normally have an incentive to expand their programs, and one way to do so is to tell lies about how much they will cost in the future. The academic specialists in any given area want to remain on good terms with the bureaucrats who have money to give out for research grants and consulting contracts. Further, they will also gain if the particular field in which they are experts expands. There will be more interest in it, and hence more students, special institutes, and research grants from outside the agency concerned. Their work is apt to be either biased in favor of expansion or, in any event, uncritical of data put out by the bureaucrats in favor of changes.[5]

In addition, they may very well feel that they understand these matters better than the common person and that a little deception is probably necessary to overcome prejudice.[6] For all of these reasons it seems dubious that the above calculations were actually made. Nevertheless, I think that if someone had engaged in careful calculations and had simply assumed that rates of growth and interest rates were likely to remain much the same, he would have concluded that the switch from the investment-type program to a "pay out as you take in"-type program was either desirable or, in any event, not particularly undesirable.

5. They may also be interested in government jobs. Carolyn Weaver Mackay, in her doctoral dissertation on origins of the Social Security Act (unpublished), refers consistently to the academic supporters of the Act before it was founded as "potential administrators."

6. For a sophisticated statement of this problem, see Thurmond Arnold, *The Folklore of Capitalism* (New Haven, Conn.: The Yale University Press, 1937). The general theme of this book is the justification of using subjectively dishonest means in order to obtain desirable goals. The references to the social security scheme are on page 193. Thurmond Arnold was a prominent "New Dealer," and I think we can take his attitude on these matters as typical of the people who were making the decisions.

There was, of course, one further special characteristic of the program. It was enacted at a time when unemployment was quite high, and the 65-year-old retirement age was a deliberate effort to get a certain number of older people to move out of jobs so younger people could have them. The extremely discriminatory provisions for working wives may have had the same general objective.[7]

All of this may seem unduly cynical, but I think we should keep in mind that government bureaucrats and academic "experts" are like the rest of us. They can frequently convince themselves that something that is in their interest is also in the interest of the public at large. They are, of course, also like you and me, in that sometimes they may sacrifice their own interests for the truth or what they conceive to be the public good. We should not, however, depend on their doing that all of the time. Still, it seems likely that the basic motive for the average person's favoring the social security program when it was started, or favoring those expansions that affected him, was the realization that he was getting a good bargain. He would pay less than the actuarially correct value of his pension. The bargain must have looked particularly good in the period (1939) when the scheme was changed from an investment program to an intergenerational transfer program.

It seems unlikely that a desire to help the poor was a major objective in the minds of most people connected with the initial Social Security Act, because, in fact, it is not even clear that it did, and if it did, it certainly did so to a very small extent. There was an arrangement under which the "payback" was somewhat higher for the poor than for the well-off, but the length of time

7. The change in 1961 to make retirement easy at the age of 62 was, I think, not an effort to deal with the unemployment problem but simply an effort to increase the employment of government bureaucrats in the agency. I have difficulty in believing that they really made the errors that would be necessary to explain their computation of the actual number of people who would retire early. It is, in this respect, on all fours with the famous double indexing that, for a number of years, led pensions to grow very rapidly. It was made essentially by a committee of bureaucrats who were nearly at the retirement age and who were aware of how easy it was for them to acquire a second social security pension to add on to their regular pension. The defense of the minimum payment for social security has, in part, been by poor people and those who are concerned for poor people, but to a considerable extent it has been bureaucrats for whom this is an extremely profitable provision if they are willing to take the necessary steps to become eligible for it. I should perhaps say that Colin Campbell, who has made a number of very helpful comments on this book, disagrees with my imputation of self-interested motives to the bureaucrats in these cases.

that you work and pay the social security tax is not relevant in computing the payout to you unless it is really quite short.

The poor are unlikely to go to college (indeed, may actually not finish high school) and, hence, begin working earlier. Further, the rich live longer. In the early days of the Social Security Act, any income earned by employment was taken, dollar for dollar, from your pension; hence, the poor person who chose to work because the pension was not, by and of itself, adequate, would find that, presumably, since his earned income was larger than the pension, he received no pension at all. Lastly, the system was very severely discriminatory against families in which the wife worked. In the 1930s and 1940s, working wives were found almost exclusively in the bottom part of the income structure. Whether this is true or not, it is clear that any help that the poor received was extremely small compared with the transfer to the present generation from the future.[8] The big transfer was certainly not to the poor.

There is, however, one very clear-cut way in which the poor were worse off. The United States, at the time the Social Security Act was enacted, was like most other countries, in that it had provisions for taking care of the poor, and the older poor would, of course, fall under them. Presumably, the poor during their working life were, to some extent, paying taxes that were being used to pay these relief payments. There is some debate as to how progressive the American tax system is now, and certainly a great deal of debate as to how progressive it was back then, but let us assume simply that people who had low incomes did indeed pay a part of those incomes out in taxes and that part of that tax payment went to help the poor. Thus, an individual who was working and had a low income would, during the period that he was working, be paying (modest) taxes to support the poor, and then when he retired, he would be taken care of by this standard aid to the poor program.

When the social security program was enacted, it changed this in two ways: (1) there was now a formal pension, and (2) the tax system now became one of the rare examples of a truly regressive tax in our revenue structure. It was a completely proportional tax on earnings, with a maximum. Thus, up to the maximum, which was until very recently quite low, they took simply a percentage of earnings. Above the maximum it took nothing; hence it was clearly regressive. There seems no doubt that if we compare the pension and the tax supporting it with the previous arrangements, the poor individual,

8. See Michael J. Boskin et al., "Separating the Transfer and Annuity Functions of Social Security," working paper, Stanford University, Stanford, California, 1981.

throughout his life, would pay in taxes a higher proportion of the amount that he eventually got back than he would have done under the previous arrangement. Further, it should be pointed out that it was the normal procedure of all administrators in the early days (only slightly modified now) to simply subtract the social security check from the relief payments (now SSI) that an older person would otherwise receive. Since the social security payments for a poor person would characteristically be lower than whatever amount of aid would normally be given locally, this meant that the poor person ended up receiving exactly what he would have received had the social security system not existed. Taxpayers who were not poor presumably benefitted from this system to some extent, since their taxes were slightly lower because the taxes on the poor were slightly higher. Poor people would pay somewhat lower taxes to support the relief system, but the payment into the social security system would be larger. The end product was almost certainly[9] that the introduction of the social security system and each and every one of its expansions made the poor either slightly worse off, or, in any event, no better off.[10] All of this changed with the 1977 amendments, which will be further discussed below.

The citizens, before the adoption of the social security system, had been making what seemed to them suitable provisions for the poor. That is, the amount being paid to the poor was the result of the political process. There is no reason why the introduction of the social security system should change the general idea of most people as to how much they will give to the poor. Indeed, as I have remarked, one of the standard arguments for social security is that it compels the poor, who would otherwise be charges on the public when they retire, to make "savings" to support themselves.

There is built into the system some tendency to help the poor, just as in the previous system. As a matter of fact, it is my opinion that social security reduced the degree to which we helped the poor, but this is controversial. It could be argued that social security left the aid to the poor the same or even increased it a little bit. What we can say for certain is that there was no great improvement for the poor. To repeat, in my own opinion, there was a modest reduction in the well-being of the poor.

As I have said above, most people, although willing to make gifts to the poor, do tend to feel somewhat annoyed about the whole process if the gifts

9. I regret to say that there are no detailed calculations with which I can make this statement more apodictic.

10. Except insofar as they received transfers from the poor of the next generation.

get above a certain amount or if they think that the poor are, at least to some extent, poor through their own fault. The person who fails to save and thus provide for old age is, to some extent, at fault in the popular mind.

I do not wish to argue that, in fact, the poor should be criticized for not making adequate savings to take care of their old age or not producing children who are willing to take care of them. The point here is that I think most people, although quite willing to take care of impecunious older people rather than letting them starve to death, nevertheless feel that it is a burden which should be shifted to the people themselves or perhaps to their children. For the person covered, the Social Security Act, in part, did shift it to the person himself.

All of the previous remarks are merely an introduction to a discussion of the future of the social security system. I am going to discuss entirely the American system, but I should say I believe that somewhat similar problems have developed elsewhere. Basically, my theme will be that a number of difficulties have arisen. One of these—but only one—is an effort to make the social security system more progressive than is actually the long-run desire of the American people. The result is the endangering of the system as a whole.

Before turning to these problems, however, I must deal with two other matters. The first is a review of the theory produced by Samuelson that we have been following so far for the social security, and the other is a discussion of some other minor factors that are making life difficult for the Social Security Administration at the moment. To begin with Samuelson, the scheme under which individuals pay taxes during their working life in order to receive a pension when they retire depends on complete faith in people who are not yet of voting age. Suppose that I begin working at the age of 20 and begin paying roughly 12 percent of my income into social security.[11] I am doing this under the assumption that when I become 65—45 years in the future—a majority of the voters then alive will present me with a pension that is suitably calculated from my tax payments. Note that there is nothing to prevent them from refraining from doing so, and all of the voters under the age of 63 at that time will have been too young to vote when I entered the system, and, hence, cannot even regard themselves as being morally bound by a promise they themselves made.

11. The social security advocates sometimes argue that the actual payment by the wage earner is only half of this amount. So far as I know, no economist agrees with them.

For many, many years, it has been alleged that this promise was an unbreakable one and that, in fact, people could safely depend on it. It does not make very much difference whether people can, in fact, safely depend on it. If they think they can, the system will continue. The problem is that in recent years the promise has begun to look a little shaky. Seventy-three percent of the population "have little or no confidence that the social security system will have the funds for retirement benefits for themselves or their spouses upon retirement."[12] The people who answered the poll's questions were opposed to basing social security payments solely on financial need rather than primarily on payroll contributions, but it is clear what they would like to have happen is not what they think will happen.

One of the reasons that social security was enacted was that a number of labor union programs that resembled social security, in that they involved fees by young members of the union to pay the pensions of older members of the union, had developed just exactly this kind of political difficulty; i.e., the younger members were resisting paying fees adequate to provide the promised pensions. This seems to have led to more labor union support for the social security program than one would normally have expected. In the period before the 1930s, labor unions in general had been rather opposed to a federal system because they regarded it as competition for their own programs. The combination of the Depression and this young member resistance meant that labor union programs were in trouble, and they thought of the federal program as bailing them out. The point of mentioning this history is that it is possible that young voters will begin acting like young labor union members in the future. Of course, the possibility is only a possibility, but there are various reasons to suspect that it may, in fact, occur.

The first of these reasons is that it would appear the program is now approaching its maximum size. There are practically no groups that are not covered one way or another,[13] and raising the pensions by raising the taxes does not, at the moment, seem to be a politically feasible proposal. It should be said, of course, that many foreign countries have higher net bundles of taxes and benefits than we do, and it is quite possible that we could raise these two amounts. There is, however, obviously a maximum that cannot be exceeded.

12. An AP poll reported in the *Richmond Times Dispatch*, Sunday, October 4, 1981, p. 14. The article also reported that in May a similar poll had indicated that 74 percent "had little or no confidence of receiving social security retirement benefits."

13. Government employees are the largest uncovered group, and they have their own pension system.

To put the matter in its most extreme form, taxes cannot exceed 100 percent of GNP. In practice, of course, the maximum will be much lower.

There is at least some evidence, however, that politically we have already reached the maximum tax. Firstly, the 1977 revision of the social security system provided a schedule for the future under which, in 1983, the replacement rate (the ratio of pension to amount earned shortly before retirement) will be significantly reduced. Further, in the current political discussion of the problems of the social security system, simply solving them by raising taxes does not seem to be a politically viable solution. Indeed, various proposals for actually reducing taxes have been canvassed. All of this may be simply a temporary phenomenon, but it may also indicate that under American conditions we have now reached the maximum tax level, and the system is, at best, going into the stable state. But whether we have now reached maximum size or we still have time, eventually we will reach it.

When the program does reach maximum size, both in membership and in percentages of income taken and income paid back in pensions, it will become much less attractive to the voter. It will no longer be possible to put part of the cost of the system on future generations. We will be in a steady state, and in a steady state the attractions of the system are largely negative (people will be badly hurt if the program is cancelled) rather than positive (people can make significant gains through expansion). Politically, this changes the atmosphere, although it is not certain that it changes it in a particularly dangerous way.

Whether we have reached this kind of maturity, either in the United States or in other parts of the world, is not certain. It depends on a subjective estimate of the total amount that can be transferred through the system without significant negative effects, both economically and politically. There are signs that we have reached a maximum right now, but these signs cannot be regarded as completely reliable. Perhaps further expansion of the tax take and the pension size is indeed possible.

There are other problems, however. Firstly, during the early years of the system the working population had been increasing in size compared with the older population. This meant that the increases in the taxes paid by the working population could be smaller in paying for a given increase in pensions than would have been possible had the two populations been growing at the same rate. This fortunate situation began changing in about 1960. The older population is now increasing more rapidly than the working population, and it looks very much as if this increase will be rapid (insofar as any demographic change is ever rapid) and continue for a considerable number of years. Thus, it will be necessary to raise the taxes to pay the guaranteed pensions[14] or cut the pensions. Currently, Congress seems to be dithering but is, to some extent, cutting the benefits. Indeed, the only real difference between the Republican and Democratic parties here is the details of the rather small cuts that they both propose.[15] This, at least temporarily, has coincided with a fall in the rate of growth of the economy. I am not at all sure that this is other than a temporary phenomenon, but it does cause some difficulties for the program.

Lastly, inflation has, for a long time, made the social security investment appear to be better, relative to private investment in financial assets, than it actually was. During a period in which people were gradually getting used to inflation, the real return on investments was much lower than the return would have been had people fully understood the inflationary situation. Institutional adjustments necessary to make it possible for the average person to make a reasonable real return on real investments had not yet taken place. We are now either entering into a period in which people are reasonably well adjusted to inflation and, hence, the institutions will provide investments with real rates of return greater than those in the social security system, or entering a period in which the inflation will stop. The latter might lead to a very misleading situation in which the real return on investments made during the inflationary period would be much higher than is really socially justifiable, with the result that the social security investments seem to be particularly bad. This, again, could make the social security system politically unpopular.

All of the factors discussed above, and another which I propose to discuss below, tend to make social security less attractive in the future than it has been in the past. This, in essence, means that the changeover point between the people who gain from the continuance of the program and those who would gain from its termination has shifted upward in the age pyramid,[16] and the result is that there are more voters who would in fact gain from termination of the program than there were before. Whether this is a majority or not is not

14. One way of raising taxes, of course, is to use other taxes to supplement the social security. This is a distinction without a difference.

15. There is another difference, of course; each one maintains vigorously that its program will protect the aged at no cost and that the other is a villainous group of people who want to impoverish the aged. The difference between the two parties is which occupies the hero and which the villain role.

16. And also, as we will discuss later, has changed qualitatively within age groups.

at all clear, but certainly the political support for the program is weaker than it was before. Another, stronger reason, which has not been much discussed in the current pother about social security, is that there has been a change in the payoff in such a way that a number of quite influential people have had their payoff reduced while another collection of relatively uninfluential people have had it increased. Specifically, in 1977, the Social Security Act was amended in such a way as to make it very much more progressive. Progressiveness was increased in two ways. Firstly, the payback ratios were changed so that people in the lower-income brackets had a much higher payback ratio than people in the upper-income brackets. Secondly, the program itself was extended well up through the income pyramid so that a number of people found their total taxes increased very sharply.

It is very hard to lay out in detail the actual effect of the social security rules, because they are extremely varying. There is, for example, ferocious discrimination against working women and innumerable special rules that affect different people. Further, as we have mentioned, the program has been gradually extended over time with the result that almost no one who is now contemplating receipt of a pension has paid at the present tax level throughout his entire life, and inflation has had a major effect.

As a sort of approximation, Table 1 shows the tax and pension for a number of incomes. Note that $29,000 gives the payment and pension for all incomes above that amount. The final column is an effort to show the degree of progression that this system implies. It shows the number of days of benefit that will be paid for by one year's tax. This is a somewhat desperate effort to get around the technical difficulties by producing a figure that is roughly comparable over income brackets. There is obviously a very considerable transfer of funds from those in the top bracket to those in the bottom.

Some of the people in the bottom bracket are persons who have fairly sizable retirement incomes, for example, federal employees who are members of the federal employees retirement program but who were employed for a short time at fairly low incomes outside the government, in essence to take advantage of this very favorable set of payouts. A much larger group, however, are people who are actually poor and for whom government support in one form or another is their principal dependence. For these people, in general, other government support is large enough so that the social security support is simply subtracted from it. For example, if you happen to be in a city and state where older, impoverished people are paid $5,000 a year and you are drawing the lowest bracket social security payment shown here, your

TABLE 1 ***Social Security Progression***

INCOME ($)	ANNUAL SOCIAL SECURITY TAX (12%) ($)	ANNUAL SOCIAL SECURITY BENEFIT[a] ($)	DAYS OF BENEFIT PAID BY ONE YEAR'S TAX
$29,000 and above	$3,564.00	$6,535.56	199
15,000	1,800.00	4,330.56	150
10,000	1,200.00	3,580.56	122
5,000	500.00	2,830.56	77
3,600	431.00	2,620.56	60

SOURCE: U.S. Department of Health and Human Services, Social Security Administration, SSA Publication No. 05 = 10088, August 1981.

[a] Benefits calculated as follows:

1. .90 times monthly earnings up to $211.00 or .9(211)12 = $2,278.80.
2. 32% of next $1,068.00 or .32(1068) = $341.76.
3. 15% of all taxable earnings beyond $3,600.00.

total income would not be higher than $5,000, since the social security pension will be taken into account in computing your poverty level.

The first thing to be said about this is that sharply increasing the total number of people who will lose from the program by bringing the higher-income people in and giving them very low paybacks is almost certain to sharply lower the political support for the program. These are people who were making rather low (from their standpoint) payments into the fund and who were expecting to receive low payments (from their standpoint) back, and the payments they would receive back were not too disproportionate to the amount they had put in. They will now pay in very much more than they did before, but the payback will only increase slightly. It should, of course, be emphasized that this group of people are quite influential in our society. I would estimate that they are, roughly, the top one-half of the population. It should be pointed out that not everyone in this group will, in fact, be particularly injured. Those who are very close to retirement probably will lose little or nothing. In other words, in this particular group, the break-even point between winning and losing has been shifted sharply upward but has not been shifted up to the point where all of them lose.

The political support for the program is further, and very sharply, reduced by this scheme. Most people are, as I have said before, somewhat charitable, but the degree to which they are charitable is limited. I doubt that these particular arrangements can be justified to the average person who will be burned by them on the grounds that they increase the payments to the poor. He probably does not want to increase the payments of the poor that much anyway.

How, then, did they get through? I think the answer to that question has to be sought in the well-known information paradox of voting. In general, it is not worthwhile for the voter to become well informed, and he is apt to pick up information rather casually.[17] Thus, various things happen that he has not heard about at all or has only thought vaguely about. The 1977 changes occurred during the period in which, for a variety of reasons, the American government was engaging in a number of programs that were intended to make the poor somewhat better off as well, of course, as to benefit a group of special interests.

From the political response since that time, the bureaucrats and politicians making these changes may have gone too far. Unfortunately, any effort to correct the program by shifting funds from the poor to the wealthy, i.e., making the payback ratio higher for the upper-income members of the program and lower for the lower-income members, would cause further difficulties for the program. The problem here, which will be discussed at much greater length below, is that any reduction of payments to any single person automatically lowers the credibility of the promise that you will indeed get your payments eventually. It begins to look like a gamble rather than a sure thing.

In any event, the upper-income groups are beginning to feel that they are paying too much, and this has occurred at a time when, for other reasons, the program was in financial difficulties. Traditionally, these financial difficulties would have been dealt with very simply by raising social security taxes. Congress, however, has recently been reluctant to raise the taxes paid by the social security–supporting part of the population. They have enacted some raises to take place in the future but have been reluctant to have any at the present. The apparent reason for this is simply that, politically, the people who lose from the program are beginning to exert political pressure that tends to cancel the pressure put on by the Grey Panthers and other groups who will gain. The exact outcome of this tension between income and outgo

17. See my *Toward a Mathematics of Politics* (Ann Arbor: University of Michigan Press, 1967) for a full discussion of this point.

in the program is not currently predictable, but it certainly does not seem likely that Congress will be willing to expand the entire program in order to increase payments for upper-income groups, which is the only way of raising the payout ratio for the upper-income groups without lowering it for the lower-income groups.

If Congress finds it necessary to actually lower the payments going to any group, and it does look as if they will have to (the only difference between the Republicans and Democrats on this issue is the details), the program suddenly loses a lot of its credibility. When you lower the payout you, in a small way, enter the last generation of the program. Up to this point, in each expansion of the program we have been able to offer to the people in the program a net gain because of the first-generation situation. Any reduction of the program imposes upon people a portion of the cost of the last generation. The people can now look forward to at least the possibility that instead of either gaining in the first generation, as most people in the program so far have, or being in the stable-state generation, in which the losses come entirely from the difference from the rate of growth of the economy and the interest rate and, hence, are not really gigantic, they will be in the last generation, in which the losses come because payments are made in taxes, and then the full return does not come in the final pension.

This was one of the problems with the various union programs that had been enacted in early times. The younger people voted against expansion and for contraction of payments to the older people, which made the younger people less confident that their descendants would pay them off, and hence the support for the program tended to shrink. The same thing could happen with social security. Let us look at the scenario that, in essence, is the reverse of the first-generation scenario in which the program is expanded because each expansion benefits people and shows signs of being a further benefit for the future. Suppose, then, that benefits are cut to some extent. This does not have to be a general cut. It could be a cut for only one group, such as the upper-income people discussed earlier.

There have been, in the history of social security, a number of cases in which minor administrative changes have led to groups being cut, but these have generally been fairly trivial in importance and certainly very inconspicuous. The cut by the 1977 income redistribution program was, for a number of people, quite significant. Further, there will have to be, or at least predictably will be, some further cut in order to bring the system into balance now.

Once such cuts have occurred and the voters have realized that they have occurred, which may take some time or may never happen, the future pension payments change from a psychological certainty to a gamble, even though the risk may not be very large. This reduces their attractiveness, i.e., moves the cutoff point between an attractive and an unattractive program up through the age pyramid. With the program less attractive, it is likely to suffer further cuts because the number of people who feel that they gain from the cuts is increased, and the number of people who would be injured by the cuts is reduced. These further cuts will, once again, lower the credibility of the payout, and one can imagine the system slowly but surely vanishing.

In a way, when a social security–type program is established, and when it is growing, there is a continuous tendency for it to grow because of the, in essence, free gift that goes to a good many of the people now alive every time it is expanded. In the stable state, there is no gain to anyone, and, in fact, everyone is losing a bit because of the interest rate differences, but the reduction of the program would be painful. Once reductions begin, however, the credibility of the promise that your pension will be paid and that it will be proportional more or less to what you put in ceases to be strong. With weak credibility and with individuals thinking of the program as a gamble rather than as an insurance policy, its political support is apt to shrink, and further reductions are possible. Each reduction lowers the credibility still further and also lowers the total amount that people will lose from further reductions. This reduces the strength of opposition by those people who still oppose, and so on until there is no more system.

Although this tendency could lead to the termination of the program, it should be pointed out that the expansion still has the advantages that it had before. The problem here is essentially one of the credibility of the promise of future payment. The lower that credibility, and every reduction in payment to anyone reduces that credibility, the more likely the system is to shrink further. With high credibility, the system has strong built-in reasons for expansion. Altogether, what one can say is that a system of this sort is highly unstable; it is apt to be either expanding or contracting at any point. We have been in a long period of expansion, and it is certainly possible that we will go into a long period of contraction.

But that is merely a possibility. Anyone looking at the history of Bismarck's invention would have to admit that there are many, many different possible outcomes. The system is now slightly over 100 years old.

Since Bismarck first introduced it, on the whole, its history has been one of growth and expansion. One hundred years is not a very long period of time; one can say that we have simply observed the childhood of the system. It is anybody's guess whether it will now continue to grow further (indicating that we have not gotten through the juvenile period), remain stable in size for a considerable time (indicating that it is mature), or begin to contract.

EDUCATION AND MEDICINE

In the last chapter, we dealt with the bulk of the welfare activities of what used to be the Department of Health, Education and Welfare. In this chapter we will take up the remaining parts, education and medicine. The three activities are indeed the largest "welfare" activities undertaken in the United States. The majority of medicine in the United States is still private, but there is a good deal of government finance and continuous talk about more. Education, on the other hand, is largely a government activity, although there is some private education. We will start with education, specifically elementary education.

Let us go back to our simple model in which everyone is born, lives to the age of 20 without doing any work, works from the age of 20 to 65, and then retires. We assume a stable population, with everybody identical, which means, of course, that each pair produces exactly two children and we shall assume they are produced on their 20th birthday. As we ignored childhood when talking about old-age pensions, we will now ignore old age and talk only about childhood. Let us begin by considering the situation with no government activity. We assume each family devotes half of its income between its 20th and 40th birthdays to support children under the age of 20. Half of that, or one-quarter of their income, goes for direct support, and the other half goes to pay for education.

It is now proposed that the entire population be taxed and this tax be used to pay for the education of the young. With our current assumptions this makes no difference in lifetime expenditures, once the transitional stage is completed. It does change the time distribution of expenditures. Instead of everyone spending one-quarter of their income on the education of their children and one-quarter on support for the first 20 years of their adult life, they will now spend one-ninth of their income on education for every year of their working life[1] while, of course, they still pay one-quarter of their income

Reprinted, with kind permission of Kluwer Academic Publishers, from *Economics of Income Redistribution*, Kluwer-Nijhoff Studies in Human Issues: An International Series in the Social Sciences (Boston: Kluwer-Nijhoff, 1983), 137–56.

1. For simplicity, I assume there is no tax on retired persons to support education. This, of course, is not true of the United States. Child allowances used in some countries tend to distribute this expenditure over lifetime, also.

for the first 20 years for the support of the children. If we consider somebody at the age of 19 contemplating his future life and making a choice between the two systems, we would not be surprised if he chose the system in which he is taxed throughout his life to pay for the education of his children. This permits a somewhat more even lifetime expenditure pattern for him.

If we look at the transition effects, however, they are almost exactly the opposite of those for the pension scheme. When the public school system or subsidization of education is adopted, those people who are over 40 years and who have already educated their children will suddenly find themselves paying one-ninth of their income in taxes for which, in a direct sense, they get no return. They are net losers, and the people between the ages of 20 and 40 are also losers to some extent, the amount of loss increasing steadily with ages between 20 and 40. In all cases, they are now paying for the education of other people's children as well as having paid for all or at least part of the education of their own children. For example, someone who is 30 years old will already have spent one-quarter of his income on the education of his children during the 10 years before the system was installed and now will have to spend one-ninth of his income for the rest of his life, which means that he will spend, in gross, considerably more than one-quarter of his income for 20 years, which was the alternative. The termination of such a scheme, once again, is the mirror image of an old-age pension, in that everyone over the age of 20 will benefit, the exact size of the benefit depending on how old they are. The total benefit may be maximum at the age of 40, less for each year less than 40 down to the age of 20, or over up to 65.

It is not necessary here to go into the problem with an interest rate, since the individual, far from saving money and receiving interest on it, in this case would find himself borrowing money in the period between 20 and 40, and using that to finance his children's education, and hence we would find the higher the interest rate, the more likely he would be to benefit from the change to public support of the school system. It is true that if the rate of growth of society were markedly higher than the interest rate, then he would be better off borrowing money to pay for his children's education and then repaying that money out of his higher income after they have graduated from school than paying one-ninth of his income throughout life. As we have pointed out, however, this is an unlikely contingency. Further, it is very difficult for young people to borrow on the sole security of their earnings at later stages in life.

Of course, grandparents are frequently interested in and willing to aid in the education of their grandchildren, even great-grandchildren, and thus it might be that in our society, in practice, after the age of 40, people would be making educational expenditures for their grandchildren and before the age of 40 people would not find it necessary to pay the entire amount, but it seems dubious that this would lead to everybody contributing one-ninth of their income to the education of children under private provisions. If it did, of course, the change to public provision would be a distinction without a difference.

All of this seems to indicate that there are no large groups that make large gains out of the institution of public education. As we will see below, there are indeed certain groups that do gain and certain groups that do lose. It seems to me that these gains, even though I am going to spend much time talking about them, cannot fully explain the institution. I think that, in part, we have here a genuine case of charitable provision.[2]

There is nothing particularly surprising in believing that people who have no children of their own may feel sorry both for parents of children, who are being hard-pressed, and for the children themselves, who might not get a very good education because their parents cannot afford it. Further, it should be pointed out that the total cost of elementary education is not really very great. The total cost of elementary education today is about 4 percent of GNP. It seems reasonable that about one-half of that is paid by parents whose children are actually in school, parents of children who will be in school shortly but are still too young, or people who expect to be parents of children in school. If we assume that grandparents, under a private school system, would be willing to make some contribution to the education of their grandchildren and that they consider at least part of their education taxes as such a contribution, then an even larger part of the total amount simply replaces private payments. This leaves us with about 1 percent of GNP, and that does not seem to be an excessive amount to be derived from charitable impulses, concerns about equality of opportunity, bureaucratic pressure by teachers' organizations, etc. At the time that the public education system was inaugurated, it did not have either the length or the elaboration that it now has, and, hence, it cost less.

There is another explanation for the development of public schooling in the United States. Confronted with a large number of immigrants whom

2. Note that I am here talking about government support of elementary education, not the particular organizational structure. What I have to say is relatively indifferent to the question of whether there is direct government provision of services or whether it hires private persons by the way of the voucher system to provide education.

they tended to think of as being both ignorant and bad Americans, 19th-century Americans decided that it was very important to "Americanize" them. The history of American education in the period from 1840 to 1860, during which it largely became a government function, indicates very clearly that Americanization and improving the quality of the votes cast by citizens were major motives. This is a clear-cut externality argument and easily justifiable in theory. It has to be said that efforts to empirically measure this externality have failed to show that it exists. These efforts, however, have mainly been made in the 1960s and 1970s, more than 100 years after the socialization of the educational system. We can hardly blame the citizens in, let us say, 1850 for believing that there were externalities of public goods connected with elementary education. After all, both Milton Friedman and I were convinced that this was so as recently as 1960.[3]

A somewhat similar approach has been taken by a number of democracies. The theory that we must "educate our governors" is frequently advanced to support public education in Switzerland, Sweden, etc. Further, most dictatorships favor widespread public education. In their case it may be partly an effort to increase the total income of the country and, hence, their power, prestige, and Swiss bank accounts. It is also, of course, an ideal opportunity to indoctrinate the children in whatever happens to be the dominant ideology. Indeed, such indoctrination is presumably the basic reason that churches always and everywhere have been much interested in education.

Thus, we may here have a case in which transfer is motivated primarily by charitable motives but secondarily by the feeling that there is a genuine externality. It should be said, however, that there are a number of other possible motives and that there is no doubt that transfers were made to people who were motivated by the desire of the recipients to receive them rather than by charity or externality considerations.

Let me begin with a rather dubious case. We have assumed that everybody has the same number of children. This is clearly not true in society, and hence the taxation of all people who own real estate,[4] for the benefit of those who have children, with the payoff depending on the number of children, resulted in a transfer to people with children, particularly with numerous children. As far as we can tell, this result was known, and the statistics indicate that people

3. I still retain an open mind on this subject. The statistical evidence does not prove the existence of such externalities, but, in my opinion, it also does not disprove them.

4. This was the original source of support for almost the entire school system.

without children tend to feel that the school system should be less well financed than do people with children, particularly those with a great many children.[5] Even here, however, it is by no means obvious that there was not a certain amount of charitable feeling involved. The people without children, or with few children, may well have felt considerable sympathy with those with many children; and, once again, it is a small amount of money. Further, the people without children may have been interested in the future of the United States and wanted to see to it that future voters were well educated.

The second transfer here would go from people who are well-off to people who are not so well-off by way of the fact that people who are well-off are apt to own more real estate than people who are not. Here, again, the statistical evidence indicates fairly clearly that people who own quite a bit of real estate tend to feel that the school system should be smaller than do people who own little real estate.[6]

There are, however, two other important groups who probably receive straight transfers. Firstly, granted that the early school system was entirely supported by real estate taxes, and that the current school system is still largely supported by them, we should note that in the short run renters are not affected by the increase in real estate taxes. Further, in this case the short run is very long. Only with the gradual reduction in the number of new housing units brought into the market will the rents rise to the point where they cover a new tax. This may take 10 to 20 years in the ordinary community. Further, a cut in real estate taxes achieved by reducing the expenditure on schools would only percolate through to the renters after a somewhat similar period.

Traditionally, a considerable portion of American citizens have been renters, before the 1930s a much higher percentage than now.[7] Thus, at the time the decision was made to socialize the school system, it was not at all clear that much of the population would bear any immediate cost. Indeed, since the votes were characteristically carried out in local communities, and Americans have always been very mobile, there was no strong reason for the

5. For example, see the survey "Attitudes Toward Year-Round School in Prince William County, Virginia," Ned Hubbell and Associates, Port Huron, Michigan, 1972.

6. Nevertheless, the people who own real estate normally do not want to abolish the school system, and here, again, I think there probably are both charitable and externality reasons involved.

7. Farms raise a special problem, but it should be pointed out that taxes on agricultural land change very slowly, and only partially get transmitted to the renters at all.

average renter to feel that he would ever have to pay the cost imposed by his vote for socializing the local school system. How important this factor was, I do not know, although my own opinion would be that it was markedly less important than the charitable and externality motives.

Another group that clearly benefitted from socialization were the teachers and educational administrators. Indeed, Edwin West's studies of the history of the development of public education out of its previous system in England seemed to indicate that this was the major, real political force. At the time education was converted to a basically government system, substantially every Englishman's child was already in school, attending private or church schools of one sort or another. Essentially, adoption of a government system seems to have been motivated very largely by teachers and government administrators.[8]

In the United States, West's work is less definitive, partly because, of course, each state and even each community had a somewhat different history, but it points to the teachers as the main motivating force.[9] The desire of the teachers to monopolize education is easy to understand. Further, teachers are by virtue of their profession accustomed to persuading people (i.e., teaching them) and tend to be moderately prominent members of their local communities. Under the circumstances, the fact that they were able to convince other people that something that was to their interest was also in the other people's interest would not surprise us. But once again, I feel that this was less important than the combination of charitable and externality motives which I have discussed before. Thus, in my opinion, socializing the school system is a case of a transfer, the basic motives of which are charity and an effort to internalize certain externalities.

When we turn to higher education, however, we find a quite different picture. The tax support of higher education is almost certainly a transfer of a sharply regressive type, i.e., a transfer up the income scale. The average taxpayer is subsidizing the education of people whose lifetime income is apt to be well above average.

Before turning to this, however, I should like to comment on two other aspects of higher education. The first of these is the fact that genuinely voluntary gifts to higher education have been, and now are, given. There are

8. Edwin G. West, *Economics, Education, and the Politician* (London: Institute of Economic Affairs, 1968).

9. Edwin G. West, "The Political Economy of American Public School Legislation," *Journal of Law and Economics* 10 (October 1967): 101–28.

many motives for these gifts. It is, for example, a way of purchasing prestige. In some cases, there may be a genuine payback, in the sense that a corporation giving a fellowship to an engineering school may find that the engineering school gives them first chance at its best graduates. Further, in early days the educational system existed primarily for the purpose of producing ministers of religion, so contributions to it were essentially religious gifts. A religious gift by a believer is, in a way, an effort to build up "treasure in heaven, where neither moth nor rust doth corrupt, and where thieves do not break through nor steal. . . ."[10]

Today the charitable gifts to education are mainly given by people whose income is far above the average for the population as a whole. From their standpoint, the gifts may be an effort to help people who are not as well-off as they are. There are, it is true, a certain number of gifts to higher education from people in the middle-income brackets, but these are relatively minor, and the universities normally solicit this kind of gift by means that imply that you are simply repaying a debt which you owe to your alma mater.

A second possible reason for maintaining universities, other than a desire to have the poor subsidize the rich, is a possibility of favorable externalities. The early universities devoted much of their attention to what they called "ethical science," which in essence was an effort to get their graduates to behave in accordance with the prevailing ethical code. I am not at all convinced that they were successful, but insofar as they were, they would be generating a genuine externality and an externality that presumably most people who held that particular ethical code would regard as positive.

Today, universities no longer engage in formal ethical indoctrination, although there is a great deal of it on a less formal level. The view that they have positive externalities would have to depend on the grounds that they somehow provided the kind of training that made their graduates leaders in the efficient functioning of democracy. This is a rather elitist point of view for which, as far as I know, no one argues very strongly.[11] There are, of course, the compulsory courses in American government that most state legislatures require, but there does not seem to be any strong reason to believe that they have much effect

10. Matthew 6:20.

11. College graduates are, of course, more apt to be leaders in their local community than people who have not been to college, but it is very hard to argue that somebody who has graduated from an engineering, medical, or business school has acquired by that education any particular special capacities to lead the country in the right direction.

Externalities could be sought in the possibility that people who have gone to college would, as a result of that, be more productive and that this additional productivity would accrue to society as a whole. This does not a priori seem unlikely, although as a college teacher I am skeptical.

A very large number of empirical tests have now been run, one way or another, on the payoff to education. I think that most people who are familiar with the literature would agree that they show no significant externalities. The benefits of education are largely captured by the person who receives the education, in that his income is higher than it otherwise would be. These tests are not, in my opinion, completely conclusive, not because they have been badly done but because the data upon which they depend are not exactly ideal. Nevertheless, people who want to argue that higher education generates positive externalities for the community bear quite a heavy burden of proof.

What we observe is a tax-financed scheme for making people who would be well-off even better off. At Virginia Polytechnic Institute (VPI), for example, people are not admitted to the university unless their grades on the College Board Examination are high enough so that they are clearly in the top 40 percent of high school graduates. Further, the university is planning on raising its cutoff level. It is fairly obvious that these people would have, throughout their lives, above-average incomes. If they enter VPI, however, they are given an education for which they pay only about 30 percent of the cost, and this education gives them the ability to earn a higher income than otherwise. The taxes that support this apparatus are general taxes which fall across the income structure in such a way that higher-income people do indeed pay more than lower-income people, but the disproportion in payment by higher-income people is much less than the disproportion in receipt of valuable capital by people who, in their lifetime earning pattern, are already in the higher-income brackets.

There is no argument in favor of this kind of income redistribution. People in favor of subsidizing higher education have normally ignored the subject. There is, however, another aspect of redistribution from the poor to the rich in which there has been a little bit of defense of existing institutions by people who normally are in favor of helping the poor.

Not only are the students in most schools selected in such a way that they have higher income prospects than has the average person, but generally (although not entirely), they come from above-average-income families. Once again, the statistics on the subject are fairly clear. Upper-income families pay more taxes than low-income families, but the number of higher-income children who are in public-supported education, let us say at Berkeley, is much more peaked than the distribution of the taxes. There are substantially no students in the higher education process in the United States who are not above, and normally very much above, average ability and, hence, probably will make a high income for the rest of their lives. There is, however, a minority of students who come from poor families. They are normally in receipt of various kinds of special aid and are indeed normally thought to be suitable recipients for charity in spite of their high prospects for good income throughout their life whether they get into college or not.

The percent of wealthy families sending children to the leading universities, or indeed to any university, is higher than that of the population as a whole. Some wealthy parents, however, send their children to private schools where tuition covers all, or at least a substantial part, of the actual educational expenditures. If we take wealthy persons as a class, consider the taxes they pay, and the return that they receive in the terms of the education of their children, the fact that some parents send their children to places like Stanford or Harvard *and* pay taxes may be taken as indicating a slight redistribution of money away from the wealthy classes. Even if we grant this point, it should be said that the effect of subsidizing students of exceptional talent is still highly regressive. Also, those particularly wealthy parents who send their children to public schools are indeed receiving a subsidy. The fact that this subsidy comes partially from other wealthy parents who have chosen to send their children to private schools does not seem terribly relevant.

Frankly, I find the fact that very few people seem perturbed at the way we run higher education today quite surprising. I have developed a habit of remarking in public lectures that all professors in the room, and they are normally my principal audience, have as a profession the increasing of the capital value of wealthy people. This sometimes leads to a little uneasy laughter, but I have never encountered either a denial that this is what we are doing or a justification for it. There may be, indeed, good arguments for this process of subsidizing the well-off, but I have not heard them. The closest that I have heard to it is the allegation that by subsidizing them you increase their income and hence increase their taxes, with the result that in the long run they pay back the subsidy.

There are, of course, arguments for providing improvements in the credit market for poor but intelligent people. The argument that they should be permitted to borrow money to get through school seems not unreasonable.

It is by no means obvious, however, that they could not do so through the private credit market. Indeed, the present government arrangements for loaning money to some poor students[12] was pioneered by a private charitable foundation that raised funds for the purpose of giving guarantees to banks which then loaned the money out at commercial interest rates. The program was highly successful until the federal government entered the business offering a subsidized loan.

A loan at less than market interest rates is just as much a subsidy as a straight grant would be.[13] But it must be admitted that the present credit market is bad, and some kind of special arrangement under which people could borrow money for their education, with provisions to make it harder for them to escape payment than it would be if they borrowed from private banks, might be sensible. In this connection, Milton Friedman's suggestion that the repayment be actuarial—that is, that you borrow the money on the condition that you pay back a certain percent of your income—is sensible. This means that if you are not very successful in later life you will not have to pay very much, but if you are very successful you have to pay a great deal.

Let us now turn to medical matters, specifically the government provision of general medical care. This is a particularly interesting case because the United States still has a good deal of what we may call the old-fashioned type of medical attention, and most of the rest of the world has what we might call the Bismarckian approach.

In the United States, with the exception of elderly people, free medical attention is provided only for the impoverished. "Impoverished" is defined rather generously in most of the United States, although the programs are state programs, and the poorer states have less money and hence define poverty less generously. People who are not poor, however, are expected to pay their own medical bills, which they normally do by way of private insurance policies. Except for the widespread existence of private insurance, this was roughly the situation with respect to medicine in Germany at the time that Bismarck introduced his general social security program, which included medical coverage. It should be said that, in a way, what Bismarck was doing

12. Not all of whom by any means are poor. Indeed, one of the things Reagan was criticized for was changing this program so it was available only to the lower two-thirds of the population.

13. See Wilson Schmidt, "The Economics of Charity: Loans vs. Grants," *Journal of Political Economy* 72 (August 1964): 387–95.

was simply generalizing programs that a number of employers, especially Krupp, had already introduced for their employees.

Medical insurance by the state, however, has some differences from the other types of welfare activity that we have been describing. Let us, once again, begin with our model in which everyone is identical and has identical lifetime expectancies, and then switch from that to a model in which, first, medical problems are not equal and, second, incomes are not equal. The model, unfortunately, will be much less informative here than it was in our two previous cases.

Suppose then, once again, our society of identical individuals with the same income, and assume that they can all expect over their lifetimes a certain amount of medical problems. The timing of the problems is not known, but the total amount is. The first thing to be said about this is that it is clearly a situation in which insurance would be sensible. If we assume that the injuries or illnesses are evenly spread over life and that they are not affected by the insurance, then a government program and private insurance would be identical, although some individuals who preferred to bear the risk themselves rather than take insurance would prefer the private insurance program.

We should note that in general the likelihood of illness increases with age. Thus, a private insurance program would, if possible, have lifetime contracts and would charge more than the actuarial risk in the early part of life in order to build up savings to use to pay for the illnesses in the latter part of life. The establishment of a government sponsored pay-as-you-go program would lead to a modest but real transfer to the older people from the younger people and, more specifically, would lead to a modest transfer to the presently voting people from future generations.

A second variable here is the actual medical expenses. In fact, they are different for different people, and to some extent they can be predicted in advance; that is, to some extent doctors can say that A is likely to have higher medical expenses than B. At the moment, in the United States, this fact is of rather little significance, because most people have their medical insurance purchased through group plans in which nobody is examined at all. The apparent reason is that the savings that can be achieved by a very healthy person, who doctors would say is less likely to become ill, are less than the administrative costs involved in giving him this kind of an option. Thus, almost everybody has the same kind of health insurance, without different programs for healthy people and unhealthy people. There is, however, a special problem having to do with people who are already seriously ill, the multiple sclerosis victim, for example. That will be dealt with after we have talked about income distribution.

Let us once again turn to our model based on Samuelson and assume now that there are two categories of people in the society, the poor who require medical help, and the well-off who would like medical help without paying for it but who can pay for it. We will start with this very simple model of income redistribution, although we will have to turn to a more complicated model shortly.

Assume then that we begin with a situation like we have in the United States, in which the poor receive more or less free medical help, but no one else does. For illustrative purposes we can assume that the poor make up 10 percent of the population. This involves a transfer from the upper-income groups to the poor, but it is a transfer that could not be made without the consent of the upper 90 percent of the population, so I think we can regard it as mainly charitable on the part of the 90 percent.[14]

Suppose that Bismarck now suggests that everybody be taxed more than they are now and that the money be used to provide free medical care for everyone. The immediate result of this is that the poor are a little bit worse off than they were before, because they have to pay more taxes. This involves a small, indeed a very small, transfer from the previous status quo in which the poorest 10 percent are now paying a small part of the medical expenses of the top 90 percent.

If we assume that the top 90 percent were carrying the type of medical insurance that most people carry, this transfer would be smaller than you might expect. Under present circumstances, in the United States, a really serious or catastrophic illness is apt to put its victim into poverty all by itself. Once he is poor he becomes eligible for the free medical service, such as it is, and as a result most people who buy insurance do not buy the very expensive type that covers the true medical catastrophe. The cost of covering these medical catastrophes would be a significant part of the total cost of any medical system. The result is that this portion of the medical bill is already covered by the state by way of the individuals' impoverishing themselves and then falling back on state aid.

14. The next few pages will contain a good deal of material that repeats the work in Chapter 6. This repetition is unfortunate but necessary since it is important to cover this area, and I suspect that most readers do not have verbatim recall.

It should be said that with respect to the long-run, catastrophic type of illness, states everywhere give rather poor treatment. Indeed, I believe this is the normal, human tendency. In a way, state hospitals, which take care of the very severely and chronically ill people, have as their real duty removing these people from the public eye. The British National Health Service actually developed a series of rules as to who was and who was not to be given large amounts of medical attention, with people whose potential for successful life was low being marked "not to be resuscitated." From the standpoint of trying to maximize total utility, this rule is probably quite sensible. It is a rule, however, that doctors, medical administrators, and politicians are extremely reluctant to say out loud, and indeed I suspect that many of the readers of this book who would be perfectly happy with the results of such a procedure—and in fact are happy with it, because it is the procedure we now use—will be deeply shocked to have it placed in writing.

I have no idea whether we should devote large resources to make people who are seriously ill, and for whom the prospects of complete recovery seem slight, as comfortable as possible or whether we should undermaintain them in hopes that they will cease to be a social charge. The reader may make up his own mind. The problem is, however, independent of whether we should have a socialized medical system, because such people will inevitably fall down the income ladder until they become poor enough to be eligible for state protection. In any event, they are a state problem.

There are certain other difficulties that the change from the aid to the poor to medical attention for everyone creates, even in our present very simple model. Firstly, the immediate effect of socializing the medical system is a sharp increase in demand for medical services. People who before economized their medical services because the services cost money now no longer have any need to do so. The size of this effect, however, in a country like the United States, where most people have medical insurance and where the American Medical Association has succeeded in preventing private insurance companies from serious efforts to keep costs down, are apt to be relatively small. Still, some method of rationing the medical services is required.

The economist first thinks of simply raising the price of medical services, but this will make no difference, since the people who are demanding the medical services—the patients—will not be affected by the price. Nevertheless, it should be said that in state medical programs in which private doctors are paid by the state, there is, at the beginning, a very sharp increase in price. This happened in the United States when the Medicare and Medicaid bills were passed. If we consider the period before these bills were passed and the period after, the elderly poor were already receiving free medical care. The basic difference inaugurated by the Medicare and Medicaid bills was that nonpoor elderly persons began receiving free medical care.[15] This meant that the demand for medical attention was sharply higher than it had been before. The elderly no longer were concerned about the prices that they paid, and everyone else had the same demand as before. The result was a sharp increase in doctors' incomes. If the same general system were extended to all the population, we can anticipate the same kind of a general jump except much larger.

The second immediate effect, almost inevitable, is a decline in the medical care available to the poor. The reason for this is that they are the only group in society whose effective demand for medicine has not changed. Before the extension of free medicine to everyone, they were the only people in society getting it and were absorbing medicine up to the point where marginal cost equalled value. As an example, in 1977, Americans earning $25,000 or more had an average of 4.8 visits per person per year to the doctor. Those with incomes under $5,000 had 5.8 visits.[16] The hospital discharge rate (the statistic used to show hospital usage) was 69 percent greater in the lowest income group than in the highest income group. Persons in the lowest income groups stayed in the hospital an average of 2.4 days more than those in the highest income group ". . . reflecting, *in part*, the poorer health of the low-income individuals."[17] Although it is, of course, true that the poor tend to be in poorer health than upper income groups, when they have free medical care and upper-income groups do not they tend to consume more medical care than their differential state of health would justify.

With general free provision, however, they have competition from other people. Further, this competition comes from people who are, in general, more adroit than the poor in manipulating government forms, getting special treatment from doctors, etc. This means that the poor not only no longer

15. As a matter of fact, the federal government put more money into aid for the poor. This is part of a long-term trend. As we get wealthier we tend to increase our provisions for the poor just as we tend to buy more other goods. No doubt improvements in the medical care for the poor would have occurred either in the year in which these two bills were passed or in some future year in any event. The basic change was the extension of aid to elderly people who were not poor.

16. *Health United States*, Public Health Service, Department of HEW, 1979, p. 177.

17. Ibid., p. 182. The italics are mine.

have as large a share of the demand for medical services as they had before, but intangible, nonmonetary values now become very important in getting medical service. Thus, one can anticipate that the poor will, in fact, not do so well as they did before.

The most striking example of this is the British National Health Service. At the time that it was inaugurated the antibiotic revolution was under way. Medicine was undergoing the largest technological improvement in its entire history. In spite of this fact, the death rate in the poorest one-fifth of the English population actually rose while the death rate for the population as a whole was going down sharply.[18] Careful sociological studies do indicate that the poor get less medical attention than the middle class, even granted that medical attention is free in England today. This is because of the greater middle-class facility with forms, political maneuvering, etc.

In England, Le Grand finds that with free medical care for everyone, the poor consume more medical care per capita than the upper-income groups but less medical care per illness. In other words, with free medical care for the poor only, the poor consume more medical care, given a particular state of health, than the well-off. With free medical care for everyone, the well-off receive more medical care, assuming that the societal state of health remains unchanged.[19]

The price mechanism cannot be depended on to bring demand and supply into accord in these circumstances. It is, of course, true that we could divert enough resources to medicine so that, individually, everyone receives medicine out to the point where it is of zero marginal value, but no state is likely to do this. This is particularly true in a democracy.[20] The individual, as a voter, realizes that additional medical attention is expensive and takes that into account in voting on how much medicine should be provided. As an individual trying to get treatment, however, he regards it as substantially free. Thus, he will vote less medicine per capita than he will try himself to absorb. As a voter, he faces a marginal cost that is the true resource cost of the

18. Gordon Tullock, "The Charity of the Uncharitable," *Western Economic Journal* 9 (December 1971): 379–92.

19. Julian Le Grand, *The Strategy of Equality* (London: George Allen & Unwin, Ltd., 1981), 36–40.

20. The following discussion is taken from James Buchanan's "The Inconsistencies of the National Health Service," Occasional Paper No. 7, London Institute of Economic Affairs, 1965.

medicine: as a customer of medicine he faces a marginal cost of zero. The fact that he acts differently in these two different spheres should surprise no one.

This leaves two other ways of rationing medical attention: administrative rules and waiting time. Both are used quite extensively. Doctors may, for example, develop quite arbitrary habits in which they simply tell their patient not to bother them. On the other hand, they may develop long lines, and the lines will grow until the marginal value to the marginal customer of the additional medical attention is equal to the marginal value of waiting in line for whatever is the necessary period of time. In England today, people requiring operations sometimes have 6- to 10-month delays, and delays of a year are by no means unheard of. Probably administrative methods are better than queuing, since, although arbitrary, they at least do not involve a net direct social waste as does queuing. Queuing is, from the standpoint of the customer, the exact equivalent of paying, but from the standpoint of society it is a net waste. It should be said here that there will also be quite extensive effects on the pay of doctors and the quality of medical treatment from this kind of change, but I would like to put that off until we have a more complicated model of income redistribution.

Let us proceed with this model and assume that instead of simply having a group of people who are, let us say, middle income and the poor, we have a distribution of incomes that is fairly broad. There are people with high incomes, people with low incomes, and all of the intermediate stages. For classification purposes only, I shall refer to these groups as the poor, the middle, the upper, and the top. The top is a very small group, perhaps one-half of 1 percent; the upper is the income group from the 80th percentile up to the top; and the middle is everyone between the 10th and the 80th percentile.

We start with a system in which the poor are receiving free medical attention, and everyone else is paying his own medical costs.[21] The poor, as we have said, probably will not be much affected by the switch from the standard charitable provision to a universal system. It will, however, have considerable distributional effects in the upper-income brackets. In the first place, although it is certainly true that upper-income people pay for more medical care and for better-quality medical care than the middle-income group, it is

21. This argument would be complicated but not be greatly changed through a gradual cutoff of medicine as incomes rose.

probable that the difference in medical expenses for the upper-income and the middle-income groups is smaller than the difference in incomes. Further, if the payment for medical attention is shifted to a tax base, the wealthy will probably pay a higher share of their income in taxes to support the medical system than do the middle people. Whether there will be a distinction in this regard of great importance between the top and the upper is not clear. Certainly, the top group will, in net, be disadvantaged, and the middle group will, in net, be advantaged if the reduction in efficiency of the medical system does not more than compensate for that.

In conversations with advocates of socializing our medical system, I find that this particular effect is the argument that seems to affect them most. They sometimes talk about preventative medicine as something that would occur under socialized medical structure, although there is no very obvious evidence that preventative medicine is worth its keep (except in preventing contagious diseases, which is a government activity anyway). Any medical activity that has large, positive externalities should, of course, either be subsidized by the state or provided by the state. Most preventative medicine does not have such externalities, and it is also true that most of it is not worth its cost. It is almost impossible to detect or prevent diseases before they occur. Indeed, those corporations that used to require their executives to undertake occasional physical examinations have usually stopped it because of the cost. There is, of course, an exception to this when the medical examination is given at a place like The Homestead, in which the benefit to the executive of having three or four days of tax-free time at The Homestead is great enough so that, from the standpoint of the company, the waste on the medical examination is paid for.

Basically, however, when I talk to people who favor socialized medicine, they argue that it is unfair for people in their position to be compelled to pay excessive medical expenses, i.e., medical expenses above and beyond their insurance policy coverage, when the poor do not. This is clearly a distributional argument which is not based on any particular concern for the well-being of the poor. Many of the people I talk to also seem to think that government medical plans would relieve them of the cost of their medical insurance. Since it would have to be paid for out of taxes, this is either a simple error on their part or a feeling that the higher-income people will be subsidizing them. In other words, the middle group would gain at the expense of the upper- and top-income groups. I believe that this is indeed correct, once again assuming that the efficiency effects do no more than offset it. There are general distributional effects of the change to a Bismarckian health program.[22] The genuine redistributional moves, however, do not benefit the truly poor of society. They may very strongly benefit people whose incomes are between, let us say, the 10th and 30th percentiles of the society and, of course, it will be possible to argue for charitable reasons that this should be done.

Let us now turn to the efficiency characteristics of the system. First, I should like to talk a little bit about the incomes of one particular group of upper-income people—the doctors.[23] The first effect of the provision of free medical attention is apt to be a sharp rise in the income of doctors because the effective demand goes up sharply and, as a general rule, the government organization has not planned on this rise and has no provisions available to deal with it. Further, the government bureaucrats who organize the scheme normally will gain if the total expenditures go up, and so for a considerable period of time they do not offer the technical advice to the politicians that would contain the cost rise.

It should be said that this is only a short-run effect and that the longer-run effect is apt to be a reduction in the income of doctors. Whether this reduction in the income of doctors is desirable or undesirable depends, in essence, on its magnitude. Always and everywhere in the world, doctors under private provision of medicine have succeeded in developing at least some cartel power, with the result that their income is above what it would be without that cartel.[24] Thus, the long-run cut in doctors' incomes is not a priori undesirable if it is kept within reason.

To return to the short-run situation, the rise in medical incomes is likely to be accompanied by a rise in the amount of leisure that doctors take and a rise in the ability of doctors to simply give orders to their patients, all of which benefits the doctors without much benefit for anyone else. Indeed, there is a net social loss, although this is very hard to measure.

22. In passing, it might be mentioned here that Bismarck probably did not help people by his program. In 1870, medical knowledge was sufficiently primitive so that in many ways you were better off if you did not see a doctor. The Bismarckian plan no doubt reduced nervous tension a good deal, but it may have led to many people being seriously injured by inept treatment.

23. What I have to say here will to a lesser extent apply to other medical technical personnel. Since the doctors' cartel is much stronger than the organizations of these other groups, the doctors normally get the bulk of the effects, both positive and negative.

24. For a contrary argument, see Cotton Lindsay, "More Real Returns to Medical Education," *Journal of Human Resources* 11, no. 1 (1976): 127–30.

The short-run effect, however, is in the long run apt to be more than offset. The government develops very considerable monopsony power to put against the doctors' cartel. Indeed, the government, if it wishes, can have much more power than the doctors. It is only sensible for government to make use of this monopsony power to lower its costs. The American government regularly does this in many areas,[25] and it is certainly true that the government medical systems have done so after a usually protracted delay. As I mentioned above, in the early stages, the program is apt to sharply increase the doctors' incomes.

This monopsony is, however, incomplete. Firstly, the upper-income people are normally permitted to get their own medicine if they want to. The situation is usually rather like that in the American school system, in which "free" education is provided for everyone, but wealthier people choose to purchase superior education privately. This means that the best doctors are siphoned off to such private practice.[26] However, the effects on the quality of doctors and on quality of treatment are quite complex, and I would like to defer discussing them in detail for a few paragraphs. This cartel power on the part of the central government can be reinforced. Canada and England have made efforts in this direction. In both cases, left wing parties are strongly in favor of making it illegal to have a private doctor. The wealthy are to be compelled to use the same facilities as the average person.

The effect of this type of measure is to extend but not perfect the monopoly. The government of England, after all, does not control Switzerland, Luxembourg, or certainly Monaco. The development of refugee medical areas for the very wealthy is thus something that cannot be prevented, although it can be delayed. What happens here is that the effort by the state to perfect its monopsony makes it harder to develop escape routes for those who can afford it. Medicine is not a single doctor who offers superior service, but a rather complex set of interlocking enterprises that provide, collectively, superior service. This is the kind of situation in which it is hardest to compete with an existing monopoly, and the state can therefore delay the development

25. See William A. Niskanen, *Bureaucracy and Representative Government* (Chicago: Aldine-Atherton, Inc., 1971), 295.

26. As a rather comic aspect of this, when I was in Hong Kong recently, I found myself in need of a doctor and went, at the recommendation of the hotel, to a collection of Swedish doctors with very elaborate offices. The doctor who dealt with me simply laughed when I said that he was a refugee from the Swedish Public Health Service.

of private competition even outside its own national boundaries. But, although it can delay it, it cannot permanently prevent it. I suppose laws could be passed requiring everyone who wished to leave the country to undergo a medical examination, but I doubt that this extreme will be resorted to.

Further, if the state is indeed successful in pushing down the incomes of doctors, this will ipso facto lower the quality of people who enter into training for doctors. The doctor who has already acquired a large volume of personal, intellectual capital that cannot be used for anything but medicine can, at least in theory, be exploited and forced to surrender the bulk of the rent on that capital to the state. However, people with the necessary talents will not take up the profession of medicine unless a suitable reward is offered.

Note here a combination of the effects of the doctors' cartel and the monopsony. In England, medical education is heavily subsidized by the state, with the result that people acquire it at much below its real resource cost. The state then takes away a large part of the rent on that education unless the doctor so trained chooses to go abroad. The whole system leads to a transfer, albeit not a very large transfer, to foreigners. Surely this is not what was intended, but politically, granted the power of doctors and the power of the state, it is not surprising.

One of the developments that has come out of this kind of state control is a habit on the part of doctors of striking and engaging in other "industrial action" to raise their incomes. Traditionally, doctors followed a differentiation policy with respect to their fees. They charged lower fees to the poor than to the well-off, and very high fees to the wealthy. Doctors always explained this in terms of their desire to be charitable, and I have no doubt that this was one of its motives, but it also was an income-maximizing policy. A doctor who was a particularly skilled surgeon could charge different people different prices because they could not trade his services among themselves.

If an automobile manufacturer tries to charge different people different prices, those who buy the car cheaply will sell it to those who are being threatened with a high price from the manufacturer. You cannot do this in heart surgery. Thus, the doctors could feel charitable with respect to their poor patients, while using a fee system which, in the long run, would give them very high incomes.[27] The various state systems eliminate this procedure.

27. The incomes would not be truly maximized if they were, in fact, being charitable to the poor, but if they got utility out of being charitable to the poor, their utility would be maximized.

The doctor receives a flat fee regardless of whom he is treating, and no longer is able to charge different people different prices.

If the doctor feels he is being underpaid and wishes to raise his income, he cannot simply raise the fees he charges across the entire schedule but must either refuse to treat state subsidized patients or go on strike. The first alternative has been quite widely used in the United States. In general, the very best doctors will not treat Medicaid and Medicare patients, because the payments to them are too low. They no longer feel that differentiating their prices would be worthwhile, because the amount available to the poor is such that they can always hire a less competent doctor, and the doctor does not get additional business by providing lower prices to the less well off. If a doctor can attract enough patients at his private rate, he will attain his income-maximizing rate. Serving poorer people at the state subsidized rate would not give a feeling of being charitable, because the poor obviously have other sources of medical support.

It should be emphasized that it is not obvious that this siphoning off of the higher-quality doctors from the government-subsidized practice is in and of itself undesirable. It seems likely that the institutions established by doctors, essentially for cartel motives, have led to most doctors being overqualified. A system in which the average doctor is a good deal less competent than the average American doctor, but where there are specialists to deal with the more difficult problems, may well be more efficient than our present structure. Thus, if the government through its monopsony power lowers the quality of the average doctor, it may be desirable. But it may not be desirable.

One of the problems in dealing with any kind of equalization of medical attention is the immense variation in quality of medicine from place to place and from doctor to doctor. In part, this is a matter of income, with the upper-income people paying higher fees and getting better medicine, but in part it is an accident. The mere question of where you live may be very important. At one time I was a professor at the University of Virginia and lived in Charlottesville, Virginia. Charlottesville is a fairly small town with a large medical school. The influence of the medical school was felt throughout the medical profession in town. Indeed, the University Hospital is by a considerable margin the largest hospital in town, and the one time that I was seriously ill I was put in the University Hospital. The medical practice there is of quite a different nature than it would be in a less well equipped town.

May I give two examples. Firstly, a friend of mine's daughter put her hand through a glass door and damaged it very badly. It was put back together by a man who had just finished writing a book on the surgery of the lower arm and hand. Secondly, in my own case, I had a case of pneumonia with a germ that had acquired immunity to tetracycline, with the result that I went to the hospital. I developed some fluid in the chest wall, and it was removed by a distinguished thoracic surgeon. Obviously, this is a very minor procedure, and I imagine that almost any doctor would have done very nearly as well as the surgeon, but it does show the quality of medical treatment that was available. Further, the ordinary doctor was subject to a number of educational and social pressures that he would not have received in a similar town that did not have a medical school. Altogether, there was a much higher quality of medical treatment there than there would be in a less favored spot. This was true for all levels of income.

Another variable is simply that different doctors are of different quality, and it is quite difficult for the average citizen to tell whether he has a good or a bad doctor. There is another minor example. My doctor in Blacksburg, Virginia, is, I think, a very good doctor, but he came to Blacksburg when it was a small town with only rural people as customers. The bedside manner he developed at that time has stuck with him now that his practice is mainly composed of university professors. I have developed considerable confidence in him, but this is in spite of, rather than because of, his normal behavior when I meet him.[28]

Thus, there is a very great variance in medical treatment. Any government program for equalizing medical treatment must, to a large extent, ignore this fact and pretend that different people with different doctors are receiving the same treatment. The man who receives an operation by Dr. Collins, of Houston, and the man who receives the same operation from a doctor somewhere else, or indeed another doctor in Houston, are assumed to have been treated the same, although this is factually a ridiculous assumption.

Efforts to equalize medical attention are more or less efforts to see to it that everybody has the same *ex ante* chance; i.e., everyone has the same gamble. It is, on the whole, unlikely that this will work, because any government program is subject to political manipulation, and one can anticipate that the politically adroit people will in fact get better doctors, but this may

28. On one occasion I had a very persistent skin rash. He appeared and told me, on looking at it, that I had an eczema. As an intellectual, I know that "eczema" is Latin for skin rash, and the treatment that he recommended seemed highly speculative. As a matter of fact, it worked perfectly.

be a minor phenomenon.[29] All that can actually be done is to assure that everyone has the same chance for the good doctoring or poor doctoring that is given to everyone else. In practice, this is not likely to be true, because doctors are apt to congregate in certain areas, with the result that geographically some areas are pretty sure to get better doctoring than others. It might be argued, however, that you have a random chance of being in a well- or badly doctored area. The situation here provides the same kind of equality as Senator Kennedy's approach to the draft. He wanted a system in which *ex ante* everybody had an equal chance of going into the Army, but where, as a matter of fact, only a small percentage would. Thus, people would *ex post* be treated very unequally, but *ex ante* they all had the same chance of either staying out of the Army or going in. Similarly, the medical system can give everyone *ex ante* the same chance of a good doctor or a poor doctor, but *ex post* some will survive while others will die.

It should perhaps be said here that I have no doubt that good doctors are a great asset and, indeed, that doctors as a whole are an asset. I am sure they lower the death rate and make the ill more comfortable and lead to quicker recovery. Note that I say I am sure this is so, because I am, but I must admit that there is very little evidence. Statistical efforts to correlate the practice of medicine with things like lower death rates have so far failed miserably. If anything, the higher the number of doctors, the more people die. The apparent explanation for this bad correlation between the quality of doctoring and health is threefold. Firstly, medicine is only one of the variables involved. After all, 90 percent of all people get well even if they are not treated. Secondly, modern medicine has developed a number of very general antigerm drugs that are so simple that almost anybody can use them, and they may well override false diagnosis because many of them will cure a large collection of diseases rather than only one. Thus, it is likely that a highly skilled doctor only makes a difference in a minority of the cases. You and I, of course, hope that if we turn out to be in that minority we find ourselves dealing with a highly skilled doctor, but, statistically, it may be hard to detect his skill.

29. There was a short period of time in Communist China in which it was argued that anybody could engage in medicine, and the newspapers presented, very proudly, examples of janitors engaging in surgery, etc. They had a rotation scheme in which the surgeon some days was the janitor, and the janitor some days was the surgeon. One can feel confident that when the local party secretary arrived for an operation, just by coincidence the chief surgeon of the hospital was acting as surgeon. Peasants might find that a janitor was called on to remove their appendix.

The third problem is that medical facilities tend to be concentrated in areas where there is a great deal of illness and death. Thus, New York City is a much more unhealthy environment than Colorado, and there are far more doctors. The death rate in New York City is, of course, much higher than it is in Colorado. Good doctoring has an effect on the death rate, but the death rate has an effect on the number and quality of doctors, too. It is statistically very hard to separate these two effects, with the result that a positive correlation between doctors and high incidences of disease and high death rates is generally observed. Presumably this would be true even under socialized medicine because, I imagine, a central planning board would concentrate more doctors per capita in New York than in Colorado, with the result that it would still appear as if doctors kill people. Other things being equal, however, good doctoring pays off in better health and lower death rates. The statistical difficulties come from the fact that other things are seldom equal, and it is very hard in this case to produce a suitable, simultaneous equation model.

The end product of our line of reasoning is that the switch from the kind of system that we have in the United States (where people pay for their own medical attention, unless they are either old or poor, and characteristically do so by insurance) to one in which the state provides the whole medical attention (such as that used in England) can be summed up fairly simply. Firstly, the effects on efficiency are ambiguous, since the existing cartel would find itself facing a monopsony purchase service, and the outcome of the squabble would be ambiguous, both on income distribution and efficiency. Secondly, there would be a modest transfer of resources away from the poor, partly by doctors concentrating on other patients and partly by an increase in taxes, but this is by no means certain. Thirdly, there would be a transfer of resources from the top income groups to the middle income groups. This is probably the principal political force behind the drive for such socialized medicine. Fourthly, the doctors would probably get a sharp increase in income in the short run and a decrease in income in the long run. Lastly, the consequences for any individual would be that his likelihood of getting good or bad doctoring would tend to be more random and less subject to his control than it is now. With the upper-income groups, this would probably mean a deterioration of their well-being; for those who today pay low prices for poor quality doctoring, it would probably mean, on the average, an increase, but in all cases the variance would increase sharply.

The theme of this book has been that the bulk of all transfers are motivated by the desire of recipients to receive the money. As far as I can see, the basic push for socialized medicine lies in the category of people who would probably benefit from it. Indeed, I notice that not only do the people from the 10th to roughly the 80th percentile in income tend to be the only people interested in the program, but the bulk of the ones who are the most interested in the program are academics and intellectuals who have a special facility in manipulating government programs. They would, in all probability, do even better than other people in their income brackets. Thus, this case is another example of the main theme. It must be admitted, however, that it seems to me that the income distributional effects of this program would be relatively modest in any direction. This may be the reason that the political pressure for establishing it has never been very strong in the United States.

ADMINISTRATIVE TRANSFERS

In the last three chapters we looked over the three programs that involve the largest "welfare" expenditures in most modern states. One of them, medicine, is not yet fully a government-supported activity in the United States, but in most other countries it is. In all of these cases there is, of course, a component of aid to the poor, but it seems likely that the poor would be better off if the programs had not been started and if the pre-Bismarckian system of income-tested aid to the poor was relied on. In this chapter we will deal with another aspect of the transfer society, more specifically what is now called rent-seeking.[1]

Almost any government activity, in addition to (hopefully) producing some general good, also affects the wealth of individuals. The defense appropriation, for example, is normally discussed in Congress at least as much in terms of where military bases will be located, what company will receive a contract for building an aircraft, etc., as in terms of the military efficiency of the forces. Similarly, police are clearly generators of public goods, but the New York police force is dominantly Irish, a fact that is not accidental. Further, the efforts all over the United States to get more blacks hired on police forces are by no means entirely motivated by a desire to improve the efficiency of the police. Patronage for the Irish and blacks is clearly involved in these decisions. But if we can see at least some transfer element in even those parts of the government that are based on a desire to provide public goods, there are many other parts of the government where there is no true public good. At the time of writing, Congress is debating—and the newspapers reporting—a proposal to raise the price of sugar and a program for peanuts that is intended to raise the price of peanuts. The discussion of these items in the press and, as far as I can see, in Congress does not carry with it even the remotest implication that these measures are in the public interest. They are

Reprinted, with kind permission of Kluwer Academic Publishers, from *Economics of Income Redistribution,* Kluwer-Nijhoff Studies in Human Issues: An International Series in the Social Sciences (Boston: Kluwer-Nijhoff, 1983), 157–73.

1. James M. Buchanan, Robert D. Tollison, and Gordon Tullock (eds.), *A Theory of the Rent-Seeking Society* (College Station: Texas A & M University Press, 1980).

discussed entirely in terms of the benefit to the sugar growers and the peanut growers, the cost to the customers, and, in the particular case of sugar, the cost to some foreign countries that will find their sugar markets restricted if the sugar scheme goes through. The arguments for these two measures to transfer wealth are entirely that the recipients want the transfer, and, indeed, have become dependent upon it. They might have to change their occupations if the government stops supporting them.[2]

It is the purpose of this chapter to look through a number of examples of this kind of transfer. We will not engage in an exhaustive analysis, because, in general, they are very complicated in detail even if the general principles are simple, but the reader should be fully aware of the fact that immense complications are present. The value of these restrictions and regulations is very hard to work out, but $300 billion a year does not seem in any sense an underestimate of their effect. Further, although this web of subsidies, taxes, and regulations, in net, surely injures the economy a great deal, it must be conceded that odd bits and pieces can be argued for on cost-benefit grounds.

Before engaging in any serious analysis of these programs, however, let us look at a few examples. In the period of the Great Depression the federal government prohibited banks from paying interest on their checking accounts. This was for banks in the more competitive parts of the United States a drastic change in their normal pattern, but clearly to the advantage of the bankers because, after all, it provided that their principal raw material, checking accounts, would be free. This restriction remained in existence from then until the late 1970s, when it began to erode, partly because of a change of intellectual climate, partly because nonbanking institutions and banking institutions outside the United States began successfully competing for depositors' funds, and partly because of inflation, which made the retention of any significant amount of money in non-interest-paying deposits impossible.

When the program was enacted, the banks were just recovering from the very serious difficulties they had had between 1929 and 1933. Present-day studies seem to indicate that the banks themselves were not badly managed; it was matters beyond their control that led to the banking catastrophe.

2. The reason these two proposals—which were contrary, on the whole, to President Reagan's philosophy—were politically viable is that the president had agreed not to oppose them in return for votes by relevant congressmen for specific programs that he favored. It is possible that the bargain, as a whole, did have public interest components even if these parts clearly do not.

At the time, however, there was a good deal of talk about unsound banks, and efforts to make them "sound" were much canvassed politically. There is no obvious reason to believe that abolishing interest rates on deposits would make banks sound except insofar as cutting any of their costs would do so. That it would benefit the banks, however, was clear, and it seems likely that the actual drive for this change came from the banking community, although I do not know of any careful studies of the matter. Certainly the banks gained.

Note that this arrangement, like so many other cases in which apparently impartial changes are made, actually did not affect everyone equally. Specifically, any business that dealt continuously with a given bank would receive no interest on its deposit in a checking account but would receive special privileges when borrowing money that were roughly proportional to the amount it kept in the checking account. This privilege was as readily extended to small businessmen as to big businessmen. In essence, whatever you maintained in your checking account gave you a lower interest rate on a proportional amount of loans. It was only the individual who had money on deposit in the bank and did not engage in regular borrowing from the bank who was not receiving "interest."

Even here, the banks in time began a policy of premiums to new depositors, more convenient banking facilities, and other services that, in general, probably consumed the same amount of resources as paying interest would have. The consumers were thus somewhat worse off because presumably they would have preferred the interest to these substitutes for it. Thus, the gain to the banks was essentially transitory, occurring only in the early days before they had expanded their facilities and service; but once they had established a banking practice in which they did not pay interest but did provide more branch banks, etc., the switching back to interest payments would, of course, be costly to them. After the first few years, the banks were probably not gaining anything at all from this restriction on their interest payments, but they would have been injured were it cancelled.

Its effective termination at the present time occurs in a period when the banking industry is in a state of considerable turmoil anyway, and the cost to the banking industry is one of their less important concerns. It is still true, however, that the average banker was opposed, albeit some aggressive and highly competitive bankers thought they could make money by undercutting.

All of this is rather typical of many of the arrangements we will describe. Firstly, there was no government budgetary cost; it was simply regulation.

Secondly, the regulation was eventually absorbed by the competitive market, with the result the beneficiaries no longer received any extraordinary returns. They were, however, in a situation where the cancellation of the benefit would injure them. Lastly, and this is very important, the whole thing went through because of public misinformation. The public image of the act was promoting "sound" banking. In fact, it was a simple transfer from the depositors to the bankers, which only made the bankers sounder in the sense that they were wealthier. Further, in the long run it did not even do that. As we shall see in our other examples, at least some misinformation is characteristic of almost all transfers.

My second example involves "voluntary" quotas on American imports. Development of the American protective tariff structure was undeniably a clear-cut example of special interests imposing large costs on the rest of society for their benefit. Since the 1930s, however, on the whole, this tariff structure has been cut back. At the same time, international transportation costs have also fallen, with the result that today the United States has a very substantial foreign trade sector instead of the extremely minor one which it had in, let us say, 1929. The exact motives for this reduction in protectionism are somewhat mysterious to me. It actually looks as if good economics finally penetrated through to policy decisions. It is, however, true that the various special interests protected by the tariffs have fought against the cuts every step of the way, and my purpose here is to discuss one of their successes—the introduction of "voluntary" quotas on our imports.

Under this system, in some area where the import of, let us say, shoes is causing difficulty for at least parts of the American industry, instead of restoring our tariffs or establishing an American government-sponsored quota on total imports, an arrangement is made with the foreign country under which it "voluntarily" restricts its exports. In many cases, the quota is genuinely voluntary in spite of my quotation marks. Suppose Korea would normally ship to the United States a million pairs of shoes, and we suggested to the Korean government that the amount be restricted to 800,000. Under these circumstances, the permit to import each of those 800,000 shoes becomes a valuable commodity. The Korean government now has the power to allocate this valuable privilege as it wishes. The efficient method, as any economist could tell the Korean government, would be to sell them at auction. Although this is economically efficient, it apparently is not politically efficient. As a general rule, allocating quota by administrative methods gives the government the power to benefit its friends.

Why, in terms of domestic American politics, this particular procedure is easier to work out than a set of tariffs or quotas is not clear. It may be the fact that we have signed various treaties agreeing not to impose such protective tariffs has actually had some effect on our policy here, although I am reluctant to credit much impact of international agreements on any democracy when strong organized pressure groups will be injured. Still, in this case, the only persons injured by the voluntary quota, as opposed to a tariff, are the American taxpayers, and they are not very well organized.

It is interesting that this quota system not only functions to restrict imports for the benefit of the American industry without producing anything in the way of a countervailing benefit to the taxpayer, but it also tends to injure the poor, although so far as I know, injury to the poor is not an objective of the interest groups who push for it. The reason for this is that it is equivalent to a tariff of so much per pair of shoes. This means that the tariff is a higher percentage of the price of an inexpensive shoe than of a higher cost shoe, with the result that it impedes the import of the cheaper shoes more than that of the more expensive shoes.[3]

As a general rule, importers of manufactured goods from areas like Korea, China, or Japan begin by aiming at the lower part of the market because they have difficulty matching the quality of the commodities in the upper end of the market. Without any restraints on import, one could predict that eventually they would tend to expand and take over the upper part of the market, too, provided they had a comparative advantage in shoes as a whole. The existence of a voluntary restraint system, however, pushes them to move rapidly toward the upper end of the line, and, in fact, they may stop providing the cheap shoes altogether. It is even possible that this accelerated development will lead to people in the upper-income brackets spending less on shoes than they would if the quota had not been put in. This, of course, comes at the expense of people in the lower-income brackets. Although the general movement of American tariffs to lower and lower levels is something that we should be very happy about, this is a neat example of the way the welfare state actually does work.

We should keep in mind that this is not viciousness on the part of the state. It is a case of resources being expended to that end. The footwear

3. John H. Suh, "'Voluntary' Export Restraints and Their Effects on Exporters and Consumers: The Case for Footwear Quotas," Working Paper no. 71, Washington University, St. Louis, Mo., 1981. This recent paper measures the welfare effect of a voluntary export restraint on the import of shoes and their antipoor effect.

manufacturers, the labor unions engaged in the production of footwear, and congressmen from districts where footwear is produced all have invested considerable resources in obtaining this particular impediment to the well-being of American citizens. Thus, the cost includes a substantial component of not only the distortion imposed on the economy by these quotas but also the cost of obtaining the quotas.

Further, there is no obvious reason to believe that resources invested in trying to manipulate Congress pay any higher for the person who invests them than resources invested in any other activity. One would assume that people would invest resources across possible alternatives until they had achieved approximate equality in expected return. Thus, one would assume that the return on resources invested in attempting to influence Congress would be about the same as the return elsewhere. This means that the bulk of the benefit that the shoe manufacturer, shoe unions, Congress, local areas, etc., obtain through lobbying is probably approximately paid for in resource investments, with the result that the net effect is that this gain is largely offset by a cost. Thus, we have the cost to the consumers and very little net gain to the producers.

The last factor is, to some extent, offset by the fact that from the standpoint of producers of shoes—and for that matter of congressmen from the shoe-producing districts—participation in the lobbying is a public good, and hence they are apt to underinvest in it. Still, the net effect of these activities is most assuredly not one of a large gain to anyone and a considerable loss to a lot of people.

Let me turn to my third example, which, thankfully, is being dismantled—the Civil Aeronautics Board (CAB). The Civil Aeronautics Board is perhaps our clearest example of a straightforward, Stigler-type, government-sponsored cartel. When it was established in the late 1930s, no one was in favor of it except the air transport industry, and the argument offered for it was that it would prevent destructive competition. The industry spokesmen did not claim that there had been any destructive competition; they simply claimed that they thought that it might occur in the future. In the intellectual climate of the late New Deal, however, almost any proposal for government action had favorable prospects in Congress, and this particular government cartel was, unfortunately, enacted.

It should be said that probably the most important single factor in all of this was the invention of the DC-3, perhaps the most successful airplane that ever flew. The DC-3 had converted the airline industry from a set of local operations, run almost on a hobby basis, into a genuine industry, and, of course, by the time the CAB law was enacted, the successors for the DC-3, the Boeing Stratocruiser and the Douglas DC-4, were well on their way into service. Thus, an industry was created that had influence and was able to press Congress for support.

Earlier congressional support for air activities had been largely support for private fliers and for various military auxiliaries. It seems to me, by the way, that if we consider the situation of the 1920s and early 1930s, the stimulation of a private aircraft industry, with lots of people able to fly, could be argued for as a perfectly genuine military asset, although conditions had, of course, radically changed in the late 1930s.

The cartel functioned just the way one would anticipate a government cartel to function. Firstly, there was a restriction of entry, and, indeed, the CAB permitted no new trunk carriers from its organization in 1937 until it was approaching dissolution. Fares were regulated and kept much above the competitive level. On the other hand, competition was not by any means totally restricted. The airlines were free to compete in service.[4] Since air transportation has an elastic demand, the total size of the industry was lower than it otherwise would have been, although it does not seem likely that most airline companies recognized this.

In addition to, in essence, subsidizing too-frequent service, the system subsidized a lot of other things. Piedmont Airlines was compelled for years to fly flights in and out of Pulaski as a requirement of keeping its permits alive. Further, to take one from which I personally benefitted,[5] first-class passengers were subsidized from the fares of the tourists. It should perhaps be said here that the existence of the tourist accommodations at all was the result of a period right after World War II in which a number of returning aircraft were permitted, for a short time, to carry passengers. They introduced cut-rate travel, and the large airlines were forced to follow in their footsteps.

In this complex collection of special privileges for owners of existing airlines (new airlines were, to put the matter mildly, discouraged), various

4. This, however, was restricted pretty much to competition by frequency of service. The CAB had regulations on such things as the kind of seat that could be installed, the kind of food that could be served, and the amount of alcoholic beverage that could be served. The only thing they did not regulate was frequency of service. The result of this, of course, was much more frequent service than was economically desirable at those prices.

5. I am a bachelor in the upper-income brackets, and almost all of my aircraft transportation flights are connected with business.

special interest groups, like the people who might want to fly out of Pulaski or first-class passengers, were only part of the subsidy for air transportation. For obscure reasons, the government—through the Federal Aviation Administration (FAA)—provided fairly sizable subsidies in the actual operation of the airlines by way of a provision of navigational and airport services. This latter subsidy was paid directly by the taxpayer while the CAB-administered monopoly was, of course, paid for by those airline passengers who were able to afford the higher rates.

The cost of this operation was very great, not least in its effect on management of the airlines. The president of a large airline tended to be not a man who knew a great deal about operating an airline, but a man who knew a number of congressmen and was capable of manipulating the CAB. This was demonstrated in the two instances in which the cartel was interrupted. Firstly, right after World War II, there was an outburst of competition from new airlines founded by war veterans. They radically changed the whole industry by the tourist ticket and a number of technical innovations. The major airlines were forced to follow in their footsteps, but were nevertheless able to reestablish their government-managed cartel and reduced these new competitors to charter and freight service.

The second burst of innovations occurred when the deregulation movement led to a sharp restriction in the powers of the CAB and movements toward its eventual termination. This led to a great shift in the airline business, with a new airline dashing in, and a number of old airlines having serious trouble. In general, it has led to a very large turnover in the higher management of the existing airlines as people who are specialists in political manipulation are replaced by people who know how to run airlines.

My fourth and last example is the elaborate set of farm programs that have done so much to spread starvation among poor parts of the world, and wealth among the owners of the better-quality American farmland. The program basically consists of two prongs. The first is a large program of research, technical assistance, and subsidized irrigation to the farmers designed to raise crop outputs. The second is a set of restrictions designed to reduce output. If we think of the objective of this program as to affect the output of farm products, this seems simply silly. If, on the other hand, we assume its objective is to raise the value of prime-quality farm real estate, then it is very sensible indeed. The research raises the output per acre, and the restrictions raise the price of the ultimate product. In both cases, the value of farm real estate is increased.

As mentioned above, starvation has been one of the consequences of this program. It should perhaps be said that starvation came only from the restrictions on output and not from the research. Further, since the end of World War II, it is not at all clear whether the net effect of these restrictions, together with the subsidies that accompany them, has been to increase or reduce total world food availability. It is perfectly clear, however, that in the 1930s the initial destruction of farm crops and then the severe restrictions on the amount that could be raised lowered world food supplies.

We, of course, had little starvation in the United States, and our traditional customers in Europe also had little starvation, but the reduction in total world food supply meant that in places like India and China there was less to eat, and the death rate must have been higher. It is quite possible that this program should rank with the work of Stalin, Hitler, and Mao among the major mass murder programs of our time. I know, however, of no serious statistics showing the actual size of the increase in the death rate.[6]

Since World War II, subsidies on prices, together with the crop restrictions and the research that made it possible to increase total product per acre, may have led to America's net food production being higher than it otherwise would have been. I am inclined to the view that this is not so, that we would have produced more food and hence that our export surpluses would have been somewhat larger without the subsidies and restrictions,[7] but it is not clear what the net effect on world food supplies was.

But let us, however, turn from this issue of what happens to foreigners, who, after all, cannot vote, and consider instead the domestic effect of the program, which perhaps is best shown by Table 1.

Table 1 is a list of more or less all our current programs, which cover about 60 percent of agriculture. Further, the total net cost is about $1 billion greater than the gain to the producers. This, of course, is a direct cash transfer. With lower prices of agricultural commodities, the consumers would presumably be consuming more than they are here, and hence the welfare triangle, in the traditional verbiage, is left out. This should add at least another $1 billion, probably $2 billion, to the net social cost.

6. It should not be terribly difficult to calculate, but the job calls for someone who knows more about agriculture than I.

7. The food would, of course, have had to be paid for. A good deal of the food, in fact, was given away under various programs designed to reduce the size of the embarrassing stockpiles of food in the United States.

TABLE 1 ***Summary Estimates of the Effects of Farm Programs in 1978/79***

COMMODITY	PERCENTAGE OF U.S. TOTAL FARM OUTPUT	RATIO OF PRICE WITH PROGRAMS TO PRICE WITHOUT PROGRAMS	COST TO TAXPAYERS	COST TO CONSUMERS	GAIN TO PRODUCERS
			(IN MILLIONS)		
Wheat	6	1.175	$1,100	$400	$1,300
Feed grains	12	1.06	1,020	700	1,500
Rice	1	1.02	10	0	10
Cotton	4	1.02	90	0	90
Tobacco	2	1.33	0	425	400
Sugar	1	1.88	−770	1,440	600
Peanuts	1	1.4	0	200	200
Cattle	21	1.035	−40	1,200	1,100
Milk	12	1.11		1,500	1,200
Wool	0.2	1.3	30	−15	15
All other	40	1.6	0	0	0
Total (or mean)	100	1.06	$1,440	$5,850	$6,415

SOURCE: Bruce L. Gardner, *The Governing of Agriculture* (Lawrence: Regents Press of Kansas, 1981), 73. Reprinted with permission of the University Press of Kansas.

The value of these special privileges is great. It is obvious why farmers favor them. It should be pointed out, however, that they are uncertain. The current situation, in which farm incomes are unprecedentedly low, illustrates this risk. That the owners of these special privileges have known that they are risky for a long time can be seen from the prices of the only case in which the privileges are actually separable from the land. Within counties, the owners of tobacco allotments are permitted to sell them or rent them to other producers. Thus, the rental or sale value of a permit to farm a certain number of square feet for tobacco can be obtained from the market. It is interesting that the sale value is only four times the annual rent. Granted that this particular kind of investment would be inflation proof, it looks as if one can buy a perpetuity in an income for only four times the value of that income instead of the ten times or more that would be apparently a correct market price.

The explanation is simple. The investment is risky because the possibility that Congress will simply repeal the act is always present. This means not only that the value of such a permit is much less than its current income would indicate, but also that the owners of the permit must devote a good many resources to trying to keep it in existence. An asset that is held at risk is one in which one must put considerable resources into defending.

The tobacco acreage restriction is intriguing for a number of reasons, not the least of which is the fact that most "consumer advocates" should be in favor of making tobacco more expensive in order to reduce the amount of cancer, and the acreage restriction certainly does so. It is a case in which a bounty is given to producers of tobacco by raising the price of tobacco to people who want to smoke. Those who feel that smoking tobacco should be made illegal, or in other ways discouraged, should be almost as much in favor of this provision as the owners of tobacco land. The only objectors would be the cigarette companies and those people who want to smoke in spite of the risk of cancer. Nevertheless, it rather looks as if this provision may fall in the near future.

Although the tobacco situation is unusual, in that we can actually measure political risk, it is clear that all of the examples that I have selected are subject to political risk. Indeed, I selected them, in part, in order to illustrate that point. The CAB is in the process of dissolution; the "voluntary quotas" are a sort of a last-ditch defense by certain industries, which would, in earlier years, have been protected by straightforward protective tariffs. The development of the federal government as a transfer mechanism in the 19th and early 20th centuries was largely a matter of protective tariffs. Their dismantling is evidence that this kind of transfer is necessarily held insecurely.

Not only is it necessary to fight to obtain these transfers, it is necessary to fight to protect them, and, on the whole, they are impermanent phenomena. All of this does not, of course, indicate they are not socially harmful; although any individual transfer mechanism of this sort is apt to be impermanent, the existence of a very large number of them has been characteristic of the government for a long time. When the government was small, as it was in the 19th century, transfers were also small, but they grew with the size of the government. Further, the risky nature of these transfers means that they never really get fully integrated into the market system as secure property. If they did become integrated into the system as secure property, then at least we would be spared the resources and political maneuvering intended to protect or destroy them. The traditional social welfare triangle would be their only cost, and the cost of political maneuvering would cease to burden the economy.

The restriction on interest payments on checking accounts is a particularly clear example of the political instability of such regulatory transfers. There was substantially no public protest when it was enacted, and there has been substantially no public criticism of it until very recently.[8] Further, I doubt that the banking system devoted very much lobbying time to defending a provision that did not seem to be subject to any attack. Nevertheless, the world changed, and to all intents and purposes, the no-interest checking account has vanished today even though legally it still exists. Whether the depositor prefers to keep his funds in a NOW account, money market fund, or one of the new common stock funds on which you can also draw checks, or, as I do, in a savings account that is electronically interconnected with my checking account, the fact remains that interest is now paid on all checking accounts where the total deposit is large enough so that the simple service of dealing with the checks does not absorb the full value of the return on the capital. If this special privilege can vanish, think how insecure the others are.

There is another characteristic that all of the special privileges I have listed in this chapter share—they are all cases where a comparatively small group of people are benefitted and where the cost is quite widely dispersed. This is rather typical of these administrative transfers, but it is by no means uniform. The reader will recall the social security system, which involves a fairly heavy cost on a very large group of people for a fairly large transfer to another very large group of people. Of course, in this case, part of the cost is concealed, since, by law, the employers are compelled to falsely inform their employees that the cost is only half of what it actually is.[9] The public education system is also a large transfer from one large group to another. Socialized medicine, if we had it, would probably also qualify. The medical aid that we, in fact, do give to older persons and to poor people is already an example.

There are a certain number of cases in which the administrative transfer is so organized that it goes from a small group of people to a large one, but they are rare. Probably the most obvious cases are the price controls on petroleum and on natural gas. Over the long run, these programs probably benefit no one, but in the early days, they imposed a very large cost on a fairly small group of people, the owners of the wells, in order to provide a small per capita benefit to an immensely large part of the population. In this case, however, although the per capita benefit was small compared with the per capita

8. I once heard Milton Friedman use it as an example of how businessmen who were in favor of free competition tend to look for government regulations to protect themselves, but this is the only public criticism I ever heard.

9. This is not quite true due to the fact that the "employers' contribution" is not included in the employees' income for income tax purposes. This would lower that portion's cost to the employee slightly.

loss to the well owners, it was nevertheless large enough to be noticeable, and the way it was administered made it particularly so. It is not true, then, that the well-organized minority always beats the unorganized majority.

The trick here, of course, is that the natural gas and petroleum regulations were very conspicuous. Most of these other special transfers are not. Further, most of them can be concealed under "public interest" rubrics. The individual voter is not motivated to understand and remember until the next election most of these provisions that injure him mildly, while beneficiaries who benefit a good deal are so motivated.

Most of these procedures are rather complicated and hard to explain. It seems likely that this complication comes from two sources: a genuine desire to have them complicated so that people have difficulty understanding them and a trade-off arrangement with other pressure groups. If we go back to the great granddaddy of modern regulatory institutions, the Interstate Commerce Commission (ICC), it is clear that the original provisions assisted the railroads in organizing functioning cartels but also provided a significant payoff to a considerable number of farmers in the United States who were benefitted by a cut in rates on their products. There were various other special groups that benefitted from special provisions in the Interstate Commerce Act, which created the ICC. No doubt, all of these things were put in in order to buy support for the basic provision. The same could be said of the original CAB policy and, indeed, most of such regulations. Further, this confusion in paying off special interest groups is not confined to the initial act. Its administration is apt to continue along the same lines. All of this makes the project very complicated and hard to understand.

The second reason for this complication is that it makes it easier to pull the wool over the average voter's eyes. This may be less important in the motivation of people who lobby for these bills, but perhaps may be more important in getting them through. They are inherently complicated, and certainly there is no obvious evidence that their sponsors try to make them simple, though I do not think that they need to complicate them more than they would be anyway. In all probability the sponsors attempt to confuse the voters more by lying about the actual intent of the bill, or its effect, than by deliberately making it complicated. The complication probably comes more from the necessity of producing a coalition of interest groups than from design. Nevertheless, the complication certainly does contribute to the difficulty of the average voter.

Frequently, the announced purpose of a bill is radically different from its actual purpose. This is a further element that helps it go through. In the period from the Civil War to about 1900, the Civil War tariffs that had revenue and protection in mind were gradually converted into a tariff system that would raise relatively little revenue and had a great protective effect. This change was normally implemented by a set of bills put in every year or so, the nominal purpose of which was "to reduce the revenue." Such bills would be introduced to change the tariff structure, and they would indeed lead to the revenue being lower than it was before. The sponsors of these bills could claim to the voters that they were lowering the tax burden of the society and could point out to the various special interest groups that the reason that the tax returns on, let us say, imports of steel had fallen was not that the rate had fallen but that the steel imports had fallen. Similar mislabeling is common in this kind of legislation.

For these bills to get through, however, we need not only all of these factors but also a certain element of intellectual confusion. As a general rule, almost all of these restrictions from the ICC to the CAB to the farm program have been popular among the intellectual community at the time they were enacted. Since most members of the intellectual community were not members of the special interest group who would gain, this popularity has to be put down to intellectual confusion.

Of course, the special interest groups had every motive to increase this intellectual confusion, but it was a "public good," and hence they could hardly invest any resources to that end. Take, for example, the farmers in the 1930s attempting to get the farm program. They would benefit from a general climate of opinion in which government intervention into the market process was thought to be good almost regardless of what it was, but if they invested any resources in attempting to provide that climate of opinion, the bulk of the return would go to other special interest groups rather than to themselves. They would be better off free-riding on other people's investment. This means that the bulk of this intellectual confusion must come from outside the special interest groups who benefit from it. There is a possible special interest group that could benefit—the so-called new class—but I would like to put off discussion for now and talk about this kind of intellectual faddism and confusion on the assumption that it is not representative of the interest of any special group.

The first thing to note here is that discussion of policy issues is extremely faddish. Once again, the morning paper[10] carries an example. President Reagan made a statement about tactical nuclear warfare in Europe that was

10. *Washington Post*, Wednesday, October 21, 1981.

simply a repetition of the official American line on this matter for the last 20 to 25 years. It is a point of view that has been endorsed in the past, and probably will be again in the future, by the *Washington Post* and by most of the rest of the establishment. He was criticized for it by the *Washington Post* and by most of the rest of the establishment. He was very highly criticized for it by the *Washington Post* as a secondary consequence of being criticized by a number of European politicians. These same politicians had endorsed substantially the same statement a few years ago. Nothing has changed except the intellectual fashion.

The reason for the fashionableness of the intellectuals is that they, like everyone else, have no strong practical motive for becoming well informed about government policy. It is desirable, if you are an intellectual, to be up on the current discussion and to have, in general, whatever happens currently to be the conventional opinions. Over time, individual critics do in fact change conventional wisdom, but this change is slow and is certainly not an unmitigated improvement. Apparently, there is a combination of a very large random walk component with a somewhat smaller movement toward the good, the true, and the beautiful. This is not to criticize the intellectual establishment; given their incentives they are behaving in a maximizing manner. We should, however, realize that error can be widely endorsed.

Special interest groups are presumably aware of this, at least subconsciously, and take advantage of whatever currently happens to be fashionable. Since they can hardly predict what will become fashionable, and in general it is not to their interest to invest money in attempting to change general intellectual fashions as opposed to opinions on some subject of narrow interest to themselves, they cannot be blamed for it, but they do benefit from it.

Here I must pick up my promise to talk about the so-called new class. The new class is the collection of professional intellectuals and civil servants who, in fact, have benefitted quite considerably from the expansion of government. Not only are there far more civil service jobs, but the intellectuals who are frequently called upon to advise, or in other ways interpret, gain from this expansion. Most of the intellectuals and civil servants are in favor of this expansion and primarily criticize it for being too slow. From this phenomenon it has been deduced that they are carrying out their "class interest."

There is no doubt that the class so defined does indeed have an interest for expansion of government. But this is a fallacy of composition. It does not follow that the individual members of the class have such an interest. Why should they invest resources in generating a public good for other members of the class? It is possible to be quite successful in the intellectual community taking an antiestablishment point of view. William Buckley and Irving Kristol are outstanding examples. It may be true that an occasional intellectual, considering some expansion of government in which he has no direct interest at all, will realize that he has an indirect interest by the increase in demand for his particular type of services and favor it. It seems unlikely, however, that this motive would be very large. Most intellectuals will be trying to maximize their own position, and that does not necessarily involve maximizing the interests of intellectuals as a class. For most intellectuals it is quite important that they be in accord, with either the intellectual community as a whole or at least some subset in it. Firstly, it is very hard to have independent ideas of your own on everything, and if you did, they probably would not be very well thought out. The division of labor suggests that you should try to learn only about a few things and get your ideas on others from "experts." The general intellectual community is, of course, full of such experts.

One can, however, just as well be a member of a subset of the intellectual community. For a long time, the Marxists have been such a subset, but on the other side there is the so-called Chicago school of economics or, to take another somewhat overlapping set, the public choice group. These provide the same possibilities for an individual to simply pick up a general set of "facts" about the world from a group that he trusts, while leaving him free, if he wants to, to contribute to the orthodoxy within the group by further work on his own. From the intellectual standpoint, this kind of structure is more or less necessary, but it is not surprising that all the people in such a group are apt to think much the same on any given issue.

As a member of the public choice group and a somewhat distant member of the Chicago group, I would say that we are reasonably scientific most of the time and that the Marxists are obscurantists. The obscurantist Marxist would deny this.[11] As a general rule, however, the intellectual community contains a very large group of people who constitute the orthodoxy, and a number of smaller groups on the edges, like the Marxists[12] or the so-called new conservatives. The main orthodoxy is the one that is of greatest immediate political importance, although the smaller groups on the edges each have the possibility of converting that main orthodoxy to their point of view. Indeed, that is their major political role.

11. This proves they are obscurantists.

12. Who are broken into a number of subcategories.

Note that this is intended as a description,[13] not as either praise or criticism. I would, of course, like everyone else, prefer a system in which the people who control our intellectual life were solely interested in the good, the true, and the beautiful, and engaged in unremitting labor to seek them out. I do not see much prospect of that in the real world, however. The individual mind is finite, and an individual intellectual can learn by his own efforts, i.e., by individual research, only a very small part of the relevant information. Of necessity, he must depend on other people for the bulk of his information, and this leads to the kind of general opinion that I have been describing. One can hope that over time the center of this opinion will gradually move toward the good, the true, and the beautiful, but there is no reason to believe it is there now or that movements are entirely in that direction. Indeed, my reading of intellectual history would indicate that large, random deviations are very common.

Let me give one very strong example of such a random deviation. When I was a boy in Rockford, Illinois, I was a very firm believer in protective tariffs and gold. The reason for this was that Rockford, at that time, was a little behind the intellectual fashion, and the dominant views of the intellectuals of 20 years before still held sway in Rockford. In this case, I was cured of these two views very quickly and easily by Henry Simons of the University of Chicago, but that these views had been orthodox among American intellectuals 20 years before I take as obvious. Further, it is not clear to me that this particular set of views was in any way inferior to what became orthodox in the late 1930s. Both were wrong, but on the whole I prefer the wrongness of the rock-hard republican intellectuals of 1920 to the wrongness of the liberal New Deal intellectuals of 1940. Those who disagree with this evaluation can consider the fact that the views that I would ascribe to the rock-hard republicans were not dominant in the United States in 1920. There had been a gradual change.

A really extreme example of the autonomous nature of such change comes not from American but from Japanese history. The Tokagawa, when they took control of Japan, set up an early version of the modern totalitarian state, with great emphasis on secret police and thought control. Nevertheless, when Commodore Perry broke Japan open in the mid-19th century, the average Japanese intellectual thought the Tokagawa regime illegitimate. It

13. For some further work along these lines, see Gordon Tullock, "The Economics of the Media," Working Paper no. CE-78-1-15, Center for Study of Public Choice, Blacksburg, Va., 1978.

appears that the Tokagawa Shogun himself shared this opinion, or, in any event, he certainly did not defend himself with any vigor against the forces that overthrew his power. The intellectual change occurred over a long period of time and in many small steps despite what would appear to be overwhelmingly strong controls. It was an example of the intellectual establishment moving in what I suppose we would have to argue was a random direction, since there is no reason at all to prefer the Emperor to the Shogun. We do not understand these movements, but we can at least observe that they exist and that they have strong effects.

It seems likely that any state of mind on the part of the intellectual community would help at least some special interest group. Further, they can very badly damage special interest groups. The present drive toward deregulation is a case in which the intellectual community's change of mind—in my opinion, very desirable—is injuring a number of special interest groups. At the moment, this drive simply seems to be a reversal of previous trends, and most of the changes, although they may indeed benefit specific groups, are also movements toward higher social efficiency. It is not safe to make predictions from trends, but it should be pointed out that the movement of England from a mercantilist society to the extremely open society of 1850 does seem to be an example of the intellectual community becoming convinced of the truth of what was then called "radicalism" and imposing it successfully on society. We can hope that something like this will happen now, but hope is different from prediction.

This has been, in a way, a digression. I believe it is necessary to have at least some comprehension of the intellectual community in order to understand the functioning of pressure groups. Their basic modus operandi is the logrolling procedure described in Chapter 4. They convince a small group of congressmen that something is to their advantage, they convince the rest of the congressmen that the cost will be very modest and that the public probably will not notice, and hence get it through. The examples I have given are, I think, good ones, but it should be said that the overwhelming bulk of this type of politics deals with much less major matters. Fairly small changes in individual regulations, special clauses in the revenue act, decisions as to where a particular military base will go—all of these are, in sum, probably much larger than the more conspicuous decisions for such things as the Interstate Commerce Commission.

The intellectual community is important because, as a general rule, getting these things through requires either the acquiescence or at least the silence of the media. If the press gets excited, the congressmen who are not directly benefitting through their constituency or, for that matter, through campaign contributions and other bribes, will become reluctant to go along, because there is a cost to them of taking an action that is unpopular. Thus, as a general rule, a movement of this sort requires that it either be secret or that it be in accordance with the current intellectual mystique. I believe, however, that this shapes the specific provisions and which special interest groups win, but does not usually change the number of such special interest groups that are successful in most cases. Of course, the example I gave of England in the early 19th century was an exception to this.

Basically then, we have a logrolling system in which congressmen trade favors. They hope to improve their electability in the next election, and by doing this they hope to benefit their constituency. Thus, anything for which the benefit to one constituency is enough so that a majority of other constituencies can be paid off will get through. If this were all, however, we would be much better off than we are. The information conditions that I have been describing mean that, in practice, a great many minor matters are advantageous to the politician, even though cost is much larger than the benefit.

If it is minor enough so that the individual taxpayer in his constituency will not feel the cost, then certainly the congressman should be willing to vote for it in return for suitable compensation, even if the trade as a whole will injure his own constituents. If, on the other hand, the press for some reason criticizes it severely, the congressman probably will vote against it because it ceases to be something that no one will notice. The general result of all of this is negative in terms of efficiency. Further, from the distributional standpoint it is probably mildly regressive. It seems likely the people who are successful in this kind of activity on the whole are more wealthy than those who are unsuccessful.

It should be noted that unfortunately the charitable instincts of the populace sometimes get involved in this kind of essentially inefficient transfer to people of upper-income status. One of the arguments being used today by people who want to retain the tobacco and sugar quotas is that if they are cancelled the farmers concerned will go into bankruptcy.[14] These farmers who might go into bankruptcy are generally upper-income people who, even if they do go into bankruptcy, have enough talent so that they will be above the average income in almost any employment they take up. The proposal that the average taxpayer, or the average purchaser of peanuts or sugar, subsidize them is a regressive proposal, but it can be argued for on charitable grounds.

14. This may well be true, and it may also be false.

The same could be said of the bailing out of Lockheed and Chrysler. In both cases, the stockholders and the employees were way above the average income in wealth and would remain above the average income and wealth even if these companies collapsed. They would, of course, have to find other employment. Thus, here is another case in which charitable instincts lead to help, or at least are one of the factors leading to help for people in the upper-income bracket by people who rank below them, i.e., regressive charitable transfers.

It should perhaps be said, however, that there is a by-product of this distribution that benefits a good many intellectuals and certainly the author of this book. As a result of the development of a large rent-seeking industry in Washington, Washington has been converted from the rather provincial city that I remember from 1948–49, when I was there undergoing training as a foreign service officer, to a highly cosmopolitan center. I can remember when practically no live theater of any sort was available in Washington, and the best restaurants were traditional American restaurants of the type one might find in a small town in the middle west. This has all changed. Today, not only are the Kennedy Center, Carter Barren, etc., available, places in which the lobbyists not only lobby but receive a federal government subsidy in doing so, but there is a spectacular set of expensive French, Italian, Chinese, etc., restaurants that an occasional visitor to the city like myself finds very attractive. From the standpoint of the midwestern laborer who pays for all of this, I suppose it is a negative transfer, but I have to admit that personally I benefit from it.

Nevertheless, the net effect of the kind of transfers dealt with in this chapter is clearly sharply negative. It is not, however, clear that there is any way of modifying democracy to avoid them. That subject will be discussed in the next chapter. Still, we would certainly want to get rid of them if we could. We do have the fact that 19th-century England, to a large extent, succeeded in eliminating them. To repeat what I said before, I believe that the sum total of all the transfers of the sort mentioned in this chapter is probably as great as the total cost of all the welfare state activities described before. Further, I think the net cost per dollar is much greater. This last sentence, which may sound confusing, simply means that I believe when some special interest gets a special favor, let us say, a higher price for tobacco, the net cost to the community of that is considerably higher than the net cost of similar size transfers under things like the social security. It is even possible that transfers under social security have no true cost to society, because the improvements in utility generated by the institution more than compensate for the inefficiency. That certainly is not true for the acreage restrictions on wheat.

GIVING LIFE

Some time ago an acquaintance of mine was told by his doctors that he would die within four months unless he had open-heart surgery. They further told him that he had about a one-in-three chance of dying under the knife if he chose to have the operation. He chose the operation and died in the intensive care unit a few hours after being removed from the operating table. Most people would refer to this as a tragic choice. It is not exactly the kind of tragic choice examined by Guido Calabresi and Philip Bobbitt in their book *Tragic Choices*, but some analysis of my acquaintance's situation will serve as an introduction to the issues that they raise.

First, the choice itself depended on the state of medical technology. One hundred years ago the doctor could have done nothing for him and probably could not even have diagnosed his condition properly. It is likely that in another 100 years medicine will have advanced to the point where he could be easily cured. The nature of the problem is in this way determined by the historical time in which it is posed. Most of the cases discussed by Calabresi and Bobbitt share this characteristic with my acquaintance's difficult choice.

Another aspect of the problem was that merely making the choice would itself be painful. Careful thought about whether one wished to live for four months or take a gamble in which one had a two-in-three chance of having a fairly long life[1] and a one-in-three chance of dying immediately would surely make anyone unhappy. People in such situations sometimes refuse to think about the problem, remarking that doctors are all incompetent, or something similar. This means, of course, that they have indirectly chosen death in four months, with the decision modified a bit by the possibility that the doctors may be wrong.

The person who, when faced with a problem of this sort, refuses to give it any consideration may be maximising his utility. The pain and suffering he would inflict on himself by careful thought about the problem might be

Reprinted, with permission, from *The Economics of Wealth and Poverty* (New York: New York University Press, 1986), 158–69.

This article first appeared as "Avoiding Difficult Decisions," review article of Guido Calabresi and Philip Bobbitt, *Tragic Choices* (New York: W. W. Norton; Toronto: George J. McLeod, 1978), in *New York University Law Review* 54, no. 1 (April 1979): 267–79.

1. My acquaintance was in his twenties.

greater than the cost of not thinking, which in his case would be death in four months. Note, however, that it is not possible for the person consciously to choose *not* to decide the basic problem because the cost of such a conscious choice would be too great. Yet conscious thought about the problem whether to think about the problem could be as painful as conscious thought about the final problem.

If we were to find people who regularly avoided decisions in such matters, an investigation of their thought processes would be an interesting one. We would probably begin by thinking that it was a study of abnormal psychology, assuming that in such a situation one should think the problem through and reach the best solution. Some reflection, however, indicates that the assumption is not necessarily valid. If persons faced with a tragic choice can quietly and without much thought bypass the problem, they will, perhaps, be happier than if they did not. Certainly, my friend would have been better off, since he would have had four additional months of life and would not have struggled with the torturous choice that faced him.

Calabresi and Bobbitt's study is an essay on avoidance. It is devoted not to the way tragic choices are made, and how they could be better made, but rather to the way in which people avoid thinking about them. This is not the description that they themselves would use, but I think it is an accurate one. To make this observation is not to criticise the book. Their subject is important, and they analyse it with great care.

The particular tragic choices the authors discuss involve social decisions about providing aid to individuals rather than, as in the example of my acquaintance above, choices made by individuals for themselves. The tragic nature of the choice arises from the fact that society is not willing to save everyone and hence must decide who will be saved. The decision process, the authors note, has two stages. The first stage, called the first-order determination, is the decision about the amount of resources society will allocate to aiding people in some tragic situation. The second stage, the second-order determination, is the choice of who will receive these particular resources.[2]

Let us examine the specific type of tragic choice in which Calabresi and Bobbitt are interested. As an example, consider the kidney dialysis machine, which can, at very great cost, allow people suffering from an otherwise fatal disease to go on living. Let us temporarily put aside the actual history of these machines and consider a hypothetical case that will help in the further analysis of the book. Suppose that a wealthy man, knowing that dialysis

2. p. 19.

machines existed and that there were many people in the community who could not afford them, decided to buy some of the machines and give their services away free.

He would have two problems, the first of which is the first-order choice of the number of machines he will purchase. Of course, in an alternative not specifically named by Calabresi and Bobbitt but nevertheless directly involved in much of their analysis, he could, instead of buying kidney machines, invest the same amount of money in some other way of reducing pain and suffering. This, however, is simply a special sub-category of first-order decision, because putting money into something other than kidney machines reduces the number of kidney machines available free of charge.

The individual wealthy man must then decide who should receive the use of the machines he has purchased. This second-order decision is of necessity a difficult one, and is indeed the "tragic choice" that Calabresi and Bobbitt analyse: whoever must make this decision decides who should live and who should die in just as direct and straightforward a way as if he were sitting on a bench and wearing a black robe. It should not surprise us that a wealthy philanthropist, in much the same way as my terminally ill friend, might wish to avoid making the final choice.

In the case of the philanthropist, unlike that of the heart patient, the decision affects not the decision-maker but other people. The motives for careful thought about a painful problem are hence much weaker than they would be were the conclusion to affect the wealthy man himself. We could therefore expect that he would, in general, try to avoid the decision but might occasionally interfere to aid some particular client who had attracted his attention. This phenomenon of interest in a few particular cases occurs in social decisions as well. Immense resources are committed to attempts to rescue pilots ditched at sea, miners trapped in pit-falls, and others in situations in which the plight of the individual attracts public attention.

When the social choice is less visible, however, the usual decision-avoidance techniques come into play. For instance, when I was in the foreign service, the areas that I served always had a large number of people who wanted American visas. But the number of such visas was restricted. The officers charged with allocating them (fortunately I was never one of them) had a number of ways of avoiding the choice process.[3] There were a number of papers to be filled out; applicants were required to sit on hard chairs for

3. Calabresi and Bobbitt cite Menotti's opera *The Consul* on more or less the same point. See p. 98.

long periods of time; and, in general, there was a lengthy delay while the applications were being taken. All this imposed a cost on the applicant, not in straightforward monetary terms (although there were some direct fees), but in terms of inconvenience.[4] In addition, the actual rules that governed the granting of visas involved a certain number of non-discretionary criteria that once again reduced the difficulty of making a decision. Leaving all these factors aside, however, the ultimate decision was made as a result of correspondence between the consuls in the field and the officials in Washington. I discovered rather early that no one was willing to admit responsibility for the ultimate decision. The people in the consulate always maintained that the choices were made in Washington, and the people in Washington always maintained that they were made in the consulates. The decision was a painful one, and responsibility for making it had been successfully avoided. Again, the avoidance of tragic choices is not confined to private decisions.

Further examination of the problems associated with tragic choices can be made if we return to our wealthy man. The decision as to who shall get the treatment is a difficult one in two respects. First, he must make the terrible choice of who will live and who will die. Second, merely making this decision reminds him that he has not spent as much money as he could have buying the machines. To use Calabresi and Bobbitt's terms, the second-order decision draws attention to the first-order decision. Our philanthropist is apt to feel guilty about the size of his gift every time he decides that someone will have to die because there are not enough machines available, unless he has exhausted all of his resources on the machines. We should not be surprised to discover that the wealthy man was concealing this problem from himself.

II

We are finally in a position to examine directly the Calabresi and Bobbitt analysis of tragic choices. The situation is identical to that of our wealthy man except that the giver is the average citizen by way of the government. This average citizen has all the problems we have canvassed above in our two simpler cases plus two more. First, in political matters the individual voter is

4. The authors discuss such non-monetary allocational mechanisms and their problems as a variant on the pure market. See pp. 92–98.

normally poorly informed. This statement is empirical in character[5] but the rationality of the average voter's ignorance may also be theoretically derived from careful analysis of the functioning of a democracy.[6]

The second additional problem is that the cost to the individual voter of any increase in the amount of resources allocated to a particular problem is generally trivial. Of course, the voter cannot afford to help everyone everywhere with a serious problem. A concerted effort, for example, on the part of Americans to raise the living standard of the average citizen of India to one-half of what we regard as the poverty level would require our diverting something like 45 per cent of the average voter's after-tax income.[7] Nevertheless, in any particular case, the cost spread over a very large number of voters is minimal. Thus, whenever the individual voter hears of someone denied the use of a kidney machine, he is apt to feel that the service should be extended because the cost to himself is small. And the decision eventually made, to provide kidney machines for anyone who needed them,[8] probably does cost the average voter only a trifling amount. Difficulties arise only if we try to generalise our attitude towards renal failure to all diseases. A willingness to spend as much to save people suffering from other diseases as we now spend for kidney problems would be very expensive for most voters.

One of the virtues of *Tragic Choices* is that it makes the dilemma or, as I shall shortly point out, trilemma clear. Resources are scarce, and we cannot help everyone who is suffering. The point is well made by the cases that draw public attention—when a person trapped in a mine disaster, or perhaps a lost explorer, is saved with the expenditure of several million dollars. We cannot possibly expend that large a sum for every person in danger.

We therefore ration the total amount of funds we make available to people in severe difficulties. Once we have decided how much we will spend—the

5. See A. Campbell, P. Converse, W. Miller and D. Stokes, *The American Voter* (abridged ed. 1964), pp. 99–102.

6. For a simple explanation, see G. Tullock, *Toward a Mathematics of Politics* (1967), pp. 100–114.

7. The figure was calculated from the UN *Monthly Bulletin of Statistics*. It is only approximate, because I did not have readily at hand any figures on family size distribution in India and hence used a four-person family as a proxy. For the reader interested in experimenting with other values, here is a simple rule of thumb. Per capita income in India is about 5 per cent of our poverty level. Every increase in Indian per capita income equivalent to 10 per cent of our poverty level would cost the average U.S. citizen about 10 per cent of his after-tax income.

8. See p. 189.

first-order problem—we must then make the second-order decision about how this rationed quantity will be allocated. Making it, however, imposes upon us the same kind of cost to which we referred above in the case of our wealthy individual philanthropist. A combination of the poor information that we expect in democratic politics, together with the fact that any individual expansion of total resources will have its cost spread over the entire electorate, means that the decision will be inherently suspect. Furthermore, in facing the second-order decisions, we may come across questions about the first-order decisions that eventually lead us to change the first-order allocation.

Indeed, it seems that the decision to universalise the availability of the kidney machines described in *Tragic Choices*[9] was reached because of questions about the way the second-order decisions were being made. But that solution cannot itself be generalised. Providing relief to everyone is possible for any particular limited class of tragic choices but not for all. Moreover, the decision to aid people in one particular tragic situation is at the same time a decision not to aid people in others.[10] We have a kind of lottery in which the government stands ready to spend a large amount of money to assist those with, for example, serious kidney diseases. But the government will then be very much more niggardly towards people who need heart shunts, even though they may be in equal danger and the cost of a shunt may be less than that of dialysis.

There is, in addition to the first- and second-order problems, a third-order problem. This third problem is the intellectual attitude we will take towards the first two. Shall we frankly admit that resources are limited and that we are going to let a certain number of people die of curable medical conditions?[11] This decision to let some people die is not, of course, inconsistent with making considerable contributions to helping people in trouble. It does, however, mean that we will have to make definite choices about who gets the aid, and that we cannot pretend it goes to everyone. The third-order decision could involve, as one alternative, simply accepting the situation. As a second alternative, we could adopt one of a large number of ways of concealing from ourselves the dilemma between the first- and second-order decisions. It is to this aspect of the tragic choice that the Calabresi and Bobbitt book is largely devoted. They analyse, frequently with much acuteness, the advantages and disadvantages of various mechanisms for making decisions about who will

9. See pp. 186–89.

10. See p. 189.

11. Or, for that matter, will we admit to letting millions starve to death in the Sahel.

receive the aid. These decisions, however, are uniformly analysed in terms of their efficiency in relieving social tension among the general citizenry and not in terms of their efficiency in reaching an optimal distribution of the aid.

Here a paradox at the heart of the authors' approach becomes evident. Efforts to solve the third-order problem, which is what this book is about, are as likely to cause social distress and unhappiness on the part of the people who must make them, as is the decision about the amount of resources to be devoted. Third-order problems thus cannot be faced openly by people who want to take advantage of avoidance techniques to conceal the actual dilemma. Calabresi and Bobbitt can talk about the techniques, and their readers can think about them, only so long as they take a cold-blooded scientific attitude inconsistent with the use of methods of concealing the decisions.

Their analysis can, of course, be thought of as an élite analysis. We, who understand these things, are considering the methods used by the general citizenry who do not, and can advise them on the methods that will maximise their utility. Utility in this case derives from a mixture of decisions on first- and second-order problems together with some mechanism for concealing the actual tragic nature of the decision. If we consider ourselves part of the group making the allocation decision, however, then the third-order tragic decision is just as tragic as the first- and second-order choices.

There is apparently no way out of the paradox. If we engage in rational thought about the choice, we will not be deceived. But avoiding deception means that we suffer a loss of utility because of the nature of the choice made. Of course, if we attempt rational thought and do it clumsily, we may be able to conceal the painful nature of the situation from ourselves. We may feel happy about our self-sacrifice (which may be genuine) in providing facilities for the poor without noticing that this means that certain other poor people, whom we could have helped with a little additional sacrifice, will die.

In tragic choice situations, rational thought in and of itself may lower overall utility even if it increases the real physical output. The poor and unfortunate would benefit if the members of our donor group behaved in a highly rational manner, because the funds chosen in the first-order choice would be distributed in a most efficient way. The donors would suffer, however, because they would be compelled to think about unpleasant problems. The other alternative, to use some method that conceals from the donors the full tragedy of the dilemma, will certainly lead to a less than optimal allocation of resources. Hence, the poor and unfortunate would be worse off although the donor group would be better off.

So far, what I have been saying has been more inspired by than directly drawn from Calabresi and Bobbitt. Yet all the elements I have discussed above are in the book—they simply are not given the same emphases of organisation or structure. In a way the authors have failed to make what we may call a fourth-order choice, namely, to discuss the tragic implications of third-order choices. Instead, they have devoted the bulk of their book to a careful and insightful discussion of the techniques actually used to conceal the problem of the first- and second-order decisions. In this discussion they assume that, in what I have called the third-order area, an implicit decision has been made that we will not directly face up to the shortage of resources and to the consequent necessity of choosing who shall live and who shall die. The book is empirical and not normative in its discussion of third-order choices. This aspect would appear to be the result of a fourth-order choice to be "cold-bloodedly scientific" in avoiding the third-order choice.

The authors ably survey the various allocation techniques that can be used. But assisting a conscious, rational choice among these techniques, which is the only practical use the book would have, would involve making a third-order decision as painful as the decisions Calabresi and Bobbitt are attempting to avoid. They do not make such a third-order decision, and the reader should note that I also have not done so. The problem is indeed a painful one.

These third-order decisions in general, unless they are decisions to face the whole matter directly in a scientific manner, have to be made sub-consciously. As in the case of my acquaintance with the heart ailment, there is no gain if one chooses to conceal with open eyes; nothing then is concealed. We would thus expect general ineptness in methods of successful concealment, simply because the choice cannot depend on careful thought.

The authors do not make a choice about whether to conceal, and, as I said before, I myself have nothing to recommend. As it is difficult to see what should be done in these cases, let us turn to the actual content of the book, the exhaustive catalogue of methods. (Note that I have just made my own fourth-order decision not to deal with the third-order problem, and that my editors have made a fifth-order decision not to deal with my decision.)

The first method the authors discuss for dealing with the problem is one included more as a straw man than for any other purpose. It is a "pure market" mechanism, which simply permits people to buy kidney machines or other costly items if they have the money and to die if they do not.[12] The

12. pp. 31–34.

obvious advantage of this method is that it solves the first- and second-order problems in one fell swoop. The decision as to who will get the machines also determines how many of them will be built. The reasons for not using this system are not absolutely clear, because it is hard to explain why we do sometimes decide to help our fellow man. But for whatever reason, the pure market solution does not appeal to many people and certainly not to Calabresi and Bobbitt.[13]

A modification of this pure market mechanism is apt to appeal to those economists willing to apply their training cold-bloodedly. Assuming that the basic problem here is one of income disparity, we could redistribute the income in society to reach some distribution that we think is optimal and let individuals spend that money as they wish. If they wish to purchase kidney machines or, more probably, purchase medical insurance that would provide a kidney machine if the policyholder needed one,[14] we would permit them to do so. If they choose to spend their money on something else and the need for a kidney machine arises, we would let them die.

Under this system the poor are given the right to make decisions about how any aid given to them will be spent. If they value something else more highly than insurance against the contingency that they will need a kidney machine in the future, we would permit them to buy it. This would surely be better for them than a kind of warden relationship in which we would force them to accept that part of the aid in kind by, for instance, lowering their income and using the difference to buy kidney machine insurance for them.

This solution, as I say, is apt to attract economists who permit their science to guide them. The objections to the system seem limited to three. One is that the poor just are not very bright and will spend their money badly, usually capsulised in the phrase that they would "drink up anything you would give them"; this point of view is rarely expressed openly, but is certainly held by many. I shall leave this one aside; I do not believe it is worth discussing.

The second objection is that as a matter of fact public charitable agencies are likely to come to the aid of a person in dire need, even if he gets into the situation by failing to buy proper insurance beforehand. We as taxpayers will often find ourselves paying for emergency treatment because we will face at that point a second-order decision whether to let the man die. Knowing that

13. See p. 31.

14. This would be very expensive but certainly not impossible.

we will behave this way, people will be less likely to buy the appropriate insurance than they would have been if we were more cold-blooded in making the ultimate decision. The donor group may thus be forced to require that persons purchase the insurance. This argument was important in the original advocacy of the social security programme, and I notice it turns up occasionally today in arguments in that field. There is no doubt, however, that it has much wider applicability.

The objection perhaps most relevant to the tragic choice analysis as set out above is that from the point of view of the donor group, the loss in utility may be greater than the gain from the betterment in the condition of the recipients. As Calabresi and Bobbitt point out, it is possible that the external costs to the donors of "the wrenching spectacle of a rich man and a poor man bidding against each other for life" may be eliminated only by a degree of wealth redistribution we would find prohibitively high;[15] the donor group might balk at the costs, both fiscal and psychological, of establishing a market-based allocation system, even when coupled with some form of wealth equalisation.

Another variation of the modified market scheme is to permit the poor person who has received some government service, let us say, the right to the use of a kidney machine, to sell the right to someone else if he feels the money is more important to him than the service. This scheme is characteristically banned, and Calabresi and Bobbitt suggest that the reason is that it puts a strain on the conscience of the donors. That the poor person would be willing to undergo great risk as a result of this type of sale indicates that his basic situation is bad indeed. This "unquiet indictment of society's distribution of wealth"[16] may cause pain to the people who have not given him more money. The donors therefore prohibit the recipient from undertaking a Pareto-superior transaction.[17] I do not know if this is the actual explanation for restrictions of this sort, but they are fairly uniformly applied by the government in the area of in-kind provision.

Another variation on the modified market method that might be used would be to permit the scarce resource, such as kidney machines, to be bought or rented, but to charge different people different prices in accordance with their wealth.[18] As a simple example (not used by Calabresi and Bobbitt),

15. p. 33.
16. Ibid.
17. Ibid.
18. pp. 98–103.

individuals might bid not dollars but hours of their income stream. Thus, if a millionaire bids 200 hours (which would cost him, let us suppose, $1 million) and a poor person bids 201 hours (the actual cash value of which is $402), the poor person wins. This method permits the use of the market while neutralising differences in wealth. It has some of the efficiency characteristics of market transactions but not all of them. And it is, of course, also non-Pareto-optimal if one prohibits resale. As far as I know, this method is not used anywhere. Calabresi and Bobbitt offer a number of administrative reasons why such "wealth distribution–neutral" markets would be extremely difficult to use in practice. Chief among these are the problems associated with assessing both the value of the benefit to the individuals concerned and the other elements of the distribution scheme, such as, in our example above, the value of an hour of a millionaire's time,[19] and with the attempt to separate price-conscious preferences from other non-price elements such as cultural preferences.[20]

A third and final "coherent" solution to allocating the scarce resource might be to distribute it by lot.[21] As Calabresi and Bobbitt point out, first come, first served is simply a special, and a rather inferior, form of lottery.[22] The lottery has not been much used for distributing positive gifts, but it has on occasion been used for conscription into the army, a situation that bears a certain resemblance to the tragic choice problem. The method first come, first served is sometimes used not as a result of conscious choice but because the people responsible can think of nothing else.

These three approaches to decision-making are all intellectually coherent, in that they attempt to apply some consistent set of values to the making of tragic choices. The remaining procedures discussed in *Tragic Choices* are less coherent. In these cases the effort to avoid thought in the area of tragic choice leads to the use of various mechanisms that conceal the actual procedures from outsiders and, in some instances, from the people making the decisions. I do not propose to elaborate the procedures they discuss, but would like merely to list some of them. One is the representative political body.[23]

19. See pp. 110–14. The difficulties associated with gauging the strength of such preferences may sometimes lead society to abandon the market in favour of other devices, such as aresponsible agencies or even "simple, muddled, collective determination[s]" (p. 109); see pp. 106–10 and text accompanying notes 24–27 below.

20. See pp. 102–3, 104–5.

21. p. 41.

22. pp. 43–44.

23. pp. 34–41.

Another is the "aresponsible agency," such as the trial jury.[24] Such bodies generally are decentralised and representative of society at large, and need not give reasons for their decisions.[25] A variation on this theme is called the "para-aresponsible agency," which has technical experts among its members.[26] Para-aresponsible agencies reduce inconsistencies of decision by the continuity of their membership, but the presence of the technical experts reduces the agency's representativeness.[27] A third method is the use of a bureaucracy that may obscure the decisional criteria.[28] Finally, various devices may be used to allocate tragically scarce resources in light of the perceived worthiness of the recipients, as measured by criteria that may be either expressed or tacit.[29] All these methods are complex and may be combined with each other in various ways. Calabresi and Bobbitt's discussion of these techniques is insightful, but the authors offer no recommendation regarding them and no general principle by which to select among them.

These discussions of less coherent methods are worthwhile reading not only for people interested in tragic choices but for people interested in government decision-making procedures in general. Many of Calabresi and Bobbitt's observations apply also to other bodies making choices that they would not classify as tragic. Government commissions appointed to deal with general policy and regulatory problems, for example, would appear to function, at least until the recent trend towards the adoption of "sunshine laws" and administrative procedure codes, in much the same way as the "God Committee" that for a while allocated the use of the dialysis machine in Seattle. The God Committee, essentially an aresponsible parajury composed of both professionals and lay persons, "chose those who . . . were most

24. pp. 57–64.

25. p. 57.

26. pp. 64–72.

27. p. 65. Calabresi and Bobbitt "suspect that while it is need for continuity which limits the degree of true representativeness possible, this lack of representativeness can be justified or explained away by invoking the need for experts" (ibid.).

28. pp. 95–97.

29. pp. 72–78. The major advantage of a worthiness approach is that it obscures the tragedy inherent in the choice. "Society announces that *it* will not choose to sacrifice lives or fundamental rights, that *it* will not violate conceptions of equality, that the sacrifices which do occur are due not to a societal unwillingness to forgo other goods but to individual failings" (pp. 76–77) (emphasis in original).

deserving to live,"[30] on the basis of loose, internally promulgated guidelines. It worked anonymously and gave no reasons for its decisions.[31] There seems to be little difference between the decision-making machinations of the God Committee and those of agencies charged with regulation in accordance with "public convenience and necessity."

It is no criticism of *Tragic Choices* to say that the discussion in this area is "wisdom" rather than "science." The authors have been unable to produce a coherent, integrated theory of the area. Since I cannot do so either, I cannot criticise them for their failure. And there is no doubt that their discussion of the pros and cons of the various decision-making schemes will leave the reader considerably better informed than he was when he began.

Altogether, the book deals with an area where government does not perform well. The reason for its poor performance in the case of tragic choices is that the task given it is impossible. Voters want to economise on expenditures in the "tragic" area. They then want these insufficient resources allocated in such a way as not to call their attention too vigorously to the fact that by economising they have caused deaths. The voters' desire to abdicate active or even visible decision-making is not necessarily irrational from the standpoint of maximising their utility. The result, however, is that rational thought is almost of necessity banned. Our wealthy philanthropist similarly desired to avoid the emotional and psychological costs of making life-and-death decisions. Incoherence in the actual allocative decision is, therefore, more or less called for. The value of *Tragic Choices* lies in its success in demonstrating that such incoherence is provided.

30. p. 187.

31. pp. 188, 233 n. 111. The committee had a few formal rules, such as state residency, but made its decisions primarily in an "unstructured" manner, considering such criteria as the recipient's age, sex, marital status, number of dependants, income, net worth, psychological stability, past performance, and future potential (p. 233 n. 111).

PART 5

WHAT TO DO—WHAT TO DO

WHAT TO DO—WHAT TO DO

So far we have described and analyzed the redistribution system in the United States, which is similar to that found in most of the world. Although I suppose that my prejudices have not been completely concealed, I have tried to make the discussion up to this point scientific rather than purely normative. In this chapter, however, I would like to discuss the kinds of reforms that we can aim for. I will try to avoid making my own values omnipresent and assume that we are attempting to maximize values that, I believe, are very widely held. These values are to be charitable to some extent, but otherwise to try and have as wealthy and efficient an economy as possible. I will have nothing to say on the degree to which we should be charitable, although I have already expressed my opinion that most people are willing to give away less than 5 percent of their income, and this opinion will remain beneath the surface in this chapter. Those who want to give away more than 5 percent or those who object to giving away more than .05 percent will, however, be able to make the appropriate adjustments.

Let us begin with the charitable component of income redistribution. To redraw an earlier figure, Figure 1 shows the population arrayed from left to right, from the poorest to the wealthiest. As a simplification I again assumed that, arranging in this order, we would obtain a straight line, which in this case is line *I*. We have some minimum living standards that we think people should not fall below, which I shall temporarily assume is line *CZ*. The net social cost, if we could simply supplement existing incomes by subsidies to the poor, would be the shaded triangle. In practice, however, people who are guaranteed an income of *C* and who have less net income are probably going to stop work unless we have elaborate administrative procedures to prevent them. Some possible procedures were discussed in Chapter 4.

Thus, the tax cost would probably be not the shaded triangle, but the total rectangle *OCZN*. Further, this is not by any means the end of the matter.

Reprinted, with kind permission of Kluwer Academic Publishers, from *Economics of Income Redistribution*, Kluwer-Nijhoff Studies in Human Issues: An International Series in the Social Sciences (Boston: Kluwer-Nijhoff, 1983), 175–87.

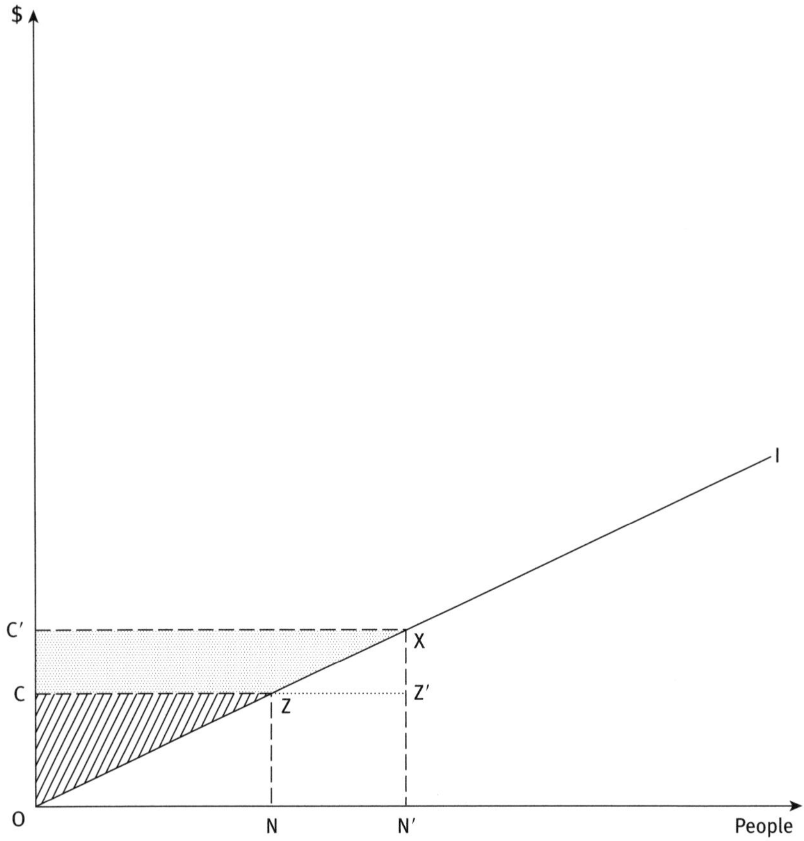

FIGURE 1
Charitable component of income redistribution

Guaranteed an income of *C* without working, some people who were obtaining a higher income by working would choose to take the lower income with leisure. In this diagram I have assumed that group is the people whose incomes lie below *C′*. If this is so, then society would lose the production of the triangle *OXN′* and pay out in taxes the rectangle *OCZ′N′*. If we could somehow make certain that the people we are subsidizing continue working and we only have to make up the difference between their product and the subsidy, then the total cost to society would be only the triangle *OCZ*. It is obvious that we can guarantee a higher minimum income with the same tax expenditure if we can assure that people whose income is supplemented do produce whatever they are capable of producing.

It seems to me that the objective of aid to the poor should be a high level of minimum income together with no leisure for the people who are on whatever subsidy we give. In other words, relief clients should continue working even if they do not produce very much. I do not think this is impossible, although it would require fairly drastic changes in our present practices. In particular, the social workers who today proclaim that they are attempting to achieve this goal would be compelled actually to work hard at it, and indeed we might want to substitute something like the Bentham-Alchian process for the social worker.

This objective is, I think, one that would be widely shared. The only question is whether it is administratively feasible. I am not sure that it is, but it seems to me that we should at least be willing to engage in a lot of experimenting aimed at that purpose. In order to engage in these experiments, I would suggest that our present relief structure be radically decentralized, with incentives for local groups to try various new techniques, and some kind of research group that looks at these techniques, applies statistics to them, and makes judgments on whether or not they are, in fact, efficient.

The decentralization could take a number of forms. Let me first discuss methods of decentralizing the administration of relief without discussing how they should be financed, and then turn to discussing their finance later. The first proposal, obviously, is that the relief be handled locally, either by state or, preferably, by city and county governments. This provides a high degree of diversity. Further, I think that administratively it is much easier for people who are members of the local community to assure themselves of whether or not individuals on relief could, in fact, work. Obviously, local administrators will have to make a certain number of arbitrary judgments on this matter, be willing to cut off people suspected of shirking, and in general exercise a good deal of discretion if we are attempting to get real product out of the relief clients. Local officials, subject to local electorate, are more likely to be capable of doing this than is a centralized bureaucracy. It requires many particular decisions, something that centralized bureaucracies are bad at.

It would seem to be highly desirable to try to experiment with the use of private rather than governmental bodies here. Traditionally, there was a great deal of aid to the poor given through private charity. In recent years, private charity, although still quite extensive, has tended to concentrate on other subjects. This is probably because so much government money goes into aid to the poor that individual charities no longer regard it as a suitable place to put money.[1]

I do not see any particular need for central supervision over these programs, although if federal government funds were provided, I presume that it would be desirable to see to it that the money actually is spent charitably. Diversion into the pockets of local aldermen should be prevented. In general, however, the objective should be to give local governments or private agencies the fullest freedom to spend the money in any way they wished, provided only that they are engaged in bona fide charitable provision. This would permit maximum diversity with the probability of the development of new techniques being maximized. Since new techniques are certainly needed in this field, this is a major advantage.

But if there is no need for central supervision beyond the simple requirement that the money not be fraudulently diverted away from charity, central investigation and inspection of them is still highly desirable—not to control but for the purpose of experiment. Statistical tests could be easily devised that would tell which various techniques used by various local groups were working best. With time, they should lead to sharp improvement.

As another possible way of getting improvements, if there is central government finance, that finance might be organized in such a way as to generate true experiments along the lines of the negative income tax experiments. Thus, if the 3,000 or so local communities are all receiving federal money for charitable purposes, a provision that 100 of the 3,000 follow one particular technique and another randomly selected 100 follow a different one would, over time, permit deductions as to which of the two techniques was more efficient. Of course, the experiments could be much more complicated than that. You would want to make sure, however, that these experiments do not develop into an effort on the part of the central bureaucracy to, in fact, exercise detailed control over a large part of the activity of the local agencies.

Let us return to the problem of finance. There seem to be three possible sources of finance: voluntary charity, local government provision through taxes, and central government provision through taxes. Going through them in inverse order, central government provision raises only one significant

1. Incidentally, charity now sometimes goes to the government rather than from it. A local Blacksburg Parent Teachers Association has been, for a number of years, making payments to the school board for purchasing various things that one would normally think were the school board's responsibility.

problem, which has to do with the incentives of local agencies. Presumably the money should be distributed on the basis of need, but we would want to avoid giving local governments a motive to multiply the number of their relief clients in order to demonstrate further "need."[2] We would like a system in which an individual local community or, for that matter, private charity—if the government is funding private charities—could gain by higher efficiency but could not gain by simply getting more customers.

I do not think this is particularly difficult. We could allocate the money on the basis of some measure of need that is not under the control of the local agency. As one example, the average per capita income of a given area would be used as the base for calculations of need. The highly efficient local agency would be able to use these funds for more elaborate charitable provision for a smaller group of people than the inefficient agency, which would find itself providing a rather low level of charity for a lot of people. Presumably, local pressures, whether through local elections or local clientele in voluntary agencies, would push the agencies in the direction of efficiency. The pressure would not, of course, be ideal from an economic standpoint, but at least it would be in the correct direction.

Finance by taxes raised by local governments does not seem to be markedly different than finance by national taxes except for two factors. Firstly, some of the areas are much poorer than others, and secondly, there is a sort of false efficiency, from the voters' standpoint, in the use of national rather than local agencies. Let us examine first the difference in the relative resources of the various areas and assume for the purpose of discussion that we are using states.

It is certainly true that California is a very prosperous part of the United States. My own personal feeling would be that if it is thought that California should not only pay for the poor in California but for other poor, the additional funds would go to California's near neighbor, impoverished Mexico, rather than more than 1,000 miles to Mississippi, which, although poorer than California, is certainly more prosperous than Mexico. In this respect, however, it would appear that my preferences are different from those of the average citizen of the United States,[3] and so I shall assume that the problem that we face here is redistribution of income inside the United States.

2. For a discussion of the same problem in a different context, see my "Competing for Aid," *Public Choice* 21 (Spring 1975): 41–51.

3. I presume they are identical with the average citizen of Mexico.

If we assume that it is desirable that money be transferred from the wealthier part of the United States to the poorer parts of the United States for purposes of relief, there seem to be three fairly straightforward techniques. The first would be for the wealthy states simply to make voluntary transfers to the poorer states. For reasons that are not clear to me, it is apparently believed that this would not work. I do not know why, if the citizens of California are willing to vote for congressmen who will make this transfer by way of the central government, they would not be willing to vote for state legislators who would do it directly. Nevertheless, that seems to be the conventional wisdom, and I shall not challenge it here.

A central government program is thus called for. The central government program must take the form of a tax and subsidy scheme, which, in net, transfers money from California to Mississippi. The simple procedure for this is a tax that falls heavily on California, which is used to pay states that have less-than-average incomes. Once again, I find that there seems to be a feeling that, politically, this is impossible. The basic program that is thought to be politically possible is one in which fairly heavy taxes are put on all of the states, and then these are administered in such a way that all of the states receive a subsidy, but California receives a lower per capita subsidy than Mississippi. I have great difficulty in seeing why this is politically more feasible than a much lower tax that, in essence, falls primarily on the wealthy states, with the returns being distributed to the poorer states. I suspect that people who argue this way are engaging in what I referred to before as well-intentioned Machiavellianism; i.e., they think they are fooling the voters in California by the scheme. I doubt that California voters are that dumb. But, in any event, assuming that they are, this scheme could be carried out fairly easily under the conditions I have given above.

Turning now to the "false efficiency," I believe it has never been discussed except in my "The Charity of the Uncharitable."[4] Individuals, if they are rational, realize that a vote means relatively little, but it means less in national elections than in state elections and less in state elections than in local elections. This provides an opportunity for an individual to take action that makes it possible for him to think of himself as charitable but does not actually cost him very much. Suppose that one has a choice among the following four actions: (1) give $100 to the poor, (2) vote in a local election to have the

4. Gordon Tullock, "The Charity of the Uncharitable," *Western Economic Journal* 9, no. 4 (December 1971): 379–92.

community tax everyone $100 and give it to the poor, (3) vote in a state election to have the state tax everyone $100 and give it to the poor, and (4) vote in a national election to have the national government tax everyone $100 and give it to the poor. An individual can, provided he is just a little bit unscrupulous in his internal calculation process, feel that he is equally charitable in selecting any one of those courses of action. On the other hand, the prospect that his decision will affect him negatively by depriving him of $100 is monotonically decreasing from the first to the last. Therefore, one would assume that he would tend to be more willing to vote for charity in a national system than locally.

Although this is true, it has the unfortunate result that he is apt to feel unhappy if the national government taxes him more than he would voluntarily give to the poor. The result is that he is apt to vote for more charity than he actually wants. Politicians facing this kind of voter would, if they were rational, choose to talk a great deal about charity but, in fact, provide relatively little. This is what we observe politicians doing in the real world, from which we deduce that both they and the voters are rational.

Granted that this is the way politicians talk and the way politicians act, it does not seem at all obvious that transferring the relief program to local levels would lead to any reduction in it except for the problem of transfers from the wealthy communities to the poor communities mentioned above. It would no doubt be resented by local politicians, and the individual voter, who is assumed in this discussion not to be introspectively clear, might also resent it because it deprives him of an opportunity to think that he is more charitable than he is.

Here, we have a rather general problem in talking about government provision of charity. Discussion of this subject frequently seems to be based on a failure to realize that the voters and the people who make individual charitable gifts are one and the same. It is true that the power distribution of people as givers and the power distribution of people as voters is somewhat different, but the result of this difference is not apt to be very great. It is true that lower-income but nonpoor people have more power in voting than they do in giving. As a counterbalance they also have the possibility of using this power to benefit themselves rather than to benefit the poor. If they choose to vote to take money from the rich that can benefit either them or some recipient of charity, it is unlikely that they will be more charitable in deciding to spend it than they will be in spending their own money. Thus, there is no obvious reason to believe that a democratic government will be any more charitable than its citizens are privately, except for the efficiency improvements in the charitable provision by government means that we have discussed above. I believe that people who think that the voter is more charitable than the private donor, although he is the same person, are not depending on Friedman's efficiency argument but on well-intended Machiavellianism. They think that the voter can be fooled into being more charitable than he would be in his private capacity.

This brings us then to our third possible method of finance—voluntary gifts. I presume, as I said above, that the voter and the charitable donor are equally charitable, but there are, of course, the efficiency advantages of using government provision. As it happens, however, these efficiency advantages can be extended by the government to private gifts by way of suitable provisions in the tax law. We already do this to a considerable extent, although with the government largely occupying the "poor" part of the charitable spectrum, relatively little private money goes there. It seems likely that the movement of the government out of this field would lead to a sharp increase in private contributions, and any desired amount could be obtained by appropriately adjusting the income tax code.

This is simply an indirect government subsidy to charity. That is the way the deductions for charitable provision are always discussed by Congress, with the basic question as, "Which is the more efficient way of handling it?" My own personal feeling in this area is that local governments are probably the most efficient way of handling the actual administration of charitable provision for the poor, but I think it is desirable to at least experiment in use of voluntary agencies. Once again, returning to my own personal preference in this matter, I would think that national government finance dispersed through local governments and voluntary agencies is the ideal system.

There are a great many other transfers that are much larger than aid to the poor. As a first category, let us examine things like the social security administration, public support of education, and public provision of medicine to the part of the population that is not poor. In the latter case, in the United States, all we do is provide for the elderly people, but in much of the rest of the world there is public provision for everyone.

These large programs can frequently be criticized on efficiency grounds, but this is pure economic efficiency. There is no reason to believe that the voters are not, on the whole, getting what they are voting for in these areas. The programs are so large, and the tax costs and benefits so conspicuous to almost everyone involved, that it is dubious that there is much deception. In this they are quite different from the kind of administrative transfers discussed in Chapter 10. These administrative transfers will be put aside for the time being.

If we look at these large programs, the first thing that we note is that they are usually rather inefficient in detail. It is hard to argue, for example, that American elementary education is in any sense the most efficient use of the money. Presumably, converting this into a competitive industry by way of some kind of tuition voucher scheme would lead to a higher net education at a lower net cost. But this is the kind of statement about general economics that I would prefer to leave out of this book, since it has nothing much to do with income redistribution, only with efficient ways of carrying out a redistribution which has already been decided on.

Let us look at these three major programs one at a time, beginning first with the old-age pension system. I cannot avoid feeling, with Senator Goldwater, that it is too bad we got into it. Once we are in, however, it is very difficult to get out. The program is politically very attractive to start because of the transfer from future generations to people who can vote right now. Once it is in existence and reaches a stable state, it lowers lifetime incomes of substantially everybody, providing only that the rate of growth is lower than the interest rate. On the other hand, terminating it would always impose a very large cost on existing voters, and the benefit would accrue, primarily, to voters in the future. Thus, the system in its pure form is an almost perfect example of a politically motivated mistake. There are great political advantages to proposing it, and once it is established there are great political disadvantages to eliminating it.

It seems likely, however, that under present circumstances the program is in grave danger. There are two basic problems. Firstly, the readjustment of the payout schedule in the 1977 amendments made the bargain a bad one for, roughly, the upper two-thirds of the population. They are not only more numerous than the lower one-third but also much more politically influential, and on a per capita basis this naturally raises doubts about the program. Once these doubts are in existence, the implicit promise that our children will pay us if we pay our parents begins to look dubious, and the advantage of the program even for the present generation begins to vanish.

The present distribution of social security paybacks can only be justified as a desire to give special payments to that part of the elderly population who are poor. Since they would, in any event, receive payments through the relief program, it seems to me politically that it is highly desirable to discontinue this arrangement. Putting the matter bluntly, a scheme under which an individual's receipts from the social security are a simple, linear function of what he has paid in in taxes, while taking care of the elderly poor by other means, would dominate. This would be cheaper because a number of people who are not themselves poor get treated as poor under the present system. I imagine this change would sharply improve the political support for the program and reduce the political risks, which would still further improve the political support.

Medicine falls roughly into three categories. The first category is the care of people who are chronically ill, which everywhere falls on the state, as it does in the United States, and which is almost everywhere provided at a lower level than charitably minded persons would regard as ideal. The second category is the provision of medical care for the poor. In this case I see no reason why we should have a special program. Income supplements to the poor, together with the possibility of obtaining income medical insurance, seems to me adequate. The desire for a special program apparently rests on the theory that the poor cannot manage their own affairs and will not buy the medical insurance. Personally, I think that the poor, although undeniably less good at handling their own affairs than other people, nevertheless are apt to handle them better than some civil servant or elected official. Nevertheless, those people who feel that the poor cannot be trusted to spend money in a way that is optimal from their standpoint, or who do not want the poor to receive optimal treatment from their standpoint but to receive treatment optimal from the standpoint of the donor of the funds, may well be in favor of provision in kind in a number of areas: medicine, housing, etc. It seems that the difference here is essentially one of preference and judgment as to the intelligence and motivation of the poor.

The third category is individuals who become severely ill and do not have resources to pay for their medicine. This is clearly an area where insurance is called for, but there does not seem to be any obvious reason why government insurance is better than private insurance. It should be said here that the current private insurance schemes are all less than optimally efficient. The basic reason for this is that they were started by the medical profession through Blue Cross and Blue Shield, and the medical profession has been able to retain considerable control over even the private programs. As a result, the laws that control these programs, influenced by the powerful medical lobby, are heavily biased towards maximizing the income of doctors rather than towards maximizing the well-being of the patients. This leads to inefficiency. Naturally, I would like to change this situation, but the problem that one faces is that it is the government influence by the doctors that is causing the inefficiency. The government, influenced by the doctors, would no doubt cause similar inefficiencies in any government program. What we must do here is take on the doctors. It is, in fact, another example of administrative transfers discussed in Chapter 10. It is an important problem, but it has little or nothing to do with redistribution of aid to the poor and a great deal with redistribution to aid by administrative means an already wealthy group of people.

Let us now turn to public education. I have already expressed my views that higher education is a highly regressive scheme for transferring funds from the people who are less well-off to those who are well-off. The only advantage I can think of this from a social standpoint is that it pays my salary. I doubt, however, that anything will be done about it, since the beneficiaries are, politically, extremely influential and, in fact, control all the communication channels, so the people who are injured by it will probably never find out they are injured.

Turning to elementary education, however, and ignoring methods of improving its efficiency (i.e., talking only about its redistributive effect), there are three different redistributions involved. The first—redistribution from upper-income people to lower-income people—is probably modest but real in the program. I emphasize the "probably" because the way that education is organized and financed in the United States makes it very difficult to measure this impact. If we are to be charitable to the poor and we believe that the charitable payments to the poor should be distributed in kind rather than in cash, then at least the bottom portion of this redistribution would be socially desirable. It should perhaps be said, however, that those children of the poor who are likely to be poor themselves the rest of their lives (i.e., the ones with relatively little talent) also gain little from the educational process. There are, of course, highly talented people who will gain a great deal from education among the children of the poor, but they are likely to be upper-income individuals in the latter part of their life.

The second redistribution is redistribution from people who have no children to those who have or from those who have few children to those who have many. I am sure this redistribution is more significant than the first one in absolute size, but I know of no formal measurement of it. It should be said that those who are worried about the population problems should criticize this arrangement severely. If you want to get people to voluntarily restrict the number of their children, discontinuing subsidies for children is a good idea. Indeed, I suppose a positive tax might be desirable.

Finally, there is the redistribution from those who are above the age where their children are in school to those whose children are still in school. It seems to me that this can best be thought of as a sort of credit arrangement in which younger people implicitly borrow money that they will repay later by paying taxes to support the school system when their children are out of school. It should be noted that such a credit arrangement could be designed without subsidizing large families by simply arranging that individual parents pay the full cost of their children's education, but that the cost be spread over their lifetimes rather than falling during the time their children are small.[5] The current system probably has relatively little effect on lifetime incomes, but is politically a little dangerous because older people have no prospect of future gains as they do in the social security system and might vote against it.

I have ignored here the possible externalities in the educational system because it seems to me that they have not been validated by empirical research. That a great many people think they exist is true, however, and this may well have an important effect on the political support of the system.

So much for these three large programs, which, individually, transfer very large sums of money. We now turn to what I have called the administrative transfers—the immense collection of minor transfers from one part of society to another by way of such things as the farm program or the Interstate Commerce Commission. I have already expressed my personal opposition to these programs, and I would like now to talk about ways by which they can be curtailed.

There are, of course, many cases in which a general tax supports the special benefit for a small group but in which the small group benefits more than the total tax. It would be preferable in these cases, however, that the tax fall on the benefitted group. This is merely one of a number of possible constitutional changes that could be made and that would tend to eliminate inefficient transfers in this group. If we could arrange for the cost of any one of these programs to fall on the people benefitted, then the people benefitted would only favor the program if their benefits were greater than the cost.

There are other reforms. Since the publication of my "Problems of Majority Voting,"[6] the bulk of my professional work has been devoted to the

5. It could, of course, also be paid by the children through a credit arrangement under which they had to repay as adults the expenditure of their education as children.

6. Gordon Tullock, "Problems of Majority Voting," *Journal of Political Economy* 67 (December 1959): 571–79.

problem of improving government efficiency. There is now a professional group, the Public Choice Society, which is largely devoted to this end. The various suggestions for improvement that have been made are mainly of a fundamental constitutional nature and unlikely to be immediately adopted. Indeed, granted their radical nature, it is probably sensible to think them over very carefully and proceed cautiously in implementing them. Still, in the long run, it is likely that progress in our government will require fairly radical constitutional changes. There is, after all, no reason to believe that a group of men, and I have the highest admiration for their capacity, who met 200 years ago solved all problems of democracy.

But if these constitutional changes are necessarily difficult and take a long time, is there anything we can do more quickly? Considering that most of the readers of this book will be intellectuals, the answer is yes. As I have pointed out, most of these administrative procedures are held insecurely, they do not last forever, and to a large extent, they require that the public either be misled into supporting them or not notice them. Thus, it is possible for the intellectual community to perform a real public service by making accurate computations on these matters and then using its control of the communications channels to inform the voters. This would surely not eliminate all of these programs, but it would reduce their number and, by raising the risk for anyone who is attempting to get money by political means, reduce the investment in that activity.

The problem with this suggestion is that intellectuals have traditionally favored these programs. The protective tariff, the Interstate Commerce Commission, the AAA in the thirties, and the establishment of the Kennedy Center in Washington are all examples of inefficient transfers from large numbers of people to small groups of people, mainly of well above average income. All were enthusiastically approved by the intellectual community at the time. Clearly, the intellectuals, if they are going to play a constructive social role in this area, must learn to behave more intelligently.

This, of course, does raise a problem. The individual intellectual cannot possibly learn in detail about all of these things, so he must pick up his knowledge from some generally respectable source. Further, in general, he has no strong motive to be well informed, while he does have a strong motive to be fashionable. Nevertheless, I do not think the problem is insolvable. What is required is an improvement in the information flow in this area. This is probably the area where the average reader can make the greatest contribution. Of course, if the average reader is in favor of these administrative transfers, he will not want to.

Having discussed in this chapter various reforms, I would like to end by a call for a particular kind of research. The modern welfare state is frequently argued for on the grounds that it helps the poor. I have not concealed from the reader my personal opinion that the welfare state helps the poor no more than its predecessors did. Helping the poor is a characteristic behavior of governments whether dictatorial or democratic. It may well be that democratic governments are more generous in this regard than dictatorial, but we do not really know. Nor do we know whether the movement to the welfare state has meant a relative improvement in the well-being of the poor. It has almost certainly retarded growth, with the result that the poor are, in absolute terms, like the rest of us, worse off than they otherwise would be, but we do not have enough research to say for certain whether it has benefitted the poor in relative terms. My opinion that it has not, and, in fact, may actually have injured them slightly, is not widely shared.

Research in this area is difficult because the details of programs for aid to the poor are not only radically different from time to time and place to place but are continuously shifting. Thus, in order to find out whether the United States in, let us say, 1850 had a poor population who were relatively worse off than they are now would require a great many different research projects aimed at specific programs. Each individual research project would have to cover a considerable time span, because the history of aid to the poor is one of a rise in aid, a gradual falling behind as the economy progresses, and then another rise. A study of one year might fall at any point in the cycle. Still, it seems to me the project is worthwhile and that a great many doctoral dissertations could be devoted to it. Until this work has been done, we will not be able to say for certain whether the welfare state benefits or injures the poor.

It seems sensible to end this book by extending the plea for specific research mentioned in the last few paragraphs to another suggestion for more research through the whole area of government redistribution. I began the book by saying that I thought research in this area was weak, largely because of a feeling that it is a matter of morals rather than a matter of science. It may be a matter of morals, but we should know as much about it as we can. I hope that readers of this book will, if they dislike the book, undertake research to disprove it, and if they like the book, undertake research along the lines suggested.

INDEX

References to bibliographic information appear in italics.

The typeface used for the text of this book is Galliard, an old-style face designed by Matthew Carter in 1978, in the spirit of a sixteenth-century French typeface of Robert Granjon. The display type is Meta Book, a variant of Meta, designed by Erik Spiekermann in the 1990s.

This book is printed on paper that is acid-free and meets the requirements of the American National Standard for Permanence of Paper for Printed Library Materials, Z39.48-1992. ♾

Book design by Richard Hendel, Chapel Hill, North Carolina
Typography by G&S Typesetters, Inc., Austin, Texas
Printed and bound by Edwards Brothers, Inc., Ann Arbor, Michigan